NICHOLAS I

AND OFFICIAL

NATIONALITY

IN RUSSIA

1825–1855

NICHOLAS I AND OFFICIAL NATIONALITY IN RUSSIA, 1825-1855

Nicholas V. Riasanovsky

UNIVERSITY OF CALIFORNIA PRESS
BERKELEY, LOS ANGELES, LONDON

University of California Press
Berkeley and Los Angeles, California

University of California Press, Ltd.
London, England

© 1959 by The Regents of the University of California

ISBN: 0-520-01065-5
Library of Congress Catalog Card Number: 59-11316

Printed in the United States of America

7 8 9 0

TO ARLENE

PREFACE

Nicholas I and Official Nationality in Russia, 1825–1855 developed from a much more modest interest in Uvarov's doctrine of "Orthodoxy, autocracy, and nationality." During my study of the Slavophiles in particular, I became increasingly aware of the paucity of our knowledge of this so-called Official Nationality frequently combined with a deprecating attitude toward it. Unable to find a satisfactory analysis of the subject, I proceeded to write my own. The book largely organized itself: an exposition and discussion of the ideology naturally occupied the central position, preceded by a brief treatment of its proponents. But Official Nationality reached beyond intellectual circles, lectures and books; indeed, for thirty years it ruled Russia. Therefore, I found it necessary to write a chapter on the emperor who, in effect, personally dominated and governed the country throughout his reign; to add a section on the imperial family, the ministers, and some other high officials to an account of the intellectuals who supported the state; and to sketch the application of Official Nationality both in home affairs and in foreign policy. Only in this manner could I bring the state doctrine and its role in Russian history into proper focus.

I might have tried to do too much. Yet I feel that I deserve indulgence at least in regard to the subjects which I did not attempt to encompass. To select one example, my discussion of Pushkin in connection with the state ideology by no means represents all that could be said about Pushkin as a thinker, let alone as a writer. Similarly, the link between romanticism and reaction which proved to be of major importance for my study does not in the least negate other connections, for instance, those between romanticism and revolution. The Russia of Nicholas I was incomparably more complex and richer than Official Nationality. The purpose of my work, however, consisted in finding what that teaching had to offer, not in exploring other topics.

I relied heavily on direct quotation from the spokesmen of Official

Nationality because I consider the general nature, manner, and tone of their statements, not only the content, to be significant. For the same reason I tried to preserve in translation the style of the original. In the troublesome matter of transliteration, I sought to follow consistently a system based essentially on that of the Library of Congress. Names of Western derivation are written in the text in their proper Latin forms.

Of the several years which it took me to gather material for this study, the most fruitful was the school year of 1954–1955 which I spent on a Fulbright research grant at the University of Helsinki. I want to thank all those responsible for the grant, as well as officials of the United States Educational Foundation in Finland, in particular Mr. Sven-Erik Sjögren and Miss Hilkka Sario. I want also to express my deep gratitude to Dr. Sulo Haltsonen, Mr. B. I. Sove, Dr. Maria Widnäs and others of the rich Slavic department of the University of Helsinki Library. I remember them as a remarkable group of scholars and friends whose help to me far exceeded any claims I might have had on their attention. I am similarly grateful to those who aided me in the British Museum Library, in the Bibliothèque Nationale and, in this country, especially in the libraries at the State University of Iowa and the University of California in Berkeley. Further, I want to thank the administrations of these two universities for their help in my work, such as the provision of research assistants.

Among the readers of my manuscript, I am, as usual, indebted particularly to my father, Professor V. A. Riasanovsky. Next I must mention my friend Professor J. F. Gilliam of the State University of Iowa, a distinguished specialist in ancient history whose contribution to this study serves to underline the fact that wisdom may often be more important than specialized knowledge. I have also profited from the searching and thorough readings of my teacher Professor M. Karpovich of Harvard University, Professor Charles Jelavich of the University of California, Dr. Barbara Jelavich, and Professors O. A. Maslenikov, C. B. O'Brien, and W. Galenson. Other valuable comments and suggestions were offered by those who read the manuscript in part, notably Professors R. J. Sontag and R. Drinnon of the University of California, Professor R. Popkin of the State University of Iowa, and Professor G. Poage of Iowa State Teachers College. My research assistants, Mrs. Janice Clark Fotion, Mr. S. Lukashevich, and Mr. F. Miller, aided me eagerly and well. My wife, Arlene, acted as a reader, a research assistant, and in general as my main helper in this entire undertaking.

NICHOLAS V. RIASANOVSKY

Berkeley, California
February 9, 1959

CONTENTS

ABBREVIATIONS USED IN FOOTNOTES

Custine: A. Custine. *La Russie en 1839*. Brussels, 1843. 4 vols.

Gogol: N. Gogol. *Sochineniya*. Ed. by V. Kallash. St. Petersburg, n. d. Vol. VIII. *Mistiko-moralisticheskie sochineniya.*

Nikitenko: A. Nikitenko. *Moya povest o samom sebe i o tom "chemu svidetel v zhizni byl." Zapiski i dnevnik.* (1804–1877 gg.). 2d ed. St. Petersburg, 1905. 2 vols.

Polievktov: M. Polievktov. *Nikolai I. Biografiya i obzor tsarstvovaniya.* Moscow, 1918.

Presnyakov: A. Presnyakov. *Apogei samoderzhaviya. Nikolai I.* Leningrad, 1925.

Schiemann: T. Schiemann. *Geschichte Russlands unter Kaiser Nikolaus I.* Berlin, 1904–1919. 4 vols.

Schilder: N. Schilder. *Imperator Nikolai Pervyi, ego zhizn i tsarstvovanie.* St. Petersburg, 1903. 2 vols.

SIRIO: *Sbornik Imperatorskogo Russkogo Istoricheskogo Obshchestva.* St. Petersburg, 1867–1917. 148 vols.

Tyutchev: F. Tyutchev. *Polnoe sobranie sochinenii.* Ed. by P. Bykov. St. Petersburg, 1913.

Tyutcheva: A. Tyutcheva. *Pri dvore dvukh imperatorov.* Moscow, 1928.

I

OFFICIAL NATIONALITY

THE SUPREME COMMANDER

Here [in the army] there is order, there is a strict unconditional legality, no impertinent claims to know all the answers, no contradiction, all things flow logically one from the other; no one commands before he has himself learned to obey; no one steps in front of anybody else without lawful reason; everything is subordinated to one definite goal, everything has its purpose. That is why I feel so well among these people, and why I shall always hold in honor the calling of a soldier. I consider the entire human life to be merely service, because everybody serves.—Nicholas I [1]

EMPEROR NICHOLAS I of Russia was a very impressive man. To use the words of a recent historian: "With his height of more than six feet, his head always held high, a slightly aquiline nose, a firm and well-formed mouth under a light moustache, a square chin, an imposing, domineering, set face, noble rather than tender, monumental rather than human, he had something of Apollo and of Jupiter . . . Nicholas was unquestionably the most handsome

---

[1] Quoted in Schilder, I, 147.

man in Europe." [2] Many of the contemporaries of the emperor
shared this extravagant judgment, eulogies of his appearance and
his presence being by no means limited to his own camp, that is,
to the Russian court circles and to their Prussian and Austrian
counterparts. For instance, Andrew Dickson White wrote in his
autobiography as he reminisced about his diplomatic service in
Russia:

> *The Czar at that period, Nicholas I, was a most imposing*
> *personage, and was generally considered the most perfect specimen*
> *of a human being, physically speaking, in all Europe.*[3]
>
> *Colossal in stature; with a face such as one finds on a Greek*
> *coin, but overcast with a shadow of Muscovite melancholy; with*
> *a bearing dignified, but with a manner not unkind, he bore him-*
> *self like a god. . . . Whenever I saw him . . . there was forced*
> *to my lips the thought: 'You are the most majestic being ever*
> *created.'* [4]

Two images stand out in the numerous descriptions of Nicholas
I: his physical beauty and his majestic bearing, the two blending
perfectly to produce one overwhelming impression. Friend and foe
alike were affected by the powerful presence of the emperor, and
some were smitten by it. A lady in waiting spoke of him as a
"terrestrial divinity." [5] A Prussian officer extolled his physical
qualities.[6] The great poet Pushkin compared Nicholas to Moses.[7]

---

[2] Grunwald, *La Vie de Nicolas I*", p. 157.

[3] White, *Autobiography*, I, 451.

[4] *Ibid.*, p. 470. More about American admiration for the emperor can be
found in Dvoichenko-Markov, "Americans in the Crimean War," *Russian
Review*, XIII (April, 1954), 137–139. See also John Motley's description:
"The Czar is deserving of all the praise I have heard of him. He is one of the
handsomest men I ever saw, six feet three inches at least in height, and 'every
inch a king.' His figure is robust, erect and stately, and his features are of great
symmetry, and his forehead and eye are singularly fine. 'The front of Jove
himself, the eye like Mars to threaten and command.' In short he is a regular-
built Jupiter." Motley to his wife, St. Petersburg, Dec. 25, 1841, *Correspondence*, I, 86.

[5] Tyutcheva, p. 96.

[6] Schiemann, II, 244–245.

[7] Pushkin, "K N. . ." (1834). *Biblioteka velikikh pisatelei pod redaktsiei
S. A. Vengerova. Pushkin.* III, 497. Gogol states explicitly that this poem
refers to Nicholas and that it was occasioned by an incident at a palace
gathering. Gogol, pp. 45–46. However, many specialists, for example, Pro-

La Ferronnays, the French ambassador, could not control his enthusiasm after his first audience with the emperor, this new and "educated Peter the Great." [8] A Polish enemy recorded how he was overcome by the stunning majesty of the Russian tsar, "the ruler of the world in appearance," and how he was unable to meet the imperial gaze.[9] The Marquis de Custine, who gained a lasting literary reputation by his violent and brilliant denunciation of the Russia of Nicholas I, was nevertheless strongly attracted by the figure of its ruler "whose head dominates all other heads . . . Virgil's Neptune . . . one could not be more emperor than he." [10]

Custine's opinion was the general opinion. Nicholas I came to represent autocracy personified: infinitely majestic, determined and powerful, hard as stone, and relentless as fate. The emperor himself believed in this image, as did most of his contemporaries and most of the subsequent historians. In the annals of mankind, few pictures have come down to us so simple, sharp, and clear as this portrait of the despotic Russian ruler.

Yet, better acquaintance changes this image. The empress, as her diary and letters testify, found many things about her husband which did not fit the general view. Close collaborators with the emperor and other people who lived long at court also discovered new facets of his personality. Historians, too, as they studied their subject more closely, came up with some unexpected results. The most meticulous of them, Professor Theodore Schiemann, produced a fine, many-sided narrative of the emperor's behavior which, unfortunately, he failed to understand or interpret in an

---

fessor W. Lednicki, discount Gogol's testimony and believe that the poem was addressed not to the emperor, but to N. Gnedich, the translator of the Iliad. I am indebted to Professor Lednicki for a discussion of this problem. The claim that the poem refers to the emperor has been maintained, e.g., in Strakhovsky "Pushkin and the Emperors Alexander I and Nicholas I," *Canadian Slavonic Papers*, I, 16–30; see especially pp. 28–29.

[8] See Schilder, I, 348, and n. 395; also Schiemann, II, 115–117.

[9] Schiemann, II, 405–406.

[10] Custine, II, 215. This attraction is apparent throughout Custine's work. The Frenchman was impressed not only by the appearance and the bearing of the emperor, but also by his voice—"unforgettable, so full of authority it is, so solemn and firm . . . this voice certainly belongs to a man born to command." *Ibid.*, p. 52.

entirely satisfactory manner.[11] Another prominent investigator
reached the conclusion that the impression left by Nicholas I was
a result of his historical role, not of his personal attributes.[12]
Still others note "failings," "exceptions," and "contradictions" in
the character of the emperor.

Those who became well acquainted with Nicholas I were struck
by the disclosure of the other side of his allegedly monolithic
personality. Furthermore, and very few went deep enough to see
it, this second side of the emperor's character, far from being
transitory or secondary, was as fundamental as the first. In fact,
the two were indissolubly linked and were always in operation
together. Nicholas I's insistence on firmness and stern action was
based on fear, not on confidence; his determination concealed a
state approaching panic, and his courage fed on something akin
to despair. The two elements of his personality were invariably
present, but they could be seen best in a time of crisis, such as
that in 1848. When the news of the revolution in France reached
Russia, the emperor's reactions were, characteristically, first, extreme nervousness and excitement verging on panic, and, second,
a demand for immediate and drastic action. As he tried to convince his brother-in-law, the king of Prussia: "Act *firmly and
promptly*, or, I am telling it to you, I am repeating it, *all is lost*." [13]
The emperor's boiling emotions could not be restricted to personal
correspondence. In the same month of March he issued a resounding manifesto, which he had composed himself, refusing to accept the modifications proposed by his chief advisers.[14] This
remarkable document began with a brief account of the new

---

[11] In fairness to Schiemann it should be remembered that he was concerned
not only with Nicholas I, but with the entire history of Russia during Nicholas's
reign. Everything considered, his four-volume study is still the best work in
the field. Schiemann used many primary sources, both in the text and in the
numerous documentary appendixes to his study, which were located in the
Prussian archives in Berlin and have since probably been destroyed.

[12] Presnyakov, pp. 87–89.

[13] Nicholas's letter to Frederick William IV was published in an appendix
to Schiemann, IV, 391–392. Italics in the original.

[14] About the manifesto see Schilder, "Imperator Nikolai I v 1848 i 1849
godakh" first published in the *Istoricheskii Vestnik* for 1899 and later as an
appendix to Schilder, II, 619–639. The text of the manifesto is given on
page 629.

"disturbances" which had arisen in the West, first in France, then also in the neighboring German states until "insolence, recognizing no longer any limits, is in its madness threatening even our Russia entrusted to us by God." Nicholas I continued:

> *But let this not be!*
>
> *Following the sacred example of our Orthodox forefathers, after invoking the help of God Almighty, we are ready to meet our enemies, wherever they may appear, and, without sparing ourselves, we shall, in indissoluble union with our Holy Russia, defend the honor of the Russian name and the inviolability of our borders.*
>
> *We are convinced that every Russian, every loyal subject of ours will respond gladly to the call of his monarch; that our ancient battle cry: "for faith, tsar, and fatherland" will now once more show us the way to victory, and that then with feelings of reverent gratitude, as now with feelings of sacred trust in Him, we shall all exclaim:*
>
> *God is with us! Understand this, O nations, and submit, for God is with us!*

This manifesto which, in the words of Baron Korff who helped the emperor draft it, contained a challenge to combat, referred to external threats which did not exist, and expressed hopes of victory while no hostilities were as yet in prospect,[15] produced a great impression both in Russia and, especially, abroad. Count Nesselrode, Nicholas I's minister of foreign affairs, hastened to explain in a special article in the quasi-official *Journal de St.-Petersburg* that the imperial proclamation should not be misinterpreted and that Russia wanted peace and had no intention whatsoever of fighting anybody, provided she were not attacked first.[16] But international suspicion proved hard to dispel. And even long after 1848 became history, scholars were still trying to discover the arcane political, diplomatic, or strategic reasons which made the Russian emperor issue his unaccountable manifesto.

Nervous fear and outbursts of aggressiveness characterized

---

[15] *Ibid.*, p. 627. Cf. Gershenzon, ed., *Epokha Nikolaya I*, pp. 124–126.
[16] The text of the article is reproduced in Schilder, II, 630–632.

Nicholas I from childhood. The future emperor was a self-willed boy who found it difficult either to study with his teachers or to enjoy himself with his playmates. Often withdrawn and shy, he insisted on having his way, refused to recognize mistakes, and flew into a rage at every obstacle. To quote an account of Nicholas's behavior during these years:

> *The games of the grand dukes were rarely peaceful; almost every day they would end with a quarrel or a fight. The irascibility and the obstinacy of Nicholas came out usually on those occasions when anything or anybody angered him. Whatever happened to him, whether he fell down, or hurt himself, or whether he believed that his wishes remained unfulfilled and that he was insulted, he would immediately use abusive words, hack with his little axe the drum and other toys, break them, and beat his playmates with a stick or with anything else at hand, even though he loved them very much, and had a particularly passionate attachment to his younger brother.*[17]

In addition to this general irritability, Nicholas I was subject to phobias. In his early childhood he dreaded officers, fireworks, thunder, and cannons. As a fully grown man and emperor he developed, following the great fire of the Winter Palace in 1837, a nervous fear of flames and smoke. And he had always to avoid heights because of the resulting dizziness. There is also considerable evidence of Nicholas's persistent horror at the sight of blood which may have influenced his behavior on the day of the Decembrist uprising and again in the Russo-Turkish war of 1828–1829.

The intensity of the emperor's nervousness was such that it gradually began to affect his excellent health and his magnificent physique. Medically Nicholas I had a good record, being almost free of serious illness, but his powerful organism began to crumble under the continuous strain: he became subject to frequent nervous ailments, usually connected with political or personal crises; he had periods of depression; he became more and more pes-

---

[17] Schilder, I, 22–23. Cf. *SIRIO*, XCVIII, 38.

simistic in his outlook; and he found it increasingly difficult to control his temper. He lost his hair early, and his appearance indicated, more and more, tension and fatigue rather than his former fitness and strength. A number of the emperor's contemporaries speak of a disastrous break in his health between the years of 1840 and 1845. It was then, in their opinion, that Nicholas I aged suddenly and lost much of his former vigor and resilience. Nicholas's death at the age of fifty-eight marked, in a sense, the culmination of this process. The emperor succumbed to an aggravated cold which his tired body refused to fight.[18]

The heavy burden of an empire lay all the heavier on the shoulders of Nicholas because of his deep emotional involvement in his task and, in fact, in everything around him. The detachment and the superior calm of an autocrat, which Nicholas I tried so often and so hard to display, were merely a false front, and frequently they failed to perform even that function. In reality, the emperor was usually seething with passions, especially with rage and with fear, but also with a kind of exultation when he felt that he was striking telling blows against the enemy. He was given to sentimentality and to tears which coursed down his cheeks, for example, when he was preparing his strange 1848 manifesto. Nicholas's violent hatred concentrated apparently with equal ease on an individual, such as the French king Louis-Philippe, a group, such as the Decembrists, a people, such as the Poles, or a concept, such as Revolution. Much has been written about the emperor's tremendous emotional involvement in the Decembrist affair, an involvement which ceased only with his death. But Nicholas I had the same general attitude in all his other relations as well, assailing with equal vehemence "the King of the French," a corrupt minor official, or a delinquent sergeant in one of his regiments. His impulse was always to strike and keep striking until the object of his wrath was destroyed.

Aggressiveness, however, was not the emperor's only method of coping with the problems of life. Another was regimentation, orderliness, neatness, precision, an enormous effort to have every-

---

[18] For a professional discussion of Nicholas's health, see the reminiscences of his personal physician, Mandt, *Ein deutscher Arzt am Hofe Kaiser Nikolaus I.*

thing at all times in its proper place. Nicholas I was by nature
a drill master and an inspector general. The army became his
love, almost an obsession, from childhood to the end of his life.
Toy soldiers and military games constituted the devouring passion
of Nicholas's boyhood, as well as of that of his younger brother
Michael. Attempts to turn his attention in other directions proved
singularly unsuccessful. Typical is the story of one assignment. In
1810 the fourteen-year-old boy was told to write a theme on the
subject that military service was only one of the careers open to
a nobleman, and that he could also enter other occupations which
were equally useful and honorable. The future emperor failed to
produce any essay at all, and his teacher finally dictated one to
him.[19]

As he grew older, Nicholas's enchantment with the army retained its full force, while his activity in that field increased
greatly. He became a most devoted and enthusiastic officer and
a lifelong expert in such things as the field manual, drill of every
sort, and playing the drum. When Emperor Alexander I put
Nicholas in charge of the army engineers, the younger brother
finally obtained a large military establishment which he could drill,
inspect, and supervise continuously. Then, in 1825, he became the
supreme commander of all the Russian armed forces, and of all
of Russia besides. The new emperor eagerly took up his vastly
expanded military functions, but he remained a junior officer at
heart. His great attachment remained the minutiae of army life:
the physical appearance of his troops, small unit drill, uniforms
with their buttons, ribbons, and colors which he proceeded to
rearrange with a most painstaking devotion to duty. As emperor,
Nicholas continued to participate personally in as many military
reviews and exercises as possible. Indeed this kind of army life
represented "as he himself admitted, his one true delight." [20] It
was also observed that the Russian emperor could not restrain
his joy when he received honorary ranks and appointments in

---

[19] The original version of this story is to be found in *SIRIO*, XCVIII, 73.
[20] This typical comment was made by Count A. Benckendorff, one of Nicholas's closest associates. His fragmentary memoirs were published as an appendix
to Schilder, II. Quoted from page 730.

Prussian or Austrian regiments, and that he insisted on having appropriate uniforms made immediately and on drilling his new troops. Time and again he surprised Prussian and Austrian officers by his perfect knowledge of their field manuals.

It was especially at large-scale military reviews that Nicholas I experienced rapture, almost ecstasy, that he felt a violent swelling of his emotions and sensed the proximity of God. For instance, his letter to the empress describing the great military celebration arranged in 1839 on the field of Borodino is a remarkable combination of precise technical information about the ceremony and of powerful religious feeling. "From the depth of my soul I prayed to God for you, for our children, for the well-being of our entire great Russian family." [21] At another huge military review, with the Austrian ambassador in attendance, the emperor, his eyes filled with tears, placed his hand over his heart, lifted his gaze to heaven and prayed loudly: "God, I thank Thee for making me so mighty, and I beg Thee to give me the strength never to abuse this power." [22]

Regimentation was not limited to the army. Nicholas made every effort to regulate minutely and precisely all phases of his own life, and he treated other people in the same manner. Everything had to be in its proper order, nothing was to be left to chance. The emperor's personality was rigid and austere, strikingly deficient in spontaneity and warmth. To quote a contemporary of Nicholas:

> . . . the usual expression of his face has something severe and misanthropic in it, something that does not put one at all at one's ease. His smile is a smile of civility which is not at all a result of gaiety or of spontaneity. The habit of repressing these feelings has become so inseparable from his very being that you see in him no awkwardness, no embarrassment, nothing studied; and yet all his words, as all his movements, follow a cadence as if he had a sheet of music in front of him. . . . There is nothing in the tone of his voice or in the construction of his

---

[21] The letter is reproduced in Schiemann, III, 373–375.
[22] Ibid., pp. 327–328.

sentences that indicates pride or dissimulation; and yet you feel
that his heart is closed, that the barrier is impassable, and that
one would be mad to hope to penetrate the privacy of his
thought.[23]

It is not surprising that, as grand duke, Nicholas never attracted
the love of his subordinates. When he ascended the throne, his
passion for regimentation and regulation became government
policy, affecting in manifold ways every single Russian and leaving a special impress on his whole reign.[24]

This minute and perfectionist ordering of everything apparently
served the emperor as a defense mechanism. He needed it because
all his life he was on the defensive. Incessantly he struggled against
his own emotions, against the Decembrists and other enemies in
Russia, against corruption and other surrounding evils, against
world revolution. Order, precise, complete order, was necessary
to keep all of these opponents down, and Nicholas I would fly
into a panicky rage not only at a report of a new uprising in
Paris, but also when a soldier was not properly groomed for a
review or a student failed to be attentive in a classroom. Custine
remarked aptly: "The emperor of Russia is a military commander,
and each one of his days is a day of battle." [25]

The military emphasis of Nicholas was, again, mainly defensive.
Even as a child "whenever he built a summer house, for his
nurse or his governess, out of chairs, earth, or toys, he never
forgot to *fortify* it with guns—*for protection.*" [26] He grew to be
the chief military engineer of his country, specializing in for-
tresses, and still later, as emperor, he staked all on making the
entire land an impregnable fortress.

Life, for Nicholas, was full of strife and frustration, and he
found it difficult to endure. Fortunately, he could obtain solace
from several sources, one of which was his extremely highly
developed sense of duty. As the weary emperor wrote to his
wife in July, 1849:

---

[23] Quoted in Grunwald, *op. cit.,* p. 35.
[24] See chap. iv below.
[25] Custine, II, 9.
[26] *SIRIO,* XCVIII, 36. Italics in the original.

*How remarkable really is my fate. I am told that I am one
of the mightiest rulers of the world, and one must say that everything, that is, everything that is permissible, should be within
my reach, that, within the limits of discretion, I should be able
to do what I please and where. But in fact just the opposite is
the case as far as I am concerned. And if one asks about the basic
cause of this anomaly, there is only one word: Duty! Yes, this
is no empty word for those who have become accustomed from
their youth to understand it as I have. This word has a* sacred
*meaning which makes all personal considerations retreat, every-
thing must keep silent in front of this one feeling, everything
must step back, until one, together with this feeling, disappears
into the grave. That is my key word. It is hard, I admit it, I
suffer more from it than I can tell—but I have been created to
suffer.*[27]

Duty, then, was the answer to the tragedy of life, and the emperor
continued to do his duty, to perform his obligations, working
indefatigably all the time, often almost in a frenzy, working to
stifle the pain which threatened to become unbearable.[28] If this
principle of duty took no account of the personal wishes of the
emperor, it proved to be equally despotic toward his people. As
Nicholas I declared concerning his Polish subjects: "They must
be made *happy* in spite of themselves." [29]

Nicholas was completely devoted to his duties, and he expected
the same degree of devotion from his subordinates. As soon as
he became the chief of army engineers, he issued the following
typical order, written in his own hand:

*Obeying the high will of the emperor I assumed, on the
twentieth day of this month of January, the position of the inspector general of the engineers. In informing the corps of engineers of this fact, I consider it my duty to confirm to all the
members of the corps that, by diligent performance of one's*

---

[27] Schiemann, IV, 208–209. Emphasis in the original.
[28] See, for instance, Nicholas's statement in a letter to Frederick William IV,
ibid., p. 56.
[29] From a letter to Frederick William IV, *ibid.*, pp. 380–381. Italics in the
original.

duties, zeal for the interests of the state, and good conduct, every-one will earn imperial favor and will find in me an eager intercessor before His Majesty. But in the opposite case, for the slightest negligence, which will never and under no circumstances be pardoned, one will be treated according to the full severity of the laws. I expect to have perpetual satisfaction from the zeal and firmness of the commanders and from the enthusiasm and complete obedience of the lower ranks. Trusting in that, I assure each and every one that I know how to appreciate the kindness of the emperor who made me the commander of such a distin-guished corps. 20th January, year 1814. The inspector general of the engineers, Nicholas.[30]

When Nicholas succeeded Alexander as emperor he continued to demand unfailing service from his subjects, and he refused to excuse anybody "ever and under any circumstances." This at-titude was all the more natural for the new autocrat because, from childhood, he had exhibited a certain ruthlessness, a lack of con-sideration for others, and an inability to see any point of view but his own. Nicholas took himself and his work very seriously indeed. And he had virtually no sense of humor. The emperor's ceaseless efforts to make everybody follow his example—a subject to be discussed later in this study—ranged from his reorganization of much of the administrative procedure of the state and his appointment of numerous high-level committees which were to consider and reconsider ways to eliminate abuses and to establish more efficient government in Russia, to early morning personal visits of various government offices intended to find out whether their occupants were at their desks on time. Punishment swiftly followed transgression. Even as a boy Nicholas came to the con-clusion that Louis XVI of France had failed in his duty because he had been lenient with evildoers.[31] Much later he stated the matter succinctly to a Polish delegation: "I am willing to forget all the evil that you have done me personally, but the emperor does not forget." [32]

---

[30] The order is published in Schilder, I, 111.
[31] *Ibid.*, p. 475 n. 23.
[32] Schiemann, III, 277.

Nicholas carried through his determination not to be soft like his unfortunate French fellow ruler and never to forget. Relentless harshness became the outstanding characteristic of his reign, and was so noted by virtually all of his contemporaries, the rebellious Herzen, the independent Samarin, the loyal Pogodin, and many others of different positions, occupations, and beliefs. Once the emperor even issued an order meant to punish a warship. The occasion was the surrender of the frigate "Raphael" to the Turks in the war of 1828–1829. The edict, addressed to Admiral Greig, ended as follows: "Trusting in the help of the Almighty I persevere in the hope that the fearless Black Sea fleet, burning with the desire to wash off the shame of the frigate 'Raphael,' will not leave it in the hands of the enemy. But, when it is returned to our control, considering this frigate to be unworthy in the future to fly the flag of Russia and to serve together with the other vessels of our fleet, I order you to burn it." [33]

In the trials and tribulations of life, Nicholas was supported not only by his powerful sense of duty, but also by his firm religious convictions. The two were intrinsically connected. Duty meant in the last analysis duty to God, the ultimate supreme commander. In relation to Providence, the Russian autocrat remained a subordinate officer determined to execute his orders well and to occupy an honorable place in the great military review to be held in the next world. Many of his efforts failed, but his conscience remained clear as long as he did not cease to try his best. And he never ceased.

God, however—so Nicholas believed—had many functions: in addition to being the last link in the chain of command and the final judge, he was an ever-present influence in the life of an individual and also his consoler. It is remarkable to what extent the emperor felt the hand of God in his day-to-day existence. As he asserted in a letter to his brother Constantine: ". . . I am firmly convinced of divine protection which manifests itself in my case in too perceptible a manner for me not to be able to notice it in everything that happens to me, and here is my strength,

---

[33] Schilder, II, 234.

my consolation, my guiding light in all matters." [34] The emperor's messages to his military commanders were full of expressions of gratitude to God for His intercession and help in war, coupled with admonitions to be humble and modest in the realization that victory was a divine gift, not a human achievement. Providence served this purpose too for Nicholas: it enabled him to bow his head with the lowly and divested him, if only for fleeting moments, of the pride and the burden of an autocrat.

On another occasion, the emperor wrote to Count P. Tolstoi on August 9, 1831: "God rewarded me for my journey to Novgorod for, several hours after my return, He granted my wife to be delivered successfully of a son Nicholas." [35] The same day, in another letter, he discussed this event as follows: "God blessed my wife granting her yesterday a happy deliverance of a son Nicholas. Our joy is great and one cannot fail to recognize, from the depth of one's soul, the mercy of God Who, through all the grief and misfortunes, sustained the health of my wife in such a marvelous manner." [36] The journey to Novgorod which the emperor mentioned as his special merit was occasioned by a revolt in that district among the so-called military colonists. The ensuing reprisals included severe corporal punishment for some two thousand six hundred rebels, one hundred and twenty-nine of them dying in the course of the chastisement.[37] The horror of it all notwithstanding, Nicholas felt that he deserved a reward because he had performed his hard duty with courage, firmness, and dispatch.

The Russian ruler was well-nigh perfect in the execution of his wearisome religious obligations. He assiduously attended long church services and in his numerous visits to the provincial centers of his sprawling empire he invariably began at the cathedral where he was received with proper, often extensive, ceremony, and which he entered devoutly and with many genuflections. All this was, of course, a matter of protocol which Nicholas would not eliminate

[34] *Perepiska imperatora Nikolaya Pavlovicha s velikim knyazem tsesarevichem Konstantinom Pavlovichem. Tom I. 1825–1829.* Vol. 131, *SIRIO*, p. 202.
[35] Schilder, II, 487 n. 451.
[36] *Ibid.*
[37] *Ibid.*, n. 450.

or even curtail. But beyond that, he found reassurance, tranquility, and joy in Orthodox church services which formed a part of his life from childhood. Nicholas loved church singing, and at times sang with the choir. He prayed, apparently with ardor and with conviction, and he followed closely every part of the ritual. In the few spare moments of his crowded schedule he read the Bible, especially the Gospels and the Epistles, daily, at least so some of his biographers assert. There is even evidence that the emperor was interested in contemporary theological writing, which is all the more noteworthy because he was not at all intellectually inclined.[38]

Nicholas was fully Orthodox in that he was devoted to the Orthodox Church in the same complete and unquestioning manner in which he was devoted to his country or to his regiment. He had none of the spiritual restlessness and cosmopolitan religious seekings of his immediate imperial predecessor. Nevertheless he appreciated Christian denominations other than his own and was keenly aware of the distinction between Christendom and the non-Christian world. He even developed a special liking for Lutheranism, the faith of his numerous Prussian relatives. Indeed, such German historians as Schiemann have noted that the emperor's religious attitude was, in certain particulars, Protestant rather than Orthodox.[39]

Nicholas's religious convictions deserve attention for several reasons. They were all-pervasive, affecting every phase of his life in an important manner. They were applied consistently and thoroughly by the emperor to many complex personal and political problems. Yet apparently he was never led to doubt these fundamental assumptions, either in youthful revolt, or in mature despair. Nicholas's faith remained always simple, blunt, and unswerving. In his own words, he believed "in the manner of a peasant." [40] The emperor fully recognized the value of religion

[38] There are, for example, some intriguing reports that Nicholas I read and liked A. Khomyakov's theology. See Khomyakov, *Polnoe sobranie sochinenii*, vol. II, *Sochineniya bogoslovskie*, p. 89 n. xi.

[39] See, for instance, Schiemann, II, 114.

[40] Barsukov, *Zhizn i trudy M. P. Pogodina*, XIII, 388.

in maintaining morality, order, and stable government, in his state as in any other. But, at least as far as his personal beliefs were concerned, the reverse relationship was the more important one: discipline, law, autocratic rule, with all their burdens and all their pains, had to go on functioning because they had been ordained by God, a superior officer from whose decision there could be no appeal. The state was to serve God, not God the state.

The emperor's sense of duty and his straightforward religious convictions were closely connected to the general sincerity and honesty of his character. His admirers presented Nicholas I as a knight in shining armor; his critics marvelled at his directness and bluntness. But even the antagonists of the Russian despot often had to admit his integrity and his truthfulness. To cite the opinion of Custine: "I do not believe that there is today on any throne a prince who detests falsehood so much and who lies so little as this one." [41] Historians have on the whole confirmed this verdict. It may be added that Nicholas I considered honesty essential even when it involved the protection of something he hated. Thus he censured the violation of the constitutions in their countries by both Charles X of France and Ferdinand II of the Kingdom of the Two Sicilies, because the two rulers had previously accepted these fundamental documents.

Nicholas's behavior was strongly affected by the Christian ethic, and also by the aristocratic code in which he was brought up. The first influence represented often an ideal to be sought, actual performance falling far short of it. But it did provide a basic frame of reference for the emperor's moral values and judgments, and it may have accounted for such aspects of his behavior as his leniency towards the Turkish prisoners of war and his insistence on the humane treatment of the population in occupied territories. The code of a gentleman emphasized honesty, honor, and proper manners. It made Nicholas react very sharply to the news that one of his generals had struck a captive enemy,[42] and, on a larger

---

[41] Custine, II, 203.
[42] Schilder, II, 480 n. 423.

scale, it led to his depending too much in his foreign policy on personal meetings between rulers and on verbal promises. In ethics as in everything else the emperor was an absolutist: the same true moral principles held sway everywhere and at all times, and nobody had the right to escape their compelling power.

Religion, morality, duty all played their part in supporting Nicholas I in his life of continuous struggle. His family contributed to the same end in a somewhat different manner, by allowing the tsar to express certain emotions and to develop certain sides of his personality which remained otherwise completely repressed. Nicholas enjoyed his family very much, and on most counts he was a good husband and a good father. His marriage to the Prussian princess who later became the Russian Empress Alexandra was a love match as well as a dynastic arrangement, and the couple remained very close to each other for many happy years. Their correspondence offers an impressive testimonial of their mutual affection as well as of the fullness with which the ruler kept his wife informed of the affairs of state and of everything else that interested him. Nicholas was, of course, the master of his family and of his household as much as of his empire, but Alexandra acquired the position of a trusted and loved companion in all matters. The emperor became similarly devoted to his children and later, as they began to grow up, he maintained his attachment to them, building them palaces, arranging appropriate marriages, and generally playing the role of paterfamilias on a grand scale. Family meant simplicity, peace, and quiet for Nicholas, and these gifts were extremely welcome after the enormous formality and strain of his exalted office. But his close relationship to his wife was particularly important. As Nicholas wrote her in 1836, after nineteen years of marriage:

> God has given you such a happy character that it is no merit to love you. I exist for you, yes, you are I—I do not know how to say it differently, but I am not your salvation, as you say. Our salvation is over there yonder, yonder where we shall all be admitted to rest from the tribulations of life. I mean, if we

earn it down here by the fulfillment of our duties. Hard as they
may be, one performs them with joy when one has a beloved being
at home near whom one can breathe again and gain new strength.
If I was now and then demanding, this happened because I look
for everything in you. If I do not find it, I am distressed, I say to
myself, no, she does not understand me, and these are unique,
rare, but difficult moments. For the rest, happiness, joy, calm—
that is what I seek and find in my old Mouffy. I wished, as much
as this was in my power, to make you a hundred times happier,
if I could have divined how this end could have been obtained.[43]

Yet even this imposing declaration of Nicholas's love for his
wife indicated that all was not well in the imperial household. In
truth, the emperor was in some ways an exacting and a harsh
husband. He found it difficult to accept the fact that his wife
often failed to keep up with his restless activity, especially as her
health declined with the years. He could hardly bear separation
from her, even for brief periods of time. The crisis in the summer
of 1845 illustrated well the attitude of the emperor, although
at the same time it represented an extreme case of his neurotic
behavior toward his wife. Trouble arose when the empress accepted medical advice to spend some time in the sunshine of
Sicily. Nicholas, who had expected that his wife would not have
to go any further away than the Crimea, was seized by one of his
attacks of panic and rage. For days the imperial family and
those around them were in extreme nervous turmoil. The stalwart
Dr. Mandt, who prescribed the foreign trip, has thus depicted
one encounter with the emperor:

He remained for a moment standing in front of me, his dark,
grey soldier's cloak was hanging loosely from his shoulders, his
naked feet were covered by slippers, which, as he had told me
once, were twenty-five years old and came as a wedding present,
his big, powerful eyes rested sadly on me—and it was as if an
electric discharge had gone through all my limbs—a tear collected
slowly there and threatened to roll over the brim; then he gripped

---

[43] Schiemann, III, 317–318. Emphasis in the original. "Mouffy" was an en-
dearing name the emperor used for the empress.

hard with his entire right hand my left forearm, squeezed it strongly and said: "Leave me my wife here!" [44]

The empress herself confided to her diary the following record of those trying days:

He had still hoped it would be the Crimea, and when the climate there appeared insufficiently strong and safe and Dr. Mandt proposed Palermo, he appeared to be beside himself, that is, in his own way and like no other man could be, not storming, or angry, or crying, but icily cold, and that towards me. He did not address to me two sentences in the course of an entire week. Those were such hard days, such a burden, such tugs at the heart that I had to become sick and nervous. But I shall write no more about this. Since last Sunday it has become better, and he is sad and talkative in the natural manner, and the best is what he told me last Thursday, when we went to the city for the last time and prayed in the Kazan Cathedral and in the fortress and again in tears in the Winter Palace, namely: "I want here to tell you, and you alone, something, and it is that I count on visiting you in Palermo, when and how I do not know as yet." [45]

The emperor's fidelity to his wife and the very close attachment of the imperial couple did not last all the way to Nicholas's death. Many reasons can be advanced for this change in the emperor's behavior. He was not only the ruler of a great empire as well as "the most handsome man in Europe," but also a charmer who enjoyed feminine company and was often at his best with the ladies. Nicholas's aristocratic code of behavior included the principle of gallantry. Time and again in the course of imperial voyages the Russian autocrat would forego various personal comforts so that female members of his wife's retinue could be better accommodated. Moreover, the emperor was extremely responsive to physical appearance, especially to feminine beauty, and he has often been described as a sensuous and passionate man. Perhaps more to the point is the probability that

[44] Mandt, *op. cit.*, p. 437.
[45] Schiemann, IV, 65.

Nicholas was seeking in a new relationship more of the re-assurance and support which he needed so badly throughout his life but which kept constantly evading him.

The emperor's choice fell on Mademoiselle Nelidov, a lady in waiting. But although observers noted Nicholas's great interest in her as early as the autumn of 1841, it took the Russian ruler several years to overcome his, and possibly her, moral scruples and establish a liaison with her. Characteristically, the intervening period was for Nicholas a time of bitter inner struggle, and one can appreciate the remark of Countess Nesselrode, the wife of the foreign minister, to the effect that she wished that the emperor would simply make Mademoiselle Nelidov his mistress and be done with it.[46] The liaison, once established, proved to be a permanent one, and it was not a secret at court. The position of the empress was all the more painful because she had to tolerate the new favorite in her entourage. Later Nicholas apparently acquired one more mistress, again a lady in waiting, Mademoiselle Kutuzov.

The emperor treated his numerous children much as he treated his wife. The relationship was a close and a warm one, Nicholas being invariably an interested and solicitous father. But, here again, the unfortunate personality of the emperor contributed to certain acute crises and tensions, for example, when the romance of his elder son and heir to the throne, Alexander, with a Polish girl threatened to spoil a projected dynastic marriage.[47]

Nicholas I had a number of artistic and aesthetic interests. He passionately admired nature, particularly beautiful southern landscapes. He became a specialist in architecture, both military and civil, and he loved to apply his knowledge of this field in practice. The emperor was brought up to appreciate art, and he developed great enthusiasm for the paintings of the Renaissance, especially those by Raphael and Titian, and for statues of classical antiquity. In music too he profited from both native ability and training.

---

[46] Countess Nesselrode to her son Dmitrii, St. Petersburg, Oct. 30, 1842. Nesselrode, *Lettres et papiers du chancelier Comte de Nesselrode. 1760–1856,* VIII, 182; hereafter cited as Nesselrode, *Lettres.* For the emperor's continuing love of the empress see, e.g., Tyutcheva, especially p. 168.

[47] This episode is discussed in a different context in chap. iii below.

He sang well, and he played the horn in a good palace quartet which the empress accompanied on the piano. Famous musicians, including Franz Liszt, were invited to give "house" concerts for the imperial family. As ruler, Nicholas did much to promote art and architecture in Russia. As to literature, his tastes ran generally to the sentimental and the second-rate. The emperor read much, trying in fact to acquaint himself with everything published in Russia and with many items produced abroad, but he had little appreciation of writing as a form of art. His judgments of books were consistently moral and political rather than aesthetic, and he missed most of the glory of the Russian literature of his day.[48]

It has been noted that Nicholas's artistic preferences formed a close parallel to his other interests and inclinations. One historian wrote: "His aesthetics is permeated with militarism as its best incarnation. His politics and his aesthetics are in a remarkable harmony: everything in line. He loved uniformity, straight lines, a severe symmetry, the regularity of design." [49] It may be added that the bay of Naples, St. Peter's, and the statues of the Vatican gallery inspired the emperor with much the same rapture which he felt at the sight of well-aligned military formations or when inspecting a mighty fortress.[50]

Life was burdensome and painful to Nicholas I. Yet, instead of rebelling violently against his surroundings, he achieved a certain adjustment by means of emphasis on the concept of duty, on religion, and on the sad lot of the Christian in this vale of tears. He also found some relief in a close relationship with his wife and with a few other people, although these human contacts in turn often led to new difficulties. It was natural for the emperor to develop a pessimistic and fatalistic outlook. His associates noted that he took little care of himself, refusing, for instance, to

---

[48] As an example see the summary and analysis of Nicholas's opinions concerning Lermontov's "A Hero of Our Times" in Schiemann, III, 411–412.

[49] Presnyakov, p. 91.

[50] Many of the emperor's impressionistic accounts of the beauties of nature and of works of art can be conveniently found in an appendix to Schiemann, IV, Anlage II. Briefe Kaiser Nikolaus' I. an die Kaiserin aus Italien und Wien. Dezember 1845—Januar 1846, pp. 366–380. The letters are in the original French.

postpone his trips at the news of assassination plots, with this typical remark: "God is my guardian, and if I am no longer needed for Russia, He will take me to Himself." [51]

As political misfortunes piled on unresolved personal conflicts, the emperor's attitude became more and more that of hopelessness and resignation. The Crimean War came as the crowning blow. When Nicholas's diplomatic system collapsed, and Russia was left alone against a hostile coalition, the weary tsar remarked: "Nothing remains to me but my duty as long as it pleases God to leave me at the head of Russia." [52] "I shall carry my cross until all my strength is gone." [53] "Thy will be done." [54]

II

Nicholas was born on the sixth of July, 1796. His parents were Grand Duke Paul and Grand Duchess Mary. Some three and a half months later, following the death of Catherine II, his father became Emperor Paul I of Russia. Nicholas had three brothers, but two of them, the future Emperor Alexander and Constantine, were nineteen and seventeen years older than he. It was only the third, Michael, his junior by two years, and a sister, Anne, who became his childhood companions and intimate lifelong friends.

Paul was extremely neurotic, overbearing, and despotic in every way. Yet it is believed that he showed kindness and consideration to his younger children, and that, in fact, he loved and cherished them tenderly. He was killed in the palace revolution of 1801 which made Alexander emperor when Nicholas was not quite five years old. The empress, on the contrary, remained formal and cold in her relationship to the young grand princes and princesses, very much in keeping with her general character. She

---

[51] From Benckendorff's *Memoirs* in Schilder, II, 665.
[52] From a letter to Frederick William IV, August 26, 1854, published in an appendix to Schiemann, IV, 434–435.
[53] In a letter to Prince Gorchakov, the commander in the Crimea; quoted in Polievktov, p. 376.
[54] *Ibid.* See also Nicholas's letter to another commander, Prince Paskevich, quoted in Schiemann, IV, 305; and Tyutcheva, p. 180.

belonged, apparently, among those human beings who combine numerous conventional virtues with a certain rigidity and lack of warmth. In the words of Count Benckendorff who knew her well:

> Demanding of herself she was also demanding of her subordinates; always tireless, she did not favor them if they appeared tired; finally, loving sincerely and constantly those to whom she had deigned to give her friendship or whom she patronized because of the inclination of her heart or of her mind, she demanded from them complete reciprocity. The only failing of this extraordinary woman was her being excessively, one may say, exacting of her children and of the people dependent on her.[55]

Nicholas's childhood, and by implication his later years as well, were strongly affected by the exacting and formal treatment which he received from his mother.

The future emperor's first guardian and instructress was a Scottish nurse, Miss Jane Lyon, who was appointed by Catherine II to take care of the infant, and who stayed with Nicholas constantly during the first seven years of his life. Described as a woman of strong, impulsive, and noble character, she probably exercised a profound influence on the child who became closely attached to her. From Miss Lyon the young grand duke learned even such things as the Russian alphabet, his first Russian prayers, and his hatred of the Poles, or at least he liked later to trace the origin of his bitter antipathy toward that people to the stories told by his nurse about her painful experiences in Warsaw in the turbulent year of 1794.

A new phase in Nicholas's life started in the years 1802–1803 when the women around him were replaced by men, and when his regular education began. General Matthew Lamsdorff, a Baltic German nobleman who had distinguished himself in military service and in administration, was put in charge of the upbringing

---

[55] Schilder, II, 186. See also *SIRIO* XCVIII, 20–21. The empress's letters of instruction to Nicholas and Michael at the time of their departures for travel or service in 1814, 1815, and 1816 are reproduced; *ibid.*, pp. 75–81, 83–87, 88–90.

of the future emperor. The choice was an unfortunate one. Whatever qualifications the new mentor might have had for his earlier
positions, he was not a suitable senior tutor for the young grand
duke: "A stern, cruel, and extremely irritable man, Lamsdorff
possessed none of the abilities required of a teacher; all his efforts
were directed towards breaking the will of his pupil and towards
going against all his inclinations; corporal punishment was prac-
ticed quite often." [56] Thus rigid and formal upbringing, based on
court etiquette, which the empress had instituted for her son
from his infancy, was supplemented by severe and formalistic
training. It is not surprising that Nicholas came to conceive of
education as a very painful and exacting process based above all
on discipline and obedience on the part of the student. As emperor, he imposed this kind of schooling on Russia.

The growing grand duke was taught a wide variety of subjects
proper to his station in life. Dancing, music, and singing were
among his first courses, and in these fields it was church singing
which appealed to Nicholas most and which he came to know
well. French lessons also started early, in 1802. At first, the
empress herself gave them to her son, performing her duties
"with great accuracy." [57] Later the Swiss, du Puget Dyverdon,
gave Nicholas more advanced training in that language. He also
taught the grand duke world history and general geography in
French. Reportedly, it was he who instilled in the future emperor
a hatred of the French Revolution. As to the Russian language,
if we exclude the rudiments learned from Miss Lyon, instruction
began also in 1802, the officer of the day being charged with the
task. Religion was added in 1803, and at about the same time
Nicholas started to study the history and geography of Russia.
In 1804, a well-known scholar, F. Adelung, began giving German

---

[56] "Nikolai I," *Entsiklopedicheskii Slovar* (Brockhaus-Efron) XXI, 119. This
is a typical estimate of Lamsdorff. For more detail see *SIRIO*, XCVIII, 26–27.

[57] This quoted phrase, as well as much information about Nicholas's education,
is taken from Schilder, I. The most important source material for these years
is to be found in *SIRIO*, XCVIII, 1–100. The volume, edited by N. Dubrovin,
is entitled *Materialy i cherty k biografii Imperatora Nikolaya I i k istorii ego
tsarstvovaniya*, and the section, composed by M. Korff, *Rozhdenie i pervye
dvadtsat let zhizni* (1796–1817 gg.).

lessons to the grand duke; later he also taught his pupil Latin and Greek. It is interesting to note that Nicholas disliked composition in any language from the start, and that he never became a master of written style in any of them, expressing himself invariably in a labored and clumsy manner.

Before long new subjects were added in rapid succession to the grand duke's curriculum. In 1804 he began to study drawing and arithmetic, in 1806 geometry, and in 1808 algebra. Physics lessons started in 1807. Nicholas was not attracted by mathematics of any kind, but he enjoyed physics, and he became an enthusiastic and highly proficient student of drawing. In the course of these years the future emperor also learned horseback riding, and he was introduced at an early age to the theater, costume balls, and other court entertainment.

The year 1809 marked another divide in Nicholas's life. The former "high school" education was replaced by something resembling a university program. Together with that change, the grand duke was deprived of the few childhood companions he had, except for his brother Michael, and an unremitting effort was made to keep him busy every minute of the day: "For this purpose special lecture tables were constructed, with a tally of daily, weekly, and monthly study hours. Not only did each teacher compose such tables, but the empress herself gave much attention to their construction, examination, and correction, a fact proved by an enormous number of extant schedules written in her hand." [58] The new curriculum included political economy taught by the well-known scholar H. Storch, logic, moral philosophy, natural law, and the history of law, as well as higher mathematics and physics. English, Latin, and Greek were added to the language program. Formal military instruction was also introduced: the distinguished general of the corps of engineers, Oppermann, supervised a number of courses which, in addition to engineering and "army service," came to include strategy.

The assertion that Nicholas was given a mediocre education which was not intended to prepare him for the throne has become a cliché in historical literature. Several scholars, however, have

---

[58] Schilder, I, 31.

challenged both parts of this statement. Polievktov, for instance, has argued that the grand duke's course of studies was both thorough and with a strong emphasis on politics, the essential subject for a ruler. Nicholas's military courses also represented, in the opinion of this historian, a necessity for a European monarch of the first decades of the nineteenth century.[59] While the issue cannot be considered settled, it is reasonable to believe that Alexander I and Empress Mary were aware of at least the possibility of Nicholas's assumption of supreme rule in Russia, and that this contingency affected the grand duke's upbringing. The picture of a completely unprepared man suddenly invested with one of the most difficult offices in the world, a picture dear to the emperor himself, is grossly overdrawn.

But, whatever the intentions of Nicholas's mentors might have been, it is clear that the young grand duke derived little profit from their work. The future emperor was an inattentive and generally poor student. This fact can be attributed not only to the deadening formalism and rigidity of the whole system of education to which he was subjected and to the grand duke's own shortcomings in character and capacities, but also to the failings of individual teachers. As a rule they were competent, sometimes splendidly competent, in their respective subjects; but they did not know how to present their material to a young man of little better than average ability who was not intellectually inclined. Nicholas made their task harder by his remarkable steadfastness, for he refused to change his habits and attitudes and was slow to acquire new interests. Throughout life, the emperor deprecated his years of study, emphasizing their tedium and the poverty of the results achieved. He even developed a lasting hatred for some of the subjects he had to learn, notably for the Latin language.[60]

The glowing exception to this record of scanty accomplishment was military science. The grand duke loved all branches of it,

---

[59] Polievktov, p. 7. See also, e.g., Kornilov, *Modern Russian History*, I, 229.

[60] Nicholas and Latin never got along well. To quote a pedagogical entry by one of the grand duke's tutors: "It was necessary to threaten a whipping and to make a great to-do about the matter in order to facilitate the conjugation of Latin verbs." *SIRIO*, XCVIII, 51; see also p. 69.

from drill to strategy, and he was fortunate in obtaining a number of skilled and stimulating teachers in that field. Perhaps Nicholas proved his military proficiency best by becoming a fine army engineer, but he also developed into an expert in several other areas of military knowledge, and, as it has already been observed, he always remained in his heart a dedicated junior officer. It should be added that the empress tried to combat her son's exclusive devotion to the army, but that in this matter, as in many others, his strong and stubborn character won out, the little story about his failure to write a theme describing careers other than military service being typical of Nicholas's attitude.

Circumstances also favored militarism. Nicholas's education, as well as that of his younger brother, was interrupted and largely terminated by the great events of 1812–1815. The grand duke shared in full the emotional lift and the upsurge of patriotism experienced by the Russians, especially of the younger generation, during the epic struggle of their fatherland against Napoleon. The future emperor, for his part, never doubted the defeat of the French invader, and he won a silver ruble from his sister Anne on a bet he made after the fall of Moscow: his wager had been that the enemy troops would be driven from Russia by January 1, 1813.[61] Of course, Nicholas wanted to join the army, but it was only in 1814 that Alexander I allowed him and his brother Michael to do so. The grand dukes, much to their disgust, were kept out of the fighting, and had to compensate themselves with sightseeing in Paris after its occupation, Nicholas as usual paying special attention to the military establishment, and with similar visits to Switzerland, the Low Countries, and to several parts of Germany. The future emperor saw many novel places and met numerous new people, including his later antagonist, Louis-Philippe, the Duke of Orleans, who, in 1814, attracted Nicholas's admiration by his happy and devoted family life. Napoleon's return in 1815 gave the grand dukes their chance to join the active army at last, but the Hundred Days were too short for that army to get into combat. Once more, the young men had to be satisfied instead with an interesting stay in Paris. Thus,

---

[61] Schilder, I, 38.

although Nicholas did not get to fight in the famous campaigns of 1812–1815, he, nevertheless, was then called to active service. The future emperor was only too willing to answer the summons, and in the years following he assumed ever-increasing responsibilities in the armed forces of the Russian Empire.

While militarism represented one major influence in Nicholas's life, another, not entirely unrelated to the first, arose from his German, especially Prussian, links. The emperor's mother was a German princess; his father descended from the ruling houses of Holstein and of Anhalt-Zerbst. He had numerous relatives in various German principalities, and he enjoyed visiting them during his trips abroad. At home, he was brought up by such Baltic Germans as Countess Lieven who supervised his care when he was a child and General Lamsdorff who was put in charge of his education. Another member of the same nobility, Count V. Adlerberg, was probably Nicholas's oldest and best friend outside the imperial family itself. Still other Germans were the grand duke's teachers, associates, or immediate subordinates in almost every phase of his activity. Most important, however, proved to be Nicholas's relationship to Prussia. It was on November 4, 1815, at a state dinner in Berlin, that Alexander I and King Frederick William III rose to announce the engagement of Nicholas and Princess Charlotte of Prussia. The solemn wedding followed some twenty months later, on July 13, 1817. The match represented clearly a dynastic and political arrangement sought by both reigning houses which had stood together in the decisive years of the struggle against Napoleon and after that at the Congress of Vienna. Nicholas, as it turned out, more than fulfilled the calculations involved in his marriage. Not only was he in love with his wife, but he became very closely attached to his father-in-law as well as to his new royal brothers, one of whom was later to be his fellow ruler as King Frederick William IV. Beyond that, Nicholas was powerfully attracted by the Prussian court and even more so by the Prussian army. He felt remarkably happy and at home in his adopted family and country which for many years he tried to visit as often as he could. This German, especially

Prussian, orientation of the Russian emperor exetcised a profound influence on his thought and on his actions.

To complete his training, Grand Duke Nicholas was sent on two educational voyages, an extensive tour of Russia which lasted from May to September, 1816, and a journey to England where the future emperor spent four months late that same year and early in 1817. The Russian trip covered much ground at great speed and was quite superficial, but it has interest for the historian because of the notes on everything seen and heard which Nicholas took following the instructions of his mother. The grand duke's observations deal, typically, with appearances rather than with causes, and they reflect a number of his prejudices, including his bitter dislike of the Poles and the Jews. It may be added that quick inspection tours, of which that of 1816 was the first, later became almost an obsession of the emperor.

The visit to England was a different matter. Nicholas stayed for the most part in London although he traveled to a score of other places, even as far north as the Scottish capital of Edinburgh. Prior to the voyage, Nesselrode had prepared a clever note on England for the grand duke, explaining that while that country was justly admired for its political institutions it also served as an excellent illustration of the fact that such institutions could never be transplanted from one state to another, the peculiar English system of government, as well as every other, being a natural result of the particular past of the given nation. This warning was probably superfluous, for although Nicholas attended the opening of the houses of parliament and in general obtained some knowledge of English politics, his only recorded comments on that score were unfavorable. The future emperor found it much more congenial to examine military and naval centers. His favorite English companion was the Duke of Wellington.

Less than a year after his return to Russia and a few months after his marriage, Nicholas was appointed inspector general of the army corps of engineers. In subsequent years he also held several other military positions, but of secondary significance. By contrast, the grand duke was delegated vast, though vague, power on those occasions when Alexander I left the country while Constantine, the other elder brother, remained, as usual, at his post in Warsaw.

There is no agreement among historians concerning Alexander I's precise intentions in regard to the imperial succession in Russia nor concerning the emperor's treatment of his young brother Nicholas. To mention the treatment first, opinions range all the way from emphasis on the solicitous help and support extended by the reigning monarch to the view that he was bent on denying any opportunity for popularity and prestige to the grand duke whom he considered a possible rival for prominence and power. Some plausible arguments support allegations of Alexander I's evil intent. For instance, it is true that he was an extremely suspicious person who remembered well the palace revolution which made him emperor by means of the overthrow and murder of his father. It is also true that the tasks assigned to Nicholas involved much painstaking work, but little distinction or glory. But all this falls far short of being solid and convincing evidence.[62] Nicholas's lack of popularity resulted from his deplorable character, not from any machinations on the part of his brother. His military preoccupation was entirely congenial to him, and it was natural in a family where all male members were passionate soldiers. It is worth noting too that Nicholas himself always retained the very highest regard for his "angelic" predecessor.[63] Alexander may well have been inconsistent in his treatment of Nicholas as in everything else, but there is not sufficient reason to consider him the grand duke's secret enemy.

As to the problem of succession, the facts are now reasonably clear, although some of their implications as well as the motives of the main actors in that drama remain subject to dispute. Paul I, who had himself long been deprived of the throne by his imperious mother, promulgated a law of succession in the direct

---

[62] Historians who accuse Alexander of wicked designs against his younger brother often merely repeat similar unsupported conjectures of some of the emperor's contemporaries, for instance, of Grech, *Zapiski o moei zhizni*, p. 425.

[63] "Angel" was the usual name for Alexander in the imperial family, and, especially in the case of Nicholas, this form of reference represented much more than simply a fashionable epithet.

male line. Alexander I had no sons or grandsons and, therefore, Grand Duke Constantine, the second brother, was his logical successor. But the heir presumptive married a Polish lady not of royal blood in 1820, and, in connection with the marriage, renounced his rights to the throne. Nicholas was thus to become the next ruler of Russia, the entire matter being stated clearly, in 1822, in a special manifesto confirmed with Alexander I's signature. The manifesto, however, remained unpublished. Instead the emperor ordered Archbishop Filaret to keep the original secretly in the Cathedral of the Assumption in Moscow, and had copies deposited in the Senate, the Holy Synod, and the State Council in St. Petersburg. In case of Alexander's death, the manifesto was to be opened and read before anything else was done. Only a handful of people were given exact information about this state secret; furthermore, although these few included such a bystander as the writer and court historian Karamzin, the two grand dukes themselves were not fully informed. To be sure, Constantine knew that he had renounced the throne, and Nicholas had received some clear indications that he was to become emperor,[64] but both brothers remained ignorant of the precise content of the manifesto and of the legal procedure chosen by Alexander to settle the issue of succession. The damaging secretiveness on the part of the reigning monarch can be best explained by the supposition that he did not consider the arrangement as necessarily final and wanted to retain freedom to change it in the future.

Following Alexander I's unexpected death in southern Russia on the first of December, 1825, Constantine and the Polish kingdom where he was commander in chief swore allegiance to Nicholas, but Nicholas, the Russian capital, and the Russian army swore allegiance to Constantine. While the behavior of the older brother was consistent and clear, that of the younger one needs explanation. As mentioned, Nicholas had been warned that he was expected to ascend the throne of Russia in due time, and the manifesto, which he now read, stated Alexander's intentions be-

⁶⁴ See especially Schilder, I, 37–38, 120–123; also, the chapter on Nicholas's accession to the throne in Polievktov, pp. 39–58.

yond any doubt. Still, there was something to be said on the
other side. The legal issue remained confused: unfortunately
Alexander's manifesto had precisely the form of a sovereign's personal will and testament in dynastic matters which Paul's law
of succession had aimed to abolish; also, it was arguable whether
a dead monarch's unpublished manifesto had validity in what
could be considered, by definition, the reign of another autocrat.
Furthermore, Nicholas was unpopular, and pressure was exerted
on him by the Governor General of St. Petersburg, Count Milora-
dovích, and others to step aside in favor of his brother Constantine
who appeared to the Russian army and the Russian people to
be the legitimate heir of Alexander. Another important, though
rather intangible, factor was Nicholas's own attitude: it seems
that he was not only reluctant to ascend the throne, but also
tried to avoid and forget the entire issue, just as he had earlier,
apparently, failed to profit by the emperor's warnings about his
future and as later he would invariably depict himself as an out-
sider suddenly thrust into the imperial office.[65] It was thus only
after Constantine's uncompromising reaffirmation of his position,
and the resulting lapse of time, that Nicholas decided to publish
Alexander's manifesto and become emperor of Russia.

On December the twenty-sixth, 1825—December the fourteenth
Russian style—when the guard regiments in St. Petersburg were
to swear allegiance for the second time in rapid succession, this
time to Nicholas, liberal conspirators staged what came to be
known in Russian history as the Decembrist rebellion.[66] Utilizing
their influence in the army where many of them were officers,
they started a mutiny in several units which they entreated to
defend the rightful interests of Constantine against his usurping
brother. Altogether some three thousand misled rebels came in

---

[65] Nicholas's behavior in regard to the imperial succession had, in my opinion,
deeper psychological roots than those recognized by the historians who suggest
that he was sullen and uncoöperative in December, 1825, because he was
offended at not having been consulted earlier on the matter.

[66] The literature on the Decembrists and their rebellion, both published
primary sources and secondary works, is enormous. In English, a convenient
account of the movement is presented in Mazour, *The Decembrist Rebellion.
The First Russian Revolution. 1825*; a reconstruction of the color and mood of
the period is attempted in Zetlin, *The Decembrists*.

military formation to the Senate Square, in the heart of the capital. Nicholas, though at first his position was a dangerous one and he had very few troops to defend even the palace itself in case of attack, rallied rapidly. Before long the mutineers were faced with troops several times their number and strength. The two forces stood opposite each other for several hours. The rebels failed to act because of their general confusion and lack of leadership; the new emperor hesitated to start his reign with a massacre of his subjects, hoping that they could be talked back into submission.[67] Verbal inducements by Miloradovich, the Metropolitan Seraphim, Grand Duke Michael, and General Voinov, the commander of the guard, all failed. As dusk began to gather on the afternoon of that northern winter day, artillery was brought into action. Several canister shots dispersed the rebels killing sixty or seventy of them. Large-scale arrests followed. Another related uprising, this time among troops in southern Russia, was also easily suppressed.

The Decembrist rebellions had slender chance of success. But they proved to Nicholas the vital and the insidious strength of his great enemy, revolution. And coming as they did at the very beginning of his reign, they formed naturally the point of departure for much of the activity and the thought of the new government. The emperor himself showed a passionate interest and played a painstaking part in the investigation and the trial of the conspirators. Indeed, he could never forget those to whom he would refer ironically as his "friends of the fourteenth of December."

Nicholas's life during the thirty years of his reign was intrinsically connected with the history of Russia, and it should be considered in that context.[68] Suffice it to say here that the autocrat's character and convictions had been formed before he ascended the throne, and that they did not change. They were now applied

---

[67] Nicholas's own explanation that he did not want to shed blood is quite plausible, although it was probably not the only consideration involved. Not the least painful aspect of the Decembrist rebellion for the imperial family rested in its shame and scandal. As poor Empress Mary kept repeating while the guns fired in the Senate Square: "What will Europe say!" Schilder, I, 292.

[68] See chaps. iv and v below.

on a much grander scale, but with the same burning zeal and deadly determination with which Grand Duke Nicholas used to drill his guards. Or, perhaps, there was a certain evolution with the years. It seems that with the passage of time Nicholas became still more irritable, even more inflexible and despotic in his ways, as well as a much sicker man. Political misfortunes culminating in the Crimean War piled ever-new burdens onto his shoulders.

Death came as liberation to the weary and harrassed Russian tsar. The fatal disease began as an ordinary cold which Nicholas caught at a court wedding late in February, 1855.[69] As usual, the emperor continued to go about his duties without taking care of his health. After a week the illness spread, affecting and paralyzing his lungs. During the night of the first of March Nicholas suddenly learned from Dr. Mandt that he had only several hours to live. The emperor accepted his fate with the utmost dignity. After confession and prayer, he proceeded to say personal farewells to the members of his family, to his few intimate friends in the capital, to the members of the imperial household including the servants, to certain soldiers who were to carry the last imperial greeting to their comrades. Overcoming pain by a tremendous effort of will, he charged his son and successor with additional final messages to be passed to different army units, in particular to the heroic defenders of Sevastopol, to the ancient city of Moscow, to his brother-in-law, the Prussian king Frederick William IV.

It was Nicholas's last hour, but his mind remained lucid, his voice calm, and he was still performing his duty. The parting salute to the troops went as follows: "Tell them that in the other world I shall continue to pray for them. I have always tried to work for their good. If I failed in that, this was not because of a lack of good will, but because of a lack of knowledge and ability. I beg them to pardon me." [70] To Alexander himself his father's

---

[69] On the basis of my estimate of Nicholas's character and in agreement with Schiemann and many other historians, I discount the opinion of those critics who believe that Nicholas may have committed suicide. This possibility is presented in Shtakelberg, "Zagadka smerti Nikolaya I," *Russkoe Proshloe*, I (1923), 58–73. Presnyakov, pp. 97–98, comments favorably on this article.

[70] Grunwald, *op. cit.*, p. 303.

last words, reportedly, were: "I wanted to take everything difficult, everything heavy upon myself and to leave you a peaceful, orderly, and happy realm. Providence determined otherwise. Now I shall ascend to pray for Russia and for you. After Russia, I loved you above everything else in the world. Serve Russia." [71] Even when the final agony began and Nicholas could no longer speak, he held the hands of his wife and his son, his eyes fastened on them in a last farewell.

The importance of Nicholas I for the ideology and the history of his reign is difficult to overemphasize. As one Russian historian stated the case: "It is not enough to say that during the rule of Nicholas government assumed a personal character. Rather, absolute monarchy at the time of Nicholas I became incarnated in his personality." [72] Or, as an English visitor observed, the emperor could declare, quite appropriately, "Russia is I." [73] But even such a tireless despot as Nicholas needed other men to teach his doctrines and execute his policies. Therefore, before we turn to the theory and the practice of Official Nationality in Russia, we shall have to discuss briefly these soldiers of the emperor.

---

[71] Polievktov, p. 376. "You" is singular in the first sentence, plural in the others, referring to the imperial family. See also the description of the sovereign's death in Tyutcheva, pp. 176–184.

[72] Polievktov, p. xi.

[73] The visitor was Thomas Raikes who journeyed to Russia in 1830. Quoted in Gleason, *The Genesis of Russophobia in Great Britain*, p. 224.

II

OFFICIAL NATIONALITY

THE MEN

*My! I see that he is simply afraid to go to the sovereign . . .
"What is he then, some sort of an animal that it is dangerous to
approach him? and how do you see him five times every day?" I
said this and let it go, just try to talk to them. "Look," she added,
pointing out to me a portrait of Orlov, "how dashing he is pictured, and yet he is afraid to speak a word!"* [1]

To CITE the judicious opinion of Professor Schiemann, there was
only one subordinate in Russia who had an independent standing in the system of government established by Nicholas, "and
that one, unfortunately for the empire, was his brother Constantine." [2] Indeed the grand duke who had renounced the throne
continued to enjoy the deference and respect paid by the reigning monarch to one who was his dynastic elder if not his superior. [3] While others were expected to be silent tools of the autocrat

---

[1] Herzen, *Byloe i dumy*, p. 247.
[2] Schiemann, II, xiii.
[3] The relations of the two are illustrated in considerable detail in their correspondence. Vol. 131, *SIRIO*.

and, unless asked, "keep their views to themselves," [4] Constantine was invited to state his opinions on various matters, and allowed to criticize the emperor. Time and again the younger brother would hasten to explain his acts and to justify his policies to the older one.

Yet, in spite of his unique position, Constantine exercised no important influence on the reign of Nicholas. He was fully preoccupied with Poland where he remained as commander in chief after the death of Alexander, visiting Russia only rarely and briefly. More important might have been the fact that, although solicited to speak on affairs of state, he had little to say and no real alternative to offer to the policies of the Russian government. For Constantine was as devoted to militarism, legitimism, and reaction as Nicholas, and perhaps even more so.[5] The grand duke was unpleasant as a person and unpopular as a public figure.[6] A perfect martinet, he was the equal of the emperor in drilling troops and in staging military reviews. Contemporaries even credited him with objecting to war because war spoils an army more than anything else, and to shouts of "hurrah" in the ranks because that might indicate too much initiative and independence on the part of the soldiers who were to obey blindly, without expressing any kind of opinion.[7] On political issues Constantine sided with the extreme Right: he believed that the punishment meted out to the Decembrists was not severe enough; he objected to the mild reforms proposed by the so-called Committee of the Sixth of December; he remained a staunch supporter of serfdom. In all such instances the grand duke merely emphasized what constituted in any case the basic orientation of the new emperor and his government. When the opinions of the

---

[4] The phrase is taken from Nicholas's resolution reproduced in Barsukov, *Zhizn i trudy M. P. Pogodina*, X, 538.

[5] On Constantine see Karnovich, *Tsesarevich Konstantin Pavlovich*.

[6] Grech's comments about Constantine in his memoirs reflected a widespread opinion: "His greatest merit was his renunciation of the throne which testifies also to his good sense. God knows where he would have dragged Russia. May the Lord admit him for this to the heavenly kingdom!" Grech, *Zapiski o moei zhizni*, p. 209.

[7] Polievktov, pp. 322–323. Custine quoted Constantine as follows: "I do not like war; it spoils soldiers, soils their uniforms, and destroys discipline." Custine, II, 214.

brothers differed, that of Nicholas prevailed, for instance, in the complex matter of the Greek War of Independence and the resulting international crisis which Constantine viewed solely in the light of his legitimist convictions.

Poland presented a special problem. Constantine, who was married to a Pole and resided in Warsaw for many years, came to like Poland which was, so to speak, his own preserve, much more than did Nicholas. But the grand duke's character and political principles, as well as the iron hand of his brother, prevented him from translating this personal preference into a liberal policy or a real rapport with the Poles. The only result was that Constantine underestimated opposition in Poland, failed to notice the rising revolutionary tide, and was caught completely unprepared by the powerful Polish rebellion. The uprising in Warsaw in November, 1830, brought the crash of the grand duke's position and in fact of an entire world which he had built around himself. His death from cholera in the following year eliminated early in Nicholas's reign the only person whom the emperor treated as an equal and an associate rather than simply as a servant.

Nicholas respected Constantine, but he was attached to Michael. As already mentioned, the emperor grew up with his younger brother who shared his studies and his games. The two had most of their interests and attitudes in common, despising homework and playing soldier every free minute. Both developed into accomplished officers, and both found that to be their favorite role. The young grand dukes also traveled and served together in 1814–1815, and later Michael was at Nicholas's side on the crucial day of the Decembrist uprising at the end of the year 1825. The brothers remained close after the elder one became emperor, this relationship ceasing only with Michael's death which came as a shattering blow to Nicholas.

Grand Duke Michael's political views were reactionary, but they were neither obtrusive nor important, because he consciously avoided state affairs, devoting himself entirely to his several military offices, notably to the command of artillery, of military schools, and of the guards. In his chosen field Michael acquired

such remarkable proficiency that the emperor considered him
his superior in army drill. But, like Nicholas and like his ideal,
Constantine, the younger grand duke was an exacting and unpopular commander, relentless in punishing every misdemeanor
and unable to control his temper. By contrast, while Nicholas's
relations with his older brother were linked to the significant
question of Russian government in Poland, those with the younger
were usually concerned with issues of no greater moment than
Michael's persistent petty tyranny over his subordinates. For
instance, in the summer of 1849, the monarch complained to his
wife: "I am informed from all sides of the deplorable effect which
the ill humor of Michael has produced among the public and
even among the troops. This is deplorable, and what can I do—
he is sick. . . . It is not at the age of fifty that one corrects such
a nervous condition." [8] And, in truth, Michael was not to be
changed. He died a month or two later from a stroke which occurred while he was taking part in a cavalry drill.[9]

The women of the imperial family had little political influence.
Empress Mother Mary who died in 1828 did considerable work
in developing education for girls in Russia, and she was also
prominent in the field of charity. But the larger state issues were
outside her province. It should be added that Nicholas was never
close to his mother, and that he would not turn to her for advice
or support. Alexandra, the reigning empress, enjoyed, as we have
seen, her husband's confidence and was initiated by him into a
tremendous variety of public affairs. Indeed, it appears that the
emperor wanted her to be his companion in everything. Moreover,
the fact that the Russian empress was a Prussian princess by origin
had itself, as has been indicated, major political significance. It
established a strong link between these two powerful East European monarchies, and it was largely responsible for the Prussian
orientation of Nicholas. Alexandra continued to contribute to

---

[8] Schiemann, IV, 201 n. 3. Cf., e.g., Nesselrode, *Lettres*, VIII, 278–279,
where Countess Nesselrode discusses, with specific examples, the same subject
in a letter to her son and states that, in retaliation for Michael's attitude,
Nicholas showed particular severity when reviewing the troops of his younger
brother.

[9] The grand duke's death is described in Barsukov, *op. cit.*, X, 280.

this closeness by maintaining affectionate relations with her family, three of whose members, her father and two brothers, ruled Prussia in succession. The empress, however, had no independent voice in politics, being merely Nicholas's admiring and obedient spouse. Her letters to her homeland, especially during the painful and turbulent years of 1848 and 1849, demonstrate with striking clarity that her views were simply those of her husband and master. As to Nicholas's mistresses, they played no part whatsoever in affairs of state.[10]

The emperor's children, especially his sons, were of some prominence by the end of his reign. They, particularly the heir, Alexander, had received a good and suitable education and had shown some ability and, in the case of Constantine, also some spirit. Alexander was almost thirty-seven years old when his father died, and he had been gradually introduced to the difficult task of ruling Russia. But, again, as long as Nicholas was alive, no dissent was allowed, the heir's behavior conforming entirely to the directions of the emperor. It is understandable that Grand Duke Alexander was considered a reactionary by his contemporaries, and that his willingness to undertake serious reforms after his accession to the throne came to many observers as a pleasant surprise.

Nicholas had few personal friends. Perhaps the most intimate was a childhood playmate, Count V. Adlerberg, who later held the position of the head of the imperial postal service, but who played no significant role in politics. In general, the emperor had a very high regard for friendship, but he kept it apart from public life. Following his aristocratic code of honor, Nicholas was a constant and reliable friend who believed that mutual esteem and attachment between men should be independent of political or other extraneous considerations. Shortly after his accession to the throne he expressed this view to the French ambassador, Count La Ferronnays, whom he addressed as "a friend who is able

---

[10] One could argue, it is true, for an indirect influence: General P. Kleinmichel's position as one of Nicholas's ministers and associates was strengthened by his role as the intermediary between the emperor and Mademoiselle Nelidov. This will be discussed briefly later in the chapter. A scintillating, first-hand description of personalities and personal relations in the imperial family, as well as of court life, is provided in Tyutcheva.

to understand me": "I do not know and cannot foresee the nature of relations which politics may establish between the Russian emperor and the ambassador of the French king. But what I can promise you on my word of honor is that Nicholas will always remain towards Count La Ferronnays the same as he has been, and I hope that this will also be true of you." [11]

Nicholas grew up as a rather lonely child, and he was slow to make friends later on. As a rule, he disliked new people. When he became emperor, he often found it difficult to adjust to changes in personnel, and to become accustomed to new associates and acquaintances. However, once a friendship developed, it usually lasted, Nicholas adhering to it with his habitual rigidity and tenacity. The emperor's distinction between private and public relations assured that while he enjoyed a number of friendships, both with Russians and with foreigners, he had no favorites. The autocrat kept political control and direction entirely in his own hands, and no relative or friend was permitted to infringe on his prerogative.

Nicholas maintained the same attitudes in his relations with his ministers and with other officials who helped him to govern Russia. General policies and decisions were the exclusive domain of the emperor. Individual assistants could venture outside their particular fields of work only on request, and even in their own departments they were subject to constant and minute harassment by their sovereign who prized them in direct proportion to their prompt and complete execution of his will. Obedience was rated very high, originality very low. Significant disagreement with the emperor remained out of the question. The autocrat's character, his political views, and the experience of the Decembrist uprising combined to install a reign of compliance and uniformity. Intellectual dissent and ideological division were pushed into the background to be expressed only in an indirect manner or in those areas where the emperor's own views were not clearly defined. In his official as in his personal contacts, Nicholas was loyal to his old acquaintances, and he

---

[11] This remarkable interview between the Russian tsar and the French ambassador is reproduced in part in Schilder, I, 343–348. Quoted from page 343.

did not like new faces. Also, in his public as well as in his private life he had a special preference for military men and the army spirit.

Subservience thus became the hallmark of Nicholas's official-dom. In the words of Prince P. Shirinskii-Shikhmatov, a minister of education late in the reign, to his assistant A. Norov: "You should know that I have neither a mind nor a will of my own— I am merely a blind tool of the emperor's will." [12] This, in the opinion of Schiemann, was essentially true also of all the other statesmen of the regime,[13] especially in its final stages. And indeed we find the same lack of initiative and imagination and the same eager execution of the sovereign's will whether we turn to the diplomats, the soldiers, the administrators, or the economists. In terms of official ideology, all of them were simply translating into practice the sacred principle of autocracy. In the judgment of a disillusioned modern historian: ". . . all the ministers of Nicholas lacked character." [14]

The emperor's loyalty to his collaborators and his dislike of new faces produced a number of important results. Nicholas tended to rely primarily on a very small group of men who were used for special missions and assignments in addition to their regular offices, who were often overburdened with work and were occasionally even denied the right to resign. One or more deaths would usually produce a reshuffle, the autocrat trying to cover the gaps with the material at hand and being invariably reluc-tant to introduce newcomers into the inner circle of government. Furthermore, it appears that once the emperor formed a favora-ble opinion of a person and accepted him into his entourage, he clung to his original estimate. This unswerving confidence on the part of their sovereign enabled such outstanding states-men as Counts M. Speranskii, P. Kiselev, and E. Kankrin to obtain impressive results in the domains of law, the organization of the state peasants, and finance respectively, in spite of many difficulties and much opposition to them and their ideas in Rus-

---

[12] Nikitenko, I, 441.
[13] Schiemann, IV, 233.
[14] Grunwald, *La Vie de Nicolas I*, p. 171.

sian society and officialdom. But the same attitude permitted many inadequate officials to occupy their posts for a very long time. This was true, for instance, of Princes A. Menshikov and A. Chernyshev, the first of whom assumed actual charge of the Russian navy for many years while the second acted as Nicholas's permanent minister of war. Menshikov began in an energetic and effective manner, but bogged down completely later on; Chernyshev never really measured up to his office, but he knew how to produce in his department the impression of order and smooth functioning which Nicholas valued so highly, and he won the appreciation of the emperor by his precise and optimistic general reports. It took the Crimean War to demonstrate the great damage done by these two appointments.

Nicholas's militarism was proverbial. The emperor naturally preferred army men to civilians, and he tried to establish the army spirit in all branches of his administration and, in fact, in the country at large. Orders for more and more groups of people to wear different uniforms—legislation which affected university students among others—represented only one symptom of this general trend. In his analysis of the Russian statesmen around the year 1850, Schiemann points out that only the minister of justice, Count V. Panin, had no military service.[15] And even if we also exclude a few other figures, such as Nesselrode whose military career had been brief and secondary to his other activities, the result is an imposing image of the militarization of high officialdom.

The commanding generals themselves, however, played no special role in Nicholas's system. Several of them, it is true, gained high prominence; and I. Paskevich who distinguished himself against the Turks in 1828–1829, the Poles in 1831, and the Hungarians in 1849, achieved great fame and signal honors. But although this Count of Erivan and Prince of Warsaw also had the good fortune of having been Nicholas's regimental commander and although the autocrat liked to address him as "father commander" and heap rewards upon him, he was nevertheless kept strictly and minutely within the confines of his particular task,

---

[15] Schiemann, IV, 247.

the army and Russian control of reconquered Poland.[16] Generals felt the iron hand of the emperor as much as everyone else.

The activity and position of Count Karl Nesselrode in the reign of Nicholas deserve special mention. The count was in charge of the extremely important field of foreign relations throughout his sovereign's thirty years of rule over Russia. In the course of his service, he attained the highest distinctions and offices in the state, becoming in 1844 Chancellor of the Empire. Nesselrode's relations with Nicholas, highly significant in themselves, also throw revealing light on the broader issue of collaboration between the autocrat and his ministers.[17]

Karl Nesselrode came from a strikingly cosmopolitan background. "Born in December, 1780, in Lisbon, to a Protestant mother and a Catholic father, he was baptized according to the Anglican rite." [18] His father belonged to the Rhenish nobility and served at several courts; his mother was a member of a prominent Jewish family in Frankfurt. Karl Nesselrode attended a lycée in Berlin, joined the Russian navy as a midshipman, and served briefly in the horse guards before he found his true vocation in Alexander I's diplomatic corps. Before long he became a very close associate of the spectacular emperor, occupying the position of his secretary, so to speak, in European relations.

Nicholas thus inherited Nesselrode from his brother. The industrious diplomat had come to represent by that time the principles of legitimacy and conservatism which inspired Alexander during the second half of his reign. Constantine and other like-minded people were strongly in favor of his continuing in the foreign office. The new emperor himself had, apparently, no objection to this collaborator. Besides, he appreciated having an experienced aide in a field new to him. The two proceeded to work jointly

---

[16] On Paskevich in general, as well as on his relations to Nicholas, see Shcherbatov, *General-Feldmarshal Knyaz Paskevich. Ego zhizn i deyatelnost.* (Numerous and valuable documentary appendixes include the correspondence of the emperor and the marshal.)

[17] Much source material on Nesselrode can be found in Nesselrode, *Lettres.* There are no books about him, but a good general account is provided in Grunwald "Nesselrode et le 'gendarme de l'Europe,'" *Trois siècles de diplomatie russe,* pp. 173–198.

[18] *Ibid.,* p. 173.

for thirty years, in success and in failure. Nesselrode took part in all the foreign affairs of the reign to such an extent that it is difficult to discern throughout the entire period any appreciable increase or decline in his position, although occasionally the emperor would act impulsively without consulting his minister and in a few instances, such as the religious conflict in Palestine over the Holy Places, he would discount the minister's judgment.

The coöperation of Nicholas I and Nesselrode was obvious, but the contribution of the chancellor to Russian foreign policy is difficult to assess. The emperor, of course, dominated in his usual authoritarian and uncompromising manner, his huge and imposing figure contrasting even physically with the tiny minister. As to Nesselrode, he distinguished himself by "pliancy, even abnegation" which were required of him to maintain his office and continue performing his important job.[19] The result was, to quote the prevailing opinion, that Nesselrode, while a convinced adherent to the ideas of legitimism and conservatism, "was not so much their original interpreter as their conscientious agent." [20] "Nesselrode did not exaggerate much when he called himself 'a modest tool of the emperor's designs, and an instrument of his political plans.' Nesselrode became the Vice-Chancellor and the State Chancellor of the Russian Empire, but he remained as formerly the secretary for diplomatic affairs." [21] However, in the judgment of a contemporary Nesselrode's "influence on the emperor was greater than the world realized because he held to his plans with a great tenacity and knew how to make them, finally, acceptable to the emperor." [22] Other critics have emphasized the restraining effect of the experienced chancellor on his impulsive and essentially undiplomatic sovereign.

Certain aspects of Nesselrode's role under Nicholas illustrate the general nature of the reign and the positions of some other ministers of the emperor. To begin with, the only theoretical

---

[19] Ibid., p. 176.

[20] Polievktov, p. 70.

[21] Presnyakov, p. 62. See also, e.g., Miliukov, Seignobos, and Eisenmann, Histoire de Russie, II, 797.

[22] The contemporary was Count Otto von Bray-Steinburg, Bavarian envoy long resident in St. Petersburg. His estimate is quoted in Schiemann, IV, 244.

difference noted between the chancellor and the monarch was
that Nesselrode was even more legitimist and conservative than
Nicholas. But there was no question of any fundamental contrast in opinion or approach. Furthermore, while Alexander I
tried various ideas in diplomacy and relied on a number of men
—Nesselrode was himself, in a sense, balanced by another close
adviser of the emperor, Capodistria—Nicholas put his faith in
one individual and a single point of view. As to the chancellor's
influence, it depended largely on his ability to mollify and modify
the views of the emperor in a manner which had usually to be
intangible enough to avoid any overt collision with the head-
strong autocrat.

Count S. Uvarov, who headed the ministry of education from
1833 to 1849 and who will be discussed later in this book, followed
Nesselrode's pattern of behavior with particular care. He was
especially insistent on presenting his views and measures as simply
a reflection of his sovereign's will, which practice, incidentally,
made it very difficult for historians to separate the ideas and
the actions of the two men. Other ministers behaved in much
the same manner. To be sure, some of them enjoyed a certain advantage in that Nicholas was less minutely concerned
with their activities than with Nesselrode's field of foreign policy
or Uvarov's domain of education. Thus the emperor evidently
let Speranskii have considerable freedom in his highly complex
and technical work of codifying law. Yet a high degree of speciali-
zation provided no guarantee of imperial noninterference. For
instance, after endorsing for many years the policies of his extremely competent minister of finance, Count Kankrin, Nicholas
dispensed with his services and appointed in his stead an obedient nonentity, F. Vronchenko, with the characteristic remark:
"I shall be myself minister of finance." [23]

The case of Count P. Kleinmichel has often been cited as an
exception to the system of administration and control established
by Nicholas. This extremely unpleasant and unpopular official,

---

[23] Schiemann, IV, 359. Prince I. Vasilchikov, the president of the Council
of State at the time, described Vronchenko rather charitably as: "of unexcep-
tionable moral character, but more a functionary than a person capable of
statesmanship." Polievktov, p. 199. Cf. Nikitenko, I, 407.

a former aide of Arakcheev, became the intermediary between Nicholas and Mademoiselle Nelidov, adopted the children of the couple, and achieved great prominence during the last years of Nicholas's reign. Moreover, while other ministers were narrowly confined to their special fields of activity, Kleinmichel ranged widely, participating in all kinds of matters. Yet a fuller understanding of his role makes it appear less extraordinary. Kleinmichel's rise began long before the emperor's attachment to Mademoiselle Nelidov, in fact during the first years of the reign. The general, according to one interpretation, clinched his high standing with the emperor by his farsighted championing of the railroads as early as the 1830's.[24] He also distinguished himself by the rapid reconstruction of the Winter Palace after the great fire in 1837, being rewarded on this occasion with the following motto for his coat of arms: "Zeal overcomes everything." In 1842 he was made director of imperial communications and public buildings, an important area of activity in which the tsar himself was deeply interested. Nicholas's increasing reliance on Kleinmichel in a great variety of matters shows no evidence of the general's special hold on the emperor, nor of his originality and statesmanship. It merely testifies to Kleinmichel's superlative ability and willingness to carry out orders promptly and without question.

Special standing was also enjoyed by the two successive commanders of Nicholas's gendarmery, Count A. Benckendorff and Prince A. Orlov. As heads of the Third Department of His Majesty's Own Chancery the two men were in charge of the new police which buttressed and permeated Russia under Nicholas, and which has often been regarded as the nerve center of the emperor's entire system of rule. The gendarme chiefs were certainly among the emperor's closest associates, and they are also usually considered among his few personal friends. In addition to their main function, both generals were successively in charge of imperial headquarters, and Orlov, in particular, was also used for special, highly important missions. The emperor's confidence in these two assistants dated from the very beginning of the reign,

---

[24] Polievktov, p. 74.

from the Decembrist rebellion to be exact: Benckendorff had warned Alexander about the revolutionary danger, and the uprising seemed to justify his knowledge and judgment; Orlov was the first to bring his regiment in support of the government to the Senate Square where he proceeded to play an important part in the defeat of the rebels. Later the generals became, in turn, the constant companions of Nicholas as he traveled indefatigably in his two-seated carriage all over Russia: until 1837 Benckendorff was almost invariably the partner of the emperor on such inspection trips; after that date Orlov usually took his place. It is probable that in the course of his reign Nicholas spent more time and discussed more matters with the two gendarmes than with any other members of his government.

Yet, once more, proximity to the emperor was not translated into effective influence or important achievement. And, again, it was an unbalanced relationship with power, direction, and drive on the one side, and passive and unimaginative execution of orders on the other. Nicholas's state may have been a police state, but professional policemen were of secondary importance at best in giving it shape and purpose. Far from resembling some of his frightening twentieth-century counterparts, Benckendorff was characterized by a certain laxity and amiability which went well with his cultural pretensions and his gallant pursuit of women. Besides, he showed great concern with the nature of his position which he wanted to make popular and praiseworthy. He even believed, or claimed to believe, as attested by the following gushing passage in his *Memoirs* dealing with a serious illness in 1837, that he succeeded in his aim:

I had the happiness to hear alive a laudatory funeral oration, and this oration, the greatest reward which a man can attain on earth, consisted in the tears and the sympathy of the poor, the orphaned, the forgotten ones, in the general compassion of all, and especially in the vivid interest of my tsar who by his anxiety and his tender care gave me the best and the highest testimony of his gracious favor. Considering the position which I occupied, this served, of course, as the best report of my eleven-year long

*management, and I think that I might have been the first of all
the heads of the secret police whose death inspired fear and who
was not pursued by a single complaint on the brink of his grave.
This sickness was for me a real triumph, the like of which none
of our dignitaries has as yet experienced.*[25]

When, in 1844, Benckendorff finally did die, the emperor's judgment confirmed the gendarme's own estimate of himself: "He
brought many of my enemies to a reconciliation and made not
a single new one." [26] And while this idyllic picture of the chief
of the secret police is much too good to be wholly true, parts of
it are upheld even by such hostile critics as the Soviet historian
I. Trotskii: "For seventeen years Benckendorff stood at the head
of the Third Department and, strange though it is, he failed to
attract—let alone the love—even the hate of those oppressed by
the Third Department." [27]

Orlov replaced Benckendorff as the gendarme commander, but
this change in leadership proved to be of little significance: "The
successor of Benckendorff, Aleksei Fedorovich Orlov, was in no
way superior to his predecessor as far as statesmanlike qualities
were concerned, while in intelligence and experience he was even
inferior to him. His sole merit was his friendship with the tsar.
But, in regard to actual work, he distinguished himself by complete indolence, and he made no impress of his own on the character of the Third Department. . . ." [28] Nicholas thus retained
complete control of the affairs of the gendarmery, while several
subordinates in the organization, notably L. Dubbelt, were particularly active in carrying out imperial policies. On his special
missions, the most famous one of which was that of 1833 to Constantinople resulting in the Treaty of Unkiar Skelessi, Orlov again
"always executed precisely the august orders avoiding initiative
of his own." [29]

---

[25] Schilder, II, 737.
[26] Schiemann, IV, 55 n. 1.
[27] Trotskii, *Trete otdelenie pri Nikolae I*, p. 118. Trotskii's opinion is based
on such contemporary judgments as that of Herzen (*Byloe i dumy*, p. 240).
[28] Trotskii, *op. cit.*, p. 120.
[29] Polievktov, p. 74. The above estimates of Orlov are standard. See, for instance, Schiemann, IV, 56, n. 1, for a similar judgment supported by the opinion

With the passage of time the special characteristics of Nicholas's regime became ever more prominent. The remaining officials of independent mind and bearing, most of them a legacy from the reign of Alexander I, died or resigned. The emperor allowed less and less criticism or even discussion of his policies. He intervened ever more arbitrarily and minutely in the affairs of the various departments. Military discipline and military obedience became the single standard of behavior in the administration.

The year 1847 marked the death of Prince I. Vasilchikov, described as the last high official in Nicholas's reign who enjoyed not only the sovereign's love, but also his esteem, and who dared speak his mind to the autocrat.[30] His high standing with the emperor resulted from the old man's character and prestige based on an impressive military record which included, incidentally, the command of the regiment in which Nicholas himself began his army service. At the time of his death Vasilchikov performed the functions of chairman of the Council of State and of the committee of ministers. In 1852 Prince P. Volkonskii, the minister of court, passed away. A very close associate of Alexander I, the prince remained during Nicholas's reign a friend of the imperial family with an easy access to the emperor and a certain freedom in his presence.

The revolutions of 1848–1849 had a profound effect on Nicholas, accentuating the authoritarian and intolerant tendencies of his regime. Even the formulator of the official ideology himself, Count S. Uvarov, came to be considered too independent and liberal to be in charge of education in Russia. The gifted minister had to resign, to be replaced by the ignorant and generally inadequate, but perfectly obsequious Prince P. Shirinskii-Shikhmatov.[31]

The quality of high officialdom had deteriorated markedly by the end of Nicholas's rule. The emperor himself complained bit-

---

of Lord Bloomfield, the British ambassador. A sharply dissenting view is that of Grunwald who expressed the highest regard for Orlov. Grunwald, *Trois siècles de diplomatie russe*, p. 185.

[30] Schiemann, IV, 102.

[31] It should be noted, however, that Uvarov's dismissal was probably produced by several different reasons. This complex episode will be discussed in chap. iv below. On Shirinskii-Shikhmatov see the quote above where the minister described himself as "a blind tool of the emperor's will."

terly about "the lack of men" as he found it more and more difficult to obtain capable assistants. Students of the reign have suggested that the tsar's extremely restrictive educational policy was ultimately responsible for this dearth of trained talent. But, while this general consideration may be partly valid, there was also the immediate, drastic, and obvious reason for the autocrat's predicament. In the summary words of one encyclopaedia:

Complaining in this connection about his loneliness, about the absence of "men," of collaborators who could be relied upon, Nicholas, however, failed to notice that the cause of this phenomenon was not so much a real lack of men, as his personal attitude towards those surrounding him, his intolerance of every original thought and independent character, his urge to lower everything and everybody to one general level. Naturally, success in service came, but for a few individual exceptions, only to self-effacing, though not at all necessarily disinterested, functionaries and to pliant and adaptable mediocrities. State activity was thus enclosed in a hopeless vicious circle trying to achieve important results by means of agents obviously unfit for the purpose.[32]

II

Nicholas I dominated his collaborators, and, in fact, dominated Russia. The imperial will drove the government and the country along the painful and unswerving path of "orthodoxy, autocracy, and nationality." No opposition or dissent was allowed. Still, one might inquire about the characters, attitudes, and interests of the men who supported and promoted the work of the emperor. Of special interest are the theoreticians and the publicists of the system who, by the very nature of their position, could not withdraw into a limited technical field of competence, but had to expound, defend, and interpret the creed and the activity of their sovereign.

The exponents of the government ideology, which came to be known as "Official Nationality," were numerous and varied in

---

[32] "Nikolai I," *Entsiklopedicheskii Slovar* (Granat), XXX, col. 216.

background and position. First mention should go to Count S. Uvarov who formulated the principles of the doctrine and, as minister of education, presided for sixteen years over its implementation in the intellectual life of Russia. A different but related kind of work in developing and spreading the official views was performed by such professors as M. Pogodin and S. Shevyrev at the University of Moscow and N. Ustryalov at the University of St. Petersburg. Prolific journalists, F. Bulgarin, N. Grech, O. Senkovskii, and others, carried government ideology to a wide audience. Popular, if not distinguished, writers, for instance, N. Kukolnik and M. Zagoskin, contributed to the same end. Much greater literary figures, Zhukovskii, Gogol, Tyutchev, and even Pushkin, were also linked, at least in part, to the official doctrine.

In character and in their approach to their task the sponsors of Official Nationality were, again, by no means uniform. Yet, certain attitudes and personality patterns stand out among them. One psychological type, common in the group, was that of a single-minded, determined, devoted, and intensely moral person. Bluntness, crudity, and lack of sophistication were usually found together with these fundamental traits. Adherence to the doctrine was, with this type, sincere, even passionate, unquestioning, and uncompromising. Deed corresponded to word; great working capacity and all the emotions were mobilized toward a single end. Good and evil, white and black, love and hate served as the main categories of feeling and thought. Life meant effort and struggle. Conviction and sense of duty supplied the inspiration in a ceaseless strife, in spite of at least a tinge of fatalism and pessimism. Nicholas I himself was a splendid example of this psychological type.

Michael Pogodin, a noted historian and journalist, was another exponent of Official Nationality who possessed basically the same character.[33] Eventually a prominent University of Moscow pro-

---

[33] Materials about Pogodin are abundant. The two chief sources are his own voluminous writings, some of them personal in character, which are listed in the bibliography, and the enormous, unfinished, twenty-two volume study, Barsukov, *Zhizn i trudy M. P. Pogodina*. The study contains hundreds of pages of excerpts from Pogodin's writings, many of them unpublished, including his

fessor and a well-known public figure, Pogodin started from a plebeian background and forced his own way in life. He was born a serf in 1800 and it was not until 1806 that the family became free when Michael Pogodin's father was emancipated by the rich and aristocratic landlord whom he served as a steward. The boy showed an early intellectual curiosity and application, learning what he could at home and being further aided by a friendly typographer and a helpful priest. In 1814 he had the good fortune to be sent to the First Moscow High School, and in 1818 he entered the University of Moscow. Pogodin proved to be an outstanding student with a special interest in early Russian history and in Slavic studies. After graduation in 1823, he wrote a dissertation "On the Origins of Russia" and defended it successfully in 1825 to receive his Master's degree. In the meantime Pogodin made ends meet by giving private lessons and by other occasional employment, and he was greatly assisted by the opportunity to spend summers with the princely Trubetskoi family where he was engaged as a tutor.

In 1826 the young man received his first appointment at the University of Moscow, and began a continuous and successful academic career which culminated in a full professorship at the University. Concurrently Pogodin earned a doctorate, became a member and an officer of several learned societies, and, finally, in 1841, was admitted to the Imperial Academy of Sciences. Pogodin began as a teacher of universal history, but in 1835 he received the new and more specialized chair of Russian history, becoming thus the first professor of that subject at the University of Moscow. In 1844 Pogodin's professorial activity came to a sudden end: as a result of administrative and faculty rivalries and squabbles, he resigned his position in a fit of temper and also, apparently, in expectation of being invited back on more favorable terms, but the invitation never came.[34] Pogodin remained, however, an academician, a noted scholar, and a prominent public

---

diary. For an estimate of Pogodin as a historian, see, for instance, Picheta, *Vvedenie v russkuyu istoriyu (istochniki i istoriografiya)*, pp. 113–116.

[34] The story of Pogodin's resignation is told in Barsukov, *op. cit.*, III, 288–291.

figure as a vigorous journalist and a champion of a certain kind of nationalist, conservative, and Pan-Slav views. He died in 1875, twenty years after the death of Nicholas I.

Pogodin's life was spent largely in Moscow, but he also traveled widely throughout Russia, often in search of historical material, and he undertook several extensive journeys abroad. The first of these, in 1835, was a landmark in establishing relations between the Moscow professor and various Slavic scholars and intellectuals outside Russia, especially in the Austrian Empire. On his later voyages too Pogodin liked to visit his Balkan friends, although he managed to travel in many other areas of Europe as well, meeting a large number and a considerable variety of people.

Pogodin's writings fall into several broad and overlapping categories. As historian, the Moscow professor is best known for his seven volumes of "Studies, Lectures, and Comments" dealing primarily with early Russian history. His political and social views found their fullest expression in numerous articles some of which were later collected into several books. Pogodin published two important periodicals: *The Moscow Messenger*, from 1827 to 1830, and *The Muscovite*, from 1841 till the late 1850's. He also produced a lengthy volume on the problems of religion, and a supplement to this volume. In his youth the professor had literary ambitions which resulted in several pieces of prose and verse, including a play, *Peter I*, and some stories. Although praised by Pushkin and certain other leading writers and critics of the time, Pogodin's fiction has no artistic significance, but it does throw additional light on his personality and beliefs. Pogodin was a popular orator at alumni dinners and other festive occasions; many of his speeches were later gathered into a book. The huge literary legacy of the Moscow professor is characterized by clumsiness, by incessant repetitiousness, and by a lack of finish and polish, most of his works giving the impression of a first draft.

From childhood Michael Pogodin was an ardent patriot and nationalist. Influenced during his early years by the romantic literature of the period, and by Karamzin's history of Russia, as well as by the cataclysmic events of 1812, he only deepened his original convictions by a study of his country's past, observation of political and social developments at home and abroad, and acquaintance with the Balkan Slavs. In time, he naturally became a devoted supporter and one of the most notable expounders of the government doctrine of Official Nationality.[35] Pogodin propounded his views with persistence and passion. He worshipped national heroes, especially Peter the Great, exulted at Russian achievements, despaired over the failings of his native land, and raged against its enemies. Political issues, such as the domestic and foreign policies of the Russian government at the time of the Crimean War, had a powerful emotional impact on Pogodin who felt compelled to express his beliefs on the matter: ". . . in order, finally, to settle my account with this miserable question which, purely by chance, diverted me from my history, inflamed my imagination, and then, for an entire year, pressed upon me as an evil spirit at night and, in daytime, constantly loomed as a disgusting phantom in front of my eyes, so that I even began to be afraid that I might go mad." [36]

As in the case of the emperor, life was hard for Pogodin. In 1845 or 1846 in a peculiar address "To a Youth," the retired professor expressed his bitterness, indeed despair, with his lot in the image of a man rolling an enormous stone uphill for the sake of humanity, which, nevertheless, either ignores or hinders, denounces, and assails him in every conceivable manner.[37] "And you will tear your garments, scatter ashes over your head, pour torrents of burning tears, howl, howl like a hungry dog under a fence, curse the day of your birth, speak blasphemy. . . ." [38] But actually this emotional outburst was as close as Pogodin ever came to blaspheming. Deep religious convictions and faith in his ideals in general kept him on his straight and difficult path in spite of all the obstacles and disappointments.[39]

Several qualities of the Moscow professor impressed his con-

[35] This ideology will be analyzed and discussed in chap. iii below.

[36] Pogodin, *Istoriko-politicheskie pisma i zapiski vprodolzhenii Krymskoi Voiny. 1853–1856*, p. 244; hereafter cited as Pogodin, *Istoriko-politicheskie pisma*.

[37] Barsukov, *op. cit.*, VIII, 263–282.

[38] *Ibid.*, p. 279.

[39] Pogodin's religious writings will be considered in chap. iii below.

temporaries. They admired especially his great vigor and energy and, together with that, his unusual capacity for work. Even Pogodin's bluntness and repetitiousness served their purpose, for they were marks of a man relentlessly determined to reach his goals. Pogodin also compared favorably with most of his colleagues and acquaintances in terms of practical sense and the resulting ability to manage financial and other worldly affairs with considerable success. Finally, he deserves credit for his sincerity and his devotion to his ideals. These last attributes were violently denied him by his opponents who preferred to regard Pogodin as a timeserver and a careerist,[40] but they are affirmed by the remarkably consequent and consistent pattern of his entire thought, work, and life.

The Moscow professor's vices were at least as pronounced as his virtues. He possessed an overbearing and uncompromising personality which made collaboration and friendship difficult. His management of his periodicals, *The Muscovite* in particular, was strikingly autocratic and arbitrary, indicating a flagrant disregard for the interests and the preferences of his associates and assistants.[41] Matters were made worse by another deplorable trait of Pogodin's character, his avarice. Often described as a natural attitude of a self-made man, it apparently had a deeper significance. In addition to being extremely loath to part with money, Pogodin remained throughout his life a great collector of different kinds of things. As a boy, he gathered bits of minerals, dried plants, and posters, together with history books and novels. As a man and scholar, he became famous for his large and very valuable collection of old Russian books and manuscripts, as well as ikons,

---

[40] Perhaps the most vicious and extreme attack along these lines was made by the famous critic and Westernizer, Belinskii. It is reproduced in Barsukov, *op. cit.*, VI, 261–262. Pogodin, of course, was vigorously defended and praised by those who shared his views. See, for instance, the eulogies of him in verse composed by F. Tyutchev and P. Vyazemskii. Tyutchev, p. 170; Barsukov, ed., *Pisma M. P. Pogodina, S. P. Shevyreva i M. A. Maksimovicha k knyazyu P. A. Vyazemskomu 1825–1874 godov*, pp. 4–5.

[41] For a discussion of Pogodin as publisher see, for instance, Dementev, *Ocherki po istorii russkoi zhurnalistiki 1840–1850 gg.*, pp. 218–220. Dementev and other Soviet critics take delight in tracing connections between the Moscow professor's high-handed direction of *The Muscovite* and his conservative and "patriarchal" ideology.

coins, and other *objets d'art*, which he obtained through incessant effort and with the help of a network of agents spread all over the country. Later Pogodin sold his treasure to the government for an impressive profit, only to begin promptly another accumulation, this time of portraits of Russian historical figures.[42]

However, Pogodin's most besetting faults consisted in his naïveté and his fantastic lack of tact. The artlessness of the Moscow professor's thought and expression baffled his contemporaries, and it tends to disarm the modern critic. For instance, as a young man Pogodin recorded in his diary his daydream of seeking out Schelling, presenting himself and begging the German sage "to enlighten him and to instruct him for the benefit of the entire North." "I am good," Pogodin would tell him, "I love learning, enlighten me. A great urge to study philosophy is rising in me." [43]

Pogodin's tactlessness was quite extraordinary. It led to constant blunders, misunderstandings, and troubles of all kinds, and it attracted the attention of virtually every friend and acquaintance. As the great writer and Pogodin's good friend Gogol summed up the case:

> If he speaks about patriotism, he speaks about it so that his patriotism appears to be venal; about the love for the tsar, which he nourishes sincerely and sacredly in his soul, he expresses himself in a manner which suggests mere obsequiousness and some sort of self-interested servility. His sincere, unfeigned wrath against every tendency injurious to Russia assumes such an appearance as if he were handing in an informer's report about some people known to him alone. In a word, at every step he is his own slanderer.[44]

Gogol even found it appropriate to utilize the death of Pogodin's first wife as the right psychological moment to urge his friend

---

[42] This phase of Pogodin's activity—as well as practically all others—is depicted in detail in Barsukov, *Zhizn i trudy M. P. Pogodina.* Boyhood collections are discussed in vol. IV, pp. 430–433. The collection sold to the government is described in vol. VII, p. 298 and vol. X, pp. 441–460.

[43] Barsukov, *op. cit.,* I, 279.

[44] Gogol, p. 22.

to reform and to renounce his two important sins, tactlessness and proneness to anger. In his answer, the Moscow professor admitted the first of these failings, remarking "I lack something." [45] K. Aksakov, the Slavophile historian, shared Gogol's bafflement: "God knows how Pogodin, with his many merits, has managed to antagonize virtually everybody. Attacks on him have often been unjust, but still people pretty generally have risen against him. It seems to me that the main cause is his inability to handle people." [46]

I. Kireevskii, another close Slavophile acquaintance, whom Pogodin had tactlessly criticized in a letter inviting a frank personal estimate of himself in return, concluded his response as follows: "By the way, until you learn all the fine points of that feeling which is known as propriety, you will never be of any use. It is not nice to end in this manner, but I have no more paper." [47] P. Vyazemskii, a prominent poet and intellectual, emphasized the same point in his comment on the Moscow professor's difficulties as a publicist: "But Pogodin is not a journalist. He lacks the tact of a journalist, although he is rich in good intentions." [48]

Pogodin's closest friend and associate, Stephen Shevyrev, shared not only his convictions and his interests, but also many of his attitudes and character traits. Born in 1806, in a gentry family, this one-time pupil in a school where Pogodin taught, became the historian's colleague at the University of Moscow, specializing in old Russian literature and in literary criticism. The two friends exerted every effort to instill admiration for ancient Russia and belief in the doctrines of Official Nationality at the University and in society, Shevyrev serving as Pogodin's intimate collaborator in different journalistic ventures. Both worked very hard, a notable instance being a joint translation of a grammar which they successfully completed in a few days of extremely intense labor,

---

[45] Barsukov, op. cit., VII, 483–487.
[46] Barsukov, op. cit., III, 298.
[47] Barsukov, op. cit., II, 59.
[48] Barsukov, ed., Pisma M. P. Pogodina, S. P. Shevyreva i M. A. Maksimovicha k knyazyu P. A. Vyazemskomu 1825–1874 godov, p. 217.

although both of them fainted in the process from overexertion.[49]

Shevyrev, as well as Pogodin, formed his fundamental convictions early and maintained them throughout life. He was also the equal of his older friend in enthusiasm, vituperation, and ardent polemic. In fact, his passionate and inconsiderate championing of his views abruptly terminated his academic career in 1857: at a meeting of the Council of the Moscow Society of Art, Shevyrev took the criticism of certain Russian ways by a Count Bobrinskii as an insult to the fatherland; blows followed words; Shevyrev emerged from the fight with a rib injury, and the scandal resulted in his dismissal from the University of Moscow.[50] The remainder of his life was spent largely abroad. He died in 1864, in Paris.

Again, as in the case of his friend, Pogodin, Shevyrev was tactless and difficult to get along with, although his principal drawback appeared to be a pompous vanity rather than bluntness and rudeness. There existed also certain more striking differences between the two men: Shevyrev has often been described as a capricious and "feminine" individual lacking the vigor and the robustness of his associate.[51] He was a poet of some merit, as well as a scholar, and he had strong aesthetic interests.

The capacities to believe simply, to work hard, and to persevere in spite of pessimism were also combined in the personality of the indefatigable journalist, publisher, educator, and grammarian N. Grech.[52] Born in 1787, he lived intensely through the nationalist upsurge of 1812 in which year a brother of his was

---

[49] Barsukov, *Zhizn i trudy M. P. Pogodina*, II, 13–14.

[50] This incident is described, for instance, in "Shevyrev, Stepan Petrovich," *Entsiklopedicheskii Slovar* (Brockhaus-Efron), XXXIX, 362–363. For contemporary comment see, e.g., Nikitenko, I, 491.

[51] He is so presented, for instance, in Soloviev, *Moi zapiski dlya detei moikh, a, esli mozhno, i dlya drugikh*, pp. 46–48. Shevyrev's own writings, some of them personal in character, provide much material about the Moscow professor. There has been no full-scale treatment of him; the most important brief accounts are listed in the bibliography. Barsukov's enormous study of Pogodin is also very valuable for those interested in Shevyrev.

[52] Grech left incomplete and disorganized but long and important memoirs (*Zapiski o moei zhizni*). He also wrote several extensive accounts of his different travels. Some other works of his, including his fiction, throw additional light on Grech's character, views, and interests.

mortally wounded on the field of Borodino. Narrow-minded, conservative by temperament, and a convinced patriot, Grech had little difficulty in adjusting to the ideology of Official Nationality, developing into one of its chief journalists. His *Northern Bee* became a leading newspaper in St. Petersburg and in Russia, and he assisted the government in other capacities as well, for instance, by writing a reply to Custine's attack on the Russian state.[53] Grech died in 1867.

Nicholas I, Pogodin, Shevyrev, and Grech were not the only proponents of Official Nationality who served their professed creed with constancy and conviction. The same was equally true of many of their collaborators. But, together with this single-minded, sincere, and persistent psychological type, the government doctrine attracted another, and in many ways opposite, kind of personality. Men who possessed it were much more sensitive and often more gifted and more intelligent than their plodding colleagues, but they lacked their consistency and reliability. In fact, they were often quite irresponsible, in thought and action, in abstract theory as much as in personal relations. They changed interests and changed sides with great ease, their lives following frequently an unconventional and even a fantastic pattern. In general they were vain and determined to be prominent and successful in the Russia of Nicholas I. They tried hard to please everybody. Yet the conventional judgment that they acted simply as unprincipled and clever careerists is not entirely correct. Far from being detached and cool manipulators, these men promoted their changeable views and projects with a certain sincerity and with a genuine enthusiasm. But they often found it difficult to distinguish between creed and fantasy, fact and fiction, right and wrong.

F. Bulgarin, a notorious journalist and writer, was such a person.[54] Bulgarin was born in 1789, in Western Russia, the

---

[53] Grech, *Examen de l'ouvrage de M. le Marquis de Custine intitulé la Russie en 1839.*

[54] Bulgarin wrote very much about himself, including six volumes of "Reminiscences" which, however, were partly fictionalized and should be handled with more than usual care. Long and useful accounts of Bulgarin are provided by his closest associate, Grech, and by M. Lemke, the historian of

youngest child in a fanatically patriotic Polish family of gentry. The boy's somewhat unbalanced and temperamental father joined Kosciuszko and was exiled to Siberia for killing a Russian general. His mother, a passionate and highly nervous woman, probably left a stronger impress on her child. In the opinion of Grech, his closest associate, Bulgarin "really loved and respected his mother, and when, on occasion, he wanted to buttress some colossal lie of his he swore during the lifetime of his mother by her grey hair, and after her death by her shadow." [55] In spite of his strongly Polish background, young Bulgarin attended a Russian military school and after that served in the Russian army, taking part in the campaign against the French in 1807 and against the Swedes in Finland in 1808. But when in 1811, because of "bad behavior," he was transferred to the retired list,[56] he left for Warsaw and enrolled there in Napoleon's Polish legion. Bulgarin fought on the side of the French in Italy, in Spain and, in 1812, in Russia.

Captured finally in 1814 by Prussian partisans, he was granted amnesty, together with other Poles, by Alexander I and soon appeared in St. Petersburg intent on making a literary career. His expurgated and "morally clean" edition of Horace's odes failed, and his attempt at historical biography proved similarly disappointing, but soon Bulgarin turned to journalism and hit his stride. He became the publisher, editor, or major contributor to more than a score of different periodicals, his fertile mind always suggesting new literary ventures. Bulgarin's most important publication was the newspaper, *The Northern Bee*, which he began to put out jointly with Grech in 1825 and which made the two men the Siamese twins of Russian journalism.[57] In addition to

censorship and the police in the reign of Nicholas I. Grech's essay "Faddei Bulgarin" is in Grech, *Zapiski o moei zhizni*, pp. 665–724. Lemke's study carries the same title and constitutes the fourth part of his *Ocherki po istorii russkoi tsenzury i zhurnalistiki*. Lemke also discussed Bulgarin in his later work, *Nikolaevskie zhandarmy i literatura 1826–1855 gg.*

[55] Grech, *op. cit.*, p. 683.

[56] Bulgarin was generally a delinquent officer, but the specific reason for his dismissal is not known. His own explanation was that he paid for his success in a romantic rivalry with his commander. Bulgarin, *Vospominaniya*, VI, 158–160.

[57] The notorious partnership of Bulgarin and Grech was immortalized by

his fame as a publicist, Bulgarin became widely known as a writer of novels and short stories, which displayed to good advantage their author's vivacity and power of superficial observation although they were sadly deficient in taste and artistry. Bulgarin missed few occasions to preach loudly Russian patriotism, morality, and enthusiastic support of the system of Nicholas I. The government responded by bestowing upon this able journalist some civil service appointments, ranks, and medals. Bulgarin died in 1859, having outlived by four years the regime under which he had made his fortune.

Many observers have noted Bulgarin's cupidity. His proliferating literary enterprises were virtually all guided by the desire to make money, and the same consideration affected most of his other activities as well. Characteristically, on one occasion Bulgarin informed an associate that he favored war against Turkey because that would bring some fifteen hundred or two thousand new subscribers to *The Northern Bee*. The journalist cheerfully accepted small bribes as well as larger ones, considering a good dinner to be a proper inducement for a favorable review.[58] But greed was not Bulgarin's only passion. It represented, rather, an aspect of his more general obsessive drive to achieve popularity, prominence, and success. The man was most notably an irrepressible braggart who tried to attract attention in every way he could. His vanity knew no bounds. His numerous war stories were full of the famous men under whom he served, both in the French and in the Russian armies. In the acid words of Herzen, Bulgarin "considered Napoleon to be his comrade in arms and always stood by him."[59] Similarly, in his literary activities, the journalist emphasized his originality and the fact that everybody else was imitating him. In addition, he boasted about his friendships with great poets and prose writers, as well

---

Krylov in his fable about "the cuckoo and the cock" who were eternally engaged in praising each other. Krylov, *Basni*, pp. 342–343. Other comments included Herzen's witty article "One mind is fine, but two are better." Herzen, *Sochineniya*, IV, 153–156.

[58] Botsyanovskii, "Bulgarin, Faddei Venediktovich," *Russkii biograficheskii solvar*, vol. "Betankur" to "Byakster," pp. 478–479.

[59] Herzen, *op. cit.*, IV, 156.

as about his own supposedly highly aristocratic lineage. Many of
Bulgarin's claims did not correspond to facts. To quote the experienced and charitable judgment of Grech: "I do not think
that he lied on purpose, but he embellished events and, after
recounting them incessantly, he himself grew accustomed to
believe that they had happened exactly as he was narrating
them." [60] It may be added that Bulgarin showed extreme sen-
sitivity to appearances and took special delight in describing
military uniforms and military men.

Bulgarin's overwhelming urge to be noticed, appreciated, and
accepted evidently stemmed from a deep-seated feeling of loneliness and rejection. As a child he had been nervous, impressionable,
and easily frightened, one terrifying experience even causing a
grave illness; [61] later he became sick in his boarding school because
he decided that his parents did not love him.[62] Loneliness also
appeared as an important motif in some of his literary works.
Nervous irritability, noticeable in his childhood, characterized
Bulgarin all his life, and on occasion it would take a more serious
turn: "At times, suddenly, without any reason at all, or because
of an utter trifle, he would be seized by some sort of frenzy;
he would become angry, scold, injure all and everybody, he would
fall into a rage. When such frenzy would take hold of him, he
would bleed himself, become weaker, and then return to his
normal condition." [63] It was difficult to get along with Bulgarin,
and especially so for his subordinates: "Bulgarin continually hired
and fired, invited and chased out his collaborators; the end result
was usually a resounding break accompanied by an undying
hostility." [64]

The journalist's peculiar nationalism—peculiar at least in that
he managed to become a zealous patriot of two hostile peoples
—was connected with his need to identify himself with some
active cause and with his ability to respond very quickly to his

---

[60] Grech, *op. cit.*, p. 696.
[61] Bulgarin, *Vospominaniya*, I, 63–64.
[62] *Ibid.*, pp. 253–254.
[63] Grech, *op. cit.*, p. 692.
[64] *Ibid.*, p. 699. Grech's own relations with Bulgarin ended in a violent
quarrel and lasting hostility.

environment. Once he left his passionately Polish home behind, the boy developed rapidly in military school into a Russian, so that his poor Catholic mother fainted when she found him, on a visit, singing liturgy in an Orthodox church.[65] However, after his service in the Russian army was terminated abruptly by his superiors, Bulgarin promptly switched his allegiance to Poland, entering the ranks of his compatriots who had joined the French. This turnabout has been interpreted as a reversion to childhood beliefs and attachments. An alternative explanation is provided by Bulgarin himself:

> With my fiery imagination and intellect eager for new experiences, with my passion for military service or, to be more exact, for war, I rejoiced at the offer of my relatives. Knowing that Napoleon uses Polish troops all over Europe, I was hoping to see Spain, Italy and, possibly, even lands beyond Europe. . . . That is what attracted me abroad! Not a single political idea entered my head: I wanted to fight and to wander. With an equal enthusiasm I would have entered Turkish or American service! [66]

After the defeat of Napoleon and the collapse of his empire, Bulgarin returned to Russia to resume his interrupted career in that country. As a sponsor of the sacred creed of Official Nationality, the journalist thundered against those Russians who were not sufficiently nationalist, correcting even their grammar and their phrasing of their native language.

However, although financially gainful, Bulgarin's standing in Russia left much else to be desired. People were repelled by his overwhelming egotism, by his constant and sickening moralizing, by his vulgarity,[67] by his complete subservience to the government. More serious charges included his informing the secret police on his rivals, although apparently the gendarmes too thought

---

[65] Bulgarin, *op. cit.*, II, 53–54.
[66] Bulgarin, *op. cit.*, VI, 224.
[67] As an example of Bulgarin's vulgarity read, for instance, his separately published essay, *Salopnitsa.*

little of Bulgarin and his assertions.[68] The journalist was not far
from the truth when he declared:

*Besides, it is very remarkable that in the course of twenty-five
years all the periodicals, whatever their total number may be
(except* The Friend of Enlightenment and Charity *which was
published by the Literary Society and the present-day* Reader's
Library), *began, developed, and ended their careers with a violent
abuse of my literary works. . . . No matter what absurdity comes
off a press, gentlemen journalists always maintain that it is in
any case* better *than my creations.*[69]

Bulgarin's life was a decline. He started out in literature as
a promising young man, a friend of the playwright Griboedov and
of some other luminaries. He ended his days as "the police spy
Vidocq," derided by Pushkin and practically every other Russian
intellectual.[70] Before Bulgarin died, his name had become a
swearword.

Bulgarin was not the only fantastic person to promote the
doctrine of Official Nationality. Senkovskii possessed as remarkable a character, and he made a similar contribution to the
government cause. Furthermore, as human beings, the two were
strikingly alike. True, Senkovskii had the advantage of marvelous
native gifts as well as of an excellent education. He quickly
became one of the first of the outstanding orientalists in Russia
and one of the youngest professors at the University of St.
Petersburg, while Bulgarin spent his youth in rather unsuccessful

---

[68] Lemke, in his above-mentioned works, analyzed in detail the relationship
between Bulgarin and the gendarmery. On the low estimate of the journalist
by the policemen see also Trotskii, *op. cit.*, p. 100. Cf. an interesting recent
article, Monas, "Šiškov, Bulgarin and the Russian Censorship," *Harvard Slavic
Studies*, IV, 127–147.

[69] Bulgarin, *Vospominaniya*, I, xiii. The Russian titles of the periodicals
were *Sorevnovatel prosveshcheniya i blagotvoreniya* and *Biblioteka dlya chteniya*,
respectively. "Better" was italicized in the original.

[70] The name, referring to a well-known French police agent of the time of
Napoleon, Eugene François Vidocq, whose unsavory memoirs came out in
1829–1830, was applied to Bulgarin by Pushkin, among others. For Pushkin's
attacks on Bulgarin see Pushkin, *op. cit.*, III, 80; IV, 550; V, 40–45. The
matter is discussed by Fomin, "Pushkin i zhurnalnyi triumvirat 30 kh godov,"
in Pushkin, *op. cit.*, V, 451–492.

army service. Talent, cultivation, and knowledge all favored
Senkovskii. Yet there were profound and basic resemblances
between the two men: both were tremendously insecure, lacking
firm foundation and lasting conviction of any sort; both were
extremely sensitive; both had an obsessive desire to attract attention and to please; both lived in a frenzy of activity, trying
out various plans and heading in all directions; both achieved
considerable temporary success, but failed to satisfy themselves,
to win the respect of other men, or to leave anything enduring
behind them. It may be added that both acted very effectively
as journalists, Bulgarin publishing the most widely read newspaper
in Russia and Senkovskii the periodical with the greatest number
of subscribers. And both were Poles performing their ceaseless
services to an alien country and an adopted ideology.

Osip Senkovskii was born in 1800, in a family of Polish gentry.[71]
His mother, who dominated and arranged the life of her pre-
cocious child, used all the means at her disposal to give him
an early and fine education. It was at the University of Vilno,
from which Senkovskii was graduated when not yet twenty, that
he developed an interest in the East, studying Arabic, Hebrew,
and other Oriental languages. In 1819 Senkovskii entered the
diplomatic service. A very brief and wholly unsuccessful marriage
was followed by two years of study and travel in the Near East,
Constantinople, Syria, and Egypt. After his return, the gifted
young man was employed for a period of time as a translator in
the foreign office, and then, in 1828, he accepted a full professorship and the chair of Oriental languages at the University of
St. Petersburg. In January, 1829, Senkovskii married again, this
time a nervous and clinging young lady who never ceased to

---

[71] The most valuable book about Senkovskii is that written by his second
wife and entitled, rather confusingly, in Russian, *Osip Ivanovich Senkovskii
(Baron Brambeus), Biograficheskie zapiski ego zheny.* Still overwhelmed by
her brilliant departed husband, Mrs. Adelaide Senkovskii presents a frank
and convincing exposition of him and of their life together, which is very
impressive indeed although not at all in the way intended. Some of Senkovskii's
letters to his wife are appended to the volume. For a bibliography of his
works see Savelev, *O zhizni i trudakh O. I. Senkovskogo.* More material can
be found in Senkovskii's own writings, in certain brief contemporary accounts,
and in the usual encyclopedias. "Baron Brambeus" was Senkovskii's favorite
pen name.

idolize him. Fortunately for the professor, his second wife, a daughter of a court banker, was also rich.

Several years were dedicated exclusively to the study of those languages which he had not as yet learned. Chinese, Mongolian, Manchurian, Tibetan, Icelandic, and other tongues occupied virtually his entire time and all his thoughts. At that time he published his scholarly works in Latin, Arabic, Persian, French, and Polish. Then too, on the occasion of the war against Turkey, he composed "A Pocketbook for Russian Warriors" (Turkish conversations, with a Russian translation).[72]

Even allowing for the exaggeration of this admiring spouse, the record of Senkovskii's first years as a professor was very impressive, a point emphasized by many commentators.[73]

But the orientalist remained restless and in search of new fields of activity. "Repose was for him equally impossible and anti-pathetic." [74] Apparently this frantic and many-sided activity represented a misdirected quest for some reassurance, haven, security. To quote again the words of his wife, as she reminisced about their courtship and about her husband's character: "In spite of the fact that he could see my love clearly, he still doubted, did not hope to be loved; he considered himself unworthy of me; he trembled at the thought of a rejection and he wanted to prolong at least the happiness of daily meetings. Such he was always, in everything, throughout his entire life!" [75]

Journalism became Senkovskii's passion. The orientalist established connections with several periodicals and newspapers, but his great prominence was linked largely to *The Reader's Library*, where he published a tremendous amount of his own writing and which he managed wholly or in part from 1833 to 1856. Senkovskii's bulky journal, modeled after the Parisian *Bibliothèque*

[72] Senkovskaya, *Osip Ivanovich Senkovskii (Baron Brambeus), Biograficheskie zapiski ego zheny*, p. 14.

[73] In addition to Savelev, *op. cit.*, see the very high estimate of Senkovskii as a scholar, together with a bibliography of his works, in Korsakov, "Senkovskii, Osip Ivanovich," *Russkii biograficheskii slovar*, vol. "Sabaneev" to "Smyslov," pp. 316–325. Korsakov's article suffers from being a eulogy.

[74] Senkovskaya, *op. cit.*, p. 131.

[75] *Ibid.*, p. 27.

Universelle, attained great popularity in Russia, even creating to some extent a new reading public from the ranks of these who had not previously touched any periodical. "Here Senkovskii placed a number of his articles on the most diverse subjects, and he filled the critical section almost entirely with his own reviews. Not satisfied with that, he changed radically all the articles sent to him, making no allowance even for the works of foreign authors," [76]—authors who included such writers as Balzac. The orientalist's entire life, and incidentally that of his wife as well, became one frenzied effort to meet publication deadlines.

While *The Reader's Library* offered a varied literary bill of fare, it contained little politics. Senkovskii was closely connected to Official Nationality and to such other journalistic exponents of it as Bulgarin and Grech; he supported the government in full measure, and he served for a period of time as one of the censors; but, as a journalist, he avoided political and, indeed, all other serious issues. Instead he devoted his periodical to amusing his readers, writing in a light style and in a jocular or semijocular vein which made even his earnest statements suspect. To make matters worse, Senkovskii lacked any independent standard of judgment and possessed abominable taste. Furthermore, being exceedingly sensitive all his life, he often reversed his estimates, reacting promptly to the latest stimulus from the outside. As to the orientalist's general political views, they manifested turnabouts and certain attitudes similar to Bulgarin's, if not as pronounced:

A Pole by birth and upbringing, a friend of Lelewel, a member of a society to disseminate enlightenment in the Polish spirit, Senkovskii not only would not sympathize with Poland, but, in the words of his acquaintance Moravskii, "could not stand the Poles and always was vicious in his remarks about them." Sent to inspect the schools in the Vilno district, Senkovskii everywhere gave strict orders "to instill in the students respect for authority and love for everything Russian." Senkovskii himself, however, did not give any indications of this love, and indeed he could

---

[76] Botsyanovskii, "Senkovskii (Osip-Yulian Ivanovich)," *Entsiklopedicheskii Slovar* (Brockhaus-Efron), XXIX[A], 531. There was no international copyright in operation.

not love Russia for he did not know it. He was perfectly cosmopolitan, with only a certain special attachment for the East which he liked because of its bright and original colors.[77]

It is not surprising that Senkovskii's position as a leading journalist and a public figure proved to be ephemeral: his tremendous output had practically no substance,[78] and the frantic effort to make people laugh could not replace conviction and serious purpose. Herzen aptly described this publicist as a purveyor of noisy fireworks, abandoned as soon as the festivities were over.[79]

In addition to scholarship and journalism, Senkovskii tried many other things. After his second marriage, he would not let his wife out of his sight for two years, devoting his entire time and talent to attracting ceaselessly her undivided attention, admiration, and affection. Later he became obsessed with purchasing and furnishing new homes for her, which had to be completely ready before she was allowed to see them. Similarly, he developed a passionate interest in giving parties. Repeated migraine headaches and, in 1833, the illness which his wife described as "inflammation of the brain" appeared to spur him on in his ceaseless quest. The orientalist became an impassioned builder of queer musical instruments, including one that was to replace an entire orchestra. Next he formulated a weird system of the structure of the universe, based on musical tones. Each new interest became all-important for Senkovskii, pushing out other occupations. The wife from whom he once could not stand separation came to be left alone for long periods of time. Although the orientalist did not resign his professorship, "he began to prepare his lectures poorly, to miss them, and his scholarly, academic authority declined with each year." [80] Journalism, however, was a

---

[77] *Ibid.*, pp. 531–532.

[78] This lack produces almost an eerie feeling as one reads through the volumes of *The Reader's Library*.

[79] Herzen, *op. cit.*, VI, 244–245.

[80] Korsakov, *op. cit.*, p. 317. Extremely nervous, irritable, overbearing, and sarcastic, Senkovskii found it difficult to get along with either the professors or the students at the University. See the comments of his colleague in Nikitenko, I, 164–165, 180, 236–237, 239. Nikitenko wrote about Senkovskii: "He is composed entirely of passions which boil and rage at the slightest push from the outside" (pp. 236–237).

somewhat different matter. In that field too Senkovskii's effort proceeded in bursts, but he kept returning to the work of a publicist from his various other occupations. His final spurt of journalistic activity occurred in the last years of his life which were also the first of Alexander II's reign. In the changed climate of opinion, Senkovskii broke into a new, liberal vein, discussing ably such questions as the need for a responsible press, a noteworthy performance for this most irresponsible journalist. He died in 1858, dictating an article as death pangs set in.

The psychological type so sharply represented by Bulgarin and Senkovskii was not confined to the journalists of Official Nationality. Some writers of that school displayed similar traits of character. What is more, the creator of the doctrine himself, Count Serge Uvarov, who lived from 1786 to 1855 and who headed the ministry of education from 1833 to 1849, also possessed a kindred personality. He was described and denounced as follows by the famous historian S. Soloviev:

Uvarov was indisputably a man of brilliant gifts, and because of these gifts, because of his education, because of the liberal mode of thinking which he derived from the society of the Steins, the Kochubeis, and of the other luminaries of the epoch of Alexander, he was capable of occupying the position of the minister of education, of the president of the Academy of Sciences, etc. But in this man the qualities of the heart did not at all correspond to the qualities of the mind. Acting the part of a noble landlord, Uvarov had nothing truly aristocratic in him. On the contrary, here was a servant who had acquired pretty good manners in the house of a pretty good master (Alexander I), but who remained a servant at heart. He spared no means, no flattery to please his master (Emperor Nicholas). He instilled in him the thought that he, Nicholas, was the creator of some new enlightenment, based on new principles, and he devised these principles, that is the words: Orthodoxy, autocracy, and nationality; Orthodoxy—while he was an atheist not believing in Christ even in the Protestant manner, autocracy—while he was a liberal, nationality—although he had not read a single Russian book in his life and wrote constantly in French or in German. Decent people close to him, indebted to him and loving him, admitted with sorrow, that there was nothing so low that he was incapable of doing it, that he was soiled on all sides by dirty acts. When talking to this person, often in the course of an intellectually brilliant conversation, one was struck by his extreme egotism and vanity. On such occasions one would be expecting that the next moment he would say that at the creation of the world God consulted him concerning the plan.[81]

This picture of Uvarov is exaggerated and incomplete, but it should not be lightly dismissed. In fact, most of Soloviev's charges are supported by many contemporaries of the gifted minister of education. It was Uvarov's pliability and proneness to compromise that De Maistre, the theoretician of reaction, singled out for attack in his interesting correspondence with the Russian.[82] Another observer, A. Turgenev, expressed in March, 1817, the following opinion of Uvarov: "I do not notice in him an urge towards the real good, but rather greed for paper immortality and for that fame which is dispensed by German and French scholarly societies and writers. He switches easily from one mode of thinking to another and . . . from his own convictions to somebody else's." [83] Uvarov's close acquaintances and admirers, such as Pogodin, deplored his vanity and his love of flattery, if not his total lack of scruples.

The aristocratic minister of education had a brilliant career which included the fields of diplomacy and finance before he was appointed to direct the intellectual development of Russia. His own schooling was of the best, and he produced some promising studies of classical subjects, in particular of certain

[81] Soloviev, *op. cit.*, p. 59. Cf. Herzen, *Byloe i dumy*, pp. 67–68, and Grech, *op. cit.*, p. 366.

[82] Stepanov, "Zhozef de Mestr v Rossii." The article was written by Stepanov; materials were published with notes by Stepanov and Vermale, *Literaturnoe Nasledstvo*, vol. 29/30 (1937), 577–726. Part III contains the correspondence of De Maistre and Uvarov (pp. 682–712), preceded by an introductory article (pp. 677–682).

[83] *Ibid.*, p. 677. See also Nikitenko, I, 321, as well as the more charitable opinion expressed by the author eleven years later on page 423 of the diary.

Greek myths. He also attained prominence by his project of an "Asiatic Academy" to explore the vast realm of Oriental studies. Young Uvarov was noticed by Goethe and by Napoleon, among others, as well as by De Maistre. In 1818 he became the president of the Imperial Academy of Sciences, retaining this position until his death. Yet, in spite of his ability and his learning, Uvarov's ideas appeaɪ to be brittle and borrowed. It was not simply that he changed them: the switch from liberalism to conservatism was characteristic of a large part of an entire generation as the "age" of Nicholas replaced that of Alexander, although Uvarov was more extreme in both periods than many of his contemporaries.[84] The discordant note was produced rather by the fact that the minister's intellectual orientation and emotional attitudes did not seem to fit his expressed beliefs. While such devoted theoreticians as Pogodin and Shevyrev hated the West, and Nicholas I hated at least large segments of it, Uvarov, the chief official promulgator of this doctrine of antagonism, combined his violent theory with a tolerant and indeed friendly personal attitude toward the great enemy.[85] Similarly, whereas the emperor and many of his followers were ready to lay down their lives for their sacred creed, the minister, this "fortunate and flexible nature," [86] evidently remained always something of a skeptic, pitying humanity deluded by its various myths.[87] In the end, the true convictions of Uvarov are no easier to determine than those of Bulgarin and of Senkovskii, and in any event, as suggested earlier, this criterion probably is not applicable in their case.

Such were the human agents of the ideology of Official Nationality. Our next concern will be the doctrine itself.

---

[84] Uvarov's early liberalism has been discussed in many works. An example of it from his own writings would be *L'Empereur Alexandre et Buonaparte*.

[85] See, for instance, his essay on "Rome" written in 1843. In Uvarov, *Études de philologie et de critique*, pp. 395–415.

[86] I borrowed the phrase from the eulogistic introduction by L. Leduc to Uvarov, *Esquisses politiques et littéraires*, p. 11.

[87] Read especially Uvarov, *La certitude historique est-elle en progrès?* The dismissed minister composed this essay in 1850.

III

OFFICIAL NATIONALITY

THE IDEAS

Our common obligation consists in this that the education of the people be conducted, according to the Supreme intention of our August Monarch, in the joint spirit of Orthodoxy, autocracy, and nationality.—Uvarov [1]

THE government ideology in the reign of Nicholas I, which came to be known as Official Nationality,[2] possessed a definite origin. It was proclaimed on April the second, 1833, by the new minister of education, S. Uvarov, in his first circular to the officials in charge of the educational districts of the Russian Empire. Uvarov

---

[1] Uvarov, "Tsirkulyarnoe predlozhenie G. Upravlyayushchego Ministerstvom Narodnogo Prosveshcheniya Nachalstvam Uchebnykh Okrugov 'o vstuplenii v upravlenie Ministerstvom,'" *Zhurnal Ministerstva Narodnogo Prosveshcheniya*, 1834, part 1, p. l.

[2] The term "Official Nationality" was not used by its proponents, nor by the early critics. Initiated by Professor A. Pypin, it obtained currency among historians late in the nineteenth century, and it has since become standard. See the important chapter "Official Nationality" in Pypin, *Kharakteristiki literaturnykh mnenii ot dvadtsatykh do pyatidesyatykh godov*, pp. 93–140. See also, e.g., Sakulin, "Russkaya literatura vo vtoroi chetverti veka," in *Istoriya Rossii v XIX veke*, II, 443–508, especially p. 445.

wrote: "Our common obligation consists in this that the education of the people be conducted, according to the Supreme intention of our August Monarch, in the joint spirit of Orthodoxy,
autocracy, and nationality. I am convinced that every professor
and teacher, being permeated by one and the same feeling of
devotion to throne and fatherland, will use all his resources to
become a worthy tool of the government and to earn its complete
confidence." [3]

The minister proceeded to propound and promote his three
cardinal principles throughout the sixteen years during which he
remained in charge of public instruction in Russia. In reports to
the emperor, as well as in orders to subordinates, he presented
these principles invariably as the true treasure of the Russian
people and the Russian state. For instance, Uvarov discussed
the matter as follows in the survey of his first decade in office,
submitted for imperial approval:

*In the midst of the rapid collapse in Europe of religious and
civil institutions, at the time of a general spread of destructive
ideas, at the sight of grievous phenomena surrounding us on all
sides, it was necessary to establish our fatherland on firm foundations upon which is based the well-being, strength, and life of
a people; it was necessary to find the principles which form the
distinctive character of Russia, and which belong only to Russia;
it was necessary to gather into one whole the sacred remnants
of Russian nationality and to fasten to them the anchor of our
salvation. Fortunately, Russia had retained a warm faith in the
sacred principles without which she cannot prosper, gain in
strength, live. Sincerely and deeply attached to the church of
his fathers, the Russian has of old considered it the guarantee of
social and family happiness. Without a love for the faith of its
ancestors a people, as well as an individual, must perish. A Russian,
devoted to his fatherland, will agree as little to the loss of a*

---

[3] Uvarov, *op. cit.* Uvarov had first formulated his three-term creed several
months earlier, in a memorandum to the emperor, dated December 4, 1832.
The memorandum followed Uvarov's inspection of the University of Moscow
and the Moscow school district and immediately preceded his appointment
to head the ministry of education. Barsukov, *Zhizn i trudy M. P. Pogodina,*
IV, 78–86, especially p. 83; Schiemann, III, 225.

single dogma of our Orthodoxy *as to the theft of a single pearl from the tsar's crown.* Autocracy *constitutes the main condition of the political existence of Russia. The Russian giant stands on it as on the cornerstone of his greatness. An inumerable majority of the subjects of* Your Majesty *feel this truth: they feel it in full measure although they are placed on different rungs of civil life and although they vary in education and in their relations to the government. The saving conviction that Russia lives and is protected by the spirit of a strong, humane, and enlightened autocracy must permeate popular education and must develop with it. Together with these two national principles there is a third, no less important, no less powerful:* nationality.[4]

It was for his long service to the three sacred principles that Uvarov was made a count. Still more appropriately, Nicholas I granted him the words "Orthodoxy, autocracy, nationality" as his family motto.

Many poets, writers, professors, and journalists proved eager to echo Uvarov's battle cry, sometimes with a respectful bow in his direction. Shevyrev, to give one example, followed the minister in 1841 in his analysis of Russia and the West for the first issue of *The Muscovite.* The Moscow professor asserted, in his usual ponderous and involved manner:

But even if we did pick up certain unavoidable blemishes from our contacts with the West, we have on the other hand preserved in ourselves, in their purity, three fundamental feelings which contain the seed and the guarantee of our future development. We have retained our ancient religious feeling. The Christian cross had left its sign on our entire original education, on the entire Russian life. . . . The second feeling which makes Russia strong and which secures its future well-being is the feeling of our state unity, again derived by us from our entire history. There is certainly no country in Europe which can boast of such a harmonious political existence as our fatherland. Almost everywhere in the West dissension as to principles has been recognized

[4] Uvarov, *Desyatiletie ministerstva narodnogo prosveshcheniya* 1833–1843, pp. 2–3. Emphasis in the original.

as a law of life, and the entire existence of peoples transpires in heavy struggle. Only in our land the tsar and the people compose one unbreakable whole, not tolerating any obstacle between them: this connection is founded on the mutual feeling of love and faith and on the boundless devotion of the people to its tsar. . . . Our third fundamental feeling is our consciousness of our nationality and our conviction that any enlightenment can be firmly rooted in our land only when it is assimilated by our national feeling and expressed by our national thought and national word. . . . Because of the three fundamental feelings our Russia is firm and her future is secure. A statesman of the Council of the Tsar, to whom are entrusted those generations which are being educated, already long ago expressed them in a profound thought, and they have formed the foundation of the upbringing of the people.[5]

In addition to *The Muscovite*, a score or more other periodicals proclaimed "Orthodoxy, autocracy, and nationality" as their articles of faith. They ranged from the fantastically reactionary, obscurantist, and nationalist *Lighthouse* to formal and pedantic government publications, such as Uvarov's own *Journal of the Ministry of Education*. A newspaper with a very wide circulation, *The Northern Bee,* and a similarly popular magazine, *The Reader's Library*, already mentioned in this study, were of particular assistance in disseminating the minister's views throughout the length and breadth of Russia. In fact, until the end of the reign of Nicholas I, Uvarov's brief formula dominated most of the Russian press.

Books followed periodicals in spreading the government doctrine. The three sacred principles appeared in many different works, in and out of context, but they became especially common in textbooks and in popularizations of the type of Bulgarin's "Russia in its historical, statistical, geographical, and literary aspects. A handbook for Russians of every class and condition." That handbook, mostly a dry compilation of facts, contained, for example, the following rhetorical passage:

---

[5] Shevyrev, "Vzglyad russkogo na sovremennoe obrazovanie Evropy," *Moskvityanin*, 1841, part 1, pp. 292–295.

Thus, the Russian state *was founded and* the name of the Russian people *was created by the introduction of the Christian faith, and not by a chance establishment of rule through conquest. That is why our* Rus *was called* holy *and the* mother *of the people, the same names that are applied to the Church. A great and salutary idea!* To be able to perform this great deed it was necessary for Vladimir and Yaroslav to establish a strong, autocratic rule, and Providence, after many trials, gave to these great men the salutary autocratic power. Faith and autocracy created *the Russian state and the one common* fatherland *for the Russian Slavs. Only faith and autocracy can constitute the glory, the well-being, and the power of Russia! Faith and autocracy are in relationship to vast Russia what gravitation is for our planet. This immense colossus, Russia, almost a separate continent, which contains within itself all the climates and all the tribes of mankind, can be held in balance only by faith and autocracy. That is why in Russia there could never and cannot exist any other* nationality, *except the nationality founded on Orthodoxy and on autocracy. They alone can establish firmly our independent and original existence. Orthodoxy strengthens the originality of the Russian people, in the midst of all the European peoples, and affirms the existence of our national language, thus preventing the Russian people from mixing with aliens and from losing its original character. Autocracy is the concentration of the strength, the will, and the thought of a numerous people scattered over an enormous territory. Orthodoxy saved Russian nationality at a time of fearful calamities, while with a decline of autocracy, with the death of Yaroslav, the power of Russia collapsed, and she became a prey of barbarians, as we shall see in our discussion of the next historical period.*[6]

---

[6] Bulgarin, *Rossiya v istoricheskom, statisticheskom, geograficheskom i literaturnom otnosheniyakh. Ruchnaya kniga dlya russkikh vsekh soslovii*, History, part 4, pp. 291–293. Although published under Bulgarin's name, the Handbook was compiled by Professor N. Ivanov. (See "Ivanov, Nikolai Alekseevich," *Entsiklopedicheskii Slovar* (Brockhaus-Efron), XIIᴬ, 763.) It is likely, however, that Bulgarin edited it and added the flourishes such as the one quoted above. In any case, the precise authorship of the passage does not matter for the purpose of illustration. Emphasis in the original.

"Orthodoxy, autocracy, and nationality" came to represent much
more than Uvarov's attempt at philosophizing, more even then
the guiding principles of the ministry of education. The formula
expanded in application and significance to stand for the Russia
of Nicholas I. Military cadets were enjoined to become "Christians," "loyal subjects," and "Russians," in that order.[7] The entire
nation was to rally for "faith, tsar, and fatherland," the phrase
used, for instance, in the famous 1848 manifesto quoted in the
first chapter of this study. The emperor himself dedicated his life
to the service of Orthodoxy, autocracy, and Russia. Everyone else
in the government was compelled to follow the monarch. At the
same time a considerable part of the educated Russian public,
led by prominent professors, writers, and journalists hoisted the
three words as their banner. "Orthodoxy, autocracy, and nationality" were interpreted to mean the past, the present, and the future
of Russia, Russian tradition as well as Russian mission, Russian
culture as much as Russian politics.[8]

One attraction of Uvarov's formula was its apparent simplicity.
It comprised only three terms, listed always in the same sequence.
The content of the doctrine of Official Nationality depended on
the meanings and the implications of these key concepts.

II

Orthodoxy, the first article of faith in the doctrine of Official
Nationality, had several basic levels of significance and numerous
connotations. In the deep, personal sense it represented, as has
already been shown in the case of Nicholas I himself, the ultimate
belief, hope, and support of man. Indeed, it was his firm faith in
God, Christ, the Divine Will, as revealed in the teaching of the
Orthodox Church, that sustained the disappointed and at times
even desperate emperor in all the trials and tribulations of his
hard life. Only Christ, only Orthodoxy, represented for the Russian monarch light, guidance, and salvation in this vale of sorrow
and strife.

---

[7] Quoted in Polievktov, p. 332.
[8] That this point of view outlived the reign of Nicholas is evident, for instance, from N. Barsukov's writings. See especially Barsukov, *op. cit.*, IV, 1–3.

Imperial convictions were shared by many lesser adherents to the state ideology. As one of them, the poet F. Glinka, stated the matter:

> Extend to me Thy hand, Father, from heaven,
> Give me firmness on my slippery footing,
> Take away my suffering with a breath of Thy love
> And show me light in the dark steppe! [9]

Or, in the words of another proponent of Official Nationality and a much greater poet, Zhukovskii: "The human soul needs God alone." [10] Even Bulgarin, hardly a religious mind himself, fell in line with this view and affirmed: "I do not claim a profound knowledge in the field of philosophy, and I confess openly that, having surveyed all philosophic schools and opinions, I find that true wisdom is contained only in the Gospel." [11]

The most remarkable religious work to come from the proponents of Official Nationality was Pogodín's "Simple Talk about Complex Things." [12] Although published in its author's old age, it represented faithfully his thinking during his entire life, consisting as it did largely of separate thoughts and short comments jotted down over a period of years and brought out in print without alteration. Pogodin's other copious writings deal with religion only in passing, but to the extent that they do so they support fully, both in general and in detail, the views expressed by Pogodin in the special volume dedicated to that subject. "Simple Talk" contained three parts: "Moral and Spiritual Aphorisms," "The Philosophers Are Asked to Explain," and "About the Crying Evil of the Day."

Pogodin started his inquiry in a characteristically blunt manner:

Life, death, the beginning, the end, good, evil, happiness, misery, the soul, immortality, the other world, faith, eternity, the uni-

---

[9] From the long poem "Carelia," in Glinka, Stikhotvoreniya, p. 271.

[10] Zhukovskii, "Vera i um. Istina. Nauka. Stati iz nenapechatannykh sochinenii," Zhurnal Ministerstva Narodnogo Prosveshcheniya, LXXXI (1854). part II, p. 9.

[11] Bulgarin, Salopnitsa, p. 6.

[12] Pogodin, Prostaya rech o mudrenykh veshchakh. The "talk" had a supplement, Pogodin, Sbornik, sluzhashchii dopolneniem k prostoi rechi o mudrenykh veshchakh.

verse, man, Christ, God!—what lofty subjects I dare to discuss!

But what other subjects are closer to man? What subjects should preoccupy us most? What problems are more intimately related to our present existence and our future fate, whatever it may be— nothingness in the opinion of fashionable philosophers, or eternal life according to the Christian teaching? [13]

The world was full of mystery:

Infinity—what is it? What spaces compose it?

How can there be anything without limits?

But one cannot imagine the limits either; what would then be beyond them?

Again mystery and unfathomableness . . .

Infinity is incomprehensible, but is the point more comprehensible?

What is the beginning? What is the end? Where is the beginning, where is the end? And what had there been before the beginning? And what will there be after the end? When was the beginning, when will be the end?

Or: everything has neither a beginning nor an end? This is still more puzzling . . .

The absence of origin in time is inconceivable.

Eternity even more so.

Limited space is inconceivable.

Limitless space is inconceivable.

The infinite divisibility of substance is inconceivable.

All this is inconceivable to us, no matter what system we adopt, no matter from which side we approach it, no matter how we turn the questions. All these are mysteries at which one's hair stands on end and one's flesh begins to creep, as soon as one starts thinking about them. . . . [14]

Pogodin emphasized repeatedly these and other such traditional problems and antinomies of philosophy and theology, but he did not limit to them his discussion of the mysterious in human

---

[13] Pogodin, *Prostaya rech o mudrenykh veshchakh*, part 1, p. 3.

[14] *Ibid.*, part 1, pp. 22–24. Emphasis in the original.

life and the universe. The entire second part of the "talk," "The Philosophers Are Asked to Explain," was devoted to premonitions, omens, prophecies, foreknowledge, the inner voice, prophetic dreams, visits by the dead, and similar supernatural occurrences. Tales of this kind were gathered by Pogodin from many sources, often from his friends and acquaintances. Unconvincing as they are, especially in the light of modern psychology, they formed an integral part of Pogodin's religious argumentation, an argumentation which stressed mystery and unfathomableness. One illustration will suffice for this section of the book. The story in question deals with Karamzin, writer, historian, and Pogodin's great hero:

Karamzin's first wife died in 1802—narrates M. A. Dmitriev in his reminiscences—Karamzin loved her passionately. Seeing the hopeless condition of the sick woman, he would now dash to her bedside, now be torn away from her by pressing work for the periodical which provided his income and was necessary for the family. Worn out, exhausted he threw himself on a sofa and fell asleep. Suddenly he sees in a dream that he is standing beside an open grave while on the other side stands Ekaterina Andreevna (whom he married later) and offers him, over the grave, her hand. This dream is all the more strange, because during those minutes, preoccupied with a dying wife, he could not even think about another marriage and could not imagine that he would marry Ekaterina Andreevna. He himself related this dream to my uncle. He married Ekaterina Andreevna in 1804.[15]

One inescapable conclusion emerged from all these mysteries of the universe and from the human inability to comprehend them:

Is it clear that our mind cannot reach these concepts? Is it clear that our mind, or rather our brain, has certain limits beyond which, outside of time and space, it cannot operate, cannot register impressions, that is, cannot understand, cannot imagine; it cannot

---

[15] *Ibid.*, part 2, p. 15.

form any concepts about existence without origin, or about in-
finity, or about limitlessness, or about divisibility . . . ?

We know, therefore, only its own limits!

*Yes, the human mind is limited, and this is precisely what the
blind, insolent pride, especially in our time, refuses to accept.*[16]

Even in the realm of ordinary human activities man's achievements were apparent rather than real. Pogodin became convinced
—and in this respect his pessimism grew with the years—that
progress had meant merely technological improvements, in particular more effective means for fratricidal strife and slaughter.
Human selfishness remained unbridled. The political system of
the world stayed as unjust and chaotic as ever. In social terms, the
situation was still more unfair and more ominous, with cataclysmic revolutions an immediate prospect. Numerous contemporary philosophies and doctrines were of no avail whatsoever.
Man had tried his best, and he was found wanting.[17]

The third part of the "talk" contained a violent polemic against
"the crying evil of the day," Russian atheists, materialists, and
nihilists who refused to share Pogodin's views, but continued to
rely on human reason and human strength. The Moscow professor struck out at his opponents in several ways. As one line
of attack he charged them with ignorance, asserting that essentially all their convictions were based merely on snatches of poorly
understood slogans borrowed from abroad. Furthermore, Pogodin
argued, even the best and the most up-to-date scientific theory
failed to resolve the basic problems of life and was full of un-
proved assumptions as well as contradictions. Developing this
theme, Pogodin undertook an extended analysis of Darwinism,
utilizing against it many arguments which were then current.
Besides, Russian nihilists failed to consider not only the theoretical assumptions of their doctrine, but also its practical implications. Materialism, determinism, and atheism were bound to

---

[16] *Ibid.,* part 1, p. 24. Emphasis in the original.

[17] The assertions contained in this paragraph are abundant in both the first
and the third parts of the "talk." Some of them will be discussed later in this
chapter.

lead to private and public license, and, eventually, to utter chaos and destruction.

Yet, while Darwinism and science in general failed to provide the answers to the most important questions asked by men, somewhere these answers had to be found: "We have here many questions without answers. Is it not clear that the answers must exist somewhere: questions can neither arise nor remain without answers: This would be nonsense. We carry in our hearts the ideal of good and we see evil ruling on earth: but there must be justice. Where then is it? Evidently in heaven." [18]

God, thus, was the great answer to the human quest. As Pogodin tried to convince his opponents: "You ascribe all creation to some force: fine, this is precisely God. Only the word is different." [19] Or, again, in a fuller statement:

That is, all the atheists, ancient and new, all the nihilists accept God. Only they call Him different names, applying their understanding of Him to different words and they argue bitterly about these words without realizing that they are all more or less in agreement and that they are denying merely the conventional term or name. But God has no name: The Existing One!

The philosophers recognize a certain creative force and cannot deny it intelligence; they revere it. This force is God. What is the highest, the holiest action of this force? Christianity. They bow, therefore, also before Christ, only covered by a different concept, in a different guise, under a different name. Is this not a misunderstanding? [20]

Pogodin's analysis led to a simple and definite conclusion: "Nothing on earth has been said, nothing done higher, purer and holier than what was said and done by the Savior of mankind, Jesus Christ. We must obey Him (here in a word is the meaning, the purpose of this book), believe Him, pray to Him, and try to live according to the commandment in the Gospel, try to improve

---

[18] *Ibid.*, part 1, p. 47.
[19] *Ibid.*, part 3, p. 131.
[20] *Ibid.*, part 1, p. 42. Emphasis in the original.

morally and mentally, the task which must be considered the only
purpose of man on earth." [21]

"Simple Talk" expressed faithfully Pogodin's own personality,
interests, and convictions. But it also presented in a typical manner a number of religious beliefs and attitudes common to many
proponents of Official Nationality. One may note first the bluntness, crudity, and naïveté of Pogodin's entire argument. These
qualities tended to characterize government ideologists in the field
of religion as well as in other fields, setting their views apart
from the brilliant religious thought of Khomyakov and his Slavophile followers. Together with the direct and artless approach,
went a strong fideistic emphasis joined to a profound suspicion
of all reasoning, even of theology. God emerged as the ultimate
answer to man's quest, the beginning and the end of human wisdom, Alpha and Omega. In their rare best moments the men
of Official Nationality, and their emperor too for that matter, did
not need the three principles: the first one alone sufficed.

The impact of Christianity was not limited, however, to the
individual soul; it also blazed its trail through history. As Uvarov
asserted in an essay on the philosophy of literature: "Christianity,
a supreme, fundamental, and established fact, alone traced a deep
line of demarcation in the annals of the human mind between
the times which had preceded it and the times which followed it.
There are, therefore, strictly speaking, only two literatures, as
there are only two orders of ideas, as there are only two civiliza-
tions: ancient civilization before Christ, and modern civilization
after Christ." [22] In the new era man, being free, could dodge
moral and religious truths, but he could no longer ignore them.[23]
Christianity provided the basic historical framework for the proponents of Official Nationality, while at the same time it indicated fundamental dividing lines in the contemporary world.

Russia could be understood only within the Christian framework. Its special legacy and treasure consisted of Orthodoxy, the
true form of Christianity. While Nicholas I and his followers

---

[21] *Ibid.*, part 3, p. 207.
[22] Uvarov, "Vues générales sur la philosophie de la littérature," *Études de philologie et de critique*, pp. 339–340.
[23] *Ibid.*, p. 350.

respected different Christian denominations and distinguished sharply between them and all non-Christian forms of belief, they underlined their conviction that only the Orthodox Church and faith were entirely correct and authentic. As Uvarov reported to the emperor, this strong, and "positive" denominational emphasis antagonized "the mystical school" which preferred to base its views on Christianity in general and which attained prominence in Russia late in the reign of Alexander I.[24] Nicholas I had a powerful feeling that he was doing the work and fighting the battle of God and His Church. Imperial manifestoes contained numerous references to Providence, and they often ended with resounding lines taken from the Christian tradition. For instance, the declaration of war on Turkey in 1853 concluded with the following words, well-known in the West in their Latin form: "In te Domine speravi, non confundar in aeternum." [25] Indeed, the link between God and Russia was considered so close that Nicholas I referred to "Russian God," [26] as did Pogodin, Zhukovskii, and some other proponents of Official Nationality. "Orthodoxy" not only stood as the first principle of the government doctrine, but it also entered as an integral part in its other two key concepts, "autocracy" and "nationality," an interrelationship which will be further analyzed later in the chapter.

The emperor and his followers were convinced that Orthodoxy set the absolute ethical norm both for the individual and for the nation. Nicholas I took his moral obligations with utmost seriousness. He was determined to be a good Christian, and he was worried by such things as the nature of his feelings toward the Decembrists or the treatment of Turkish prisoners of war. The emperor never tired of admonishing his soldiers to be humane in war, especially in their dealings with the population of occupied

---

[24] Uvarov, Desyatiletie ministerstva narodnogo prosveshcheniya, 1833–1843, pp. 106–107. Uvarov did not discuss "the mystical school," and he was careful not to criticize the late emperor directly, but his meaning is unmistakable.

[25] As another example of this use of religion see the 1848 manifesto quoted in chap. i above.

[26] See, for instance, Nicholas I's letter to Paskevich quoted in Schilder, II, 385. Zhukovskii was delighted to find this expression in P. Vyazemskii's poem and discussed it at length; Zhukovskii, Polnoe sobranie sochinenii v odnom tome, pp. 168–171.

territories. Indeed Christian principles were not to be forgotten even in combat. In the words of an imperial order to the Russian soldiers at the outbreak of the war against Turkey in 1828:

Warriors! Fighting against civilized people, skilled in combat, you obtained undying glory winning not only by courage alone, but also by kindness. Unquestioning obedience to superiors, strict observance of order, and charity toward the vanquished were always the distinguishing traits of Russian soldiers. That is why peaceful citizens everywhere were so glad at your coming and, vanquished by you, called you liberators. Now too you will retain this precious fame: stretching a friendly hand to the fellow Orthodox, strike down the stubborn enemies, but spare the unarmed and the weak; spare the possessions, the homes, and the very temples of your enemies even though they profess a different faith. So orders our faith, the Sacred teaching of the Savior! One who wins over embittered enemies by mildness and kindness, one who defends an orphan or a widow, will, together with the bravest, be close to my heart.

Russian warriors! You will not deceive my expectations. God is with us; he crowns with victories valor and justice!—Nicholas [27]

Furthermore, throughout his life Nicholas I was bent on improving himself morally and spiritually; and while one may question the result of his efforts, there is no reason to doubt his sincerity or persistence. Moral improvement represented also the constant, though elusive, goal of Pogodin,[28] and of numerous other adherents of Official Nationality. The emperor and many of his followers believed in the Divine presence, participation, and guidance in their daily lives, and this spurred them on in the eternal struggle of the Christian trying to win his salvation.

Projected outward, self-improvement meant moralization and didacticism. The literature of Official Nationality teemed with moral lessons intended to edify and instruct the reader. Crude at their best, these lessons became extremely cheap and vulgar

---

[27] The order constitutes appendix IX in Schilder, II, 777.
[28] This theme recurs in Barsukov's huge study of Pogodin, as well as in Pogodin's own works.

when dispensed by such shady and facile journalists as Bulgarin. That irrepressible writer produced innumerable moral tales praising virtue, castigating vice, and satirizing human foibles. The brunt of Bulgarin's attack was directed at luxury, at ignorance, especially the ignorance by the Russians of their native land, and at their slavish imitation of the West, France in particular. His greatest commendation went to truthfulness, a circumstance of some interest in the light of his own character.[29] The good invariably found their reward and the evil their punishment, all accounts being correctly settled in this world as well as in the next.

While Bulgarin moralized glibly and even flippantly, Gogol's spiritual search evidenced sincerity and obsessiveness bordering on derangement. Yet the immortal writer joined the notorious journalist in urging upon the Russian public the ethical doctrine espoused by Nicholas I and his government. What is more, the two teachers even presented their argument in much the same naïve and clear-cut manner. Gogol's contribution to Official Nationality consisted in his *Selected Passages from Correspondence with Friends* which came out in 1847. The book produced a sensation. Westernizers, liberals, and radicals, headed by Belinskii, assailed Gogol for his alleged betrayal of his own principles, and of progress and civilization in general. Much of their venom stemmed from their earlier misunderstanding of Gogol who, in fact, had never shared their views and whose devastating descriptions of Russia had issued from his weird psychology and satirical genius, not from any ideology of the Left. In any case, the new Gogol became a heavy liability—indeed a nightmare—to his forward-looking friends and admirers. The opposite camp rejoiced. Shevyrev and his associates realized that the great writer had committed himself unreservedly to their cause, and they hailed the book as a new and higher stage in his development. Yet they too were forced to add at least a measure of criticism to their praise. They were disconcerted not by Gogol's fickleness, but

---

[29] In praise of truthfulness, see especially Bulgarin's tale, "Bednyi Makar, ili kto za pravdu goroi, to istyi iroi," *Sochineniya*, V, 111–170. Didactic and satirical literature had become very prominent in Russia in the eighteenth century.

rather by his utter faithfulness to the moral doctrine of the Right. For in Gogol's strange mind and peculiar book this doctrine was transformed into a caricature of itself, but a caricature that was both appropriate and revealing.[30]

Selected Passages from Correspondence with Friends resulted from its author's moral earnestness. As Gogol explained to his readers in the Preface:

My heart tells me that my book is needed and that it may be useful. I think so not because I have a high opinion of myself or assume an ability to be useful, but because never before have I felt such a strong desire to be useful. On our part it is sufficient to extend the helping hand; the help is brought not by us, but by God Who bestows the power of word upon the weak. Thus, no matter how insignificant or contemptible my book may be, I have allowed myself to bring it out into the world, and I ask my fellow countrymen to read it several times. At the same time I beg those of them who have the means, to buy several copies and to distribute them to those who are themselves unable to purchase it. On this occasion the latter should be informed that all money in excess of the expenses for my forthcoming journey will be assigned, on the one hand, to aid those who, similarly to me, will feel the inner need of traveling to the Holy Land for the coming Lent and who will not be able to accomplish this undertaking with their own means alone. On the other hand, the money will be used to help those whom I shall meet already on their way thither and who will all pray by the Holy Sepulchre for my readers, their benefactors.[31]

Selected Passages contained discussions of many topics ranging from the nature of Russia and the mystique of autocracy to everyday problems and cares. Much of the volume was written in the

---

[30] The most famous attack on the book was made by Belinskii in his remarkable "Letter to Gogol," *Sobranie sochinenii v trekh tomakh*, III, 707–715; see also pp. 687–706. Shevyrev expressed his views in "Vybrannye mesta iz perepiski s druzyami N. Gogolya," *Moskivityanin*, 1848, no. 1, Literary Criticism, pp. 1–29. Much valuable material about the controversy over Gogol's work can be found in Barsukov, *op. cit.*, VIII, 519–619.

[31] Gogol, p. 4. *Selected Passages from Correspondence with Friends* constitutes the bulk of the eighth volume of Gogol's *Works*.

artificial, elevated style which not infrequently plagued Gogol's literary work. The entire book was replete with moral and practical advice. A governor general was urged to eliminate bureaucratic formalism in his province and instead to deal with his subordinates in a personal, patriarchal manner. He had, for instance, to explain to them the meaning of duty, a gratifying subject, for, as Gogol asserted: "It will be possible to discuss the duty of man to the point that it will appear as if they were discoursing with angels in the presence of God Himself." [32] Such talks were to be conducted in Russian, not the fashionable French. The governor was further advised to explain to the gentry within his jurisdiction the true and noble role of their class in Russia and to enjoin them to enter the service of the state. Finally, the governor was to reëstablish the ancient position of custom, tradition, and the Orthodox Church itself in the lives of the Russians entrusted to his care. This, again, was to be accomplished simply by his noble example and counsel.

A wife, who, in the opinion of Gogol, lacked firmness of character, received the following precise instructions:

Take the entire household economy upon yourself; let income and expense be in your hands. . . . Divide your money into seven almost equal piles. In the first pile there will be money for rent with the heating, water, firewood, and everything that relates to the building and the cleanliness of the yard. The second pile will contain money for the table and all the food with the cook's wages and supplies for everything that lives in your house. The third pile—the carriage: the vehicle itself, the coachman, horses, hay, oats, in one word, everything that belongs to this department. The fourth pile—money for dress, that is, everything necessary for both of you to go out or to stay home. In the fifth pile will be your pocket money. In the sixth pile money for special expenses which may occur: a change of furniture, the purchase of a new carriage and even help to some of your relatives, if they suddenly develop a need for it. The seventh pile is for God, that is, money

---

[32] *Ibid.*, p. 163. The letter to "One occupying an important position" takes up pp. 152–172 of the volume.

*for the church and the poor. Make it so that these seven piles
remain unmixed, as if they were seven separate ministries. Keep
an expense account separately for each one, and under no circumstances borrow from one pile for another.*[33]

Provided this rule were observed for a year, in spite of all the lures
and embarrassments, and provided it were accompanied by some
other attempts to organize life and by appropriate prayer, firmness of character was bound to be achieved. What is more, the
lady in question was likely to revaluate her needs in the course
of the year, to develop a more modest way of living and to devote
in the future greater sums of money to the church and the poor.
    But the most extraordinary piece of advice befell a landlord:

*Take up the task of a landlord as it should be taken up in the
true and lawful sense. First of all, gather the peasants and explain
to them what you are and what they are: that you are the landlord
over them not because you want to rule and be a landlord, but
because you are already a landlord, because you were born a landlord, because God will punish you if you were to exchange this
condition for any other, because everyone must serve God in his
own place, not someone else's, just as they, having been born
under authority, must submit to the same authority under which
they were born, for there is no authority which is not from God.
And right then show it to them in the Gospel so that they all
down to the last one will see it. After that tell them that you
force them to labor and work not at all because you need money
for your pleasures, and, as a proof, burn right there in front of
them some bills, and make it so that they actually see that money
means nothing to you. Tell them that you force them to work
because God decreed that man earn his bread in labor and sweat,
and right there read it to them in Holy Writ so that they will
see it. Tell them the whole truth: that God will make you answer
for the last scoundrel in the village, and that, therefore, you will
all the more see to it that they work honestly not only for you,
but also for themselves; for you know, and they know it too, that,*

---

[33] *Ibid.*, pp. 140–141. This letter occupies pp. 139–143 of the volume.

once he has become lazy, a peasant is capable of anything—he will turn a thief and a drunkard, he will ruin his soul, and also make you answerable to God. And everything that you tell them confirm on the spot with words from Holy Writ; point with your finger to the very letters with which it is written; make each one first cross himself, bow to the ground and kiss the book itself in which it is written. In one word, make them see clearly that in everything that concerns them you are acting in accordance with the will of God and not in accordance with some European or other fancies of your own.[34]

Nicholas I, Uvarov, Pogodin, Shevyrev, Gogol, and even Bulgarin, as well as many others, all wanted to educate their fellow countrymen morally and spiritually, to make them good Christians and perfect Russians. The main means for the achievement of this purpose were the family and the school. The family had an indispensable part to play in this process of upbringing. As the emperor declared in the celebrated manifesto which announced the execution of the five Decembrists:

Let parents turn their entire attention to the moral education of their children. Not enlightenment, but mental idleness, more noxious than physical idleness, but the absence of firm principles must be held accountable for this wilfulness of thought, the source of violent passions, this destructive luxury of semiknowledge, this urge towards fantastic extremes, the beginning of which is the decline of morals, and the end perdition. All the efforts, all the sacrifices on the part of the government will be in vain if home education does not prepare the character and does not coöperate with the purposes of the government.[35]

A strong, Christian family provided the foundation for state ideology and for the state itself.

The school was to continue and develop the work of the family. Uvarov and his subordinates had numerous and varied tasks,

---

[34] *Ibid.*, pp. 121–122. Other advices to the landlord continue until the end of the letter on page 128.

[35] I used the text of the manifesto as it was published at the time in *Severnaya Pchela*, no. 85, July 17, 1826.

duties, and plans,[36] but, again, the moral element dominated their perspective. Their chief function was to produce right-minded subjects for the Russian empire, and Uvarov discussed this crucial matter in detail in some of his reports to the monarch.[37] Religion and morality appeared prominently in the official orders and regulations of the ministry of education,[38] as well as in its *Journal* where they were combined, often incongruously, with dry, administrative summaries and specialized, scholarly articles. Right principles and good conduct held the center of attention in the Russia of Nicholas I. Tyutchev expressed official opinion when he observed that in Russia especially the government, as well as the Church, had to take charge of human souls.[39]

The family and the school had to coöperate in order to perform their educational task successfully. Shevyrev, who was a specialist in pedagogy as well as in literature, developed this important point in his University of Moscow commencement address of the sixteenth of June, 1842, entitled "Concerning the Relationship of Family Education to State Education." [40] Shevyrev eulogized the family. The Old Testament demonstrated its great role among the Chosen People. China owed to it its unique and astounding durability. Roman power and glory rested on the family, and Rome collapsed as the family declined. But the greatest affirmation of the family came with the birth of Christ and the rise of

---

[36] See chap. iv below for a brief discussion of the activities of the ministry of education.

[37] Uvarov's annual reports were published in *Zhurnal Ministerstva Narodnogo Prosveshcheniya.*

[38] See, for instance, "The Rules for the Guidance of Individuals Maintaining Private Schools in the St. Petersburg School District": "Pravila dlya rukovodstva lits, soderzhashchikh chastnye uchebnye zavedeniya v S. Peterburgskom uchebnom okruge," *Zhurnal Ministerstva Narodnogo Prosveshcheniya,* Sept., 1847, pp. 27–36.

[39] Tyutchev, p. 366. Cf. the remarkably similar educational theory and practice in the Austrian empire in the reign of Francis I; Rath, "Training for Citizenship in the Austrian Elementary Schools during the Reign of Francis I," *Journal of Central European Affairs,* IV (July, 1944), 147–164.

[40] Shevyrev, *Ob otnoshenii semeinogo vospitaniya k gosudarstvennomu. Rech proiznesennaya v torzhestvennom sobranii Imperatorskogo Moskovskogo Universiteta, 16 iyunya 1842, Ordinarnym Professorom Russkoi Slovesnosti, Doktorom Filosofii i Chlenom Pedagogicheskogo Instituta, Stepanom Shevyrevym.* The address took up almost a hundred printed pages.

Christian teaching. Christianity sanctified the family by the example of the Savior himself and by the sacrament of marriage, while the doctrines of the Fathers of the Church explained its surpassing importance. However, even Christian nations failed to develop the family to its full potential. In England, for instance, it was disfigured by primogeniture and by the tremendous authority of the husband over the wife; and in France it was subordinated to the interests of society at large. Fortunately, the Slavs in general and the Russians in particular were indissolubly linked to the family. This union stemmed from their special character as well as from their entire history. Russian fortunes waxed and waned with those of the ruling families in the country, and the entire past of the nation was based on the great institution of the family.

Still, there existed one other basic element in Russia, the state. It had a role to play in the education of the Russians, supplementing the function of the family. More specifically, state schools performed a fourfold service: they added the concepts of duty, necessity, and social obligation to free development in the home; they could compensate for some of the failings and shortcomings quite common in the family environment, for families, as well as other institutions, rarely measured up to the ideal; they brought into unity and conformity the great variety of private backgrounds and attitudes; they offered tremendous educational opportunities, far beyond the resources of any family.

Furthermore, the correct education of a Russian corresponded in its main stages, that is, family, school, and finally the synthesis of the two in a mature outlook, to the history of the Russian people. The whole nation had existed in a secluded and informal family manner until Peter the Great turned it toward the West and imposed the tutelage of the state over the thoughts and the actions of his subjects. With Nicholas I, the final stage was reached: Russia entered the period of a harmonious synthesis of its ancient heritage and its more recent acquisitions from the West, of the family and the state. Shevyrev could well conclude: "Thus from the entire development of Russian life there stems the obvious necessity of a joint march of the family and the state in a new period of education which it is the task of our generations to get started." [41]

This great dialectical truth had immediate practical applications. Shevyrev accompanied it with the following shrill appeal to the parents of the typical University of Moscow student: "If you have sent him to us from afar, parents, oh! hasten, hasten after him hither at the first opportunity: he needs your presence more now than when he lived in the seclusion of a school. . . . Look: at the time when we begin to influence his mind with scholarship, violent passions start boiling in his heart, doubts penetrate his thoughts, life is luring him from all sides into the tempting snares of its enticements!" [42]

Because Orthodoxy was the foundation and the ideal of Russian education, both the family and the school had to be linked as closely as possible to the Church. Shevyrev, who himself came from a very religious gentry family, stressed the importance of organized religion in the home:

To establish firmly the Christian element in the family, it is necessary to introduce into the family complete Christian teaching, both as regards life itself, and as regards external ceremony. . . . Further, the most frequent possible, incessant contacts between the family and the Church are necessary. This is especially true of religious services in the home, which represent a beautiful and special characteristic of our denomination, a characteristic which shows that our Church has apprehended most wisely the peculiarity of Russian family life and has deigned to bestow upon the home all of its services, except the Mass. The more often a family is sanctified by prayers, the more often it is marked by the sign of the cross and by the blessings of the clergy, the more powerfully will the holy essence of religion penetrate, by means of external senses, into the souls of the children.[43]

---

[41] Ibid., p. 76.
[42] Ibid., p. 84.
[43] Ibid., p. 78.

As to the school, there also "the entire temple of popular education is to be sanctified by the altar of God, by the cross, and by prayer." [44] Even after the end of Nicholas I's reign, at the time of Alexander II's reforms, Pogodin insisted that education of the masses in Russia must be based exclusively on the Church.[45] Here again Gogol expressed the extreme form of this line of reasoning: he declared that peasants should not be educated at all, that the words of a priest were more useful to them than all the books, and that learning should be provided only for those few among them who had the ability and the urge "to read the books in which is inscribed God's law for man." [46] And Gogol's obscurantist position was not very far from that of the ministry of education which aimed to teach different Russians only what was proper knowledge for men of their social condition.

It is not difficult to understand why the appeal to "Orthodoxy" in the doctrine of Official Nationality has frequently been considered a gigantic fraud. Religion was used to preach obedience to the emperor, the officer, and the landlord. The government which taught meekness and charity distinguished itself by despotism and brutality. Even the Church was effectively controlled by the state and generally did its bidding. Benckendorff, the chief of gendarmes, reflected official thinking when he remarked concerning the establishment of a new university in Kiev: "Kiev was selected as the place for the new university, this city being, on the one hand, the ancient cradle of Orthodoxy and, on the other, the headquarters of the First Army, which offered all the necessary facilities for the surveillance of a large gathering of young people." [47]

The charges that Official Nationality misused religion are based on facts, and they are very important. Indeed, they cannot be

---

[44] Shevyrev, *Istoriya Imperatorskogo Moskovskogo Universiteta*, pp. 469–470.

[45] See especially Pogodin's speeches in the Provincial Zemstvo Assembly in 1868. Pogodin, *Rechi, proiznesennye M. P. Pogodinym v torzhestvennykh i prochikh sobraniyakh, 1830–1872*, pp. 390–395, 401–406. Hereafter cited as Pogodin, *Rechi*.

[46] Gogol, p. 125.

[47] Schilder, II, 680.

gainsaid. Yet, they do not tell the full story. Nicholas I and many
of his followers believed in Orthodoxy. They understood it in
a limited manner, and their performance fell far short even of
their understanding. But the ideal and the profession of faith
remained. It fell to those living in the twentieth century to witness the work of governments which denied moral principles as
such. On the basis of this later experience, allegiance to Christianity, or to another moral teaching, has acquired a new significance. Professing a creed can be a great force in the history of
mankind, even the greatest, except living it.

III

Autocracy was the second article in the creed of Official Nationality. The law of the land declared: "The Tsar of all the
Russias is an autocratic and absolute monarch. God Himself
commands us to obey the Tsar's supreme authority, not from
fear alone, but as a point of conscience." [48] Or, to quote from the
military statutes dating back to the reign of Peter the Great:
"Article 20. Whoever utters blasphemous words against the person of His Majesty, whoever deprecates His intentions and His
actions and discusses them in an unseemly manner, he will be
deprived of life by decapitation.—Commentary. For His Majesty
is an autocratic monarch Who need answer to no one in the
world for His actions, but Who possesses power and authority
to govern His states and His lands, as a Christian ruler, according
to His will and judgment." [49]

Even pithy, legal formulations of autocracy usually included
two items: the absolute nature of imperial power and the link

---

[48] *Svod Zakonov Rossiiskoi Imperii*, vol. I, art. 1.
[49] Quoted in an appendix to Schilder, I, 758. For the Swedish origin of this
formulation, see Miliukov, *Gosudarstvennoe khozyaistvo Rossii v pervoi chetverti XVIII stoletiya i reforma Petra Velikogo*, pp. 500–501 n. Cf., for instance, the "small catechism" composed in 1832 for the education of the
rebellious Poles and reproduced partly in Schiemann, III, 202 n. E. g., "Question 5. What kind of obedience do we owe to the emperor? Answer: a perfect,
passive, and boundless one in all matters. . . . Question 12. How does God
consider a failure in respect and loyalty to the emperor? Answer: as the most
horrible sin and the most dreadful crime."

between the emperor and God. For, in the last analysis, God provided the foundation for the authority of the tsar. Most proponents of Official Nationality were well aware of the connection. Such statements as "the heart of the tsar is in the hand of the Lord," Pogodin's special favorite, indicated this awareness. It also found expression in the constant joining of the images of the monarch and of God, one of the most common motifs in the poetry and the prose of Official Nationality. Typically, in such composite pictures the tsar was represented as the absolute ruler of his great realm yet begging guidance and support from the ultimate ruler of the world, God. Panegyrics which, forgetting the chain of command, spoke of the tsar as himself a god were relatively few in number, subject to criticism for their lack of taste, and fair game for the censors.[50] One example taken from the works of Grech should suffice to illustrate the official position. The journalist is describing the great military review held on September 14, 1834, to celebrate the unveiling of a monument to Alexander I in St. Petersburg:

At the sight of this rare spectacle (never before had such a large number of troops been gathered in St. Petersburg) one spontaneous thought entered the minds of all those present: what means moves and inspires these enormous forces, gives them unity and harmony, preserves order and organization among them, produces earnestness, gives birth to the exalted will to die for the fatherland? This means is the unity of the will of the Mover of these forces, their obedience to the One; He, on His part, invested in earthly authority and power is asking for Himself, in humility of spirit, aid, inspiration, and blessing from above! [51]

Some writers of Official Nationality undertook a more thorough analysis of the mystique of autocracy. Zhukovskii declared emphatically: "In the Christian world autocracy is the highest level of power; it is the last link between the power of man and the power of God." [52] True autocracy had a twofold nature: absolute

---

[50] Evidently Nicholas I himself disapproved of such extravagant praise and wanted it censored out. See Nikitenko, I, 223.

[51] Grech, *Sochineniya*, III, 443.

[52] Zhukovskii, *op. cit.*, p. 171.

dominion over men for whom it represented divine authority, yet complete and voluntary submission to God. Because of this submission, "human law becomes *divine truth,* for it derives from an authority permeated by divine truth." [53]

Gogol discussed the same subject as follows:

Why is it necessary that one of us should acquire a position above all others and even above the law? Because law is wooden; man feels that law contains something harsh and unbrotherly. One will not get far merely with a letter-perfect execution of the law. But none of us should break the law or fail to comply with it. That is why we need supreme grace to mitigate the law, and it can come to men only in the form of absolute power. A state without an absolute monarch is an automaton.[54]

Indeed it was the task of the ruler to love all his subjects, and love them equally well. He alone could perform this function because he was equidistant from them all, and because such love represented his direct moral obligation. He alone could suffer for and with all of his people, he alone could bring them cure. "The people will be fully cured only where the monarch will apprehend his highest significance—to be an image on earth of the One Who Himself is love." [55] Gogol pointed to David and to Solomon as illustrating the true function of the ruler.[56]

The view of the tsar as the Christian conscience of Russia found acceptance among many government ideologists and was developed by some of them to suit their particular needs. For example, Ya. Rostovtsev in his "Instructions for the Education of Students in Military Schools" advanced the following argument for absolute obedience to the emperor: because supreme authority was the public conscience of Russia, its decisions in public affairs were as morally binding on the individual as were the dictates of his own conscience in his private life.[57]

---

[53] *Ibid.* Italics in the original.
[54] Gogol, p. 45. Gogol ascribes this argument to Pushkin, but himself agrees enthusiastically with it.
[55] *Ibid.,* p. 49.
[56] *Ibid.,* p. 358.
[57] Rostovtsev's theorizing is summarized in Presnyakov, pp. 13–14.

The belief in autocracy also received support from several other lines of reasoning. Especially pervasive among the proponents of the state creed was their conviction of the inherent weakness and even wickedness of man and of the resulting need for a strong, authoritarian rule over him. As is true of most conservative or reactionary teachings, Official Nationality was a profoundly pessimistic doctrine. Its low estimate of humanity fitted neatly into the Christian framework, if at the expense of neglecting certain basic aspects of Christianity. One of Uvarov's favorite arguments, in his classical research as well as in his other writings, dealt with the fall of man from his initial state of grace, the fact "which alone contains the key to all history." [58] Pogodin, whose deep disillusionment in mankind was noted earlier, found everywhere "proofs of the fall of man (which continues in us), of our impaired nature." [59] Grech's *Memoirs* refer to mankind as a "despicable and ungrateful tribe" [60] and note, in connection with Alexander I's Bible Society, that "human viciousness turns even a medicinal drink into poison, and by its machinations extracts damage and poison from the Word of God." [61] Even Senkovskii's allegiance to Official Nationality has been credited to his skeptical view of the Russian people. [62] The same pessimism and disillusionment constituted, as has already been shown, fundamental traits in the personality of Nicholas I himself.

Because men were feeble and perverse, they had to be driven by a benevolent supreme authority in order to achieve desirable social ends. Pogodin combined loud praise of the Russian people, which is to be discussed later, with some reservations on the subject. As early as 1826 he observed: "The Russian people is marvelous, but marvelous so far only in potentiality. In actuality it is low, horrid, and beastly." And he went on to assert that Russian peasants "will not become human beings until they are forced into it." [63] Pogodin kept repeating this kind of refrain

[58] Uvarov, *Essai sur les mystères d'Eleusis*, p. 30.
[59] Pogodin, *Prostaya rech o mudrenykh veshchakh*, p. 91.
[60] Grech, *Zapiski o moei zhizni*, p. 209.
[61] *Ibid.*, p. 365.
[62] Korsakov, "Senkovskii, Osip Ivanovich," *Russkii biograficheskii slovar*, p. 321.
[63] Barsukov, *op. cit.*, II, 17.

throughout his life. For instance, he complained in 1856, after a discussion of the deficiencies of the educational system in Russia: "What will you do: a Russian must have intelligent prodding and supervision from the outside." [64] Bulgarin joined Pogodin in urging the imperial government to prod the people; for example, to force the peasants in northern Russia to live in good, clean, comfortable houses such as those common in the Ukraine.[65] Grech proclaimed dogmatically: "Men are not angels; there are many devils among them. Therefore, police, and a severe police, is a necessity both for the state and for all private individuals." [66] And he commented as follows on the reign of Nicholas I:

Pepper too is required in a salad! Alexander was too meek, replacing during the first years firmness of character with kindness and compassion. This is too good for the vile human species. Now there, I love our Nicholas! When he is gracious, he is really gracious; but when he hits, then willy-nilly they sing: "God, save the Tsar!" Truthfulness, directness, sincerity compose, in my opinion, the greatness of any person, especially of a tsar. Why be crafty, when one can issue orders and use the whip.[67]

In fact, while social betterment depended on government initiative, the state had a still more immediate and fundamental task to perform: to preserve law and order. Bulgarin wrote with unusual conviction:

It is better to unchain a hungry tiger or a hyena than to take off the people the bridle of obedience to authorities and laws. There is no beast fiercer than a raging mob! All the efforts of the educated class must be directed toward enlightening the people concerning its obligation to God, to lawful authorities and laws, toward the establishment of the love of man in the heart, toward the eradication of the beastly egoism inborn in man, and not toward exciting passions, not toward generating unrealizable

---

[64] Barsukov, ed., *Pisma M. P. Pogodina, S. P. Shevyreva i M. A. Maksimovicha k knyazyu P. A. Vyazemskomu 1825–1874 godov*, p. 58.
[65] Bulgarin, *Vospominaniya*, III, 62.
[66] Grech, *op. cit.*, p. 104.
[67] *Ibid.*, p. 211.

hopes. Whoever acts differently is a criminal according to the law of humanity. One who has seen a popular rebellion knows what it means.[68]

The government knew. Nicholas I and his officials proceeded to emphasize above all the perfect maintenance of discipline and order, punishing relentlessly all opposition and disaffection. In theory too Tyutchev and other ideologists stressed the role of the Russian emperor as the mainstay of law, morality, and civilization against individual license, subversion, and revolution.

It is worth noting that in addition to postulating the autocrat as the ideal form of supreme government, the proponents of Official Nationality put their faith in general in men rather than in institutions. As Pogodin explained the matter:

There is no institution or law which cannot be abused, something that is being done promptly everywhere: therefore, institutions and laws are not as important as the people on whom depends their functioning.[69]

One educated, zealous, active superior—and the entire department entrusted to him is, under the system of publicity, aiding other departments by its example, organization and training of officials. One governor with such qualities—and one fiftieth part of Russia is prospering, a second, a third—and all the people cannot recognize themselves, they will be the same and yet not the same in this general uplift.[70]

Except for "the system of publicity" which found no favor in the eyes of the emperor, Pogodin's statement represented faithfully the convictions of Nicholas I and of his associates. More than that, such a view was basic to their entire management of Russia. And Pogodin's argument, it may be added, repeated almost verbatim the opinion of Karamzin, in particular his famous assertion that the true need of Russia was fifty good governors.[71]

[68] Bulgarin, *Vospominaniya*, I, 14–15.
[69] Barsukov, *Zhizn i trudy M. P. Pogodina*, V, 22.
[70] Pogodin, *Istoriko-politicheskie pisma*, p. 268.
[71] Karamzin, "O drevnei i novoi Rossii v ee politicheskom i grazhdanskom otnosheniyakh," in Pypin, *Obshchestvennoe dvizhenie v Rossii pri Aleksandre I*,

The great emphasis on morality and moralizing in the doctrine of Official Nationality resulted partly from the fact that that ideology had nothing else to offer in the way of political improvement. Moral talk, under these circumstances, can be interpreted either as a dead end or a subterfuge.

Autocracy found justification not only in religion and in the nature of man, but also in history. The proponents of Official Nationality showed a remarkable awareness of history and the historical approach. Nicholas I himself read avidly everything dealing with the Russian past, both original documents and secondary works. It was in his reign that chairs of Russian history, as distinct from world history, were established in the universities of the empire, and large sums of money were devoted to the gathering and publication of source materials. Historians and historians of literature, such as Pogodin and Shevyrev at the University of Moscow and Nicholas Ustryalov at the University of St. Petersburg, made important contributions to the development and dissemination of the ideology of the state. Academic writing was supplemented by journalism and by fiction. The age of romanticism proved to be especially favorable in Russia, as elsewhere, to historical drama, novel, and story. Their quality ranged from such rare masterpieces as Pushkin's *Boris Godunov* to Zagoskin's trite novels, Kukolnik's feeble plays, and even Bulgarin's insipid tales about the early Slavs. Most of these works were very poor history, but they helped to provide sustenance and form to the interest in the past which represented a distinct characteristic of the age. And many of them attained success with the public. History, in one form or another, became the center of attention and controversy. "The historian represented"—in the words of Pogodin—"the crowning achievement of a people, for through him the people came to an understanding of itself." [72]

It is not surprising that, turning to history, the ideologists of Official Nationality, especially the more superficial among them, found the decisive role of autocracy, or at least of strong mo-

appendix to chap. iv (pp. 479–534, especially p. 528). The influence of Karamzin on Official Nationality will be discussed later in this chapter.

[72] Pogodin, *Historische Aphorismen*, p. 8.

narchical government, everywhere. Bulgarin's *Handbook* asserted that Rome had fallen because the Roman Senate had refused to recognize imperial succession as the hereditary right of a single family,[73] that Arabic Caliphates had similarly declined because their rulers had failed to maintain their proper authority,[74] that the superiority of the ancient Germans over their neighbors had stemmed from their possession of hereditary, not elected, chieftains.[75] "The most secure foundation of states is hereditary succession to the throne of a single family. This has been proved by both Ancient and Modern History." [76]

The Russian past had a special relevance to the Russian present. The Russian state came into existence: "In the middle of the ninth century (in the year 862) when the Northern Slavs felt, in their turn, the need of autocracy, although they did not understand its entire scope, did not comprehend that the power and the well-being of a people depend exclusively on the concentration of its will and its intelligence in one person, the person of the father of the people, the hereditary head of a great family." [77]

The work which presented best the salutary impact of autocracy on Russia was Karamzin's brilliant twelve-volume *History of the Russian State*, unfinished at the time of its author's death in 1826.[78] Karamzin held the position of official historian, and he also won immense favor with the reading public. Repetitions of his theme and variations on it became extremely common in the reign of Nicholas I. Autocracy received incessant praise for binding the Russians together and leading, or driving, them to new prosperity, power, and glory. Highly representative of this approach was Ustryalov's *Russian History*, which Uvarov adopted as a textbook in the schools of the empire and which he commended enthusiastically in a report to the monarch.[79]

---

[73] Bulgarin, *Rossiya v istoricheskom, statisticheskom, geograficheskom i literaturnom otnosheniyakh*, History, part 1, pp. 10–11.
[74] *Ibid.*, part 3, pp. 178–181.
[75] *Ibid.*, part 4, p. 279.
[76] *Ibid.*, part 1, p. 11.
[77] *Ibid.*, part 2, p. 402.
[78] Karamzin, *Istoriya gosudarstva rossiiskogo*.
[79] Ustryalov, *Russkaya istoriya*. For the minister's praise see Uvarov, *Desyati-*

Autocracy represented, thus, the main lesson of Russian history. It allowed of no exception or compromise. Characteristically, Nicholas I himself affirmed that he preferred a republic to a constitutional monarchy: the first could be a "sincere" form of government, the second was "a lie." [80] Furthermore, no group or class within Russia could have any special standing in the eyes of the emperor. All were equally his humble subjects. Gogol emphasized the religious importance of the fact that the tsar was "equidistant" from every Russian; others praised its political and administrative implications, Bulgarin, for example, asserting: "One of the most salutary aspects of monarchical rule is that the monarch can, in spite of circumstances, raise a man from the dust, place him on the step next to the throne, and crush the scepter of his power if he uses it for evil." [81] "Before the autocratic monarch, as before God, all subjects are equal." [82]

Some proponents of Official Nationality were willing to allow that other systems could work well in other countries, for instance, in England,[83] but insisted that they were inapplicable in Russia. Grech even concluded that "cold, rational, moral, and prosaically-Protestant" peoples, such as the English, the Swedes, the Danes, the Northern Germans, and the North Americans, all lived happily and prosperously under the representative form of government; but Romance and Slavonic nations had to be ruled by the stick.[84] Only Pogodin and a few other government ideologists who were close to the Slavophiles thought at times that "the voice of the people," in the form of a *zemskii sobor* or otherwise, would be a desirable addition to the Russian political system. This "voice,"

---

letie ministerstva narodnogo prosveshcheniya, 1833–1843, pp. 97–98. Uvarov notes that Ustryalov's textbook is especially useful in "the Western region," for Ustryalov emphasized the ancient allegiance of this area to Russia. Cf. Nikitenko, I, 279. Ustryalov's discussion of the reign of Nicholas I was corrected by the emperor in person.

[80] Custine, II, 114.

[81] Bulgarin, *Sochineniya*, I, 166.

[82] *Ibid.*, p. 210. Bulgarin also quoted Napoleon to the effect that everything should be done for the people, nothing by the people. Bulgarin, *Vospominaniya*, VI, 280 and n.

[83] Cf., e.g., the treatment of England in Nesselrode's note mentioned in chap. i above.

[84] Grech, *op. cit.*, p. 445.

however, was to buttress autocracy by bringing it closer to the masses, not to curb it.[85]

The entire history of Russia foreshadowed and justified Nicholas I's regime, but its direct line of descent stemmed from Peter the Great. The proponents of Official Nationality, from the monarch himself downward, admired, almost worshipped, the titanic emperor. The historians among them, Pogodin, Shevyrev, and Ustryalov, paid special attention to his personality and reign. Pogodin, to take the most interesting example, fell in his youth, if not earlier, under the fascination of the great reformer, this "Russian to the highest degree," the "human god."[86] Later, although specializing in an earlier period of Russian history, he taught a course on Peter the Great's reign, collected documents related to it, and wrote on the subject both as historian and as publicist. The reforming emperor even inspired Pogodin to compose a tragedy in verse, "Peter I," which dealt with a particularly painful episode of Peter's life, his condemnation of his own son Alexis to death, and which was written as an apotheosis of the great emperor's sense of duty and of his services to Russia.[87]

It is remarkable to what extent Pogodin was emotionally involved in his subject. Thus, he asserted that he had difficulty writing the second act of his play because he was afraid of his inadequacy and because he could "virtually see" Peter opening the door and menacing him with his proverbial club.—"One shudders

[85] See especially Pogodin, "Potrebnosti minuty," *Istoriko-politicheskie pisma*, pp. 314–317. The belief that autocracy was the proper form of government for Russia was not limited at the time to proponents of Official Nationality, or to Russians. It was held, for instance, by Henry Middleton, the United States minister to St. Petersburg from 1820 to 1830, who thought that absolute monarchy was the only possible system for the huge, heterogeneous, and backward Russian empire. See Raeff, "An American View of the Decembrist Revolt," *Journal of Modern History*, XXV (Sept. 1953), 286–293.

[86] See especially Barsukov, *op. cit.*, I, 56, 211; II, 293. Shevyrev fell under the same spell as Pogodin. For instance, in 1829, at the age of twenty-three, he noted in his diary: "Each evening certainly, and sometimes in the mornings too, I assign it to myself as an unfailing duty to read the life of Peter the Great and everything related to him." And he added the categorical imperative: "Be such a man as Christ, be such a Russian as Peter the Great." The diary was never published. This account with its quotations is from "Shevyrev, Stepan Petrovich," *Russkii biograficheskii slovar*, vol. "Shebanov" to "Shyutts," pp. 19–29. Quoted from p. 22.

[87] Pogodin, *Petr I.*

even to pronounce this name." [88] Again, the professor told his
students that it had proved almost beyond his power to prepare
an introductory lecture on the great emperor: "When I stood
face to face with this gigantic colossus, my spirit sank, I could
not collect my strength to survey at a glance the totality of his
actions in order to compose for you an introduction to his history.
And, believe me, this is not a piece of rhetoric." [89] Peter the Great
also haunted Pogodin on his trips abroad where the historian
tried to see the places visited by the emperor. Characteristic was
his pilgrimage to the famous little house in Zaandam:

> . . . then suddenly my guide exclaimed: "Well, here is the
> house of your Peter the First!" . . .
> My heart contracted, tears came to my eyes, I could hardly
> breathe as I opened the gate . . .
> With a tembling heart I crossed the threshold, for a long time
> I could not collect my senses . . . So this is where our Peter
> lived and worked! So this is where he thought and dreamed about
> Russia! How pure, how noble he was here! . . .
> I bowed to the ground to the Great One and left his sanctuary
> with a full heart.[90]

Still Pogodin, as well as his friend Shevyrev, knew and loved
old Russia too well to be completely uncritical of Peter the Great
and of his work. Pogodin tried repeatedly to strike a balance between the old and the new, between the virtues of ancient Russia
and the merits of Peter's reform.[91] This task became all the more
urgent when the Slavophiles proceeded to mount their attacks on
the emperor, and the professor had to meet the charges of his
close acquaintances and collaborators. These attempts to compromise, to present "the two sides" of the issue only demonstrate
further the extent to which Pogodin remained in Peter the Great's
thrall. It was in 1841, and in connection with some discussions
with the Slavophiles, that Pogodin decided to set down in an

---

[88] Barsukov, op. cit., III, 254.
[89] Barsukov, op. cit., V, 181.
[90] Pogodin, God v chuzhikh krayakh, part IV, pp. 14–15.
[91] An early effort on the part of Pogodin to resolve this problem is recorded
in Barsukov, op. cit., I, 211.

authoritative manner his estimate of Peter the Great.[92] In his essay,
"Peter the Great," he wrote:

> The Russia of today, that is, European Russia, diplomatic,
> political, military, commercial, industrial, scholastic, literary—is
> a creation of Peter the Great . . . Wherever we look, everywhere
> we meet this colossal figure which throws a long shadow over our
> entire past and even eliminates old history from our field of
> vision—which at this moment is still stretching, as it were, its
> arms over us and which, it appears, will never drop out of sight,
> no matter how far we advance in the future.[93]

After several grandiloquent pages, Pogodin turned to a more
mundane exposition of his subject:

> Yes, Peter the Great did much for Russia. One looks and one
> does not believe it, one keeps adding and one cannot reach the
> sum. We cannot open our eyes, cannot make a move, cannot
> turn in any direction without encountering him everywhere, at
> home, in the streets, in the church, in the school, in the court, in
> the regiment, at a promenade—it is always he, always he, every
> day, every minute, on every step!
>
> We wake up. What day is it today? January 1, 1841.—Peter
> the Great ordered us to count years from the birth of Christ,
> Peter the Great ordered us to count the months from January.
>
> It is time to dress—our clothing is made according to the fashion
> established by Peter the First, our uniform according to his model.
> The cloth is woven in a factory which he created; the wool is
> shorn from the sheep which he started to raise.
>
> A book strikes our eyes—Peter the Great introduced this script
> and himself cut out the letters. You begin to read it—this language
> became a written language, a literary language at the time of Peter
> the First, the earlier church language being pushed out.

---

[92] "Petr Velikii," in Pogodin, Istoriko-kriticheskie otryvki, pp. 333–363
(this and succeeding references are to vol. I). This essay was originally published in the first issue of the Moskvityanin. For the background of the article
see Barsukov, op. cit., VI, 5–6. The relationship between Pogodin, Shevyrev,
and the Slavophiles is discussed in N. Riasanovsky, "Pogodin and Ševyrëv in
Russian Intellectual History," Harvard Slavic Studies, IV, 149–167.

[93] Pogodin, Istoriko-kriticheskie otryvki, p. 335.

Newspapers are brought in—Peter the Great introduced them.

You must buy different things—they all, from the silk necker-chief to the sole of your shoe, will remind you of Peter the Great: some were ordered by him, others were brought into usage, im-proved, carried on his ships, into his harbors, on his canals, on his roads.

At dinner, all the courses, from salted herring and potatoes which he ordered grown to wine made from grapes which he be-gan to cultivate, will speak to you of Peter the Great.

After dinner you drive out for a visit—this is an assemblée *of Peter the Great. You meet the ladies there—they were allowed into masculine company by a command of Peter the Great.*

Let us go to the University—the first secular school was founded by Peter the Great.

You receive a rank—according to Peter the Great's Table of Ranks.

The rank gives me gentry status—Peter the Great so arranged.

I must file a complaint—Peter the Great prescribed its form. It will be received—in front of Peter the Great's Mirror of Justice. It will be acted upon—on the basis of the General Reglement.

You decide to travel abroad—following the example of Peter the Great; you will be received well—Peter the Great placed Russia among the European states and began to instill respect for her; and so on, and so on, and so forth.[94]

In summary, everything in and about contemporary Russia derived from the titanic reformer. He had the key and the lock. Yet, though the importance of the first emperor could not be subjected to doubt, critics had appeared recently to challenge the particular form change took under Peter and to regret his sharp break with the past. Pogodin went on to reply to these cavilers in no uncertain terms: Peter's reform was necessary if Russia were to survive in the world. This was obviously true as far as the army and the navy were concerned, and this applied also to other fields of state activity which, in addition, were closely linked to the first two. "Had Peter not preceded him, would it have been possible

---

[94] *Ibid.,* pp. 340–342.

for Alexander to fight Napoleon?" [95] Besides, Western enlightenment had been penetrating Russia to an ever-increasing extent before Peter; Peter's policies represented largely a continuation of
those of his predecessors and were to be explained as part of a
fundamental historical process. Peter the Great was impulsive and
violent at times, but even his outbreaks of temper were usually
justifiable. Everything considered, it took remarkable impudence
to question the specific measures and directives of the gigantic emperor—"As to me, I would not undertake for anything in the
world to offer a different plan of the battle of Poltava, another
project of the Treaty of Nystadt." [96] True, Russians after Peter
the Great proceeded to worship the West and to forget their own
nationality. But this had not been the attitude of the reformer himself, and he could no more be blamed for the later aberration than
Guttenberg be held responsible for noxious books.

Furthermore, Peter's work was to form an integral part of the
glorious Russian synthesis of the future: ancient Russia had possessed enormous riches and gifts which, however, represented only
one half of the total legacy of the ancient world, the Eastern or
Greek half; Peter the Great added the remaining Western portion
of the inheritance to the treasury of his native land; the third and
final epoch was already dawning—it would mark the abandonment of mere imitation of the West and the construction of a
new, organic Russian culture on the basis of all the assembled
wealth of the past.

Pogodin finished his essay with an account of the praise heaped
upon Peter the Great by Russians and foreigners alike, but especially by the great Russian writers. The concluding words belonged to Lomonosov:

*To whom then shall I liken our hero? Often I have meditated
about the nature of the one who by the almighty wave of his hand
rules the sky, the earth, and the sea; his spirit breathes, and waters
flow; he touches mountains, and they rise. But there is a limit
assigned to the thoughts of man! They cannot reach Divinity!*

---

[95] *Ibid.*, p. 346.
[96] *Ibid.*, p. 350.

Usually he is pictured in human form. Well, then, if we must
search for a man who is, according to our understanding, like
God, I find none, but Peter the Great.[97]

Pogodin's preoccupation with Peter the Great was dull, blunt,
crude, and obsessive; Pushkin's treatment of the reforming emperor was brilliant, graceful, sensitive, but also obsessive. The
difference emphasized the chasm between awkward prose and
magnificent verse, and, beyond that, between mediocrity and
supreme genius. Yet both writers were under the spell of the great
emperor, and the themes they kept repeating in their works show
profound similarities. Pushkin dealt with the reformer of Russia
in such accomplished pieces as "Poltava" and "The Bronze
Horseman," as well as in notes, letters, and conversations. He
was working on a history of Peter the Great when he was killed in
a duel. Pushkin's Peter, as well as Pogodin's, was above all the
glorious hero of Poltava, the almost superhuman leader of his
country, who gave Russia a new life and a new history, symbolized
by St. Petersburg, Pushkin's beloved city. He stood for reform,
light, progress, for the present strength of the nation, and for
its future destiny. Still, Pushkin, like Pogodin, had certain reservations to make. Only they were produced not by any love of ancient
Russia—for Pushkin was a Westernizer by taste and outlook—but
rather by a concern for the common man writhing in the clutches
of the leviathan emperor and state. In his extensive study of
the time of Peter the Great, the poet became increasingly impressed by the ruthlessness and cruelty of the overwhelming monarch and his measures. Pushkin's own life seemed to repeat the
same tale: he found himself controlled, restricted, directed, and
generally hounded at every turn by Peter the Great's state and
by Peter's successor, another powerful and autocratic emperor,
Nicholas I.

These elements, and, no doubt, many other, went into the
making of Pushkin's masterpiece, "The Bronze Horseman." In

[97] *Ibid.*, p. 363. In this article Pogodin also urged that a university chair
devoted to Peter the Great be established in Russia, just as there was a Dante
chair in Italy (p. 357). There is little doubt that he would have been eager
to occupy the new position himself.

this story of a poor, ordinary man, Eugene, who lost his beloved in a St. Petersburg flood, went mad, dared challenge the bronze statue of the builder of the city, and then ran in mortal terror pursued by it, the poet presented both the might and the harshness of Peter the Great and of Russian autocracy. While extending sympathy to the unfortunate Eugene, Pushkin depicted the Bronze Horseman as an infinitely majestic, an almost divine figure, the greatness and permanence of whose work the poet affirmed powerfully in the introduction. The astounding lines dealing with the emperor, not those describing Eugene, were to remain a treasure of Russian verse. Pushkin's tale is a tragedy, but its composite parts are not evenly balanced: above all rises the autocratic state sweeping on to its grand destiny, undeterred by the obstacles of nature, such as swamps and floods, and impervious to the pain, the sorrow, and even the opposition of the individual, exemplified by Eugene's miserable plight and his pathetic rebellion. Pushkin's "Bronze Horseman," as well as his treatment of Peter the Great in general, represented his closest approach to the doctrine of Official Nationality.[98]

Pogodin's and Pushkin's enormously high estimate of Peter the Great was shared by all proponents of the state ideology, the only distinction being that most of them eulogized the reforming emperor without any reservations or qualifications whatsoever. Their characteristic attitude was expressed, for instance, in N.

---

[98] Pushkin, "Mednyi Vsadnik," *op. cit.*, III, 473–482. My interpretation of the poem is, in broad outline, a common one, restated recently, for example, in Bowra, "Pushkin," *Oxford Slavonic Papers*, I (1950), 1–15. There are variations on the theme, as well as different interpretations. An ingenious twist is suggested by V. Bryusov, a famous literary figure himself, who argues that Pushkin is entirely on the side of Eugene and that Eugene's revolt against autocracy is successful because it forces the Horseman to abandon his majestic aloofness and to leave his eminent, shrine-like position in order to pursue the enemy. Bruysov's reasoning, however, fails to convince. See Bruysov, "Mednyi Vsadnik" on pages 456–476 of the above-mentioned volume of Pushkin's *Works*. Views similar to Bruysov's were expressed recently in the valuable work by Lednicki, *Pushkin's Bronze Horseman*. For a sharp contrast to Bruysov's and Lednicki's opinion see, e.g., Vernadsky, " 'Mednyi Vasdnik' v tvorchestve Pushkina," *Slavia*, II (1924), 645–654. The enormous bibliography on Pushkin contains numerous and detailed discussions of various matters which I barely mention. My purpose is simply to indicate what I consider to be the essential point of contact between the great poet and Official Nationality.

Atreshkov's essay published in January, 1833, in *The Northern Bee*.[99] The essay was aimed at those who claimed that Peter the Great's precipitous turn to the West had damaged Russian nationality, and the author wasted no time in assailing his antagonists. After making certain allowance for criticism by ignorant foreigners, he continued in the following manner: "But you, my countrymen, remember, before you pronounce the blasphemous accusation, that you are talking about Peter, the greatest of geniuses, about Peter, the creator of our glorious fatherland, the sole cause of its might, the source of your well-being and of that of your descendants! Remember that with him you are condemning the foundation and the cornerstone of the building which he erected!" [100] Following this broad hint that an attack on Peter the Great might be treason as well as sacrilege, Atreshkov proceeded to disprove to his own satisfaction all the charges against the reforming emperor. In concluding his article, he ran short of comparisons and of words sufficiently strong to praise "divine Peter":

> But show me another Peter, founder of the state, lawgiver, general, astronomer, statesman, trader, artist, artisan, and at the same time untouched by any egoism or lust for glory. He renounced for the sake of the enlightenment and the well-being of his subjects all the worldly blessings of a mortal and a monarch. He sacrificed for them his incessant forty-year long labor, the endurance of constant dangers, and finally his only son. There never was his like. He is the crown of creation, the glory of mankind, the cause of the existence and the happiness of Russia.[101]

It is understandable why even Pogodin, in spite of his own tremendous admiration for Peter, found himself at odds on this subject with some other proponents of the official view. For instance, the Moscow professor was angered by Kukolnik's play,

---

[99] Atreshkov, "Nekotorye vozrazheniya kritiku naschet izmenenii Petrom Velikim natsionalnosti russkikh," *Severnaya Pchela*, nos. 7 and 8, Jan. 10–11, 1833.
[100] *Ibid.*
[101] *Ibid.*

"The Orderly," and especially by the following lines in it referring
to Peter the Great:

> *I saw how the Great Anatomist*
> *Split open the decrepit body of Russia,*
> *Changed her rotten insides,*
> *Put together her cleansed members,*
> *Skilfully bandaged her all properly,*
> *Lifted her by the shoulders, put her on her feet,*
> *And—the Muscovite steppe, the China of Europe,*
> *For the marvelous achievements of her monarch,*
> *Is promoted universally to an Empire!* [102]

But when Pogodin accused Kukolnik of insolent ignorance of
pre-Petrine Russia, Bulgarin rose quickly to the defense of the
playwright.[103] In the opinion of most proponents of Official
Nationality, it was impossible to overpraise Peter the Great or his
achievements. "In our opinion, in the entire history of mankind
there has been nobody like Peter the Great. Compared to him,
even Napoleon is a dwarf!" [104] "Everything that has been done
following his lead has proved great and useful; everything done
contrary to his plans has collapsed of itself!" [105]

Nicholas I himself participated fully in this overwhelming and
blind veneration of Peter the Great. His enthusiasm for the reformer of Russia may have already been stimulated at the age
of seven or eight by I. Golikov's collection of materials about
Peter.[106] In any case, it lasted until Nicholas's death, the monarch
admiring his predecessor in an unreserved and almost religious
manner. Peter the Great was constantly on Nicholas I's mind:
Nicholas read voraciously about Peter, referred to him often, and
tried to emulate him. Two examples should be enough to illustrate

---

[102] Kukolnik, "Denshchik," *Sochineniya dramaticheskie*, III, pp. 189–330.
Quoted from page 296. Elsewhere in the play Kukolnik made the same point
more gracefully: "Great, divine work! Over our dark country Peter is lighting
an artificial sun!" *Ibid.*, p. 288.

[103] For the controversy see *Severnaya Pchela*, no. 78, April 9, 1852.

[104] *Ibid.*

[105] Bulgarin, *Vospominaniya*, I, 201.

[106] Schilder, I, 475 n. 25.

this lifelong devotion. After reading the manuscript of Pogodin's play "Peter I," written in 1831 and full of gushing praise of the reformer of Russia, the monarch wrote the following resolution: *"The person of Emperor Peter the Great must be for every Russian an object of veneration and of love; to bring it onto the stage would be almost sacrilege, and therefore entirely improper. Prohibit the publication."* [107] In 1839 there was a crisis in the imperial family: the heir to the throne, Alexander, would not give up his Polish mistress and agree to a dynastic marriage. On that occasion Nicholas I told his wife in a letter: "But for me the state counts above everything else; and much as I love my children, I love my fatherland much more still. And, if this becomes necessary, there is the example of Peter the Great to show me my duty; and I shall not be too weak to fulfill it." [108] These lines, ominous in the light of the fact that Peter the Great had his son Alexis condemned to execution from which he was spared only by his sudden death in prison, may be attributed to a momentary depression. Yet the appeal to the example of the great reformer was both characteristic and revealing, perhaps especially so in this dreadful instance. Alexander, however, finally followed the will of his father, thus settling the matter without recourse to the emperor's model of autocracy.

Nicholas I's admiration for Peter the Great and his desire to follow in the footsteps of his famous predecessor found reflection in the literature of Official Nationality. Comparisons and connections between the two emperors were discussed and glorified by numerous writers of the period ranging from poets, Pushkin included, to such historians as Raphael Zotov.[109] In fact this subject became one of the favorite themes of what may be described as the cheap patriotic press. Publicists defending Nicholas and his Russia against foreign criticism similarly considered it their duty to stand up also for Peter the Great, a function eagerly undertaken, for instance, by Grech in his attempt to refute Custine's attack

---

[107] Barsukov, *op. cit.*, IV, 13. Italics in the original.
[108] Quoted in Schiemann, III, 376.
[109] Zotov, *Tridtsatiletie Evropy v tsarstvovanie Imperatora Nikolaya I,* especially vol. II, pp. 312–313. On Pushkin in this connection see, for instance, Schilder, II, 16.

on Russian government and life.[110] Scholars of a much later time, quite free from the dogma of Official Nationality, continued to discover significant parallels between the two emperors. Polievktov, to give one example, stressed the fact that the reign of Nicholas I marked, in Russian history, the high point of absolutism and of its consistent application to government and life—"with the likely exception of the epoch of Peter the Great." [111]

Peter the Great occupied a unique position in the ideology of Official Nationality. He was the founder and, so to speak, the patron saint of Imperial Russia; it was his name that was paired most often with that of the ruling monarch, Nicholas. But there were other imperial predecessors who also deserved remembrance and praise, two especially: Catherine the Great and Alexander I. Catherine merited high consideration because of her achievements in international relations and in spreading enlightenment in Russia. But Nicholas I disliked her as a person; [112] and the treatment of her in official ideology remained formal and correct rather than warm and enthusiastic. Alexander I, on the other hand, was presented as an ideal Christian as well as a great ruler, Nicholas I himself in particular almost worshipping his elder brother. In the literature of Official Nationality, Alexander was eulogized as the savior of Russia and the world from Napoleon, and as "the angel" who brought humanity into warfare itself, whose manifestoes directed his subjects to return good for evil, and who spared Paris even though the French had devastated Moscow.[113]

---

[110] Grech, *Examen de l'ouvrage de M. le Marquis de Custine intitulé la Russie en 1839*, pp. 22–23, 71–74. Custine had stressed the role of the great reformer in the creation of modern Russia which the Frenchman detested. "Here the spirit of Peter the Great dominates the spirit of all men." Custine, II, 23.

[111] Polievktov, p. viii.

[112] Nicholas I condemned Catherine's immorality and probably also her usurpation of the throne. Cf., e.g., Schiemann, I, 5, n. 1, and *SIRIO*, XCVIII, 6.

[113] Such praise of Alexander, especially on moral grounds, was extremely widespread. As typical short references see Bulgarin, *Vospominaniya*, II, 207–208; Shevyrev, *Znachenie Zhukovskogo v russkoi zhizni i poezii*, pp. 41–45; or Grech, *Sochineniya*, III, 419. Longer discussions include: Uvarov, *L'Empereur Alexandre et Buonaparte*; Grech, "Biografiya imperatora Aleksandra I," *Sochineniya*, III, 149–186; Strakhov, "Aleksandr Pervyi, Ovsoboditel Otechestva i Evropy," *Syn Otechestva*, XIV (1814), part XXI, contemporary History and Politics,

Politically he was pictured as a staunch conservative, a great builder and supporter of the legitimist alliance in Europe, the liberal aspects of his reign being conveniently omitted.

Peter the Great, Catherine the Great, Alexander I, and, of course, Nicholas I were mentioned prominently and often by the proponents of the state ideology, especially on ceremonial occasions. For instance, on the twenty-ninth of December, 1826, at a session marking the centenary of the Imperial Academy of Sciences, Uvarov in his presidential address extolled at length the virtues and the achievements of the departed rulers.[114] He paid special attention to Peter the Great, the real founder of the Academy, but he also lauded the contribution to the enlightenment of Russia made by Peter's successors. Uvarov declared in the concluding part of his speech:

If death does not break everything that links the perishable to the immortal, all the ties which attach this restricted and transitory life to the luminous existence of a life that has no limits and no end; if the feelings of pure and noble souls who here below burned with a holy love for their native land are not absorbed without return by the celestial origin to which they have now risen; the shadow of Peter, the shadow of Catherine, and that of Alexander glide at this moment, let us not doubt it, over this sanctuary of the sciences which they established and preserved.[115]

Nicholas, the fourth member of the imperial series, did not have to glide for he was present in person to listen to Uvarov's address and to celebrate the centenary. The setting of this solemn occasion emphasized, very appropriately, the same four sovereign figures: "At the end of the new hall of the Academy dedicated

---

pp. 60–64; Fedorov, "Chuvstva rossiyanina pri vesti o konchine Aleksandra I," *Syn Otechestva*, CI (1826), no. 1, part IV, Rhetoric, pp. 81–93. There is a recent article discussing Alexander's army regulations and the behavior of Russian troops in France. Lukacs, "Russian Armies in Western Europe: 1799, 1814, 1917," *American Slavic and East European Review*, XIII (Oct. 1954), 318–337.

[114] Uvarov, *Discours du Président de l'Académie Impériale des Sciences, prononcé dans la séance solennelle du 29 decembre 1826, a l'occasion de la Fête seculaire de l'Académie.*

[115] *Ibid.*, pp. 7–8.

by this solemn ceremony rises a colossal bust of *Peter I*. On either
side of it one sees a full-length portrait, one of Emperor *Nicholas*,
the other of Emperor *Alexander*. An autograph manuscript of
Catherine II was placed on the table in a gilded bronze casket." [116]

The autocratic empire of Peter the Great, Catherine the Great,
Alexander I, and Nicholas I possessed certain special characteristics
which were emphasized time and again by the ideologists of the
state. The enormous size, huge population, and vast natural resources of Russia provided the material for many boasts which
also frequently underlined the fact that the tremendous Russian
power was fully coördinated, controlled, and directed by a single
man. In the rhapsodic language of Pogodin:

Russia! What a marvelous phenomenon on the world scene!
Russia—a distance of ten thousand versts in length on a straight
line from the virtually central European river, across all of Asia
and the Eastern Ocean, down to the remote American lands! A
distance of five thousand versts in width, from Persia, one of the
southern Asiatic states, to the end of the inhabited world—to the
North Pole. What state can equal it? Its half? How many states
can match its twentieth, its fiftieth part?

Russia—a population of sixty million men, that is, those who
could be counted, not including those who remain as yet un-
counted; a population which increases by a million every year and
will soon reach one hundred million. Where do you find such
numbers? . . .

Russia—a state which contains all types of soil, from the
warmest to the coldest, from the burning environs of Erivan to
icy Lapland; which abounds in all the products required for the
needs, comforts, and pleasures of life, in accordance with its present
state of development—a whole world, self-sufficient, independent,

---

[116] *Ibid*. The description of the setting precedes the text of Uvarov's speech,
page not marked. Italics in the original. Cf. E. Tregubov's poem celebrating
the coronation of Nicholas I where the poet extolls the emperor for uniting
in his person the virtues of his predecessors, Peter, Catherine, and Alexander.
Tregubov, "Na vseradostneishii den svyashchennogo koronovaniya Ego Imperatorskogo Velichestva Gosudarya Imperatora Nikolaya Pavlovicha," *Syn
Otechestva*, CVIII (1826), no. XIV, pp. 180–182. See also the ending of
B. Fedorov's above-mentioned essay.

absolute. Many of these products are such that they have con-
stituted separately the sources of the well-being of entire large
states in the course of centuries, while Russia has them all to-
gether.—Of gold and silver, which are virtually exhausted in
Europe, we have mountains, and in reserve complete untouched
mountain chains. Iron and copper—let them name whatever
amount they want, and next year it will be delivered without fail
to the Nizhnii Novgorod fair. Bread—we can feed all of Europe
in a hungry year. Timber—we can rebuild her, if—God forbid—
she burns down. Flax, hemp, leather—we shall dress and shoe her
. . . Is it necessary to mention cattle, fish, salt, fur-bearing ani-
mals? What is it that we cannot supply to others? And all this
we see, so to speak, on the outside, on the surface, nearby, under
our eyes, at hand, and what if one were to go deeper down, look
further! Do not we constantly hear rumors that in one place were
found deposits of coal several hundred versts in length, in another
marble, in a third diamonds and other precious stones! . . .

While some countries could not make effective use of their resources: "This is not at all true of Russia. All its forces, physical
and moral, compose one enormous machine, arranged in a simple,
convenient manner, and directed by the hand of a single man, the
hand of the Russian tsar who can at any moment with a single
motion start it, give it any direction and attain any speed he
wishes." [117]

Russian autocracy was not only immensely powerful and
perfectly coördinated, but also thoroughly patriarchal. Pogodin
liked especially to dwell on this subject:

There it is, I shall add here, the secret of Russian history, the
secret which not a single Western sage is able to comprehend.
Russian history always depicts Russia as a single family in which
the ruler is the father and the subjects the children. The father
retains complete authority over the children while he allows them
to have full freedom. Between the father and the children there

---

[117] Pogodin, "Pismo k Gosudaryu Tsesarevichu, Velikomu Knyazyu, Alek-
sandru Nikolaevichu, (nyne tsarstvuyushchemu Gosudaryu Imperatoru) v 1838
godu," *Istoriko-politicheskie pisma*, pp. 1–7.

can be no suspicion, no treason; their fate, their happiness and their peace they share in common. This is true in relation to the state as a whole, but one notices a reflection of the same law also in its parts: the military commander must be the father of his soldiers, the landlord must be the father of his peasants, and even servants in the house of every master were called children of the house in the expressive old language. As long as this union is sacred and undamaged, so long there is peace and happiness—as soon as it begins to waver, no matter where, there appear disorder, confusion and alarm.[118]

Again, in a speech to the heroes of Sevastopol, Pogodin exclaimed: "We are all one family. Here [pointing to a portrait of the tsar] is our father, kind, gracious, benevolent, decorated with flowers. Long live Holy Russia!" [119] And, year after year, at the annual University of Moscow alumni dinners Pogodin urged that patriarchal relations be established between the faculty and the students at his alma mater instead of the existing "foreign," formal attitude with its exclusive concern for the student's academic progress.[120] Gogol echoed the Moscow professor, insisting: "Do not forget that in the Russian language . . . a superior is called father." [121]

Nicholas I shared this belief in the patriarchal nature of Russia, in the personal ties binding the Russians together and in his role as the father of the great family. For example, in 1850, on the twenty-fifth anniversary of the Decembrist rebellion and of his own assumption of the crown, the emperor addressed the Preobrazhenskii guard regiment in the following terms: "You, Preobrazhentsy, I thank most especially. You know what remarkable fortune brought us together so that we form one joint family, and my family belongs to you, just as you belong to me. Here you see three generations—he grasped at this point the hands of the Grand Duke, heir to the throne, and of his eldest

---

[118] Pogodin, *Rechi*, p. 90.
[119] *Ibid.*, p. 198.
[120] *Ibid.*, pp. 241, 607; 167. The last reference is to Pogodin's speech in 1846 in Odessa at a dinner given to him by his former students at the University of Moscow.
[121] Gogol, p. 163.

son—now you know whom you have to serve. Serve them as you
have served me, and your children will serve my children as you
have served me." [122] Nicholas I spoke loudly, holding back the
tears; everybody around him wept.[123] In the same fatherly, though
this time reproachful, mood the emperor would explain to the
manufacturers that they must take care of their workers [124] or up-
braid young Samarin for denouncing the Baltic Germans.[125]

Paternalism not only pervaded many activities of the monarch,
but was also delegated by him to his subordinates. The administrators, the teachers, and especially the police were all to
provide paternal protection, supervision, and guidance to the Russian people. As Nicholas I instructed Prince Orlov, the head of
the gendarmery, in the case of Ivan Aksakov whose letters were
found to contain criticism of the existing order in Russia: *"Call
him in, read to him my remarks on the subject, enlighten him, and
let him go."* [126] "Tsar-father," the common popular term for the
ruler of Russia, was more than a superficial epithet in the reign of
Nicholas I, although its practical implications were often stern
and even grim.

Militarism represented another important characteristic of
Russian autocracy. Like most modern dynastic states, the empire
of the Romanovs was largely a result of long and successful wars.
The acquisition of the imperial title itself was linked to Peter the
Great's victory over Sweden in the decisive Great Northern War.
But while Peter the Great remained, as usual, the supreme patron
saint, militarism and patriotism of the time of Nicholas found
their direct and inspiring antecedents in the reign of Alexander.
It was above all 1812, the *annus mirabilis*, that cast its long shadow
over the thought and the writings of Official Nationality.[127] A

---

[122] Quoted in Schiemann, IV, 235.
[123] *Ibid.*
[124] The autocrat's remarkable speech to the Moscow manufacturers in 1835
was summarized by Benckendorff in his *Memoirs.* Schilder, II, 699.
[125] The best account of the reprimand which Nicholas I delivered in person
to Samarin is in Nolde, *Yurii Samarin i ego vremya,* pp. 47–49.
[126] Barsukov, *op. cit.,* X, 509. The original Russian is still more succinct,
containing only the predicates without the objects. Italics in the original.
[127] Probably carried away by his patriotism, Nicholas I strained diplomatic
relations and came close to insulting France in his "Order to the Troops"

good illustration of this influence can be found in the periodical
A Son of the Fatherland which continued to come out until 1852.
This journal was founded in 1812, by Grech at the suggestion of
Uvarov, and its name reproduced a phrase from the letter Grech
received from his brother after that brother had been mortally
wounded in the battle of Borodino.[128] Militarism, patriotism,
nationalism, hatred of the French, friendship toward the German
—especially the Prussian—allies, and other attitudes characteristic
of the last years of the war against Napoleon were all carried by
Grech and his periodical from the reign of Alexander into that
of Nicholas.

Most proponents of Official Nationality were at least interested
in military affairs, even if they did not have the *condottiere* past
of Bulgarin, and they often used warlike terminology where
ordinary words would have sufficed. Uvarov, in a report to the
emperor, referred to the Kievan University of St. Vladimir as "an
intellectual fortress" and spoke of "giving a decisive battle" to the
spirit of Poland.[129] Zhukovskii described the relationship between
the tsar and God as "an offensive and defensive alliance." [130] A
special case was that of Stephen Burachek, a former naval officer
who introduced naval terminology into his obscurantist periodical,
The Lighthouse.

The doctrine of Official Nationality proclaimed that all Russians were boundlessly devoted to their ruler; but it emphasized
above all the dedicated attachment of the Russia soldiers to the
tsar. As an old campaigner expressed it in one of Bulgarin's stories:

*To make a bayonet charge, to assault a battery, to deploy into
combat formation, to amuse oneself by an exchange of fire, all
this, under the eyes of the tsar himself, is not a battle, but a feast!
You see, the tsar's eye is the proprietor's eye. To God and to the
tsar—we are all alike children: you, gentlemen, the elder ones, and*

at the great celebration of the Borodino anniversary in 1839. The Order was
published in *Severnaya Pchela*, no. 195, August 31, 1839.
    [128] See Grech, "Nachalo Syna Otechestva," *Zapiski o moei zhizni*, pp. 290–
306.
    [129] Uvarov, *Desyatiletie ministerstva narodnogo prosveshcheniya 1833–1843,*
pp. 130, 159.
    [130] Zhukovskii, *op. cit.*, p. 171.

*we the younger. Whether a colonel distinguishes himself, a captain
or a simple soldier, it is still the same joy for the heart of the tsar,
the same glory for Orthodox Russia. It was read to us how our
father-tsar himself deigned to reward simple soldiers with medals;
how he himself was concerned for the wounded, and, in the case
of the invalids, ordered that they should be provided for even
back home. Where you have the tsar's kindness, there you have
God's blessing and the commander's solicitude. One sorrow I shall
take with me to the grave, namely that I had no occasion to fight
under the eyes of the tsar himself.*[131]

Tales of the heroism of Russian soldiers and of their supreme
devotion to the emperor abounded in the literature of the period;
such journals as A Son of the Fatherland even set apart special
sections for them.

Poetry competed with prose. One versifier, M. Markov, restated
the sentiments of the old campaigner in the following manner:

> *Burning with love for you,*
> *With a soul alien to base flattery,*
> *The Russian knows no higher honor*
> *Than to die under the eyes of his tsar.*[132]

F. Glinka taught a succinct moral lesson in a poem in which a
young widow told her children about their departed warrior
father:

> *He went thither, to the bright abode of the Heavenly Tsar*
> *Because here he had been faithful to the earthly tsar.*[133]

Autocracy represented the foundation of Russian government,
the political essence, so to speak, of Russia. But the application
of this concept extended beyond the boundaries of the empire of

---

[131] Bulgarin, *Sochineniya*, XI, 236.
[132] Markov, "Russkii Tsar," *Biblioteka dlya Chteniya*, VIII (1835), 7. It
may be added that while Bulgarin specialized in prose, his only lines of verse
known to me deal precisely with the theme under discussion: "Strong through
its faith and its oath,/ Our good Russian people/ Will shed its blood bravely/
For the sacred tsarist family./ A soldier's life is at the tsar's disposal/ We
shall all die for the tsar!/ We are glad to fight in the open field,/ And we
are not afraid of the seas!" Bulgarin remembered this youthful effort in
Bulgarin, *Vospominaniya*, VI, 111.
[133] Glinka, *op. cit.*, pp. 52–53.

the tsars. On the world stage autocracy became legitimism. As will be shown in some detail in the fifth chapter, Nicholas I and his followers considered themselves true defenders of the established, legitimate, international order against any transgression. They were determined to uphold the arrangements of the Congress of Vienna and the victorious reaction abroad as well as at home. Problems of Russian foreign policy were numerous and exceedingly complex. Yet, at least in times of crisis, when only the essentials mattered, the ideologists of Official Nationality saw the international situation in a remarkably simple manner. For instance, Tyutchev wrote in April of the cataclysmic year of 1848:

> In order to understand the meaning of that supreme crisis which has now gripped Europe, one should realize the following. For a long time now only two real forces have existed in Europe— revolution and Russia. These two forces are at present counterpoised against each other, and, perhaps, tomorrow they will join battle. No negotiations, no treaties are possible between them; the existence of one of them means the death of the other! On the outcome of the struggle which has begun between them, the greatest struggle which the world has ever witnessed, will depend for many centuries to come the entire political and religious future of humanity.[134]

Autocracy thus determined, in the opinion of the proponents of Official Nationality, the Russian position and the Russian role in the world. Orthodoxy here, as elsewhere, was joined to autocracy. For, as Tyutchev and many other theoreticians explained, the Russian autocratic state was indissolubly linked to that authentic form of Christianity, whereas revolution was above all antiChristian. However, one complication remained: in addition to "Orthodoxy," and "autocracy," the state ideologists had to make allowance for the difficult and controversial principle of "nationality." It is to this last key concept that we must now turn our attention. As we shall see, at least one of its interpretations proved to be incompatible with simple-minded legitimism.

---

[134] Tyutchev, "Rossiya i revolyutsiya," in Tyutchev, pp. 344–351; quoted from p. 344.

IV

"Nationality" was at the time and has since remained the most obscure, puzzling, and debatable member of the official trinity. While "Orthodoxy" and "autocracy" were relatively precise terms referring to an established faith and a distinct form of government, "nationality" possessed no single, generally accepted meaning. It has been most often interpreted as merely an appendage to "autocracy," an affirmation that the Russian people were docile and obedient subjects of their tsar and their landlords.[135] According to this view, it served mainly as a propaganda device and possessed no significance of its own. Indeed, it has been equated by some simply with the defense of serfdom.[136]

This assessment of "nationality" is largely valid, but incomplete. For in addition to its reactionary, dynastic, and defensive connotations, the term also had a romantic frame of reference. And on the romantic plane "Russia" and "the Russian people" acquired a supreme metaphysical, and even mystical, importance, leading to belief in the great mission of Russia, to such doctrines as Pan-Slavism and such practices as Russification. Theories attempting to buttress the antique Russian regime met German idealistic philosophy with its dizzying new vistas. It followed logically that the two views of "nationality," which we may call "the dynastic" and "the nationalistic," were in essential contradiction to each other. This contrast and antagonism found expression in the strife between different groups of government ideologists. It was reflected more subtly in the change of position by certain proponents of the state views, while in still other instances the contradiction remained concealed and implicit. In general, the concept of nationality accounted for the tensions and conflicts within the government doctrine.

Yet in spite of their differences, the proponents of Official

[135] See, e.g., Presnyakov, p. 58, or "Nikolai I," *Entsiklopedicheskii Slovar* (Brockhaus-Efron), XXI, 119–124, especially p. 120.
[136] Uvarov's emphasis on serfdom as, together with autocracy, the foundation of Russia has been noted by many specialists. It will be discussed later in this chapter.

Nationality enjoyed a measure of agreement as they defined and expounded the nature of Russia and the Russian people. To begin with, they emphasized that the subjects of the tsar felt and expressed overwhelming devotion to Orthodoxy and autocracy. Shevyrev, for instance, declared: "I have become accustomed to feel, at the mention of the Russian people, a certain calm, and that not only back in my own fatherland, but also all over Europe. The reason is that I indissolubly connect two concepts with the name of the Russian people: unqualified submission to the Church, and the same devotion and obedience to the ruler." [137] Pogodin, in his turn, listed the fear of God, devotion to their faith, and piety among the distinguishing characteristics of the Russian people.[138] Tyutchev declared even more emphatically: "Russia is above all a Christian empire. The Russian people is Christian not only because of the Orthodoxy of its beliefs, but also because of something even more intimate than belief. It is Christian because of that capacity for renunciation and sacrifice which serves as the foundation of its moral nature." [139]

The alleged ardent affection of the Russians for their ruler formed an especially frequent subject for discussion among the ideologists of the state. As Nicholas I himself announced in the famous manifesto which reported the execution of the five Decembrists:

This design did not correspond to the character, did not correspond to the ways of the Russian people. Concocted by a handful of monsters, it infected their immediate companions, depraved hearts, and insolent fantasies. But in ten years of evil

---

[137] Quoted in Dementev, *op. cit.*, p. 185.
[138] Pogodin, *Rechi*, pp. 39–40. As a young man Pogodin had noted with pride that Russian soldiers away on a campaign preferred starvation to breaking a fast. Barsukov, *op. cit.*, I, 94.
[139] Tyutchev, p. 344. Ustryalov, dutifully underlining all the principles of Official Nationality, summarized the character of the Russian people as follows: "profound and quiet piety, boundless devotion to the throne, obedience to the authorities, remarkable patience, a lucid and solid intelligence, a kind and hospitable soul, a gay temper, courage amidst the greatest dangers, finally, national pride which had produced the conviction that there was no country in the world better than Russia, no ruler mightier than the Orthodox tsar." Ustryalov, *Russkaya istoriya*, II, 15.

*efforts it did not penetrate, could not penetrate further. The
heart of Russia has remained and will always remain inaccessible
to it. The name of Russia will not be disgraced by treason to
Throne and Fatherland. On the contrary, We saw on this occasion new examples of devotion, We saw how fathers did not
spare their criminal children, how relatives rejected and brought
to justice the suspects; We saw how all the estates united in one
thought, one wish: trial and punishment of the criminals.*

*In a state where love for the Monarch and devotion to the
Throne are based on natural traits of the people, where there
exist laws native to the land and a firm rule, all the efforts of
evildoers will be futile and mad: they can conceal themselves in
darkness, but at their first appearance, rejected by common indig-
nation, they will be crushed by the might of the law.*[140]

The manifesto may have been guided largely by wishful thinking
and even by propaganda. But it also expressed the emperor's
general view of his subjects. As Nicholas I wrote in 1831, in a letter dealing with his journey to supervise the reëstablishment of
order and the punishment of rebels in the so-called military
settlements: "Observe that, except for Orlov and Chernyshev, I
was alone among them; and all lay flat, their faces to the ground!
That is the Russian people for you!" [141]

Uvarov carefully pointed out to the sovereign, time and again,
that enthusiastic devotion to the throne reigned among all those
under the jurisdiction of the ministry of education. For instance,
on one occasion he reported:

*Quite often I would interrupt the lecture of a professor and
conclude it with a moral exhortation of my own. My discourse
would always encompass the person of the Monarch, devotion to
the Throne and the Church, the necessity of being a Russian in
spirit before trying to become a European in education, the possibility of combining the unshakable loyalty of a subject with
higher learning, with the enlightenment that belongs to all*

---

[140] The manifesto was published in *Severnaya Pchela*, no. 85, July 17, 1826.
[141] The emperor's letters to Count P. Tolstoi about the rebellion in the
military settlements constitute appendix XXIV in Schilder, II, 612–616;
quoted from p. 615.

*peoples and all centuries. And always, I dare to affirm it, general
exaltation met my unexpected, chance remarks.*[142]

Or, to cite a particularly touching episode which occurred in
Vilno where the Russian government was struggling against Polish
culture and influence:

*When, on the day of my departure, I ordered that all the
students of the institutions in Vilno under my authority, some
1,000 persons in number, be gathered in the palace courtyard, a
pupil of the boarding school for the gentry, Bronskii, stepped
forward from the ranks and in the name of his comrades greeted
me with a brief address. After having said, in excellent Russian,
that they thank me for my visit, that they thank me for my fatherly
treatment of them, he added in conclusion: "Be also and always
our protector in front of the Most Gracious Monarch. Tell Him
that we remember Him, that we love Him, that we shall be worthy
of Him, that we too are His good children . . . ."—Here this
thirteen-year-old youth dissolved in tears and rushed to embrace
me. Of course, not a single spectator remained unaffected by this
expression of sentiment, which was undoubtedly unfeigned and
flowed straight from the heart.*[143]

Shevyrev proved as eager as Uvarov to express his own devotion
to the throne, as well as that of his colleagues and students, for
instance, when two sons of the emperor came to one of his lectures.[144] Gogol insisted that special high and majestic lyricism
appeared suddenly in the works of Russian poets when they
touched upon the great and specifically Russian theme of love
for the tsar.[145]

Pogodin repeatedly contemplated and discussed this remarkable
sentiment. For instance, in 1841 he noted in his diary, in connection with Nicholas I's visit to Moscow: "To the Kremlin. With

---

[142] Barsukov, *op. cit.*, IV, 83.
[143] Uvarov, *Desyatiletie ministerstva narodnogo prosveshcheniya, 1833–1843*,
p. 151. Emphasis in the original.
[144] Shevyrev, *Istoriya Imperatorskogo Moskovskogo Universiteta*, pp. 507–
508.
[145] Gogol, pp. 43–53.

the people. Thought about the idea of the tsar who, as far as we are concerned, cannot sin, against whom nobody complains, whom nobody accuses. This is an article of dogma, although not a written one. And I doubt that they understand it. How enormously much one can accomplish with this idea!" [146]

Pogodin's most enthusiastic outburst resulted from a similar visit by the heir to the throne, in 1837:

The doors of the Cathedral of the Assumption open; preceded by torches, the Metropolitan comes forth holding a Cross in his upraised hands. Behind him the Grand Duke with uncovered head, with lowered eyes, followed by the worthy City Governor of Moscow, by the preceptors and the teachers, and by the most eminent statesmen. Oh, how handsome he was in this minute! What beauty radiated from his young, open face! How much goodness and happiness this gentle smile promised! . . . And what sacred thoughts awoke in a Russian mind. . . . The thought about him, and about the Russian people, the youngest son of humanity, firm and fiery when a skillful hand sets in motion the sacred strings of its heart, a fresh and energetic people which, at a signal from its tsars, is ready to fly to its death as to a nuptial feast, a people which has still retained all the freshness of feeling now when the time of raptures has passed for Europe, and the century has enveloped itself in egoism. "Our father, our father!" exclaimed grey old men leaning on their crutches and trying to catch with their fading eyes the movements of the August Youth. "Our father"—these simple words contain the entire meaning of Russian History. Do not boast to us, the West, of your famous institutions! We honor your great men and recognize duly their benefactions to humanity, but we do not envy them, and we point proudly to our own: unto the West that which is Western, unto the East that which is Eastern. [147]

In connection with this visit, Pogodin was requested to prepare for the imperial guest an essay about Moscow. He concluded it as follows:

---

[146] Barsukov, *op. cit.*, VI, 4.
[147] Barsukov, *op. cit.*, V, 4.

But why have I begun this moral description of Moscow?
Moscow will reveal itself directly to the Grand Duke for whom
I have had the happiness to write this note. When the imperial
standard on the Kremlin Palace announces His arrival, when
the great bell of the Cathedral of the Assumption begins its
solemn tolling, and the Tsarist square is covered by countless
Orthodox people, when a unanimous hurrah! *roars like thunder*
at the sight of the longed-for august first-born of Moscow, let
Him look carefully into these faces, let Him listen attentively to
these sounds: He will hear in them, He will read in them, more
clearly than in all the chronicles, our History. He will comprehend
through them, more correctly than on the basis of all the statistical
data, the secret of Russian power. He will learn in this great
moment of revelation, what is Moscow, what is the Russian man,
what is Holy Russia. Its limitless future will unveil itself in front
of Him, as will His own high destiny, and His young, pure, kind
heart will rejoice with the highest and the most sacred feelings
which a Tsar can possess in this world.[148]

Bulgarin participated actively in the general chorus, reiterating
loudly that loyalty and love of the ruler stood out as distinguishing
traits of the Slavs in general and the Russians in particular.[149] The
Polish journalist's patriotism extended even to a utopian society
he described. There, after a festive dinner when only fruit, des-
sert, and wine remained on the table: "The professor rose from
his chair, approached a wall, pressed a spring, and a lovely melody,
as if played by several harps, charmed my ear. After the prelude,
women began to sing in a chorus the hymn of the fatherland;
men in half-voice repeated the words of the hymn: tears rolled
spontaneously from my eyes. After the singing was over, I could
not refrain from praising this custom." [150]

As editor and publisher of *The Northern Bee*, Grech distinguished himself by articles of his own authorship on such subjects

---

[148] Pogodin's essay "About Moscow" is in Pogodin, *Istoriko-kriticheskie
otryvki*, pp. 131–159, quoted from pp. 158–159. "August first-born of Moscow"
referred to the fact that the grand duke had been born in Moscow. Italics in
the original.
[149] See, e.g., Bulgarin, *Sochineniya*, I, 11; V, 36; VI, 43.
[150] *Ibid.*, VI, 128.

as the death of Alexander I, the passing away of his wife, Empress Elizabeth, and of the Empress Mother Mary, the coming of age of the heir to the throne, Alexander, and the unveiling of the great monument to Alexander I.[151] All these rhetorical essays breathed the spirit of utmost loyalty and devotion. Furthermore, Grech expressed bitterness when rulers were treated in a different manner. Thus he denounced Auber's opera "A Masked Ball, or the Death of Gustavus III" as utterly disrespectful to the eighteenth-century Swedish king, who was made to engage in an amorous intrigue and die by the hand of the insulted husband. Grech concluded: "In this case even the music of the spheres will echo in the soul as a screech of a wheel that needs to be oiled." [152]

Other periodicals followed *The Northern Bee* in their devotion to the throne, the poets rivaling the prose writers. Works of verse glorifying the emperor and his family and singing the love of the Russian people for their rulers included a few good pieces, notably by Zhukovsky, and a great deal of trash. The sentiments which this poetry meant to convey found their summary, for instance, in a stanza from M. Markov's "The Russian Tsar":

> *How sweet it is with a flaming soul*
> *To love Thee, to marvel at Thee,*
> *And to pray the Creator for Thee:*
> *May He, for our sake, prolong Thy years.*[153]

The emphasis on the special character of the Russian people was joined to a general pride in Russia. Nicholas I and his followers stressed the virtues and the glory of the Russians, Russian history, institutions, and language. Language stood out as a vital issue because of the general acceptance of, and even preference for,

---

[151] These articles were gathered as "Articles on Contemporary Subjects" in Grech, *Sochineniya*, III, 407–444. They received prominent mention in Grech's official biography compiled for his jubilee in 1854: *Nikolai Ivanovich Grech. Biograficheskii ocherk*, pp. 31–32. The author of the biography is not given, but apparently it was A. Viskovatyi.

[152] Grech, *Sochineniya*, III, 34.

[153] Markov, "Russkii Tsar," *Biblioteka dlya Chteniya*, VIII (1835), 8. A pathetic example of this devotion to the imperial family is provided by the poem which Tyutchev tried to compose shortly before his death. I. Aksakov, *Biografiya Fedora Ivanovicha Tyutcheva*, pp. 14–16n.

French in Russian educated society, and because of the multi-
lingual nature of the Russian state. The emperor ordered the use
of Russian at court functions.[154] The government, and especially
the ministry of education headed by Uvarov, embarked on a great
program of spreading the knowledge of Russian in the non-
Russian areas of the empire.[155] Writers and journalists supported
the same cause. Bulgarin, to take one example, satirized repeatedly
the ignorance on the part of the Russians of their own native
language and land and their snobbish preference for everything
French.[156] Many others made similar attacks, the figures of the
young Russian fop and, especially, of the French tutor serving
as the common object of ridicule and, in the case of Pogodin,
even of hatred.[157] As the playwright Kukolnik admonished his
countrymen:

> *He who is ashamed of his native tongue*
> *Will also be ashamed of his parents.*

Some preferred French because of a desire to brag or because they
followed blindly the current fashion. Although bad enough, they
were not the worst offenders.

> *But those, who are capable of thinking,*
> *But on purpose do not speak Russian—*
> *Well, in this case it is no longer boastfulness,*
> *It means that they no longer feel like Russians!*
> *These are as trees without roots,*
> *The withered sycamore of the parable . . .*[158]

---

[154] Concerning the application of this order see Grunwald, *La Vie de Nicolas
I*er*, p. 160 n. 2; and Custine, II, 279.

[155] This subject will be discussed in chap. iv below.

[156] See especially Bulgarin, *Sochineniya*, VII, 1–48; VIII, 26–52, 163–220;
XI, 1–119.

[157] Pogodin's deep antagonism to French tutors and other foreigners dated
from his own days as a private teacher. Barsukov, *op. cit.*, I, 68–70. Criticism
of Francomania was, of course, already widespread in Russian literature in
the eighteenth century. The more notable examples then included Fonvizin's
play, "A Brigadier," and some writings of Catherine the Great herself. I am
impressed, nevertheless, by the great vogue of such criticism in the reign of
Nicholas I.

[158] Kukolnik, *op. cit.*, pp. 234–235.

Other nationalities of the empire had to learn the Russian language for a different reason: it represented a great unifying bond in the tsar's huge and heterogeneous realm.[159]

But the proponents of Official Nationality did not limit their championing of Russian to patriotic or utilitarian grounds. They went on to assert that it excelled other languages and to elaborate this point in detail. Grech, in his capacity of grammarian, affirmed that "our language—one can say this confidently—is superior to all the modern European languages." [160] These languages, in fact, showed every kind of deficiency, from the excessive regularity, control, and alienation from their own popular sources, characteristic of the Romance languages, to the unnatural, foreign admixtures in Polish and Czech.

In what majesty then does Russian appear among all these tongues! It consists of a pure, regular, rich popular dialect utilizing all the treasures of the ancient church language which had been formed following the Greek pattern, but which remained close to the language of the people. It has developed out of itself, without any alien admixture; it possesses all grammatical forms in abundance; it can imitate ancient meters; it is expressive, free in its flow, noble, solemn, and at the same time fresh and melodious. In other languages one must avoid expressions and turns of phrase of the common people: in our case one may and should seek them and use them.[161]

It is not surprising that Grech's colleague, Bulgarin, had everyone know Russian in his utopian world of the future. As a member of that blessed society explained to the author: "The Russian language, which without a doubt holds first place in melodiousness and in the richness and the ease of word construction, is the language of poetry and literature in all the countries of the globe." [162]

Gogol contributed a similar sweeping eulogy of Russian:

---

[159] An early and explicit statement of this view which came to dominate the Russian government can be found in Professor A. Kaisarov's "Address about Love for the Fatherland," (Rech o lyubvi k otechestvu), *Syn Otechestva*, 1813, no. XXVII, part I, pp. 3–20.

[160] Grech, *Sochineniya*, III, 290.

[161] *Ibid.*

[162] Bulgarin, *Sochineniya*, VI, 130.

Finally, our extraordinary language itself is still a mystery. It contains all tones and all shades, all transitions of sounds, from the hardest to the softest and the most tender. It has no limits, and, being alive as life itself, it is able to garner riches every minute, obtaining, on the one hand, solemn words from the church-Biblical language, and, on the other, selecting at will neat expressions from its countless dialects scattered over our provinces. It is thus able, in one and the same speech, to attain heights inaccessible to any other language and to descend to the simple level tangibly felt by even the densest person. A language which is in itself already a poet. . . .[163]

Shevyrev undertook the task of establishing the nature of his countrymen on the basis of their tongue, devoting to this enterprise a lecture on "the Russian language—an expression of the spirit and the character of the Russian people." [164] The professor began in a characteristically romantic manner with the assertion that nothing expressed nationality as well as language. "Language is the invisible image of the entire people, its physiognomy." [165] While Shevyrev did not intend to deal with this profound subject in its entirety, he had certain relevant suggestions to make concerning the Russian language and the Russian people. The richness and multiplicity of sounds in the Russian language and the resulting ability of Russians to learn other tongues with unparalleled ease indicated the Russian destiny of bringing together and assimilating culture and enlightenment from all European countries. Russian had no articles, a fact which emphasized its living quality, its special adaptability to conversation rather than writing. "Our speech is broad, sweeping, as is also our national character." [166] Similarly, in Russian the present was the only true tense, whereas the past and the future represented merely artificial constructions. This demonstrated clearly the concrete, practical, living nature of Russian, for in practice only the present exists,

---

[163] Gogol, p. 219.

[164] The lecture served as the introduction to the course in Russian literature which Shevyrev presented to a Russian audience in Paris, in 1862. Shevyrev, *Lektsii o russkoi literature*, pp. 1–19.

[165] *Ibid.*, p. 3. Cf. Pogodin, *Istoriko-politicheskie pisma*, p. 28.

[166] Shevyrev, *op. cit.*, p. 5.

other tenses belonging to the realm of abstract thought. The weak
development of the conditional mood in Russian corresponded to
the popular dislike of legalism, of written agreements in particular.
Complex aspects of Russian verbs also contained a remarkable
lesson:

> *Aspects provide the possibility of either condensing action into
> a single second of time, or of expanding it over the greatest
> stretch imaginable, or, finally, of expressing it as incomplete or as
> complete. . . . Is there not reflected in this ability to condense
> or to expand the factor of time that quality of the Russian people
> which enables it sometimes to condense centuries into decades,
> years into months, months and days into moments? The Rus-
> sian people sits for thirty years riveted to a spot, like Ilya of
> Murom, and then suddenly gets up as a valiant warrior ready for
> every glorious deed.*[167]

The belief in the unique qualities of the Russian people and
the Russian language led naturally to a view of Russia as a distinct
and separate entity, standing in sharp contrast to "the West," to
"Europe." And, indeed, all proponents of Official Nationality sub-
scribed to some such view. But it was the romantic nationalists
among them who emphasized the dichotomy and constructed
an elaborate intellectual edifice on the basis of it. As Shevyrev
stated the case in his celebrated article in the first issue of *The
Muscovite*: "The West and Russia, Russia and the West—here
is the result that follows from the entire past; here is the last word
of history; here are the two facts for the future." [168] Pogodin, the

---

[167] *Ibid.*, p. 7. Romantic analysis of the Russian language and exuberant
praise of it, characteristic of Official Nationality, were by no means limited to
its proponents. The Slavophiles, Konstantin Aksakov in particular, engaged in
the same task, and Shevyrev referred to Konstantin Aksakov in the article
under discussion. Russian was eulogized at different times by many other intellectuals, especially writers, the most famous examples being Lomonosov
and Turgenev. As to the Ilya of Murom image, the proponents of official
nationality emphasized frequently the great daring of the Russians and their
ability to rise suddenly to the occasion and "do the impossible." See, e.g.,
Pogodin, *Rechi*, p. 74; Bulgarin, *Sochineniya*, XI, 140–141; Gogol, pp. 228–
229.

[168] Shevyrev, "Vzglyad russkogo na sovremennoe obrazovanie Evropy,"
Moskvityanin, no. 1, 1841, p. 219.

historian, explained the difference between the two in his usual dogmatic manner: Western states were based on conquest which bequeathed division, oppression, and strife to their subsequent development; Russia was created by a free invitation to the rulers with the resulting unity, concord, and harmony. An illustration served to illuminate the point:

> *Invitation and conquest in that rough, wild period were, let us admit it, very closely related, much alike, divided only by a thin line—but still divided! Look at two seeds: they are almost identical; it is only through a magnifying lens that one can notice a fine distinction—but give them their term, give these seeds time to develop, to grow, and you will see that an oak will come out of one of them, and from the other a palm or some tender and fragrant plant; and the fine distinction of the seeds will reveal itself strikingly in the flowers and in the fruits.*[169]. . . *Our state was founded on love, the Western states on hate.*[170]

The original contrast between Russia and the West underwent further accentuation throughout their subsequent histories. Because Russia had escaped conquest, the Russians remained free and in possession of their land while in the West native peoples became slaves. Furthermore, because Russian rulers had few retainers and, being on friendly terms with the people, did not depend on them, aristocracy and feudalism never developed in Russia. In fact, the entire class struggle which plagued Western history reaching its crescendo in modern times, remained alien to peaceful Russia. In that happy land: "All the people were distinguished only according to their occupations, equally accessible to everyone, while they enjoyed the same political and civil standing in their mutual relations and with regard to the prince." [171]

Various "physical" and "moral" factors contributed further to the unique destiny of the Russians. The enormous size of Russia made rapid invasion impossible and at the same time assured land in abundance for all, thus eliminating one of the greatest reasons

---

[169] Pogodin, "Parallel russkoi istorii s istoriei zapadnykh evropeiskikh gosudarstv," *Istoriko-kriticheskie otryvki*, pp. 55–82; quoted from p. 62.

[170] *Ibid.*, p. 74.

[171] *Ibid.*, p. 68.

for strife. Their huge numbers also added strength to the Russians, and made it possible for them to assimilate all comers. For the same reason foreigners, even when they represented the ruling group, were forced to respect the people. Russia offered no luxuries or riches, only basic natural products in return for hard work: therefore, ambitious conquerors directed their steps elsewhere, for instance, to Constantinople. The Russian climate too had a providential effect on Russian history: "The severe, cold climate forced the inhabitants to live at home, near their hearths, in the midst of their families, and not to bother about public affairs, the affairs of the market place where they would go only in case of dire need. They left everything willingly to the prince and to his boyars and thus avoided all collisions and discords." [172] The flatness of the landscape itself contributed to social equality among the Russians; all Russians lived under similar conditions; there were no mountains on which to erect castles, even no stone, for that matter, only combustible wood. The landlocked nature of Russia helped the country to maintain for many centuries its separateness.

As to moral factors, the Slavs were by their very nature quiet, peaceful, and patient.[173] Similarly, Orthodoxy, in contrast to Catholicism, emphasized calm, contemplation, tolerance, and a withdrawal from the world of politics. Russia also differed from the West because she was young and fresh: "In our case the new secular enlightenment was grafted to a fresh, wild tree; in their case, to an old and rotten one. Their building was built on ruins, ours on virgin soil." [174] All comparisons led to one inevitable conclusion: "How many differences were placed in the foundation of the Russian state compared to the Western ones! One cannot

---

[172] *Ibid.*, pp. 77–78.

[173] The proponents of Official Nationality loved to characterize the Russian people as peaceful. This suited well their Christian ideal as well as their political doctrine which stressed obedience of the masses. Yet they also liked to praise Russian military valor, with the result that some of them, e.g., Bulgarin and F. Moroshkin, described the Slavs and the Russians as generally warlike. See, for instance, Bulgarin, *Rossiya v istoricheskom, statisticheskom, geograficheskom i literaturnom otnosheniyakh*, History, part 2, pp. 41–42; Bulgarin, *Vospominaniya*, VI, 269; Moroshkin, *Istoriko-kriticheskie issledovaniya o russakh i slavyanakh*, pp. 161–163.

[174] Pogodin, *op. cit.*, p. 80.

decide which are the more powerful: the historical, the physical, or the moral ones! Well then, how mighty they must be as they act on one another, mutually strengthen one another, move towards the same end!" [175]

And Pogodin kept repeating this important point throughout his life: "We have a different climate from the West, a different landscape, a different temperament, character, a different blood, a different physiognomy, a different look, a different way of thinking, different beliefs, hopes, wishes, pleasures, different relations, different conditions, different history, everything different. . . ." [176]

The proponents of Official Nationality all proclaimed the peculiar nature of the Russian people to be their devotion to the altar and to the throne. They took pride in Russia, the Russian language, and Russian history, and they loved to contrast their peaceful and calm fatherland to the restless and turbulent West. In particular, they insisted that class struggle and revolution could never find any application in Russia. But beyond these weighty affirmations agreement ceased. Those ideologists of the state who thought above all in dynastic terms limited their interpretation of "nationality" to the above-mentioned postulates. Their attitude was entirely defensive: "nationality," as well as other doctrinal principles, served as buttresses of the existing order. The nationalists, on the other hand, strove to combine this loyalty to the Russia of Nicholas I with the broad and dizzying vistas of the emerging romantic nationalism. "Nationality" meant for them not only the legendary past and the strait-jacketed present of Russia, but also its glorious, Messianic future. The Russian people were the bearers of that great mission, not merely obedient pawns in the hands of their masters. Russia expanded to become Slavdom, Russian destiny advancing to the Elbe, Vienna, and Constantinople. Indeed, the entire world was to be recast in response to this call of fate, through blood and iron if necessary. The Messianic Russian future called for an adventurous, aggressive, even

---

[175] *Ibid.*, p. 81.
[176] Pogodin, *Istoriko-politicheskie pisma*, p. 254. Cf., e.g., Zhukovskii, *op. cit.*, pp. 164–168.

revolutionary, foreign policy which represented the very opposite
of the conservative and legitimist orientation of Nicholas I and
his government.

The dynastic view was represented by Nicholas I himself, as well
as by most members of his government and his court. It also
found expression in such loyal press as *The Northern Bee* with its
well-known editors Grech and Bulgarin. The nationalist wing was
led by the Moscow professors Shevyrev, and, especially, Pogodin,
and it included the poet and publicist Tyutchev, as well as numerous participants in *The Muscovite*. The members of this latter
group stood close to the Slavophiles, although they remained
separated from them, primarily by the issue of the nature and
role of the Russian state.[177] Moreover, judging by Barsukov's
meticulous listing of Pogodin's contacts and other evidence, they
enjoyed considerable support among the Russian public. Romantic, nationalist ideas penetrated even the Russian government, and
that on an increasing scale, affecting some of the ministers and
other high officials; although they never grew strong enough to
replace the essentially dynastic and *ancien régime* outlook of the
emperor and of most of his aides.[178]

Uvarov, in his key position of minister of education, reflected
these opposing influences in a striking manner. An aristocrat by
origin, a reactionary by conviction, a man fully identified with the
existing Russian regime, he nevertheless patronized nationalistic
professors, himself dabbled in romantic ideology in composing the
famous triple formula, and wanted to play the role of an intellectual abreast of, and indeed leading, his times. The revolutions
of 1848 made him recoil from nationalism and toe the line of
extreme Russian reaction. Yet his support of official policy was
found to be insufficiently complete and single-minded and, in
1849, Uvarov was forced to resign his ministry.[179]

[177] On the relationship between this group and the Slavophiles, see N.
Riasanovsky, "Pogodin and Ševyrëv in Russian Intellectual History."
[178] See chaps. iv and v below for a further discussion of this topic.
[179] The dismissal of Uvarov will be discussed in chap. iv. As an example of
the treatment of "nationality" in Uvarov's *Journal of the Ministry of Education* see Pletnev, "O narodnosti v literature," *Zhurnal Ministerstva Narodnogo
Prosveshcheniya*, part 1, 1834, pp. 1–30.

The difference between the two points of view came out strongly, perhaps in an exaggerated manner, in the following question of terminology. While Holy Russia was exalted as their key symbol by the nationalists, Bulgarin quoted Count E. Kankrin, the minister of finance of German origin, as saying: "If we consider the matter thoroughly, then, in justice, we must be called not *Russians*, but *Petrovians*. . . . Everything: glory, power, prosperity, and enlightenment, we owe to the Romanov family; and, out of gratitude, we should change our general tribal name of *Slavs* to the name of the creator of the empire and of its well-being. Russia should be called *Petrovia*, and we *Petrovians*; or the empire should be named *Romanovia*, and we—*Romanovites*." [180] And Bulgarin added his own opinion to the minister's suggestion: "An unusual idea, but an essentially correct one!" [181]

According to all proponents of Official Nationality, the Russian people had a narrowly circumscribed role. They were to act within the confines of an autocratic regime, to remain obedient and grateful children of their tsar, as well as devoted and heroic soldiers of their officers. Still, even in this estimate of the Russian people subtle differences appeared between those who thought in terms of the traditional dynastic state and those who burned with the new flame of nationalism. The first group tended to be entirely reactionary in its approach: serfdom was defended as an indispensable pillar of Russian society, the education of the tsar's subjects was not to exceed what was proper for their social position, and in general the people were to be kept in their place and to remain merely pliant material in the hands of their masters. The nationalist ideologists of the state accepted on the whole the existing Russian order, but they also envisioned some possible modifications of it, such as the abolition of serfdom. They wanted to spread education among the masses, to make all people active

---

[180] Bulgarin, *Vospominaniya*, I, 200–201. Italics in the original.
[181] *Ibid.* This was not the only proposal to rename Russia "Petrovia." A little later one historian even argued that, in recognition of the services of Nicholas I, the country should be renamed "Nikolaevia." Zotov, *op. cit.*, II, 312–313. On "Holy Russia," see especially Cherniavsky, " 'Holy Russia': a Study in the History of an Idea," *American Historical Review*, LXIII: 3 (April, 1958), 617–637.

and enthusiastic participants in the destinies of Russia. They believed in a popular autocracy, in a real union in thought and action between the tsar and his humble subjects. And they came to be opposed to aristocracy, as an obstacle to this union and a class phenomenon which had no place in the true Russian society.

Social and economic reaction in the reign of Nicholas I centered largely on the issue of the defense of serfdom. As Uvarov, who in this debate represented the extreme Right, formulated the matter: *"Political religion, just as Christian religion, has its inviolable dogmas; in our case they are: autocracy and serfdom."* [182] He referred to this controversial subject very often and at least on one occasion discussed it in detail with a few friends who had gathered at the minister's estate of Poreche.[183] Pogodin, one of the guests, wrote down fifteen separate headings under which Uvarov explained the problem of serfdom, arguing for the retention of that institution. The minister claimed that there was no need for abolition, and he stressed the enormous practical difficulties of such a reform, but his main emphasis remained on the indissoluble link between autocracy and serfdom. Pogodin recorded the following arguments, among others:

> *The question of serfdom is closely linked to the question of autocracy and even monarchy.*
>
> *These are two parallel forces which have developed together. Both have the same historical beginning; both have equal legality . . .*
>
> *Serfdom, whatever one may think of it, does exist. Abolition of it will lead to the dissatisfaction of the gentry class which will start looking for compensations for itself somewhere, and there is nowhere to look except in the domain of autocracy . . . Peter I's edifice will be shaken. . . .*

---

[182] Barsukov, *op. cit.*, IV, 38. Italics in the original.

[183] This talk of Uvarov, as recorded by Pogodin and reproduced in Barsukov's work, is our best source of information concerning Uvarov's views on serfdom. Barsukov, *op. cit.*, IX, 305–308. For a discussion of Uvarov's position see, e.g., Melgunov, "Epokha 'ofitsialnoi narodnosti' i krepostnoe pravo," in Dzhivelegov, Melgunov, and Picheta, eds., *Velikaya Reforma. Russkoe obshchestvo i krestyanskii vopros v proshlom i nastoyashchem*, III, 1–21, especially p. 2. Cf. Schiemann, IV, 9–10.

Serfdom is a tree which has spread its roots afar: it shelters both the Church and the Throne.[184]

A number of other high government officials joined Uvarov in defending serfdom, and so did certain publicists of the Right. As late as 1859 Grech argued that, although serfdom was unjust, "the liberation of wild slaves, under conditions of complete moral disorder, of a lack of true, spiritual religion, and of the corruption of our minor officials, will bring upon Russia complete ruin and countless misfortunes." [185] Nicholas I himself held the identical view.[186] Even Henry Middleton, the American representative, expressed sentiments later formulated by Uvarov when he reported to Washington:

Add to this that it seems most natural that the present body of the Nobility should incline to bear with the autocracy placed above it, in order to enjoy the benefits of the servage beneath it. While on the other hand the Crown, however disposed, from many considerations both moral and political, to elevate the condition of the serf, will yet be careful not to do anything which shall tend to change the relations by means of which autocracy is rendered so necessary in the state.[187]

Education served as another area of reactionary theory and practice in the reign of Nicholas I. The emphasis lay, again, on keeping the masses in their proper place. As Uvarov explained the activity of his department to the emperor: "The difference in the needs of the different estates and conditions of people leads inevitably to an appropriate delimitation among them of the subjects of study. A system of public education can only then be considered to be organized correctly when it offers opportunities to each one to receive that education which would correspond to his mode of life and to his future calling in society." [188] Others, in and

[184] Barsukov, *op. cit.*, IV, 38.
[185] Grech, *Zapiski o moei zhizni*, p. 499.
[186] Government policy in regard to serfdom, as well as other government policies, will be discussed in chap. iv.
[187] Raeff, *op. cit.*, p. 293. Emphasis in the original.
[188] Uvarov, *Desyatiletie ministerstva narodnogo prosveshcheniya, 1833–1843*, p. 8. For identical views fostered by the Austrian government see Rath, *op. cit.*, especially pp. 156–157.

out of the government, were more outspoken than the urbane minister. Benckendorff, the chief gendarme, bluntly told Nicholas: "Russia is best protected from revolutionary disasters by the fact that in our country, from the time of Peter the Great, the monarchs have always been ahead of the nation. But for this very reason one should not hasten unduly to educate the nation lest the people reach, in the extent of their understanding, a level equal to that of the monarchs and would then attempt to weaken their power." [189]

Gogol's obscurantist position in education, which included the affirmation that the great majority of the people should remain illiterate and that the masses "in truth, should not even know whether there are any books except church books," created a scandal among Russian intellectuals.[190] V. Dal, another and a far less important writer, produced a similar controversy when he, much like Gogol, declared publicly that education was more likely to spoil than to improve the peasants, at least for the time being.[191]

By contrast, the nationalists had more confidence in the Russian people and happier plans for them. Though no ardent emancipationist, Pogodin argued against Uvarov in favor of abolishing serfdom,[192] added highly critical comments to his account of the minister's defense of that institution,[193] and welcomed the great reform.[194] Pogodin's plebeian, even serf origin, gave him a different perspective on the matter from that of the aristocratic Uvarov and other court dignitaries. Shevyrev, who, like his Slavophile friends, had an old and honorable gentry ancestry, joined Pogodin in praise of emancipation, devoting to it one of

---

[189] Schilder, II, 287.
[190] Gogol, p. 125. See the discussion of this subject in sec. ii of this chapter.
[191] About this controversy see Dementev, op. cit., pp. 374–375.
[192] Barsukov, op. cit., VI, 158.
[193] Barsukov, op. cit., IX, 305–308.
[194] See, e.g., Pogodin, Rechi, pp. 230–232; and Pogodin, Stati politicheskie i polskii vopros (1856–1867), p. 465. That Pogodin considered serfdom a tremendous threat to peace and order in Russia is clear from Pogodin, Istoriko-politicheskie pisma, pp. 261–262. As a young man Pogodin had written a tale, "A Pauper," depicting the abuses of serfdom (Barsukov, op. cit., I, 329).

his most enthusiastic poems.[195] In education, too, Pogodin urged the interests of the people, arguing that general education was a necessity if Russia were to survive as a modern state. His admonition became a shrill cry in the dark days of the Crimean War.[196]

Pogodin believed, as we have already seen, that true Russian society had to be classless. He held to this conviction throughout his life, in large things and in small. It inspired much of his historical writing as well as his attacks on class exclusiveness delivered at gentry assemblies and elsewhere.[197] And it also made him insist at an annual University of Moscow alumni dinner that such occasions should be made less expensive and more democratic.[198] Aristocracy was evil because it could shackle the people and threaten the monolithic nature of the Russian state. Talent had to have opportunities for advancement, no matter where that talent originated. Peter the Great gave the fullest application to this important principle of statecraft, and it also formed the foundation of the might of England, as Pogodin explained in his essay on Disraeli.[199]

But, in addition to the leaders which it could produce, the people itself was important.[200] Whether in the form of a *zemskii sobor*, or by other means, the people could advise and support the tsar, could back him fully and directly in all his undertakings. "In

---

[195] See his poem "19 fevralya" in Shevyrev, *Stikhotvoreniya*, pp. 197–198. Tyutchev expressed similar sentiments in a briefer, but better piece, "To Emperor Alexander II," Tyutchev, p. 197.

[196] See especially Pogodin, *Rechi*, p. 240; *Istoriko-politicheskie pisma*, pp. 218–219, 286.

[197] See especially Pogodin, *Rechi*, pp. 380–388.

[198] *Ibid.*, pp. 217–218.

[199] See Pogodin "Disraeli," *Stati politicheskie i polskii vopros* (1856–1867), pp. 214–217. "Disraeli—prime-minister, the head of the English government! Disraeli, a Jew by origin, a writer, a gentleman of the press—something that is still worse and lower in the eyes of some—by his mode of life! . . . Here is the basis of English power and dominance! Here is the guarantee of the well-being of the aristocracy itself! They know how to detect merit, wherever it may appear; they look for it sharply and sensitively in all the backwoods; they are ready to obey any intelligent voice, no matter from which direction it comes." (*Ibid.*, p. 214.)

[200] Cf. the Slavophile views on government and people.

other words: we think that every supreme authority, even the wisest, will become still wiser when assisted by the voice of the entire people." [201] And Pogodin liked to repeat the famous democratic dictum: *vox populi, vox Dei.*[202]

The Baltic Germans represented an issue over which the nationalist and the dynastic outlooks clashed sharply. These descendants of the Teutonic Knights enjoyed an exceptional and dominant position in their provinces, and they also played a major role in the Russian state at large, occupying a great number of important posts, especially in the diplomatic service, in the army, and at court. The Baltic barons provided solid support for Nicholas's entire system. Yet they became anathema to the rising nationalist spirit. Pogodin followed the Slavophile Samarin in violent attack on this dangerous "foreign" element.[203] He demanded the abolition of the special privileged status of the Germans in their corner of the empire as unnecessary, oppressive, archaic, and insulting to the Russian people and the Russian state. He urged further a rapid Russification of the Latvian and Estonian majority of the provinces which hated its ruthless German masters and longed for closer ties with the Russians. Only thus could the area be safeguarded from the German menace. "The Russification of the Ests, the Livs, and the Kurs is a political necessity, and one must be blind not to see that! . . . The Slavs have let slip the Oder, the Vistula, the Pregel, even the Memel—it is necessary, then, to insure in good time the Dvina. . . . That is, it is necessary at any price to Russify the Letts and the Ests, and as quickly as possible. *Caveant consules, ne quid respublica detrimenti capiat,* I exclaim to our statesmen." [204]

---

[201] Pogodin, *Rechi*, p. 388. Pogodin prefaced this statement with the assertion that it did not contradict at all the principle of autocracy.

[202] See e.g., Pogodin, *Istoriko-politicheskie pisma*, p. 139, p. 191; *Stati politicheskie i polskii vopros* (1856–1867), p. 164. By contrast with this praise of the people, one may cite Bulgarin's opinion: "Those who saw the Russian people on a rampage are convinced that the alleged freedom has never led to any good, and that all great and useful deeds have been accomplished under the firm authority of the rulers." Bulgarin, *Rossiya v istoricheskom, statisticheskom, geograficheskom i literaturnom otnosheniyakh*, History, part 4, p. 211.

[203] See in particular Pogodin, *Ostzeiskii vopros. Pismo M. P. Pogodina k professoru Shirrenu.*

[204] *Ibid.*, pp. 108–111.

Tyutchev shared Pogodin's sentiments toward the Germans
in general and those in the Russian service in particular. He
assailed with the greatest venom Nesselrode, Nicholas I's foreign
minister:

> No, my dwarf, unparalleled coward,
> No matter how much you shiver and lose courage,
> You with your soul of little faith
> Will not be able to entice Holy Russia. . . .
> The world destiny of Russia,
> No, you cannot dam it! . . .[205]

While the nationalists vituperated, those who thought in terms
of a traditional dynastic state were more than satisfied with the
Baltic Germans. Bulgarin, for instance, after a visit, gave a glowing
account of their provinces. He admired especially the patriotism
of the people, the general love for learning, the complete integrity
of the officials, the excellent system of justice, and the fine development of agriculture.[206] Grech too had a high regard for the Baltic
Germans, noting in particular that their success in the Russian
service was a result of their superior education.[207] For a variety of
reasons Nicholas I and his government found it difficult to maintain a consistent policy in regard to the Baltic Provinces, a subject which is to be discussed later in this study. But the personal
preferences of the emperor and of most of his aides were not with
the nationalists. The monarch himself lectured Samarin on the
impropriety of his attack on the Baltic Germans and emphasized
their value for Russia.[208] He is even supposed to have asserted:
"The Russian nobles serve the state, the German ones serve
us." [209]

---

[205] See Tyutchev's poem "Na grafa Nesselrode" in Tyutchev, p. 193. Nesselrode, to repeat, was of German, though not Baltic German, origin.
[206] Bulgarin, Sochineniya, XI, 185–195.
[207] Grech, Zapiski o moei zhizni, pp. 352–353.
[208] Nolde, op. cit., pp. 47–49.
[209] Presnyakov, p. 9. "Us" refers to the imperial family. No source is cited.
See also Miliukov, Seignobos, and Eisenmann, op. cit., p. 737. Schiemann,
quoting Senator K. Lebedev, ascribes this statement to the heir, Grand Duke
Alexander, later Emperor Alexander II. Lebedev went on: "As soon as the
monarchic principle is destroyed in Russia, the Germans will no longer be

Pogodin wanted to destroy the German element in the Baltic Provinces of the empire, but he also opposed Estonian or Latvian nationalism. The realm of the tsars had to be a Russian state. As a young man he had already expressed his uncompromising hostility to all alien elements in Russia.[210] As an old and embattled publicist he kept repeating that his country was not a *gesammtes Vaterland*, such as Austria, but Holy Russia. "No, the Russian monarch was born, grew out of the Russian soil. He won all the territories together with the Russian people, through Russian toil and Russian blood!" [211]

But while romantic nationalism was in many ways exclusive, it tended to be inclusive and to expand in one direction: a people became identified with its race, both the concept of race and the identification having been greatly bolstered by the development of modern philology.[212] Therefore, the rising Russian nationalism developed in the direction of Pan-Slavism. After the summary of enormous Russian power presented earlier in this study, Pogodin continued triumphantly:

And what if we add to this number thirty million of our brothers, that is, brothers and cousins, the Slavs who are scattered all over Europe, from Constantinople to Venice and from Morea to the Baltic and the North seas? The same blood flows in the veins of these Slavs as in our veins. They speak the same language as we do. Consequently, according to the law of nature, they sympathize with us. In spite of the geographic and the political separation, they constitute, on the basis of origin and language, one moral whole with us! Let us subtract this number from our neighbors, Austria and Turkey, and after that from all of Europe, and let us add it to our total. What will be left to them, and how much shall we have? Thinking halts, breath is taken away! A ninth part of the entire

---

able to live in it. The disappearance of the German party will be the clearest sign of the disappearance of autocracy, of the absolute rule of the tsar!" Schiemann, IV, 62–63.

[210] Barsukov, *op. cit.*, I, 56.

[211] Pogodin, *Stati politicheskie i polskii vopros* (1856–1867), pp. 476–487, quoted from p. 487.

[212] Words such as "family" and "tribe," rather than "race," were used by the proponents of Official Nationality. I think, however, that their meaning in this context can be best rendered in present-day English by "race."

*inhabited earth, and almost a ninth part of the entire population.
Half the equator, one quarter of a meridian!* [213]

The Slavs were, according to Pogodin, the most ancient inhabitants of Europe known to history. Their antiquity could be
safely deduced from their huge numbers, their enormous geographic spread, and the originality and richness of their language,
because all these characteristics required a very long time to develop. Later invaders obliterated much of Slavic culture and
achievement in all but eastern Europe, notably Russia, leaving
in many areas only some place names and other fragmentary
evidence to testify to the great Slavic past.[214] Ancient writers,
such as Procopius and the emperor Mauricius, already recorded
certain basic Slavic virtues: sincerity, simplicity, and the absence
of viciousness or of flattery in their character.[215] The Slavs were
above all a family people, a point emphasized especially by
Shevyrev. Slavic family life stood close to the ideal, being distinguished by a pervasive patriarchal spirit, by the great virtues
and the very high social standing of women, and by the absence
of such horrible, but widespread, primitive practices as infan-
ticide.[216] Unfortunately the Slavs also had significant deficiencies
of long standing, two in particular: a lack of concord among
themselves and an exaggerated receptivity toward foreign influences.[217] These failings, added to the fact that the Slavs were
by nature peaceful tillers of the soil rather than bloodthirsty
warriors, tilted the historical balance against them and in favor

---

[213] Pogodin, *Istoriko-politicheskie pisma*, p. 2; see also, e.g., pp. 115–117; and
Pogodin, *Sobranie statei, pisem i rechei po povodu slavyanskogo voprosa*, p. 128.
[214] Pogodin, *Sobranie statei, pisem i rechei po povodu slavyanskogo voprosa*,
pp. 25–35. This typically romantic emphasis on the antiquity of their people
can be found in the writings of many proponents of Official Nationality. An
extreme case of it, as applied to Russia, is provided by Moroshkin who argues
that the Russian state already existed at the time of Herodotus, that the Russian
gentry was the oldest in the world, and that "*Russian history must serve as the
point of departure for every kind of European history!*" Moroshkin, *op. cit.*,
p. 162; italics in the original. Cf. the treatment of the Slavic past by the
Slavophiles, especially by Khomyakov. See N. Riasanovsky, *Russia and the
West in the Teaching of the Slavophiles*, pp. 71–75.
[215] Pogodin, *op. cit.*, p. 31.
[216] Shevyrev, *Ob otnoshenii semeinogo vospitaniya k gosudarstvennomu*, pp.
57–74.
[217] Pogodin, *op. cit.*, p. 31.

of their violent and aggressive neighbors. Some lands lost entirely their Slavic character; in others the population remained Slavic, but it was brought under the yoke of invaders, such as the Germans and the Turks. Heroic resistance, exemplified by the Hussite wars, proved of no avail. The enemies, especially the Germans, "hostile to the Slavs because of some physiological quality," [218] won repeated victories in their ruthless campaign to exterminate their rivals.

But the tragedy of Slavdom was finally coming to an end; a reversal of fortune appeared in sight. The Russians had not only succeeded in escaping the fate of the other Slavs, but they also proceeded to construct, in spite of all obstacles, the mightiest state in the world. That state was at last coming into its own, and it was bound to assert itself strongly on the international scene. The other Slavs too were finally showing signs of awakening to their joint destiny. The rising force of nationalism that was bringing the Germans and the Italians together could not stop on the Elbe or on the Dalmatian border.

In the course of some fifty-five years of ardent adherence to Pan-Slavism,[219] Pogodin several times changed his programs for Slavdom and revised his hopes on the subject. His demands ranged from a real unification of the Slavic world under the scepter of the Russian tsar, to some vague federation, and even to mere insistence on full civil and cultural rights for the Slavs within alien empires. Political crises in eastern Europe repeatedly brought Pogodin's enthusiasm and expectations to a fever pitch, while the passage of years with their sequence of hopes betrayed contributed to a certain disillusionment and moderation.[220] But through it all Pogodin remained faithful to his belief in the

---

[218] *Ibid.*, p. 24.

[219] Barsukov quotes an entry in Pogodin's diary, dated as early as February 6, 1821: "Talked with Kubarev about the unification of all the Slavic tribes into one whole, into one state. Let another Peter be born—he will find another Suvorov, and the party will be over. With 500,000 he would settle the affair. The main thing is to take them from the Austrians." Barsukov, *op. cit.*, I, 56. Later Pogodin declared that Slavdom was his Alpha and Omega. Barsukov, *op. cit.*, V, 330.

[220] Pogodin's voluminous writings on Slavdom are mentioned in the footnotes and in the bibliography.

brighter Slavic future and in Russia as the great agent and leader
of the Slavic destiny. "If Germany considered itself bound to
liberate its blood brothers, Germans, from the very light yoke
of the Danes who are not alien to them by origin, and not only
free them morally, but separate them physically and add them
to its own body; is it not just, is it not obligatory, is it not lawful,
is it not necessary for Russia to act in the same manner in relation to the Slavs oppressed by Moslem Turkey?" [221]
Russia was the natural leader of the Slavs for a number of reasons. Its enormous population, size, resources, and political power,
together with the subjugation, poverty, and misery of the other
members of the Slavic family made Russia the obvious champion
of their joint cause. Beyond this, Russia, because of its very bulk
and good fortune, remained free of the petty rivalries and jeal-
ousies which plagued the other Slavs. Only Russia, therefore,
could serve as their broad-minded and disinterest guide.[222] The
Russian language too could be used to advantage as the literary
language of all the Slavs. It was the tongue of by far the most
numerous and historically successful Slavic people; it also combined—so Pogodin asserted—"the qualities of virtually all other
western and eastern dialects into which the Slavic language is
usually divided"; and it stood closest to the original speech of
the ancient Slavs.[223] Orthodoxy, in turn, represented the true
religion of Slavdom. Pogodin suffered personal mortification from
the fact that many Slavs, such as the Poles, the Czechs, and
the Croats, gave their allegiance to Roman Catholicism, and he
tried on many occasions to lay this issue to rest by declaring
that Russia did not dream of interfering with other peoples'
religious beliefs and that she considered all Slavs, regardless of
their creed, as brothers.[224] Yet his own convictions and aspirations
came out only too clearly, for instance, when he tried to prove
to the Czechs that Hussitism had been really a striving toward
Orthodoxy.[225]

---

[221] Pogodin, op. cit., p. 23.
[222] Ibid., pp. 48–49.
[223] Ibid., pp. 41–42.
[224] As an example of such pronouncements see ibid., pp. 48–49.
[225] Pogodin, "Pri prazdnovanii pyatisotletnei godovshchiny Gusovoi, v sobranii

The entire miraculous history of Russia pointed to its great Messianic future.[226] Its late appearance on the world stage meant that time for a change of scenes had finally come. The long period of Russian historical growth and preparation promised all the more abundant results.[227] Indeed, Russia not only represented Slavdom in its striving for a place in the sun, but—in a typically romantic paradox—it stepped forth also as the champion of all mankind, for Russia was panhuman by its nature and could thus become the moral leader and the impartial judge of the strife-torn world. Only Russia could lead all the nations on earth to a true Christian enlightenment.[228]

Tyutchev shared to the full Pogodin's beliefs and hopes in regard to Russia and Slavdom. He developed his views in several articles and, more imaginatively, in many poems.[229] For instance, in verses addressed to the famous pioneer of Czech nationalism, Hanka, Tyutchev began by asking the crucial Pan-Slav question:

> *Must we always remain in separation?*
> *Is it not time for us to come to our senses*

Slavyanskogo Komiteta, v Moskve, 25 avgusta 1869 goda." (*Ibid.*, pp. 140–151.) Tyutchev held identical views: I. Aksakov, *op. cit.*, pp. 143–146; Tyutchev, pp. 348–349, and the poem "To the Czechs, on the Huss Anniversary," (*ibid.*, pp. 212–213). See also Petrovich, *The Emergence of Russian Panslavism, 1856–1870*, pp. 88–90.

[226] Pogodin delighted in emphasizing the "miraculous" and providential nature of Russian history. See, e.g., Pogodin, *Istoriko-kriticheskie otryvki*, pp. 10–14, 147–155; or Pogodin, *Rechi*, pp. 271–272, 274. He asserted that: "No other history contains in itself so much of the miraculous, if one may use this expression, as Russian history." (Pogodin, *Istoriko-kriticheskie otryvki*, p. 10.) And on another occasion, in a speech following a hearty dinner, Pogodin exclaimed: "Russia—a miracle! The Russian people—a miracle! The Russian language—a miracle! The Russian stove which bakes in its own manner—a miracle! Russian history—a miracle! . . . Let us review in our minds the last ten years; what miracles have occurred and are occurring in front of our eyes! how? what? wherefrom? for what reason? why? one cannot puzzle it out, cannot understand it, one can only gape at the marvel and cross oneself!" (Pogodin, *Rechi*, p. 272.)

[227] *Ibid.*, p. 10.

[228] *Ibid.*, pp. 38–41; see also Pogodin, *Istoriko-kriticheskie otryvki*, pp. 431–432; Pogodin, *Istoriko-politicheskie pisma*, pp. 11–13, 238–240; Pogodin *Stati politicheskie i polskii vopros* (1856–1867), pp. 272, 283. Cf. Shevyrev, "Vzglyad russkogo na sovremennoe obrazovanie Evropy," pp. 219–296; and Gogol's views on Russian Messiahship, Gogol, pp. 228–229.

[229] Tyutchev's "political" poetry was collected in Tyutchev, pp. 179–226.

> *And to extend our hands all around*
> *To our blood relatives and friends?* [230]

The poet went on to depict in darkest colors the tragic past and present of disunited Slavdom, and then turned to the epoch-making achievement of the man who "on the heights of Prague, with a modest hand, lighted a lighthouse in the darkness." [231]

> *Oh, what rays suddenly*
> *Illumined all the lands!*
> *The entire Slavic world*
> *Rose in front of us,*
>
> *A marvelous day began to shine*
> *On the mountains, the steppes and the sea littorals,*
> *From the Neva to Montenegro,*
> *From the Carpathians to beyond the Urals.*
>
> *Dawn is breaking over Warsaw,*
> *Kiev has opened its eyes,*
> *And Vyšehrad has started to converse*
> *With the golden-domed Moscow.*
>
> *And the sounds of fraternal dialects*
> *Have again become understandable to us.*
> *The grandsons will witness the realization*
> *Of that which the fathers saw in their dreams!* [232]

Again, in a poem "To the Slavs" Tyutchev declared:

> *Even though by a hostile fate*
> *We are separated,*
> *We are still one people,*
> *Sons of a single mother;*
> *We are still blood brothers . . .*
> *This is what, this is what they hate in us:*

---

[230] *Ibid.*, p. 187.
[231] *Ibid.*
[232] *Ibid.*, pp. 187–188.

> To you they cannot forgive Russia,
> To Russia—they cannot forgive you!
>
> They are worried, to the point of fear,
> That the entire Slavic family,
> Facing both enemy and friend,
> Will declare for the first time:—this is I! . . .
>
> He is alive—Supreme Providence,
> And His judgment has not been exhausted . . .
> And the word "Tsar-Liberator"
> Will move beyond the Russian border! . . .[233]

Tyutchev's belief in Russian and Slavic destiny had strong mystical overtones:

> It is not the noise of a rumor spreading among the people,
> It is not news born in our family—
> It is an ancient voice, a voice from above:
> "The fourth age is already at its termination,—
> It will be completed, and then the hour will strike!"
> And the vaults of ancient Sophia
> In resurrected Byzantium
> Will again shelter the altar of Christ.
> Throw yourself down in front of it, oh, tsar of Russia,
> And rise as the tsar of all the Slavs! [234]

The result of this transformation staggered one's imagination, as Tyutchev emphasized in another poem, "Russian Geography":

> Moscow, and the city of Peter, and the city of Constantine—
> These are the sacred capitals of Russian tsardom . . .
> But where is its end? and where are its borders
> To the North, to the East, to the South and toward sunset?
> They will be revealed by the fates to future times . . .
>
> Seven internal seas and seven great rivers! . . .
> From the Nile to the Neva, from the Elbe to China—

[233] Ibid., pp. 207–208.
[234] Ibid., p. 191.

From the Volga to the Euphrates, from the Ganges to the
Danube . . .
This is Russian tsardom . . . and it will not disappear with the
ages
As the Holy Spirit foresaw and Daniel foretold.[235]

The Polish question upset the calculations and challenged the
most cherished beliefs of the Russian Pan-Slavs. The inclusion
of a large part of this Western Slavic people in the realm of
the Russian tsar resulted not in the blessed fulfillment of a
brotherly union, but in the most bitter antagonism and strife.
Something had definitely gone wrong. Pogodin tried, with pain
and passion, to resolve this tragic problem.[236] He explained again
and again that the great hostility between the two neighbors came
from a misunderstanding, that they had a joint historical destiny,
that the intrigues of their common enemies who feared their
linked strength were largely responsible for their fratricidal struggle. Pogodin admired the patriotism of the Poles, and he also
regarded them as an extremely gifted people. He urged that they
be given every consideration by the Russian government, although
this applied only to ethnic Poland proper, while the so-called
"Western region" where the Poles constituted merely an upper-
class minority was to be treated as an integral part of the Russian
nation. Alternatively, as Pogodin saw that the Poles would not
listen to his appeal, he suggested independence for Poland. Only
after the unsuccessful Polish rebellion of 1863 did Pogodin become
completely disappointed in the Poles and accept the official
government view which required firm and oppressive control of
Poland on grounds of Russian national interest.[237] He also found
an explanation for the failure of this experiment in brotherhood:

[235] *Ibid.*, p. 190. The last two selections represent interesting poetic examples
of the theme of "Moscow, the Third Rome." Tyutchev believed in the destiny
of Russia as the new universal empire, the heir of Rome and Byzantium.
[236] See especially Pogodin, *Stati politicheskie i polskii vopros* (1856–1867).
Pogodin also discussed the Polish question frequently in his writings on the
Slavs in general, and less often in other works.
[237] On the impact of the rebellion of 1863 on the Russian Pan-Slavs, notably
on Pogodin, see Petrovich, "Russian Pan-Slavists and the Polish Uprising of
1863," *Harvard Slavic Studies*, I, 219–247, as well as Petrovich, *The Emergence
of Russian Panslavism, 1856–1870.* Professor Petrovich draws a number of distinctions which I could not include within the scope of a single paragraph.

the Polish gentry which dominated the land was alien, probably Celtic, rather than Slavic. These prehistoric invaders never became mixed with the conquered Slavic masses, always retaining their contempt for and their separateness from them. And, unfortunately, these foreigners, with their undying hatred of Slavic Russia, directed the policies of Poland throughout her history.[238] Tyutchev's attitude toward the Poles paralleled closely that of Pogodin, being characterized by the same personal involvement, hope, and grief.[239]

The ambitious program of the romantic nationalists promised struggle and war, but they accepted willingly, even eagerly, this inevitable development. They could afford to do so because they were convinced that Russia, especially Russia together with the other Slavs, was invincible. In the case of Russia, the way could be discerned clearly by every thinking person, only the will was still lacking. As Pogodin suggested in 1838 to the heir to the throne:

Let us now compare the forces of Europe with the forces of Russia which we have already discussed, and let us ask what is impossible for the Russian monarch.

One word—an entire empire does not exist; one word—another empire is wiped off the face of the earth; a word—and instead of them a third one appears from the Eastern Ocean to the Adriatic Sea . . .

It is known that our present monarch, your august father, does not think about any conquests, about any acquisitions. But I cannot, I dare not omit to remark as a historian that the Russian tsar now, without plans, without wishes, without preparations, without stratagems, calm in his study in Tsarskoe Selo, is closer than Charles V and Napoleon to their dream of a universal monarchy, a dream which they entertained at the height of their glory, after thirty years of efforts, deeds, and successes.[240]

---

[238] Pogodin, *op. cit.*, pp. 330, 473–474, 528–529.
[239] See especially his poem "On the Capture of Warsaw. August 26, 1831": Tyutchev, pp. 183–184.
[240] Pogodin, *Istoriko-politicheskie pisma*, pp. 10–11. The empires in question are the Turkish, the Austrian, and the Russian Pan-Slav empire of the future.

Or, as Pogodin argued on another occasion, emphasizing that in 1812 Russia had defeated "all of Europe": "Having repulsed victoriously such an attack, having liberated Europe from such an enemy, having brought him down from such a height, possessing such resources, not dependent on anyone and necessary for all, can Russia fear anything? Who will dare contest her preëminence, who will prevent her from deciding the fate of Europe and of the entire humanity, if only she would so desire?" [241]

The overwhelming might of Russia confronted a shattered, declining, and, indeed, dying West. Pogodin loved to draw general sketches of Western weakness and collapse as pendants to his enthusiastic depiction of the collossal power of his native land.[242] Shevyrev outdid his friend on the subject of the decline of the West, especially in the article in the first issue of *The Muscovite* where he declared:

Yes, in our sincere, friendly, close relations with the West we fail to notice that we are dealing, as it were, with a man who carries inside himself a vicious, contagious disease, who is surrounded by an aura of noxious exhalation. We exchange kisses, we exchange embraces with him, we share with him the meal of thought, we drink the cup of feeling . . . and we fail to notice the poison concealed in this carefree intercourse, we do not scent in the joy of the feast the future corpse which is already exuding an odor! [243]

It was the duty of the philosopher "to strike the bell of contemporary history" and to cry out again and again: "Europe is dying!" [244]

---

[241] Pogodin, *Istoriko-kriticheskie otryvki*, pp. 3–4.

[242] See, e.g., Pogodin, *Istoriko-politicheskie pisma*, pp. 7–9. In his play, "Peter I," Pogodin made the great emperor speak as a Pan-Slav drunk with Russian power and the weakness of the West; Pogodin, *Petr I*, pp. 125–127.

[243] Shevyrev, "Vzglyad russkogo na sovremennoe obrazovanie Evropy," especially p. 247. This remarkable passage may have given rise to the expression "putrefying (or putrid) West." See Struve, "S. P. Shevyrev i zapadnye vnusheniya i istochniki teorii-aforizma o 'gnilom' ili 'gniyushchem' Zapade," in *Zapiski Russkogo Nauchnogo Instituta v Belgrade*.

[244] Shevyrev, *op. cit.*, p. 245.

Shevyrev explained that the decay of the West began when Rome broke away from the universal church, continued with the Reformation and the French Revolution, and culminated in the general collapse of religion.[245] Tyutchev also proclaimed the contest between Christianity and atheism to be the main issue of the day. The decision in this struggle between Orthodox Russia and the godless West could not remain in doubt, the poet welcoming the explosive events of 1848 as the blessed consummation, as the unmistakable call for Russia to assume her true place in the world:

And when has this mission been more clear and more obvious? One can say that God has written it in letters of fire on this sky all darkened by storms. The West is disappearing, everything is toppling down, everything is being destroyed in a general conflagration: the Europe of Charles the Great and the Europe of the treaties of 1815; Roman Papacy and all the royal houses of the West; Catholicism and Protestantism; faith long since extinct and reason reduced to absurdity; order henceforth impossible, liberty henceforth impossible; and on all these ruins of its own making civilization committing suicide by its own hand. . . .

And when we see emerging from this immense deluge this empire, as if it were the Holy Ark, still more immense, who can then doubt its mission, and should it be for us, its children, to display skepticism and cowardice? [246]

Although the nationalistic proponents of Official Nationality emphasized the fundamental dichotomy and antagonism between Russia and the West, their attitude toward individual European countries showed extensive variation. They saw two immediate and supreme enemies: Turkey and Austria. The first did not even belong, properly speaking, to the West, although it enjoyed Western protection and sponsorship. Turkish tyranny over the

---

[245] This analysis of the decline of the West was identical with that of the Slavophiles. See N. Riasanovsky, *Russia and the West in the Teaching of the Slavophiles.*

[246] These were the concluding paragraphs of Tyutchev's well-known article "Russia and Revolution," Tyutchev, p. 351.

victimized Slavic subjects reflected all the primitive brutality and
viciousness of these Asiatic invaders. It could never be justified
in the eyes of God or man. But the rule of the Austrians over
their millions of Slavs was no less despotic and inhuman, if
somewhat better camouflaged. The Austrians represented the
Germanic element which had been waging war against Slavdom
for many centuries; and they aimed once more to deprive their
neighbors and rivals of all national and racial identity. While
Turkey specialized in the mutilation of Slavic bodies, Austria
directed its endeavors toward the destruction of the Slavic soul.
It was Austria, therefore, which Pogodin hated with an almost
pathological hatred, that repeatedly found its way, in and out of
turn, into his diverse writings. He was convinced that: "Russia
has no enemy as bitter as Austria. We can make a business deal
with England, we can reach an agreement with France; with the
Austrians the only possible settlement is through combat, that is,
through death." [247] In addition to the Austrian Germans, the
Hapsburg state contained another mortal foe:

> This enemy is Hungary, I mean Magyar Hungary. Of all the
> enemies of Russia this is perhaps the one that hates her with the
> most furious hatred. The Magyar people—in which revolutionary
> fervor has come to be joined in a most strange combination to
> the brutality of an Asiatic horde and about which it can be said
> as much as about the Turks that it is merely camping in Europe
> —lives surrounded by Slavic peoples which are all equally odious
> to it. [248]

Prussia was not at the time as violently anti-Russian as Austria,
but potentially it represented a more formidable antagonist for
it served as the greatest concentration of the German element.
As Pogodin explained the matter: "For Austria, Russia is the
danger; for Russia, the danger is Prussia which has more strength,
spirit, education." [249]

Because the Germanic neighbors were the mortal enemies of

[247] Pogodin, *Istoriko-politicheskie pisma*, p. 224.
[248] Tyutchev, p. 350. Pogodin, on his part, also noted the hostility of the
Magyars, but he thought little of their prowess. Pogodin, *op. cit.*, p. 52.
[249] *Ibid.*, p. 56.

Russia, France could be enlisted as the natural ally of the great
Slavic state. Pogodin kept speculating throughout his life as to
the course European history would have taken had Russia made
a deal with Napoleon after smashing his invasion in 1812; he
deplored the German orientation of the Russian government;
and he kept advocating a change in Russian diplomacy, a change
which did occur some fifteen years after his death with the Franco-
Russian alliance of the early 1890's.[250] England, on the other
hand, was more of an enemy than a friend as far as the radical
Russian nationalists were concerned. Pogodin and his associates
had much admiration for Great Britain, and to some extent their
attitude toward that strange island country always remained
ambivalent, but in general they placed it in the hostile camp.
They objected in particular to the English support of Turkey; to
the fact that Great Britain had enjoyed an enormous imperial
expansion, yet would not recognize the legitimate interests of
Russia; to the alleged crass materialism of the English and their
single-minded worship of gold.[251] Partly because they considered
it a counterweight to England, they often spoke and wrote kindly
of the United States.[252]

Russian nationalists were consistent enough to affirm the rights
of nationalities other than their own. Pogodin even declared that
he wished well "to every European nationality without distinction:

[250] Pogodin stated his views on France and on other countries on many different occasions. See in particular Pogodin, *Stati politicheskie i polskii vopros*
(1856–1867); and Pogodin, *Istoriko-politicheskie pisma.* In contrast to the
official attitude, there apparently existed in Russia at the time of Nicholas I a
strong popular sentiment favoring an alliance with France. Schiemann, IV, 21–
22.

[251] In one of his earliest works, Pogodin had already come to the conclusion
that in England everything was done by means of and for the sake of gold.
Pogodin, *Historische Aphorismen*, p. 29. Later he criticized Khomyakov, the
Slavophile, for praising England, as well as for blaming France, to excess.
Pogodin, "Neskolko slov po povodu pisma g. Khomyakova ob Anglii," *Moskvityanin*, VI (1848), no. 11, Scholarship, pp. 1–10. Cf. Zhukovskii's essay
on "Russian and English Policies." Zhukovskii, *op. cit.*, pp. 174–178.

[252] See especially Pogodin, "Rech, proiznesennaya v Dume, na obede, v chest
amerikanskogo posolstva," *Rechi*, pp. 262–264; and Pogodin, *Istoriko-
politicheskie pisma*, pp. 233–234. For a more critical view of the United States
emphasizing the lack of respect for authority in that country, see "Vzglyad na
Severo-Amerikanskie Soedinennye Shtaty," *Syn Otechestva*, CLXXX (1836),
172–192.

German, French, Italian, Slavic, Greek, Wallachian, Scandinavian, and so on, and so forth." [253] He, as well as Shevyrev, extended special sympathy to Italy and Italian unification, Pogodin proclaiming on one occasion: "A sincere, pure, full sympathy to the fate of Italy, a passionate, unqualified wish that she would become free as soon as possible from the alien, hated yoke, and that she would receive the independence which belongs to her according to all the rights, that she would receive the opportunity to develop unhindered her mighty strength, to advance along the road of success, and to utilize all the gifts with which nature has so richly endowed her." [254] The Moscow professor liked to ask such blunt questions as: "And if in Italy, Italy will dominate, rather than Austria or France, will that not be more lawful and more just?" [255]

But, in a typical nationalist contradiction, Pogodin and his friends came out against the independence of those nationalities which lived within the Russian Empire. We have already seen their attitude toward the Estonians and the Latvians as well as in the much more complicated case of Poland. Similarly, Pogodin refused to recognize the Ukrainians and the Lithuanians as separate peoples. The Ukrainians were so much like the Great Russians and so closely associated with them throughout history that the two could not be cleft asunder.[256] The Lithuanians were simply too weak to exist independently and had, therefore, to join the Russian state.[257]

It is noteworthy that Pogodin identified himself not only with the Russian people and with Slavdom, but also with the so-called white race, or, as he often put it, "the tribe of Japheth." As a young man he had already come to the conclusion that: "It is impossible

---

[253] Pogodin, *Stati politicheskie i polskii vopros* (1856–1867), p. 66.

[254] *Ibid.*, p. 64.

[255] Pogodin, *Istoriko-politicheskie pisma*, p. 114. Pogodin discussed Italy many times, devoting to it a number of special articles, e.g., "The Italian Question," "Good Wishes to Italy," and a clumsy, but sincere, eulogy, "In Memory of Cavour." Pogodin, *Stati politicheskie i polskii vopros* (1856–1867), pp. 44–67, 116–123, 124–127.

[256] *Ibid.*, pp. 385–388.

[257] *Ibid.*, pp. 374–375. However, although an ardent nationalist, Pogodin believed that at some future date a world federation would be established, the Holy Alliance and the international congresses of the early nineteenth century serving as its precursors. See, for instance, p. 109 (*ibid.*).

to educate Africa and Asia, except by fitting out an army from all of Europe and sending it on a crusade against them. Let Europeans occupy the thrones of the Ashantis, the Burmese, the Chinese, the Japanese, and let them establish there a European order of things. Then the fate of those countries will be decided. And why should this not be done? . . . The happiness of mankind depends on it." [258]

Pogodin held this belief steadfastly throughout his life, reacting to various political developments in terms of his basic conviction. Highly characteristic was his response to the news of the Sepoy Mutiny. Pogodin explained that the first reports of the rebellion evoked joy in Russia, a fact easily understandable in the light of all the damage and injury done to Russia by England in the immediately preceding years. A certain countess even promised to make a pilgrimage to the Holy Trinity Monastery on foot, just so the English would be made to suffer more. But, once detailed information from India reached Russia:

. . . we forgot immediately that the English were our enemies, and saw in them only Europeans, Christians, sufferers; we saw in them an educated people which is threatened by barbarians— and a general compassion, a general sympathy expressed itself everywhere.[259]

From the point of view of humanity, as Europeans, as Christians, as an educated people, we wish success to the English, we wish that they would establish firmly their rule in India, and that they would extend it, as far as they can, in Asia, in Africa, and in America. We wish that the other European nations would succeed in exactly the same manner and would gain footholds more and more powerfully in the other continents which must take to their bosoms, in the form of numerous well-organized colonies, the overflow of European population, and thus rescue old Europe from the troubles, worries, and dangers which are caused by crowding, by pauperism, and by the proletariat. Shem

---

[258] Barsukov, *op. cit.*, II, 17.
[259] Pogodin, *op. cit.*, p. 16.

and Ham, according to the word of the Scripture, must bow to Japheth.[260]

Several years later, commenting on world politics, Pogodin declared: "To establish European influence in Africa—this is a success for enlightenment; and I shall be glad to see Spain acquire Fez and Morocco, France Tunis and Tripoli, and England Sahara for that matter, where she will most likely find ways to create plantations." [261] At the same time that Pogodin urged a European conquest of the world, he stressed the duties and the responsibilities of this white man's burden: government in colonial areas had to be guided by the true interests of the natives, not by motives of economic exploitation, as had too often been the case.[262]

Russian imperial interests lay in Asia. Pogodin made that point in his usual blunt and direct manner: "Let the European peoples live as they best know how, and manage in their lands as they please; whereas to us belongs, in addition, half of Asia, China, Japan, Tibet, Bokhara, Khiva, Kokand, Persia, if we want to, and perhaps must, extend our possessions to spread the European element in Asia, so that Japheth may rise above his brothers." [263]

The far-reaching ambitions of the romantic nationalists stood in sharp contrast to the thinking of Nicholas I and of his government on international affairs and to their foreign policy, which will be discussed in the fifth chapter. That policy was based on the legitimist principles of Paul I which found further development and expression in the reign of Alexander I, contributing to the creation of the Holy Alliance as well as of the Quadruple, and the later Quintuple, alliances and the series of international congresses which these alliances produced. Nicholas I was determined to follow in the footsteps of his brother. When the widening gulf between the eastern and the western European

---

[260] *Ibid.*, p. 21.
[261] *Ibid.*, p. 92.
[262] See, e.g., Pogodin's further discussion of the matter in the two instances just cited.
[263] Pogodin, *Istoriko-politicheskie pisma*, pp. 243–244.

powers made joint action impossible, the Russian emperor unhesitatingly took his stand with Austria and Prussia in defense of the Vienna settlement and the *status quo*. The nationalist aspirations and plans of Pogodin and his friends challenged at almost every point the dynastic, legitimist orientation of Nicholas I and of his associates. For instance, while the romantic nationalists proclaimed the Germans to be the mortal enemies of their country and race, the monarch had, as we have seen, the closest and friendliest ties with these Germans, especially with the Prussians. Indeed, when in 1817 he had welcomed his bride, the Prussian princess, across the Russian border and reviewed on that occasion her military escort, he had proclaimed: "My friends, remember that I am one half your countryman, and that I am a member, as you are, of the army of your king." [264] Nicholas retained his attachment to Prussia throughout his life, and he remained a friend of Austria until the very last years of his reign and the tragic diplomatic crisis leading to the Crimean War.[265] Loyal journalists echoed the same sentiments. Bulgarin, for example, contended that the presence of Germans near them and among them had exercised a great beneficial influence on the Slavs, for the Germans built cities, developed commerce and crafts, and taught the Slavs the virtues of exactitude, economy, moderation, cleanliness, and order.[266] The writings of Grech similarly contained outspoken praise of the Germans, especially the Prussians, and of German culture.[267]

Pan-Slavism also served to divide the nationalistic from the

---

[264] Schilder, I, 85.

[265] It may be noted that Nicholas I liked Tyutchev's essay "Russia and Germany" with its emphasis on Russian beneficence toward Germany and the absolute necessity for Germany to be friendly to Russia, but he disapproved of other political writings of the poet. Tyutchev, p. 16; Stremoukhov, *La Poésie et l'idéologie de Tiouttchev*, pp. 134–136; I. Aksakov, *op. cit.*, p. 31 and n. Pogodin's prayer was that Germany might become, at last, repugnant to the emperor "as she has become to all of us, his loyal subjects." Pogodin, *op. cit.*, p. 205.

[266] Bulgarin, *Vospominaniya*, VI, 267–271. By contrast, Shevyrev argued that the Germans passed only vicious customs to the Slavs. Shevyrev, *Ob otnoshenii semeinogo vospitaniya k gosudarstvennomu.*

[267] See, e.g., Grech, *Sochineniya*, III, 86–107. See also Uvarov, *L'Empereur Alexandre et Buonaparte*, pp. 24–25.

dynastically minded proponents of Official Nationality. Although Uvarov promoted Slavic studies and patronized Pogodin and some other nationalistic professors, he never accepted their program of active support for the national awakening of various Slavic peoples.[268] In fact, in 1847, following the discovery and destruction of a radical Ukrainian group of Pan-Slavs known as the Brotherhood of Cyril and Methodius, Pan-Slavism was officially branded a false and dangerous teaching. Uvarov explained this decision to a special meeting of the faculty of the University of St. Petersburg and also in a ministerial circular. He admitted the cultural value of Slavic studies, then continued:

But this Russian Slavism must keep apart from any admixture of political ideas. Then the remaining principle, hidden in its depth, will be our state principle, on which throne and altar are firmly grounded, our properly Russian principle, the Russian spirit, our sacred treasure. . . . Holy Russia lived through distress and suffered alone; alone she shed her blood for the Throne and for the Faith; alone she advanced with a firm and rapid step on the course of her civic development; alone she rose to fight the twenty nations which invaded her borders with fire and sword in their hands. Everything that we have in Russia belongs to us alone, without the participation of other Slavic peoples who now stretch their hands toward us and beg for protection, not so much from an inspiration of brotherly love as from the calculations of a petty and not always disinterested egoism. . . .

Is not the name of the Russian more glorious for us, that famous name of ours which, since the foundation of our state, has been repeated and is being repeated by millions of people in their social life? Let the name of the Russian be heard in the uni-

---

[268] After his visits abroad, especially to Slavic lands, in 1839 and again in 1842, Pogodin presented to Uvarov reports about his voyages which included detailed plans for influencing world public opinion favorably for Russia, for helping Slavic scholars and cultural undertakings, and the like. A summary of the first report reached the emperor, who rewarded Pogodin with a gift of money, but none of the recommendations were translated into action. The second report remained in the ministry "because of too sharp a disagreement with the general opinion." Pogodin, *op. cit.*, pp. 15–69, quoted from p. 69. Barsukov, *op. cit.*, V, 395.

versities as it is heard among the Russian people which, without
any cunning philosophizing, without the imagined Slavdom, has
retained the faith of our fathers, the language, the ways, the
customs, the entire nationality. . . .[269]

Nicholas I demonstrated more forcefulness than his minister
in condemning Pan-Slavism. For instance, he penned the following comment on the dossier of Ivan Aksakov, the noted Slavophile
and Pan-Slav who had just been arrested because of some sharp
criticism of the Russian system found in his correspondence:

Under the guise of a sympathy for the Slavic tribes supposedly
oppressed in other states there is hidden the criminal thought of
a union with these tribes, in spite of the fact that they are subjects
of neighboring and in part allied states. And they expected to
attain this goal not through the will of God, but by means
of rebellious outbreaks to the detriment and destruction of Russia
herself. . . . And if, indeed, a combination of circumstances
produces such a union, this will mean the ruin of Russia.[270]

The differences between the two groups kept increasing during
the thirty years of Nicholas I's reign. As liberalism advanced and
revolutions surged through Europe, those who thought in dynastic
and legitimist terms became ever more pessimistic and ever more
on the defensive. Their one remaining purpose was to protect the
status quo, to hold the line, with a determination born of despair.
But the nationalists looked at the world in quite a different
manner. Excitement, optimism, and hope served them as daily
bread. They welcomed the age of gigantic, "tribal," wars.[271] They

---

[269] Barsukov, *op. cit.*, IX, 235–237. Italics in the original. Nikitenko summarized the meaning of Uvarov's words as follows: "Our nationality consists in
a boundless devotion and obedience to autocracy, while western Slavdom
must not excite in us any sympathy. It has its own way, and we have our way.
We hereby most solemnly abjure it. Besides, it does not deserve our sympathy,
because we established our state without it, without it suffered and rose to
greatness, whereas it remained always dependent on others, could not create
anything, and has now finished its historical existence." Nikitenko, I, 373. See
also Uvarov's report to the emperor on the Brotherhood published in French
in Luciani, trans., *Le Livre de la Genèse du peuple ukrainien*, pp. 74–80.
[270] Barsukov, *op. cit.*, IX, 279. Passage italicized in the original.
[271] See, e.g., Pogodin, *Stati politicheskie i polskii vopros* (1856–1867), p. 309.

demanded an aggressive and sweeping foreign policy suitable to the occasion instead of what they considered to be timid, puny, and trifling measures of their government. The two groups were reacting to the same development, the death of the old and the coming of the new order in Europe, but their reactions were diametrically opposed.

The Crimean War marked the climax. Pogodin and his friends saw it as the long-expected Armageddon. Government policy had proved its utter and complete bankruptcy, leaving Russia without a single ally against a mighty coalition; new and radical measures were clearly in order. The nationalists thirsted for war, Pogodin even praying that another country, Austria, might join the ranks of the enemies—"For I am convinced that as long as Austria is not against us, God is not as yet with us." [272] Russian objectives left no room for vacillation or compromise. They had to include, according to Pogodin, a complete destruction of the Turkish Empire, the liberation of the Slavs, and the formation of a great Slavic federation headed by Russia with the capital in Constantinople. In particular, there could be no turning back on the issue of the Slavs:

We came to the Danube and we stood there for a long time; we could not make the decision to cross.—But then, finally, someone pushed us in the neck and, willy-nilly, we crossed to the other side. . . .

And on the other side, look, people run to meet us, with bread and salt, with crosses and holy water. There a bell struck which has not been heard for four hundred years, the first ringing for a church service sounded, the first cross rose over an Othodox church. Well then? Will you allow this cross to be taken down? Well then? Will you allow the tongue to be torn out of this bell? No, this cannot be and this will not be.[273]

Love of man, kinship, community of faith, gratitude combine with our own present historical and political necessity to wage a war against Turkey, to which this discourse of mine is dedicated.

---

[272] Pogodin, *Istoriko-politicheskie pisma*, p. 118.
[273] *Ibid.*, p. 115.

*Tell me then, all of you who have even a drop of warm blood,
in whom a human heart beats—all of you who were born in pain
out of the wombs of your mothers—Hottentots, Eskimos, Pat-
agonians, diplomats, politicians, what war can be more honorable,
more humane, more holy! Forward! God is with us! . . .*

*Here is our purpose—Russian, Slavic, European, Christian!
As Russians, we must capture Constantinople for our own
security.*

*As Slavs, we must liberate millions of our older kinsmen,
brothers in faith, educators and benefactors.*

As Europeans, we must drive out the Turks.

*As Orthodox Christians, we must protect the Eastern church
and return to Saint Sophia its ecumenical cross.*[274]

The magnitude and the importance of the war called for an
all-out effort. Pogodin demanded that Russia should reverse her
policy completely and proclaim herself the champion of nationalism and freedom in Europe. "Start an uprising in Turkey, in
Austria, in Greece, in Poland—and Italy will rise herself, perhaps
also France: you wanted war—well, here it is for you. . . . The
choice, it seems, is not a difficult one; to have all of Europe
against us, or set one half of it against the other?" [275]

Russia had to make a clean break with her recent diplomatic
past.

*Hurry your flight, then, Napier's bomb: we need a signal to
move to new quarters, to exchange northern swamps for that land
where oranges bloom and platans rustle. Come, Napier's bomb
—you will probably fall, according to the law of Nemesis, on the
ministry of foreign affairs! How we shall be grateful to you! Burn
with your burning fire which the English have lighted in hell,
burn all our notes including the Vienna one, all the protocols,
declarations, confidential accounts, conventions, instructions, reports, and all our political relations with Europe! Let everything
be burned with fire! Qui perd gagne!* [276]

---

[274] *Ibid.*, pp. 186–187.
[275] *Ibid.*, p. 200; see also p. 336.
[276] *Ibid.*, p. 191. To quote another, and perhaps still more striking, example

Internally too the country had to be mobilized for the supreme struggle. Pogodin insisted that the government, especially the emperor, had to speak to the people plainly and directly, to inspire everyone to full participation in this decisive war for Russia and Slavdom. The tsar, in turn, was to listen to the voice of the people, in the form of a *zemskii sobor*, or otherwise. Court expenses were to be cut in half; others, especially the rich and the famous, were to make similar sacrifices; all festivals, entertainment, gaiety were to be postponed for the duration; Russians were to give up buying foreign imports, "so that not a foot would be set in foreign stores." [277] "Let us embrace privations and need, even hunger and cold, for a period of two or three years; let us be patient through all; let us suffer, work, serve, wherever one fits best, wherever one understands most, as long as one has the strength." [278]

It was to be a total war to the bitter end.

V

The doctrine of Official Nationality reflected faithfully much of Russian, and also of general European history. It represented, in its foundation, the ideology of the dynastic *anciens régimes* which ruled most of Europe for several centuries. In the case of Russia, however, this system had a definite point of origin in the reforms

---

of Pogodin's passionate emotional involvement in the Crimean War: "Consequently, they threaten not only Kronstadt and Sevastopol: they must be expected everywhere—in the church and in the bedroom, when teaching and when praying, at dinner and at supper, in the temple and in the pit of the stomach, over the head and in the heart, at noon and at midnight, on weekdays and on Christ's Holy Sunday." *Ibid.*, p. 109.

[277] *Ibid.*, pp. 314–340, quoted from p. 335.

[278] *Ibid.*, p. 335. The attitude of the government toward Pogodin's demands can be best seen from its policy which completely failed to implement them. There were, however, also some written statements of the official point of view. Most interesting is Nesselrode's defense of the ministry of foreign affairs against Pogodin's attack: "Zashchita politiki Rossii i polozheniya, prinyatogo eyu v Evrope," published as an appendix to Pogodin, *op. cit.*, (French original on pp. 3–10, and a Russian translation on pp. 10–16). For Nicholas I's reaction to Pogodin's writings about the Crimean War, see Barsukov, *op. cit.*, XIII, 117–118. Although Pogodin's violent attacks on government policy could not be published at the time, they were copied and received considerable circulation.

of Peter the Great. Hence the unmeasured glorification of the famous monarch by Nicholas I and his followers, the glorification that stopped short only of deifying Peter. The eighteenth-century legacy of enlightened despotism played a cardinal role in the dogma of Official Nationality. The ruler always knew best, and he directed his superior wisdom to the endless and thankless task of running the state in the true interests of his subjects. Everyone else, regardless of rank or function, had to serve the same common purpose with complete obedience and dedication. The Age of Reason also contributed to Nicholas's regime a certain pragmatic emphasis, a distrust of philosophic systems, a belief in the rational approach to the business of government, a passion for organization, clarity and precision, and the cosmopolitan element so well exemplified by the French-speaking Russian court with its multinational background.

While the eighteenth century provided one of the two basic components of the doctrine of Official Nationality, the other was produced by the first decades of the nineteenth century, the period of restoration, reaction, and romanticism. Indeed, the teaching of Nicholas I, Uvarov, and their underlings can be fairly considered as the Russian version of the European reaction against the French Revolution and Napoleon. Legitimacy, tradition, and order set out to combat revolution, change, and chaos. Religion acquired new importance as the chief bulwark of the established system threatened by critical intellect and radical passion. In Russia this meant a new glorification of Orthodoxy, the first item in the official trinity, just as in France it signified a return to Roman Catholicism. An attack on reason and individualism, and a historical cult emphasizing the uniqueness and sacredness of native institutions were also brought forth as underpinnings of the existing regime, in the autocratic empire of the tsars as much as elsewhere.

All these ideas and arguments were closely linked to the new cultural climate in Europe, the climate of romanticism. But that *Weltanschauung* had still more portentous gifts to offer, above all nationalism. Educated Russians developed a sensitive pride in their people and their country and a penchant for comparing favorably everything that was their own to everything foreign. Some of them, however, went much further and embraced the nationalist gospel of the German thinkers with its involved and cloudy philosophy and its racist and activist practical implications. Between those who used certain romantic doctrines to support the existing order and those who were willing to follow romantic nationalism wherever its dizzying flight might lead, there could be no compromise, in Russia or in other lands. Still, it took much time for this basic antagonism within European society to reveal itself to its full extent, and more time for that society to reach the end of the long and eventful journey from Metternich to Hitler.

Official Nationality formed, thus, part and parcel of the general European evolution, a point illustrated in a striking and enlightening manner by a summary consideration of the relationship between its proponents and other European intellectuals. In brief, the Russian doctrine represented, as indicated above, a provincial branch of the continent-wide reaction to the eighteenth century, French revolution, and Napoleon. Russian thought participated in the joint struggle against the new France, her ideas and her legacy, just as did the Russian government and the Russian army. The common nature of the enterprise implied close relationship and coöperation on the intellectual as well as on the military and political fronts. Furthermore, while in practice the Russian role in defeating Napoleon and after that in maintaining the *status quo* was second to none, in the realm of theory the Russian product suffered by comparison with the works of the brilliant reactionaries who wrote in French and of the indefatigable German nationalist professors. The West possessed a richer cultural heritage, a greater abundance and variety of writings in political theory and political philosophy, and more freedom of expression. It was, therefore, natural for the ideologists of the Russia of Nicholas I to learn and borrow from other lands, following in the footsteps of their more liberal eighteenth-century ancestors.

The cosmopolitan upbringing of the Russian educated class made this task of acquisition direct and relatively simple. The

Russian intellectuals of the time usually knew French fluently, German very well, and they often enjoyed some competence in other European languages. They established and maintained contacts with Western thinkers, traveled widely in "Europe," and followed with perseverance and passion its political and cultural development. It is also worth noting that none of the proponents of Russian state doctrine demonstrated much originality or creative ability as ideologists, thus failing to win for that school the relatively independent and important position within European romanticism which belonged, for instance, to the Slavophiles. The end result was that the teaching of Official Nationality both formed an integral part of the European cultural climate of the period and leaned very heavily on reactionary and romantic thought in other lands, this dependence being equally evident in its general outline and in numerous particulars.

Uvarov, the gifted minister of education and creator of the official doctrine, offers an excellent illustration of this relationship between Russia and the West. His fine education, his facile, inquisitive, and impressionable intellect, and his many prominent acquaintances in a variety of countries, made him a full and eager participant in the intellectual and ideological life of the continent. Uvarov wrote usually in French or in German, and while his contemporaries, as well as subsequent critics, questioned his Russian style and his acquaintance with native authors,[279] his knowledge of western European—especially French and German—literature and scholarship, was apparent to all. The Russian aristocrat cherished his contacts with foreign luminaries, in particular with Goethe, to whom he dedicated his book about a Greek poet and about whom he delivered a presidential address at the Imperial Academy of Sciences.[280] Uvarov experienced, as has already been indicated, the strong impact of liberalism associated with the French Revolution and Napoleon as well as with the

---

[279] See, e.g., Barsukov, op. cit., VI, 42, as well as S. Soloviev's bitter estimate reproduced in chap. ii above.
[280] The book was Uvarov, Nonnos von Panopolis der Dichter. Eine Beytrag zur Geschichte der Griechischen Poesie. The dedication is to be found on pp. iii–iv. Uvarov's speech, "Notice sur Goethe," was published in his Études de philologie et de critique, pp. 357–374.

wars of liberation against that mighty conqueror. His evolution
into a theoretician of reaction and of the state reflected the
general intellectual development of Europe, a development in
which such different figures as Wordsworth and Metternich
participated, and it was very strongly influenced by many Western
romanticists. The same or similar influences can be easily detected
in Uvarov's more scholarly works, whether they deal with the
classical world or with Asiatic cultures. Of the leaders of reactionary thought, Uvarov knew best De Maistre, who spent the
years from 1803 to 1817 in Russia as ambassador from the House
of Savoy. There remains correspondence between the two for the
years 1810–1814, with De Maistre commenting on several of
Uvarov's pieces and Uvarov discussing the ambassador's *Essai sur
l'origine divine des constitutions*. It is noteworthy that De Maistre
considered his younger Russian acquaintance to be a man of
exceptional ability, perception, and promise who unfortunately
did not have the strength of character to develop fully his basic
convictions and was much too prone to vacillation and compromise.[281] Uvarov also knew the thought of other theoreticians of
the Right, ranging from Chateaubriand whom he admired and
to whom he referred prominently in his writings,[282] to secondary
figures like Louis Bautain, the author of such books as *Philosphie
des lois au point de vue chrétien*, published in 1830, and *Philosophie du christianisme*, published in 1835.[283] Works of a
number of leading German and British scholars guided Uvarov's
classical investigations, while his extravagant praise of the cultures
of Asia was borrowed from such giants of German romanticism

---

[281] See the discussion of Uvarov in chap. ii. The best and the fullest treatment
of the relationship between De Maistre and Uvarov is in Stepanov, *op. cit.*,
where the extant correspondence is reproduced. The best known of the letters
contains De Maistre's criticism of Uvarov's project of an Asiatic Academy and
can also be found in Uvarov, *op. cit.*, pp. 49–66.

[282] Uvarov, *L'Empereur Alexandre et Buonaparte*, p. 1.

[283] The well-informed Nikitenko noted, in 1834, in his diary: "In the third
issue of 'The Journal of the Ministry of Education' there was published an
article of a Strasbourg professor of philosophy, Bautain. He says that all
philosophies are nonsense, and that everything must be learned from the Gospel. The minister declared that all professors of philosophy and of the
disciplines related to it, in all our universities, must be directed by this article
in their teaching." Nikitenko, I, 244.

as Friedrich Schlegel and Herder who must also have influenced some of his other views.[284]

The case of Pogodin was very different from that of Uvarov. Of plebeian rather than aristocratic origin, Pogodin failed to acquire the minister's graceful manners and cosmopolitan polish, never learned any foreign language even approximately as well as his mother tongue, and left Russia for the first time only at the age of thirty-five. Yet, essentially, Pogodin experienced the influence of the West and reflected certain general currents of European thought as much as Uvarov. A reading of Pogodin's works will demonstrate the great range of the Moscow professor's acquaintance with the intellectual development of Europe and his passionate interest in it, an interest which included Proudhon as well as Hegel, Lamennais as well as Arndt, and Darwin as well as Byron and Walter Scott. Pogodin's first journey to the West was followed by others, the Russian historian indefatigably touring everywhere, learning all he could, and establishing contacts with numerous intellectuals. On his initial voyage, in addition to all other activities, Pogodin attended many lectures at the University of Berlin.[285] As already noted, Pogodin's special line of interest and contribution was his establishment of relationships with numerous Slavic scholars, in particular in the Austrian Empire. Also distinctive was his fondness for journalism and his prompt response throughout his life to a great variety of items appearing in the press of different European countries. As historian, Pogodin participated in the great revival of that field in the nineteenth century, profiting from the lectures of Ranke and

[284] Uvarov refers specifically to Schlegel's, *Ueber die Sprache und Weisheit der Indier*, Heidelberg, 1808, as by far the most remarkable work on India ever published, and to "the famous Herder" as the man who in his *Geist der hebraeischen Poesie* seized best the essence and the import of Hebrew literature. Uvarov, *Études de philologie et de critique*, p. 31 n. 2, and pp. 34–35. De Maistre criticized Uvarov bitterly for praising Herder, whom the Catholic reactionary considered "one of the most dangerous enemies of Christianity." Uvarov, *op. cit.*, p. 56. Stepanov believed that Uvarov obtained from Friedrich Schlegel, whom he met in 1808 in Vienna, the ideas that religion formed the center of the spiritual life of man, and that philosophy and poetry were aspects of religion, while mysteries and myths represented its core. Stepanov, *op. cit.*, p. 680.

[285] Barsukov provides a detailed account of these voyages as well as, in general, a tremendous wealth of material on Pogodin's interests and contacts.

Savigny, among others, and from the writings of numerous other Western scholars, such as Thierry and Guizot.[286] As thinker, he followed faithfully one of the main ideological currents of the age, romantic nationalism. Pogodin's youthful worship of Schelling, mentioned in the second chapter, blossomed into a lifelong devotion to the concepts of nation and national mission, a creed quite similar to that of many German professors. And, as in the case of those professors, this philosophy led to far-reaching and brutal political demands.

Shevyrev experienced much the same impact of the West as Pogodin, his basic orientation and many of his particular interests being very similar to his friend's. But he was the more philosophically and aesthetically inclined of the two, and he made a special effort to introduce Friedrich Schlegel's exposition of the history of poetry and Schelling's and Baader's philosophic doctrines to his Russian students and readers.[287] Shevyrev's works contain references to numerous Western contemporaries, ranging from the leading German and French authors, as well as such British writers as Carlyle, whose account of the French Revolution he endorsed,[288] to various little-known continental scholars and

---

[286] Pogodin spoke of Guizot "marking the beginning of a new age in historical science." Pogodin, Istoriko-kriticheskie otryvki, p. 422.

[287] In 1840 Shevyrev presented an account of Schelling's teaching in The Journal of the Ministry of Education. Shevyrev, "Izvlechenie iz pisem ministru narodnogo prosveshcheniya," Zhurnal Ministerstva Narodnogo Prosveshcheniya, 1840, part 1, sec. IV, pp. 1–14. See also, e.g., his reference to Schelling in Shevyrev, "Vzglyad russkogo na sovremennoe obrazovanie Evropy," p. 284. Shevyrev referred to Baader in terms of high praise in the same article (p. 286) and expounded his teaching at some length in Shevyrev, "Khristianskaya filosofiya. Besedy Baadera," Moskvityanin, 1841, no. 3, pp. 376–437. Shevyrev mentioned prominently his personal discussions with Schelling and Baader, those with Baader continuing for three months. It is interesting that Shevyrev used both Schelling and Baader to refute Hegel. See also Chizhevskii, Gegel v Rossii, pp. 228–230. Shevyrev published his defense of the Russian Orthodox Church, in the form of a letter, in Baader's well-known study, Der morgenlaendische und abendlaendische Katholicismus, "Aus Einem Schreiben des Herren Doctor und Professor Etienne de Chévireff in Moscau an den Verfasser d.d. 22 Februar 1840," (Baader, Gesammelte Schriften zur Religionsphilosophie, IV, 204–218). Shevyrev began his scholarly career by translating, with two friends, the study by Tieck and Wackenroder, Herzenergiessungen eines kunstliebenden Klosterbruders. Later he emphasized the historical approach in literary criticism.

[288] Shevyrev, "Vzglyad russkogo na sovremennoe obrazovanie Evropy," p. 242.

publicists. Shevyrev possessed a rare knowledge of Italian literature and thought, having spent several years in Italy as a young man and having returned to that country on later occasions.[289]

Tyutchev was another Russian nationalist intimately connected with the West and Western culture. After being graduated from the University of Moscow and joining the diplomatic corps as a youth, he spent much of his life abroad, chiefly in Munich where he resided for sixteen years in succession and for several more years intermittently, roughly from the age of nineteen to the age of forty. He was married twice; first to a Bavarian lady and, after her death, to an Alsatian one. Although a great Russian poet, Tyutchev wrote his political articles in French. At the time when the Tyutchevs lived and maintained a salon in Munich, that Bavarian city developed, under the patronage of Louis I, into an outstanding cultural and intellectual center. The new university contained such leading romanticists as Schelling, Baader, and Oken who affected Tyutchev profoundly and in a variety of ways—natural philosophy, nationalism, and different metaphysical, historical, and religious views all forming parts of this manifold influence.[290] The Russian poet enjoyed the favorable opinion of Schelling, the friendship of Heine, and the acquaintance of a number of other important intellectuals, including the Byzantine scholar Fallmerayer who emphasized the significance of the Slavs in the Balkan peninsula and predicted a great future for them.[291] Indeed, it has been suggested that even Tyutchev's

---

[289] But he seldom referred to Italian sources in his discussions of general intellectual problems. As an exception see the mention of Vico in Shevyrev, *Lektsii o russkoi literature*, p. 14.

[290] For Schelling's impact on Tyutchev see especially Sechkarev, *Schellings Einfluss in der russischen Literatur der 20er und 30er Jahre des XIX Jahrhunderts*, pp. 99–106. Baader's long and intimate contacts with Russia are outlined, for instance, in Masaryk, *The Spirit of Russia. Studies in history, literature, and philosophy*, I, 286. For a detailed treatment presenting in particular the links between Baader and the Russia of Nicholas I and emphasizing his contacts with Shevyrev see Benz, *Die abendlaendische Sendung der oestlich-orthodoxen Kirche*. This recent book was expertly reviewed in Chizhevskii, "Baader i Rossiya," *Novyi Zhurnal* XXXV (1953), 301–310. Baader's letters to Uvarov were published in Susini, *Lettres inédites de Franz von Baader*, pp. 451–461.

[291] Fallmerayer's historical works, especially his theory of the Slavic origin of modern Greeks, are well known. His prediction of the future Slavic hegemony

glorification of Russia was nourished by the high regard for his
native land, his people, or his church, expressed in one fashion
or another by Schelling, Baader, and Fallmerayer.[292] But the poet's
intellectual horizon was not limited to Munich. For instance, according to one interpretation, he derived his fundamental dichotomy between Christianity and Revolution—Revolution representing the rebellion of the ego against every authority and
above all against God—from Fichte, Michelet, and Louis Blanc.[293]

Uvarov, Pogodin, Shevyrev, and Tyutchev all contributed to
various romantic currents and crosscurrents which swept over
Europe in the nineteenth century; and they were all influenced
in a fundamental manner by different Western intellectuals. The
same can be said, on the whole, about other proponents of
Official Nationality; the link to the West being affected in each
instance by specific personal circumstances, such as German background and Lutheran faith in the case of Grech, Zhukovskii's
immersion in romantic literature and his marvelous ability to
translate and adapt Western originals from many lands, or the
cosmopolitan, aristocratic upbringing in the tradition of legitimism, Restoration, and the Prussian alliance of Nicholas I
himself. Western influence was precise and particular as well as
general and basic. To select a few examples among many, Zhukovskii used the conclusion of Johann Mueller's world history as the
starting point of his discussion of autocracy; [294] Pogodin relied

in the world was made in 1830 in Fallmerayer, *Geschichte der Halbinsel Morea
im Mittelalter*, I, v. On Fallmerayer and Tyutchev see Rauch, "J. Ph. Fallmerayer und der russische Reichsgedanke bei F. I. Tjutcev," *Jahrbuecher fuer
Geschichte Osteuropas*, I, no. 1, 54–69. Bulgarin, or rather Ivanov, depended
heavily on Fallmerayer in his account of the Slavic past. Bulgarin, *Rossiya v
istoricheskom, statisticheskom, geograficheskom i literaturnom otnosheniyakh*,
History, part 2, pp. 73 ff.

[292] Stremoukhov, *op. cit.*, p. 119. The Slavophile Ivan Aksakov, on the other
hand, emphasized repeatedly "the miracle" of Tyutchev's retaining his "true
Russian nature," writing Russian poetry and developing "a Russian ideology"
in spite of his long life abroad, constant use of French, and other intimate
ties with the West. I. Aksakov, *op. cit.*, in particular, pp. 40, 85. For the latest
notable contribution to the discussion of the Western and the Russian elements in Tyutchev see Weidle, "Tyutchev i Rossiya," *Zadacha Rossii*, pp. 169–
200.

[293] Stremoukhov, *op. cit.*, p. 125–126. On De Maistre and Tyutchev see
Stepanov, *op. cit.*, p. 617.

[294] Zhukovskii, *op. cit.*, p. 171.

on Thierry to prove the importance of conquest in the development of the West; [295] Shevyrev appealed to a German specialist
in defense of Christian education,[296] and to one Polish and two
French writers to provide evidence for his eulogy of the simple
society of the Slavs.[297] Even Shevyrev's extravagant account of
the decline of the West was borrowed, in part, from a French
publicist, Philarète Chasles.[298] When, after the revolutions of
1848, the government decided to isolate Russia completely from
the intellectual development of the rest of Europe and proceeded
to institute a ban on philosophy, Nikitenko noted in his diary:
"Again a persecution of philosophy. It has been proposed to limit
its teaching in the universities to logic and psychology, entrust-
ing both to the clergy. The Scottish school is to serve as the
foundation." [299]

There existed many differences of opinion and appreciation
among the proponents of Official Nationality as far as various
Western intellectuals were concerned. Field of interest, degree of
acquaintance, general taste, and special likes and dislikes all
played a part in their judgments. However, at least one divergence
in estimate carried important implications and deserves notice.
It refers to German idealistic philosophy. The nationalists thought
highly of this philosophy, above all of Schelling. Pogodin's and
Shevyrev's admiration for that complex thinker dated at least
from their membership in the early 1820's in a group of youthful
romantic enthusiasts known as the Lovers of Wisdom,[300] while
Tyutchev felt the direct impact of the master in Munich. *The
Muscovite* paid homage to Schelling, and to Baader, as well as
to some other romantic philosophers, especially of the more

---

[295] Pogodin, *Istoriko-kriticheskie otryvki*, pp. 57–58 ff.
[296] Shevyrev, *Ob otnoshenii semeinogo vospitaniya k gosudarstvennomu*, p. 21.
[297] Shevyrev, *op. cit.*, pp. 57, 69–70.
[298] Shevyrev, "Vzglyad russkogo na sovremennoe obrazovanie Evropy," pp.
242–245. See also Struve, *op. cit.* In all the instances mentioned above
the borrowings are explicit and acknowledged.
[299] Nikitenko, I, 395.
[300] There is no monograph on the Lovers of Wisdom. A considerable amount
of material is scattered in different works. See, e.g., Koshelev, *Zapiski*, pp. 12 ff.
for a brief account by a member; Sakulin, *Iz istorii russkogo idealisma: Knyaz
V. Odoevskii*; and Koyré, *La Philosophie et le problème national en Russie au
début du XIXe siècle*, chap. iv, pp. 137–152.

religious and mystical kind. Shevyrev's and particularly Pogodin's fascination with Schelling reached the ridiculous extremes mentioned previously. In terms of doctrine this adulation found expression in the following set of assertions shared by the nationalist ideologists of the state with the Slavophiles: "Only Russia is in the full bloom of her forces, in the age of maturity; she must begin from that point which Europe has now reached. Schelling, the crown of European enlightenment, its greatest, so to speak, effort, who is now devoting himself to the Christian religion, is destined, it seems, to pass this enlightenment on to Russia for further development, for consummation." [301]

Nicholas I and most of his dynastically oriented followers, on the other hand, paid no attention to Schelling and were suspicious and critical of the entire German idealistic philosophy.[302] Uvarov, as on so many other occasions, occupied an ambivalent position: for instance, he showed, as already noted, a great appreciation of

---

[301] Pogodin, Rechi, p. 39. Recently a scholar commented: "It is striking to observe the manner in which an early Russian writer on this subject like Pogodin consciously attempted to apply Schelling's philosophy of nature to history. Indications of such an attempt are to be found in the papers of the young Pogodin as early as the spring of 1824. It was during the following three years that he developed the ideas for his 'Historical Aphorisms' and translated the 'Introduction to History' of Ast, a German disciple of Schelling who was already applying the ideas of his master to historical development. In 1827, Pogodin published his 'Historical Aphorisms,' in which he affirmed that history is governed by laws in very much the same manner that the physical world is: each people and each state must, sooner or later, pass through definite stages of development which are part of the universal historical process." Thaden, "The Beginnings of Romantic Nationalism in Russia," American Slavic and East European Review, XIII (1954), 517–518. Pogodin also wanted at one time "to encompass Schelling's entire system in an epic poem 'Moses'." Barsukov, op. cit., I, 280–281. The poem, naturally, was to be dedicated to Schelling. Among the German poets, Pogodin and his friends especially admired Schiller. Barsukov, op. cit., I, 90. In 1856, Shevyrev composed the following verses: "Blessed is he who loved Schiller / Who spent his youthful years with him / And who dedicated the spring feast of life / To the singer of dreams and of passionate freedom." Shevyrev, Stikhotvoreniya, p. 192. On the influence of Schiller in Russia, see especially Malia, "Schiller and the Early Russian Left," Harvard Slavic Studies, IV (1957), 169–200.

[302] For a striking example of Nicholas I's outbursts against German intellectuals, see Grunwald, La Vie de Nicolas Ier, p. 261. Of the journalists, Bulgarin showed the most contempt for and antagonism to the philosophers, wishing mankind "more common sense than contemplative philosophy" (Bulgarin, Sochineniya, VII, 183) and denouncing Hegel and Schelling (Bulgarin, Vospominaniya, VI, 281–283). See also Bulgarin, Sochineniya, VI, 109–110.

Herder, but he was willing to dismiss Kant as illegible and obscure.[303]

While the writings of the proponents of Official Nationality contain many foreign names representing major sources of inspiration and influence, only one Russian author can be placed by their side. This distinction belongs to Karamzin who, late in life, added great popularity and prominence as a historian to his widespread literary fame. Karamzin's unfinished, twelve-volume *History of the Russian State*, which began to come out in 1816 and continued to be issued until shortly after his death in 1826, became the classic history of the romantic age in Russia and a best seller. Karamzin's position of official historian emphasized the connection between him and the entire historical tradition of Official Nationality developed by such scholars as Pogodin, Shevyrev, and Ustryalov. The writer's political beliefs, expressed notably in his *Memorandum about the Old and the New Russia*, submitted to Alexander I in 1811,[304] as well as in his *History*, made him the outstanding Russian exponent in his generation of autocracy and of the strong, patriarchal state. Finally, Karamzin even came to be considered by some Russian intellectuals as a shining example of Christian and civic virtue and as a moral guide.

Pogodin showed special devotion to Karamzin. This admiration began in boyhood; and when Pogodin, then a high school student, saw the famous writer for the first time, with several friends in a museum, he fell into "a certain state of numbness," walked after them without being able to collect his thoughts, and followed them to their carriages.[305] When several volumes of Karamzin's *History* came out in 1818, Pogodin used a ruse to obtain enough money from his relatives to finance the purchase.[306] In 1825, he dedicated his own first scholarly study, a dissertation on the origin of Russia, to his ideal, writing to him as follows: "From

---

[303] Uvarov cited Goethe to that effect and endorsed his opinion. Uvarov, *Esquisses politiques et littéraires*, pp. 214–215.

[304] Although the *Memorandum* was not published until much later, it was in the 1830's that it became generally known to the educated Russian public.

[305] Barsukov, *op. cit.*, I, 29.

[306] *Ibid.*, pp. 29–30.

you I began to learn the good, language, and history. Allow me
then to dedicate to you, as a sign of sincere gratitude, my first
work." [307] As a professor, Pogodin urged his students: "Study,
study Karamzin, and concentrate on him; do not begin writing
without knowing by heart a hundred pages of his works." [308]
He himself based his lectures on Karamzin's *History*,[309] read and
reread the famous work throughout his life, gathered all the
information he could about it and about its author,[310] and insisted that Karamzin deserved more honors in his native land:
an anniversary celebration, a monument in the center of Moscow,
a scholarship in his name.[311] Pogodin even swore by Karamzin,[312] and listed "Karamzin's heart," together with "Newton and
his binomial theorem, Raphael and his ideals, Mozart and Don
Giovanni, Peter the Great's will, Voltaire's wit," and "Napoleon's
intelligence," as the most wondrous products of creation.[313]

Pogodin presented his general estimate of Karamzin in 1845,
in Simbirsk, at the unveiling of a monument to the famous writer,
when the Moscow professor was asked to deliver "A Historical
Word of Praise of Karamzin," a speech to which he assigned
much significance.[314]

---

[307] *Ibid.*, p. 294.

[308] *Ibid.*, VI, 301.

[309] Shevyrev, *Istoriya Imperatorskogo Moskovskogo Universiteta*, p. 545.

[310] See, e.g., Pogodin's letter to V. Karamzin, the writer's son, asking in
minute detail about his father's working habits, mode of life, character, tastes.
"I must know his entire day, from morning to night." Barsukov, ed., *Pisma
M. P. Pogodina, S. P. Shevyreva i M. A. Maksimovicha k knyazyu P. A.
Vyazemskomu 1825–1874 godov*, pp. 128–129 n. 87.

[311] *Ibid.*, pp. 66, 77, 82, 85–86. This book provides, in general, a wealth of
material on Pogodin's interests in Karamzin. Pogodin, *Rechi*, p. 276.

[312] Barsukov, *Zhizn i trudy M. P. Pogodina*, VIII, 100.

[313] Pogodin, *Prostaya rech o mudrenykh veshchakh*, p. 25.

[314] As Pogodin wrote to Vyazemskii in 1840: "My word of praise for Karamzin is still unfinished. Will you believe me that I take it up some five times a
year and that each time fear drives me away? I cannot manage it. I turn every
word around. . . . It is complicated! Great is the responsibility!" Barsukov,
ed., *Pisma M. P. Pogodina, S. P. Shevyreva i M. A. Maksimovicha k knyazuy
P. A. Vyazemskomu 1825–1874 godov*, p. 35. After Vyazemskii approved the
text, Pogodin expressed his delight, adding that he had never wanted to succeed so much as on this occasion (*ibid.*, p. 40). He was extremely well pleased
with the results of his speech. Pogodin, *Rechi*, pp. 265–268. The address was
published (*ibid.*, pp. 45–96). See also Pogodin's speech delivered in 1866, in
the Academy of Sciences, "About Karamzin as Man and Citizen," *ibid.*, pp.
149–162.

Yes, Karamzin did not resolve the fate of battles, but he resolved complex problems of our state system, problems which are more important than all conceivable victories in the world.

Yes, Karamzin did not extend the boundaries of the empire, but he extended the boundaries of the Russian language which contains the most firm foundation of our might, the sure promise of a most brilliant glory.

He did not discover new sources of revenue, but he discovered new sources of pleasure in the heart, pure, beautiful humane pleasures which cannot be purchased by any treasures of the Old or the New World.

He did not compose laws, but he inspired respect for them and taught how to live so that no laws would be necessary for men.[315]

In addition to Pogodin, Shevyrev,[316] Tyutchev,[317] Prince P. Vyazemskii, and many other Right-wing intellectuals of the reign of Nicholas I had the highest regard for Karamzin. The same was true of the emperor himself.[318] Karamzin's powerful appeal had a solid basis: he had been both an archconservative and a romantic nationalist; indeed, in a sense he had combined Orthodoxy, autocracy, and nationality. But Pogodin and other nationalists of Official Nationality did not follow the famous writer blindly. Notably, they eliminated Karamzin's emphasis on aristocracy, replacing it by the vision of a monolithic Russian state composed only of the tsar and his people.[319]

The problem of the social and economic background of the doctrine of Official Nationality has generally been treated in too simple a manner. The ideology has been considered as a rationalization and an intellectual prop of the prereform Russian society, based on serfdom and dominated by the landlords.

---

[315] *Ibid.*, p. 48.

[316] Barsukov, ed., *op. cit.*, p. 147.

[317] See his poem "For N. M. Karamzin's Anniversary," where he begs the historian to be his "guiding, inspiring star," Tyutchev, p. 203.

[318] Kornilov even wrote: "Karamzin's views served as the basis of Nicholas's internal policy." Kornilov, *op. cit.*, p. 241. See also Polievktov, p. 60.

[319] This romantic concept of the *Volk*, developed principally by German thinkers, represents the main difference between the historical views of Karamzin and those of Pogodin and his friends. For a recent analysis of Karamzin's thought emphasizing its Age of Reason foundations, see Pipes, "Karamzin's Conception of Monarchy," *Harvard Slavic Studies*, IV (1957), 35–58.

Marxist historians in particular have developed this class interpretation, using it both to explain the nature of Official Nationality
and to indicate its relationship to other teachings of the time.
For instance, it has been argued that the government doctrine
represented, more specifically, the position of the upper, most
reactionary layer of the gentry, while the Slavophiles expressed
the views of its middle, somewhat more moderate, stratum.[320]
Yet, though this approach may be valid to an extent, any historical
analysis of the ideology of Official Nationality should make full
allowance for the fact that it stood, first and foremost, for the
opinions and the interests of Nicholas I and his government.
That government maintained close links with the landlord class,
but the two were by no means identical. The principle of autocracy, with its emphasis on the absolute obedience of all the
Russians to their monarch, provides a striking illustration of this
point.

Moreover, the sharp intellectual cleavage among the state
ideologists over the dogma of "nationality" also had certain social
aspects that further indicate the complex nature of the movement. The dynastic wing enjoyed its greatest strength among the
aristocrats of the court and the high officials of the state, and
it could count on the allegiance of the Baltic German nobility
and of many other non-Russians.[321] The romantic nationalists,
on the other hand, were led by intellectuals; and they found
increasing support among students, army officers, and other young
educated Russians. The second group possessed a much humbler
background and a much wider appeal than the first. The proponents of the dynastic view centered in St. Petersburg, the
capital; the nationalists, in Moscow.[322]

---

[320] Rubinstein, "Istoricheskaya teoriya slavyanofilov i ee klassovye korni,"
*Trudy Instituta Krasnoi Professury. Russkaya istoricheskaya literatura v klas-
sovom osveshchenii*, I, 53–118.

[321] See, e.g., Bulgarin's eulogy of General K. Benckendorff, the gendarme's
brother, who did not fit at all the pattern of emerging Russian nationalism.
His dying wish was to be buried in Stuttgart, by the side of his wife, on whose
magnificent tomb he had inscribed: "*Nur sie!*" Bulgarin, *Sochineniya*, III,
244–256. The gendarme himself was naturally hostile to *The Muscovite*.

[322] Romantic praise of Moscow by the Slavophiles, as well as by other nationalists, was very common. The best example for our purposes is Pogodin's
article "About Moscow." Pogodin, *Istoriko-kriticheskie otryvki*, pp. 131–159.
For a contrasting Official Nationality evaluation, giving preference to St.

The basic attitudes of the two wings of Official Nationality were
also different. The legitimists, as has already been noted, looked
to the past and dedicated themselves to the struggle against
revolution in the name of the existing order. Their defensive
mentality found appropriate expression in Uvarov's famous ad-
vocacy of "intellectual dams" [323] and in his assertion that he
would die with a sense of duty fulfilled if he could succeed in
"pushing Russia back some fifty years from what is being prepared
for her by the theories." [324] But the nationalist intellectuals
pointed to the future and envisaged quite another role for themselves. As Tyutchev noted with heavy sarcasm: The world had
been forced to accord Russia a place in the sun; only the philosophy of history had not yet deigned to do so.[325] Therefore,
a new philosophy of history, a new ideology was to be created,
both as a matter of justice and for the more important purpose
of bringing into the consciousness of the Russians their true
nature and their providential mission.[326] Pogodin, Shevyrev,
Tyutchev, and their friends, as well as many romantic thinkers
in other lands, meant to be the prophets of the chosen people.
In Russia, as elsewhere, romantic nationalism was largely the work
of crusading professors, publicists, and students. Pogodin, again,
reflected best this new position of the intellectual: he urged the
establishment of a chair of current affairs in the universities,
"for the closest possible applied unity of lectures and life," [327]
explained repeatedly how professors should use their knowledge
to support the policies of their country,[328] and even suggested that
congresses of historians and other specialists "attempt solutions

Petersburg, see Grech "Moscow Letters," *Sochineniya*, III, 231–258. See
also Lednicki, *op. cit.*, pp. 43–48.
[323] Uvarov used this phrase in his report on the inspection of Moscow University and the Moscow School District in 1832, on the eve of his appointment as minister of education. Quoted in Barsukov, *Zhizn i trudy M. P.
Pogodina*, IV, 85.
[324] Nikitenko, I, 267.
[325] Tyutchev, p. 337.
[326] On the significance of this "bringing into the consciousness," see especially Shevyrev, "Vzglyad russkogo na sovremennoe obrazovanie Evropy,"
pp. 292–296.
[327] Pogodin, *Rechi*, pp. 618–620, quoted from p. 620.
[328] *Ibid.*, pp. 15–18, 21–44; Pogodin, *Istoriko-politicheskie pisma*, pp. 28–45.

of certain political problems, closely related to scholarship." [329]
The Moscow Slavonic Benevolent Committee, founded in 1858,
and of great importance subsequently for the development of
Pan-Slavism in Russia, owed much to Pogodin.[330]

The doctrine of Official Nationality belonged with the numerous reactionary and romantic teachings which flooded Europe
in the first half of the nineteenth century. Its chief historical importance, however, lies in the fact that it became for thirty years
the program of the Russian government. For good or ill, Nicholas
I applied relentlessly the principles of "Orthodoxy, autocracy, and
nationality," as he understood them, both in his own vast empire
and in his activities in the world at large.

---

[329] Pogodin, *Stati politicheskie i polskii vopros* (1856–1867), p. 475.

[330] Because of his remarkable practical ability, his business interests, and his
concern with Russian merchants, Pogodin has sometimes been cited not only
as an intellectual, but also as a representative of the middle class in a more
general sense.

The contrast described in this paragraph relates to one of the fundamental
cleavages in modern European history. For a recent provocative discussion
of this entire subject, see Arendt, *The Origins of Totalitarianism*.

IV

OFFICIAL NATIONALITY

HOME AFFAIRS

"Everything must proceed from here."—Nicholas I pointing to his breast.[1]

> *. . . At full height,*
> *Illumined by the pale moonlight,*
> *With arm outflung, behind him riding,*
> *See, the bronze horsemen comes, bestriding*
> *The charger, clanging in his flight.*
> Pushkin, The Bronze Horseman.[2]

THE REIGN of Nicholas I was all of a piece. In the judgment of Professor Schiemann, the Russian emperor stood out as "the most consistent of autocrats." [3] Students of the period have preferred on the whole either to treat the entire thirty years of Nicholas's government of Russia as a single unit or, when they found sub-

---

[1] Quoted in V. Riasanovsky, *Obzor Russkoi Kultury*, part II, issue I, p. 161.
[2] Translated by Oliver Elton, *Verses from Pushkin and Others*, London, 1935. Used with permission of Edward Arnold (Publishers) Ltd.
[3] Schiemann, II, xii.

divisions desirable, to minimize the importance of this partitioning and to emphasize the continuity of imperial policies and
outlook. The usual dissection of the reign slices it into three
chronological segments: the first years, from Nicholas's accession
to the throne to 1830 or 1831 while the emperor was learning his
task and considering his future steps; the long stretch from 1831
until another revolutionary year, 1848, during which the established system achieved its full expression; and the bitter last seven
years when the Russian government tried desperately to ward off
all threats to the old regime at home and to meet challenges from
abroad. Yet, as pointed out by Polievktov, these subdivisions refer
to the tempo and the methods of imperial policy, not to its basic
orientation or its objectives.[4]

The ideas and the actions which gave this substantial unity
to the reign of Nicholas I had firm roots in Russian history. The
Russian Empire as it existed until the revolution of 1917 was
founded by Peter the Great who stressed absolutism, unquestioning service to the state by all, and the monarch's personal
participation in everything as much as did his admiring nineteenth-
century successor. Weakened by a number of feeble sovereigns
and by the liberal veneer of the age of Catherine, the principle
of autocracy reappeared in an extreme, even pathological, form
during the brief rule of Nicholas's father, Paul, whose attitude
toward his subjects was epitomized in his alleged assertion that
in Russia only that man was important who was speaking to the
emperor, and only while he was so speaking.[5] Furthermore, Paul
added an intense preoccupation with dynastic rights and with

---

[4] Polievktov, pp. 65–66. See also, especially, the studies of Schiemann,
Kornilov, and Presnyakov, as well as the nine-volume *Istoriya Rossii v XIX
veke* (Granat). The reign of Nicholas I occupies most of the first and second
and parts of the third and fourth volumes. The contributions include an excellent general analysis of the internal policy of Nicholas I by Professor
A. Kizevetter (vol. I, pp. 169–231). The latest general treatment of the
subject is S. Okun, *Ocherki istorii S.S.S.R. Vtoraya chetvert XIX veka*. My
purpose in this chapter and the one following is not to add materially to
these and other weighty works on the period, but merely to indicate certain
connections between the word and the deed of the emperor and his assistants,
between the theory and the practice of Official Nationality.

[5] On Nicholas's attitude toward Paul see, for instance, Grech, *Sochineniya*,
III, 409 n. 1.

legitimism in general to the official Russian viewpoint introducing, notably, a strict law of succession to the throne in direct male line in place of Peter's utilitarian practice of selection by the ruler. Alexander, the immediate predecessor of Nicholas, began as a liberal, but ended as a reactionary. Nicholas proved willing, indeed eager, to forget the constitutional plans and the attempts at reform in the reign of his brother, while he continued the conservative policies which characterized the second half of Alexander's reign. Alexander also bequeathed to Nicholas the Prussian orientation, the tradition of the Holy Alliance, and the new position of Russia as a mainstay of the restored and legitimist Europe. Many important functionaries, such as Nesselrode, Benckendorff, and Kankrin, who had reached the highest rung of office in the reign of the elder brother, continued their work in that of the younger. Official theory which praised Peter the Great and Alexander I as the chief creators of the existing Russian system corresponded to political reality.

The doctrine of Official Nationality reflected a certain stage in the development of the Russian state and of its ideology. It presented faithfully the beliefs of Nicholas I and of his assistants, and it found manifold expression in the policies of the emperor's government. Of its three key principles, autocracy possessed the most immediate and obvious political significance, and autocracy became the watchword of Nicholas's entire system. Simple in concept, it proved to be varied in application and complex in execution.

In contrast to Alexander who showed repeated interest in curbing absolutism in his domain and who had prospective constitutions prepared by such statesmen as Speranskii and Novosiltsov, Nicholas demonstrated a deadly determination to preserve the existing political system. After the accession of the new emperor to the throne and the Decembrist rebellion, any questioning of autocracy in Russia came to be considered subversive. The faithful subjects of the tsar could indulge instead in that patriotic and quasi-religious praise of absolute rule which was outlined in the preceding chapter. Nicholas not only failed to contribute to the development of constitutionalism and constitutional thought in Russia, but he tried his best to eliminate all such pernicious vestiges from the Russian past. Thus during the great codification of law in his reign, the emperor issued express orders to omit everything referring to the constitution granted briefly by Empress Anne in 1730 and to certain other undesirable episodes.[6] Again, after the suppression of the Polish rebellion and the occupation of Warsaw, Nicholas wrote as follows to Prince Paskevich, the Russian commander, concerning Novosiltsov's constitutional project which the Poles had found and published:

Chertkov brought me a copy of the constitutional project for Russia found in Novosiltsov's papers. The publication of this paper is most annoying. Out of a hundred of our young officers ninety will read it, will fail to understand it or will scorn it, but ten will retain it in their memory, will discuss it—and, the most important point, will not forget it. This worries me above everything else. This is why I wish so much that the guards be kept in Warsaw as briefly as possible. Order Count Witt to try to obtain as many copies of this booklet as he can and to destroy them, also to find the manuscript and send it to me. . . .[7]

The Polish uprising of 1830–1831 and its suppression, which provided the background for this expression of imperial concern, meant the end of the Polish constitution. Nicholas had inherited it from Alexander, and he proceeded to honor it for a number of years in spite of his great distaste for it. But the emperor decided that the Polish rebellion annulled all former arrangements and, after the victory, he applied autocratic rule to Poland.

The political system of Russia at the time of Nicholas contained no restrictions on the absolute power of the monarch. Still, the

---

[6] The banned items included the oath of allegiance of February 21, 1730, the manifestoes of October 5 and October 17, 1740, a draft of the manifesto of July 6, 1762, and several others. Polievktov, p. 257. The emperor even objected on various occasions to the word "freedom" and its various derivatives, including the set expression "free agriculturists" used to designate the serfs who had been emancipated by their masters in accordance with the law of 1803, as "incompatible, in a certain sense, with our state system." SIRIO, XCVIII, 258, 282.

[7] The letter, written on September 14, 1831, is quoted in Schilder, II, 390. Emphasis in the original.

emperor worried lest some institutions or administrative arrangements in his native land might tend to infringe on the sovereign's
prerogative. Also, he generally demanded immediate execution
of his will, being impatient of deliberation, consultation, or other
procedural delay. Nicholas wanted to define precisely the exact
field of activity of every official and every agency and to keep
them all strictly within the confines of their specific duties. And
he would interfere with the proper course of state business to
obtain prompt compliance and quick results.

The Committee of Ministers suffered a certain limitation of
its competence during the autocrat's reign.[8] The State Council
too lost in importance; the emperor, when sending to it legislative projects for discussion, occasionally added such comments
as his expression of hope that there will follow "no disadvantage
of excessive debate" and even the direct order: "I wish this to be
accepted." [9] The phrase "having listened to the State Council,"
which had been introduced by the original statutes of the Council
as a part of the formula of imperial confirmation of legislative
acts, disappeared from the 1842 redaction of the statutes.[10] The
Senate fared worse, attracting repeatedly the hostility of the emperor. Nicholas himself undertook to supervise the proper legal
operation of the machinery of the state, while the Senate came
to be reduced more and more to its purely judicial functions.
After listing the impressive series of measures introduced by the
emperor to facilitate direct control and regulation of all government and administration in Russia, an official historian of the
Senate adds dryly: "Under such conditions not much room was
left for Senate supervision." [11]

---

[8] According to Professor Seredonin, the sovereign "insisted that the ministers
should be merely the strict executors of his will, of his wishes. . . . One
may say that Emperor Nicholas killed the committee of ministers, reduced
it to the status of almost his private chancery." Quoted in Florinsky, *Russia,
a History and an Interpretation*, II, 768.
[9] Polievktov, p. 221. The entire fine chapter on "The State Machinery
in the Reign of Emperor Nicholas I" (pp. 209–225) deserves special notice.
[10] *Ibid.*, p. 222. For the autocrat's authoritarian treatment of the State
Council, see also *SIRIO*, XCVIII, 117, 118, 122, 248.
[11] Gogel, "Krug vedomstva i ocherk deyatelnosti Pravitelstvuyushchego
Senata," *Istoriya Pravitelstvuyushchego Senata za dvesti let, 1711–1911 gg.*,
vol. III, *Pravitelstvuyushchii Senat v XIX stoletii do reform 60-kh godov*, p. 505.

Nicholas's treatment of his ministers, of the State Council, of the Senate, and of the entire administration of the land reflected a fundamental characteristic of his rule: a preference for arbitrary personal actions and decisions in place of established legal procedure. The emperor believed that a good Christian conscience accomplished more than legal formalism and that sturdy common sense produced better results than all "abstractions." [12] These attitudes in the government of Russia represented appropriate practical counterparts to the doctrines of Official Nationality which emphasized men, not institutions, and glorified paternalism as the special virtue of the Russian way of life. Many observers as well as later commentators, however, refused to share the opinion of state ideologists. The charge of arbitrary action became a leading item in the indictment of Nicholas's regime both by contemporaries and by subsequent historians.[13]

Impatient and dissatisfied with the regular channels of government, the emperor relied to a large extent on certain special measures and devices to carry out his intentions. As one such method, he made an extremely extensive use of *ad hoc* committees standing outside the usual state machinery. The committees were composed, typically, of a handful of the most trusted assistants of the emperor, and, because these were very few in number, the same men in different combinations formed and reformed small groups throughout Nicholas's reign—much as is the practice today in college faculties. Only death provided an assured escape from this duty. The committees, as a rule, carried on their work in secret, adding further complication and confusion to the already cumbersome administration of the empire. In the words of a specialist:

---

[12] As Nicholas asserted: "In my opinion, good morality is the best theory of law. It must be in the heart independently of these abstractions and must have religion as its basis." And he "disliked organically all theories and abstractions" which, to use his own words, "are later either forgotten or find no practical application." Ammon, "Nikolai I," *Entsiklopedicheskii Slovar* (Granat), XXX, col. 212. Nicholas's statements, both the first one and that quoted by Ammon, are taken from Baron M. Korff's notes reproduced in *SIRIO*, XCVIII, 30.

[13] For example, this accusation inspires Custine's work, and it occurs repeatedly in diplomatic dispatches. Among historians, Schiemann made the most of this point.

A secret committee usually arose to draft a project of a law concerning this or that pressing major issue. The project produced by the committee, after passing through the State Council and sometimes even omitting this stage, usually gained the confirmation of the monarch, regardless of the decision of the highest consulting body, and became law. While the matter passed through all these stages—and on occasion the process became very much drawn out—the secret committee sometimes acquired the standing of a highest administrative agency, and the corresponding lower agencies referred to it as to their highest authority. Intruding, with their opinions protected in advance by august approval, into the sphere of activity of the State Council, the secret committees of the time of Nicholas interrupted by their administrative practice the mutual relations of the organs of the central government and, so to speak, completed the work of destroying the regular system of the highest state institutions, the task largely performed by His Majesty's Own Chancery.[14]

The first, and in many ways the most significant, of Nicholas's committees was that established on December 6, 1826 and lasting until 1832. Count V. Kochubei served as its chairman, and the committee contained five other leading statesmen of the period. In contrast to later committees which were assigned a narrower field of activity, the Committee of the Sixth of December had to examine the state papers and projects left by Alexander, to reconsider in that connection virtually all major aspects of government and social organization in Russia, and to propose improvements. The painstaking work of this select group of officials led to negligible results: entirely conservative in outlook, the committee directed its effort toward hair-splitting distinctions and minor, at times merely verbal, modifications; and it qualified drastically virtually every suggested change. Even its innocuous "law concerning the estates" which received imperial approval was shelved after criticism by Constantine.[15] This laborious futility became the characteristic pattern of a great majority of subse-

---

[14] Polievktov, p. 224. His Majesty's Own Chancery will be discussed next.
[15] The proceedings of the Committee were published in vols. 74 and 90 of *SIRIO*. Its work is brilliantly analyzed in Kizevetter, *op. cit.*, pp. 175–192.

quent committees during the reign of Nicholas I, in spite of the
fact that the emperor himself often took an active part in their
proceedings.[16] The failure of one committee to perform its task
merely led to the formation of another. For example, some nine
committees in the reign of Nicholas tried to deal with the issue
of serfdom.

His Majesty's Own Chancery proved to be more effective than
the special committees. Organized originally as a bureau dealing
with matters which demanded the sovereign's personal participation and supervising the execution of august orders, the Chancery
grew rapidly in the reign of Nicholas I. As early as 1826, two new
departments were added to it: the Second concerned with the
codification of law, and the Third with the administration of the
newly created corps of gendarmes. Both additions had important
and lasting results: the legal code was successfully produced and
remained in force until 1917, while the Third Department contributed more than any other agency in giving to the reign of the
willful autocrat its particular tone and point.[17] In 1828 the Fourth
Department appeared for the purpose of managing the charitable
and educational institutions under the jurisdiction of the Empress Mother Mary. Eight years later the Fifth Department was
created and charged with handling the reform in the condition
of the state peasants; after two years of activity it was replaced
by the new Ministry of State Domains. Finally, in 1843, the
Sixth Department of His Majesty's Own Chancery came into
being, a temporary agency assigned the task of drawing up an
administrative plan for Transcaucasia. The Chancery served Nich-
las I as a major means of conducting a personal policy which bypassed the regular state channels. In the judgment of a leading
authority:

*In this consecutive growth of His Majesty's Own Chancery it
is impossible not to see an expression of the idea that only the*

---

[16] On the emperor's participation in committee work see especially "Imperator Nikolai v soveshchatelnykh sobraniyakh. (Iz sovremennykh zapisok
stats-sekretarya barona Korfa)," *SIRIO*, XCVIII, 101–283. Some reasons
for the futility of committee activity will be considered later in this chapter.

[17] The Third Department of His Majesty's Own Chancery will be discussed
briefly later in this chapter.

usual or long established branches of administration can be en-
trusted to the management of the ministries, whereas every new
departure in the state, exceeding the limits of current adminis-
trative practice, must be introduced outside the regular order,
must be placed under the more immediate supervision and direct-
ing guidance of the monarch himself.[18]

In addition to the secret committees and the Chancery with
its several departments, Nicholas I relied heavily on special emis-
saries, most of them generals of his suite, who were given different assignments and sent all over Russia to execute immediately
the will of the emperor. They too operated outside the regular
system and represented an extension, so to speak, of the emperor's own person.[19]

As to local administration, Nicholas directed his efforts toward
its greater standardization and more effective subordination to
the center. By an edict issued in 1837, the governors of the
provinces received increased powers as officials uniquely in charge
of and responsible for their particular areas. Provincial boards
were subordinated to the governors and became executive agencies
losing their former consultative and somewhat independent character. These and certain other measures emphasized the bureaucratic way at the expense of Catherine the Great's more complex
organization meant to attract participation of the local gentry.
Some historians even speak of a transformation of local administration in the reign of Nicholas I, very much in line with the general character of government activity. "Centralization and personal decision—thus one may characterize the condition of the
state system in the reign of Nicholas." [20]

The emperor's control and organization of Russia assumed both
a paternal and a military nature, these two aspects emerging in
sharp relief in government practice as well as in official theory.
As the father of his people, Nicholas refused to be restrained by
procedural formalities or legal obstacles, and he felt himself su-

---

[18] Kizevetter, *op. cit.*, pp. 195–196.
[19] According to one count, their number increased from 75 to 400 in the
course of the reign. Tarasov, *Nikolaevshchina* (*Vremya Nikolaya I*), p. 4.
[20] Polievktov, p. 225.

premely qualified to settle every issue by his own personal decision. Militarism, as has already been indicated, colored the entire outlook and activity of the emperor resulting not only in an emphasis on the army, but also in an attempt to introduce military organization and principles in the state at large. Almost all assistants of the emperor were also military men who, together with their sovereign, used military terminology in civilian functions and thought naturally in terms of direct orders, unquestioning obedience, and personal responsibility for one's command.

New categories of Russians, including students, were put in uniforms, the jurisdiction of military courts was increased, military schools multiplied, and whole administrative departments, such as those of land surveying, forestry, transportation, mining and engineering, received a military organization. In a broader sense, Nicholas I considered all his officials—ministers, governors, or postmasters—as army commanders entrusted with and accountable for their respective units. Changes in the structure of certain ministries emphasized the same point as the reform of provincial government: the fullness of authority of the man in charge, in this case the minister, and an abolition of the vestiges of collegiate rule. And the same tendency spread to the lower echelons of the administration. As one intelligent observer remarked, the government, apparently, "set itself the task of disciplining the country." [21]

---

[21] Nikitenko, I, 88. Nikitenko's comment deserves to be quoted more fully as an example of the impression which the emperor's militarism produced even on his conservative and completely loyal subjects: "There was no high position or office in the state, but that the appointment to it was given by preference to a man with thick silver or golden epaulets. These epaulets were recognized as the best guarantee of intelligence, knowledge, and ability even in those fields where, it would seem, special training is necessary. Convinced of the magic power of the epaulets, their wearers raised their heads high. They became filled with belief in their own infallibility and boldly cut the most complicated knots. First themselves educated in the spirit of a strict military discipline, later preserving this discipline in army ranks, they introduced the same principle of absolute obedience into the administration of a peaceful, civil society. In this respect, it is true, they were merely assisting the purposes of the government which, apparently, set itself the task of disciplining the country, that is, of bringing it to such a condition that not a single person in it would think or act except following a single will. As a result of this, so to speak, barracks system each general, no matter which branch of administration he had been called to manage, tried first of all and

But the principle of autocracy found its most striking expression in the indefatigable activities of Nicholas I himself. The emperor not only performed with utmost conscientiousness the usual functions of a sovereign, but served also as his own chief inspector of state, traveling unceasingly over the length and breadth of his vast empire. Furthermore, he demanded full details in ministerial and other reports and participated in person in countless minutiae of Russian government, administration, and life, ranging from military uniforms and drill to the erection of new buildings in St. Petersburg and new churches all over the country. In addition to guiding the generals, the ministers, and other officials, Nicholas I often directed capital firemen as they fought dangerous conflagrations, and he was never more the autocrat than on that summer day in 1831 when he set out to bring to order a raging mob crazed by the fear of cholera. In Russian history only Peter the Great tried to do more, and more different, things in person than Nicholas.

The emperor's conduct of state business was, in the technical sense, exemplary. He virtually never failed to read carefully, consider, and sign with a minimum of delay all the papers that required his attention, devoting to them, if necessary, the nights after days of military maneuvers or the brief stops on his tireless journeys all over Russia. Nicholas found time to make a tremendous number of marginal comments, and he even would correct writing errors. According to tradition, no state documents perished in the great fire of the Winter Palace in 1837 because the monarch had examined everything pertaining to current business and had returned these materials to appropriate officials.

Nicholas's constant inspection trips all over Russia usually followed a set pattern. The emperor liked to travel very rapidly, often at night, accompanied on many occasions only by his chief of gendarmes, first Count Benckendorff and later Prince Orlov, and a bare minimum of drivers and orderlies. Upon arrival he went immediately to pray in the local cathedral or church and then

---

most of all to instill as much fear as possible among his subordinates. Therefore, he scowled and frowned, talked brusquely and, for the slightest reason, and sometimes without reason, raked one over the coals."

proceeded to examine government offices and such public institutions as hospitals, schools, and prisons. This examination resembled in every essential an army inspection and formed a complement to the endless drills and reviews to which the monarch subjected his military establishment. Orders, punishments, and rewards followed promptly. Occasionally the emperor visited special attractions such as a manufacturing exhibition in Moscow or a fair in Nizhnii Novgorod. Nicholas believed that this burdensome and even dangerous traveling—for he was incapacitated for several weeks by one accident and lucky to escape injury and perhaps death in several other instances [22]—served its purpose. He thought it especially important to come as a bolt from the blue, or, to use his favorite Russian phrase, as snow on one's head. As he explained matters to the empress in a letter written from Kazan on August 21, 1836: "Fifteen days have now passed since I left you, but I have seen and done much. We are not wasting our time. This manner of traveling, when one can bear it, is really good, because one sees everything, and they never know when or where I am going to arrive. They expect me everywhere, and if everything is not well, they at least try to make it so." [23] Yet the evaluation of this imperial activity by Count G. Barante, the French ambassador, seems more realistic:

It is always routes covered with extreme haste, religious ceremonies performed with ostentation, military reviews, and brilliant

[22] For the emperor's travels see Benckendorff's *Memoirs* appended to Schilder, II. Benckendorff served as a constant companion of Nicholas, and he included in his account numerous travel notes dictated to him by the emperor, who later read carefully and corrected the work. The accident which resulted in an injury to the emperor and its aftermath are described on pp. 757–762. Another accident, this time in the Caucasian mountains, when the monarch escaped harm, but might have easily lost his life, is depicted on p. 754. As to the extent of the sovereign's travels, there exists the following curious computation for all but the last five years of the reign included in the Minister of War Prince A. Chernyshev's report of the work of his ministry from 1825 to 1850, a report which is deluged with statistics: "In ceaseless activity, Your Imperial Majesty, during twenty-five years, deigned to traverse in the course of august journeys: 124,486 versts by land, and 12,850 by sea; out of this total, 114,640 versts within the empire, and 22,696 abroad." *SIRIO*, XCVIII, 317. One *versta* is not quite two-thirds of a mile.

[23] Schiemann, III, 476. Nicholas's letters to his wife during the years 1830–1838 compose the ninth appendix to the volume.

festivals; never an attentive examination of the administration, of the local needs, of the condition of commerce and industry, never a detailed and truly instructive conversation with civil officials or with the leading inhabitants. The visits to public educational and charitable institutions are also nothing but rapid tours where only external order and neatness can be appreciated. In a word, for such voyages the appearance is sufficient in almost all things, something that everyone knows and says. The country gains no advantage from them. It means enormous expenses added to a budget already insufficient for legitimate needs or to the burden on the localities. Nobody, at least not in the educated classes, sees in this anything but a need for continuous distraction and novelty, a more and more restless physical activity.[24]

In addition to the usual rounds of inspection, the emperor would often rush to meet an emergency. He hurried on many occasions to fires in the capital, to Moscow when cholera swept that city, to the riot which the same dread disease produced in St. Petersburg, to the sites of rebellion in the military colonies. In these urgent instances Nicholas I acted in a particularly direct and authoritarian manner. Thus in the autumn of 1830, he led for ten days in person the struggle against cholera in Moscow, introducing and enforcing various administrative, medical, and sanitary measures and contracting a mild case of the disease in the process. Still more striking was the emperor's intervention during the following summer in the cholera riots in St. Petersburg after a crazed mob stormed a temporary hospital, killed several doctors and routed Count Peter Essen, the governor general of the city who tried to restore order. Proceeding in a carriage and in the company of several high officials to Haymarket Square, the center of the riot, Nicholas brought the crowd of some five thousand people to their knees, upbraided them in his most sweeping manner and obtained docile obedience from them.[25]

---

[24] *Ibid.*, p. 463. Barante's reports to his government during the years 1830–1837 constitute the seventh appendix to the volume. The Frenchman was a noted historian as well as a diplomat. Most of the recent students of the reign of Nicholas I agree with this evaluation of the sovereign's inspection trips.

[25] See, e.g., Schilder, II, 306–311, 362–370 for the events in Moscow and in St. Petersburg respectively.

These brave acts of direct imperial intervention received extravagant praise from official ideologists, and they have been highly considered by some discerning critics of the monarch.[26] Still, there are reasons to believe that even this immediate and, so to speak, pure exercise of autocracy failed to achieve its purpose. For instance, Schiemann has criticized Nicholas's actions in Moscow which included the punishment of an excellent doctor because his hospital reported more deaths than any other with the result that for days no deaths were reported from Moscow hospitals, and the imposition of a virtually impossible quarantine on the city, fortunately, modified in application by its governor general, Prince D. Golitsyn. As to the St. Petersburg riot, Schiemann claims that the emperor in his address to the people forgot to do the most important thing, namely to enlighten them about cholera, and even unwittingly confirmed the rumors of poisoning by his reference, in a different connection, to the unruly French and Poles: the people reacted by catching and bringing to police headquarters, confident that they were executing the will of their tsar, foreigners and other suspicious-looking individuals.[27]

Nicholas I not only paid the most painstaking attention to the huge and difficult business of government, did his own inspecting of the country, and rushed to meet all kinds of emergencies, but he also maintained a special interest in certain selected fields of activity. The army, in particular, remained the emperor's passion. A junior officer at heart, Nicholas began his reign with a meticulous reform of military uniforms in which he literally counted each and every button.[28] He went on to engage, throughout the thirty years of his rule, in an endless round of drills, reviews, inspections,

---

[26] As examples of praise by government ideologists see Barsukov, op. cit., III, 208–214, and Grech, Examen de l'ouvrage de M. le Marquis de Custine intitulé la Russie en 1839, p. 40. Approving critics include Polievktov, pp. 185–186 and the author of the article on Nicholas I in the Brockhaus and Efron encyclopedia (p. 123).

[27] See Schiemann, III, 32–35, and 144–149 for the German professor's description and discussion of the developments in the old and in the new capital respectively. His criticisms are on the whole well-taken, although he appears to stretch a point when he argues that Nicholas was in no personal danger in Haymarket Square (pp. 147–148). See also Okun, op. cit., pp. 60–62.

[28] For this reform see, e.g., Schiemann, II, 106–108. The role of militarism in Nicholas's life was discussed in chap. i above.

and other military trivia. The emperor showed an interest in strategy, and he participated in the planning of several campaigns as well as of numerous maneuvers, but he appeared to be engrossed first and foremost in the minutiae of army life. Although the European monarchs of the period were in general much pre-occupied with their military establishments, Nicholas's devotion proved to be so extreme that official ideologists had to come to the defense of their sovereign. For example, Grech, addressing a foreign audience in his reply to Custine, wrote as follows: "The face of the emperor is bronzed by the sun: on the basis of this the marquis tells us that he passes the major part of his life in the open air, in reviews, or in rapid journeys. It is nothing of the sort: the major part of his life is dedicated, in his study, to affairs of state. Military exercises represent merely a recreation for him, and this recreation is so insufficient that lately doctors have been forced to advise him to take walks in addition." [29]

Engineering, architecture, building of every kind stood out as another major interest in the life of Nicholas. Again, this fascina-tion dated back to his childhood, was developed further in the course of his training as a military engineer, and had been fully formed by the time he ascended the throne. As sovereign, Nicholas alloted large sums for building in his empire and supervised actively practically all architectural and engineering work done anywhere by the state and even private construction in St. Petersburg and several other places. He patronized a number of architects, such as C. Thon and A. Stackenschneider, and wanted to introduce his favorite architectural models as standard through-out the realm. The emperor's taste tended to be varied and eclectic. He felt powerfully the attraction of the monumental and severe classical style, but he also admired the light architecture of Italian villas, as well as other current fashions, and he came to sponsor, especially in the construction of churches, Thon's ques-tionable attempt to revive the native Russian tradition. A. Benois, the best authority on this as on so many other subjects, draws another distinction: the monarch insisted on severe majesty in public buildings, yet he had a personal preference for simplicity

---

[29] Grech, *op. cit.*, p. 46. One is strongly reminded of Eisenhower and golf.

and comfort.[30] Nicholas I showed interest in art, his most lasting contribution in this field being the construction of a fine building to house the great imperial Hermitage collection, and the opening of this museum to the public.

Another area of vital concern to the emperor defies precise definition. Nicholas I exhibited a minute and passionate interest in different kinds of matters related to all sorts of people: not only subversion, or possibility of subversion, but also breaches of morality, as well as the usual promotions, awards, rewards, and punishments. The monarch liked to think in terms of individuals rather than institutions or legal abstractions, and this in turn accentuated the personal character of his autocracy. Beginning with the famous case of the Decembrists, Nicholas I paid un-flagging attention to all opponents or suspected opponents of his regime often directing police investigations, personally confronting the culprits, and prescribing their punishment, even to the exact place of exile. Similarly, in his capacity of chief protector and arbiter of public morals, the sovereign interfered in individual and private matters and issued at times such remarkable rulings as the one which declared, after the annulment of a marriage: "the young lady shall be considered a virgin." [31] It was especially through the gendarmes of the Third Department of His Majesty's Own Chancery that Nicholas I extended his control over everyone in Russia. However, although a tremendous number of matters was brought in this manner to the attention of the emperor, and although there exists a voluminous record of his participation in them, one instance will have to suffice to emphasize the extent and the pointlessness—some would say imbecility—of this system of personal intervention.

Certain peasants informed the local authorities that they knew of a cellar where a treasure was buried. A request was next made

---

[30] Benois and Lanceray, "Dvortsovoe stroitelstvo imperatora Nikolaya I," *Starye Gody* (July–Sept., 1913), 173–197; see especially p. 173. On govern-ment building see Kleinmichel, "Istoricheskoe obozrenie putei soobshcheniya i publichnykh zdanii s 1825 po 1850 god," *SIRIO*, XCVIII, 530–591.

[31] Quoted in Grunwald, *La Vie de Nicolas Ier*, p. 169. The emperor must have had the legal status of the lady in mind, but the episode is characteristic of his blunt intervening in the personal affairs of his subjects.

to the central office to assign an officer of the gendarmes to investigate the claim. The chief of the corps reported the matter to the emperor who decided: "Declare to the informers that if they are telling nonsense they will be treated as insane. If they assume this risk, and if they insist, then send him." Accordingly a lieutenant colonel of the gendarmes went with the peasants to look for ،he treasure, but failed to find it. The frightened informers pleaded that they had spoken on the basis of tradition and omens, that they had not visited the cellar themselves but believed others and that, in any case, treasures could not be found without a magic herb. Again the case went, step by step, to the sovereign. Nicholas ruled: "Because it was promised that they would be treated as insane, send them for a year to the nearest asylum." [32]

Prompt punishments and rapid rewards formed an integral part of the emperor's minute and personal participation in the affairs of his country. Typically, Nicholas summarized a segment of one of his inspection journeys as follows to Benckendorff:

We reached Bobruisk late at night. On the morning of the twelfth of August I inspected the Fifth Infantry Division and the fortress works. Both here and in Duenaburg I look at them with particular joy; everything I planted has already grown into enormous trees, especially Italian poplars. The hospital enraged me. Imagine, the functionaries had taken for their own needs the best part of the building, and what had been intended for the sick was turned into the halls of the supervisor and the doctors. For that I put the commandant into the guardhouse, dismissed the supervisor and taught everybody a lesson in my own manner.

On the next day, after an inspection of two engineer battalions and a temporary hospital, following a liturgy in the camp, we darted to Chernigov, where I only entered the cathedral, and on the fourteenth of August, at nine in the evening, we alighted at the Monastery of the Caves in Kiev.

---

[32] This episode is taken from Trotskii, *op. cit.*, pp. 114–115. Declaration of insanity, made famous by its application to Chaadaev, was used repeatedly as punishment in the reign of Nicholas I. For a defense of this measure in the case of Chaadaev see Grech, *op. cit.*, p. 104, where the journalist argues that it represented, surely, the best way to mortify the insolent author, to reform him, and to teach a lesson to others. For general comment see Presnyakov, p. 50.

I reprimanded Count Guriev who, instead of meeting me in front of the Monastery, remained waiting by the quarters assigned to me, on the right flank of the guard of honor. He did not like my reprimand, but it was a deserved one.[33]

The inspection of the Caucasus during the same year of 1837 produced one of the most striking instances of imperial punishment and, incidentally, also of reward. Again in Nicholas's own words:

Thus, Prince Dadian, a son-in-law of Count Rosen and my aide-de-camp who commanded a regiment only sixteen versts from Tiflis, drove soldiers, and especially recruits, to chop wood and to cut grass, not infrequently on the property of other landlords, and then did business in this plunder in Tiflis itself, under the eyes of his superiors. Besides, he forced soldiers' wives to work for him and he built, with the labor of the soldiers, a mill instead of barracks, and he did not even share with the poor lower ranks the considerable sums alloted to him for the purpose. Finally, this fine fellow, instead of training the two hundred recruits given him, forced them, barefoot and without uniforms, to tend his sheep, oxen, and camels. This was really too much, and as soon as the first news of it reached me, I sent my aide-de-camp Vasilchikov to the spot, his investigation disclosing things exactly as I have now told you. In view of these abominations, it was necessary to show an example of strict retribution.

During the parade I ordered the commandant to tear off Prince Dadian, as unworthy to remain my aide-de-camp, the aglet and my monogram and to send him, directly from the square, to the Bobruisk fortress for immediate arraignment by court-martial.

The emperor went on to tell Benckendorff how sorry he was to apply this extreme form of punishment, but that he believed that the circumstances required it, and that the chastisement of one who was both an aide-de-camp to the sovereign and a son-in-law of Rosen, the chief civil administrator of the Caucasus, would serve as a salutary warning to all others. Nicholas concluded: "In any case, I felt fully the horror of this scene and, in order to mitigate

---

[33] Quoted from Benckendorff's *Memoirs* in Schilder, II, 741–742.

that which was cruel in it for Rosen, I called up, right there on the spot, his son, a lieutenant of the Preobrazhenskii regiment decorated with St. George's cross in the assault on Warsaw, and made him my aide-de-camp in place of his unworthy brother-in-law." [34]

School inspections assumed the character of military reviews, and they could be equally frightening. To quote from Nikitenko's diary: "Today Nicholas visited our First High School and expressed dissatisfaction. Here are the reasons. The pupils were studying. He entered the fifth class where teacher Turchaninov was teaching history. During the lesson one of the pupils, the best, by the way, both in conduct and in achievement, listened attentively to the teacher, but only leaning on his elbow. This was taken to be a breach of discipline. . . . The curator was ordered to fire teacher Turchaninov." Another breach of discipline occurred in a class in religion, where a student sat leaning on the table behind him. In the end, the curator himself was forced to resign. [35]

And, resuming the sad story of the First High School at a later date:

The sovereign arrived angry, went everywhere, asked about everything, with the obvious intention of finding something wrong. He did not like the face of one of the pupils.—"What sort of an ugly Chukhon mug is this?" he exclaimed, looking at him with fury. In conclusion he told the director:

"Yes, in appearance you have everything in order, but what mugs your pupils possess! The First High School must be first in everything: they have not that vivacity, that fullness, that nobility which distinguishes, for instance, the pupils of the Fourth High School!" [36]

An imperial visit to a similar military school for boys found things in disorder and resulted in the loss of his company command for one officer, while another was sent to the guardhouse for

[34] *Ibid.,* pp. 753–754.
[35] Nikitenko, I, 231–232.
[36] *Ibid.,* p. 338. "Chukhon" refers to a Finnish tribe living in the vicinity of St. Petersburg. Nikitenko gave the director as his source for this story.

a week and could not be promoted until the death of Nicholas. But the following year the school was prepared.

Besides, after the sovereign's first visit we fixed wires with bells along all the staircases on all the floors, so that, as soon as the emperor's carriage appeared from Haymarket Square, all our bells began to ring. The emperor remained very well satisfied with order; having gathered around himself the youngest students, he joked and talked with us and gave us leave to go home for three days. Those pupils who remained in the institute went, at school expense, to the theater and to the circus.[37]

The juxtaposition of reward and punishment, displayed during the imperial visits to this school or in the course of the episode involving Prince Dadian and the younger Baron Rosen, characterized Nicholas's interference in the affairs of his country. Punishments struck the popular imagination most and became an indissoluble part of the image of Nicholas's Russia.[38] Yet, the emperor dispensed rewards with equal dispatch. Impulsively he piled up honors on such heroes as victorious Marshal Paskevich, and he bestowed lavishly on the select the highest aristocratic

---

[37] Nikiforov, *Vospominaniya iz vremen imperatora Nikolaya I*, pp. 38–40. Cf., e.g., Driesen, "Iz starykh arkhivov," *Krestovyi Pokhod vo Imya Pravdy, Russkaya Zhizn*, no. 167, Jan. 30, 1958.

[38] The popular attitude toward the government and its officials was reflected in the following incident described by the Slavophile Khomyakov in one of his letters: "Three days ago the Bolshoi Theater burned down, and, it appears, more than twenty persons died, including quite a number of children. . . . On the roof a man enveloped by flames was about to perish. A house painter, having crossed himself, climbed with a rope up a gutter and saved the doomed man. The people wept and threw money into his hat, some two hundred silver rubles. At this point an adjutant of Zakrevskii approached him and asked him to come to the Count, in order, of course, to receive a reward. The unfortunate hero howled: 'Have mercy on me! Why should I go to the Count? I am not guilty of anything.'—while the people shouted: 'We shall not give him to the police,' and so forth. He was barely induced to go. This was told by that same adjutant who took the hero to the governor of the city." Khomyakov, *Polnoe sobranie sochinenii*, VIII, 324–325. Barsukov recounts the same story and adds that later Nicholas I himself received the hero in his study. The emperor began with the words: "*Thank you for the good deed. Kiss me and tell me how God helped you.*" And, after listening to the hero's account, he concluded: "*Depart with God, and if there is need for it, come to me whenever you want.*" Barsukov, *op. cit.*, XII, 457–464; quoted from pp. 463–464. Italics in the original.

title, that of Prince.[39] The virtues and achievements of obscure people also often received their appropriate recompense from the ubiquitous sovereign. In addition to the instances already cited, the following case, told by Nikitenko, illustrates well the all-pervasiveness of the monarch's paternal supervision:

> In the Catherine Institute there is a girl Popandopulo, some fourteen years old. She learned from newspapers about the death of her brother, killed in a battle with the Turks. Her friends expressed their sympathy, and one of them asked her: "Are you sorry for your brother?" "Why be sorry?" she answered: "He perished for tsar and fatherland." The sovereign was informed of this, and His Majesty allotted to the girl Popandopulo, until her marriage, a pension of one thousand rubles—"for religious and loyal sentiments," as it is stated in the official document. In addition to that, at the time of her graduation from the Institute, she is to be given another thousand rubles, and the Court is to be informed of her marriage when a dowry will be provided for her.[40]

The great exertion on the part of the emperor failed to bring desired results. Even those components of the system to which the sovereign had devoted most attention betrayed his expectation. The army represented an outstanding instance. In spite of all the august efforts, it proved to be totally unprepared for the Crimean War. Indeed endless reviews and perfection in drill availed little against the better-armed, -equipped, and -led Allies. As many contemporaries and later writers observed, the military pastime of the emperor appeared to be an end in itself unrelated to the true functions and purpose of the military establishment.[41] If this

---

[39] Nicholas I granted the title of Prince to sixteen persons, the previous highest total awarded by a sovereign having been four in the reign of Paul; after the death of Nicholas I, the title was never again granted. The Russian word is *knyaz*. For a contemporary criticism of Nicholas's system of rewards as much too bountiful, see Gershenzon, ed., *op. cit.*, p. 170.

[40] Nikitenko, II, 429.

[41] Some such criticism is to be found in almost every work on the reign of Nicholas I. For a particularly sharp instance see Schiemann, II, 249–250. The most brilliant and extreme attack on the emperor's parade ground militarism was made by Mickiewicz in "The Review of the Army" which forms a part of his *Digression*. On the horrible conditions in the army and the high death rate see K. Kutuzov's report reproduced in Gershenzon, ed., *op. cit.*,

is too harsh a criticism, Nicholas I nevertheless remains condemned of superficiality and blindness. Only appearances mattered at imperial parades; only the real quality counted in war.

Other instances of direct imperial participation were often equally unsatisfactory, if less tragic. The monarch's interest in and support of architecture had some happy consequences, but many specialists complained about his taste as well as his penchant for imposing it rigidly on his subjects, for instance, when he ordered Thon to prepare models of churches for two hundred, five hundred, and one thousand persons which were to be imitated by all the architects of the empire. Nicholas's constant inspections, again, did not go beyond appearances, and his direct intervention in all kinds of things, with the resulting rewards and punishments, was always arbitrary and frequently misguided and unjust.[42] More important, all these personal efforts of the emperor could not seriously affect the enormous amount of corruption and mismanagement present in his far-flung realm.

Recent historians have elucidated with much detail and precision these weaknesses of Nicholas's rule. But long before their judgments were passed, Pogodin marked the death of his emperor with an article entitled "The Tsar's Time." The state ideologist wrote:

A miserable system which, together with unexpected blows from the outside, carried the late Emperor Nicholas to the grave! In a fit of boundless zeal for the good of the fatherland he wanted to do everything himself, worked for almost thirty years without thinking about himself, and fell a victim of the tsar's duty which

---

pp. 158–171; especially pp. 163–167. On connections between the general reactionary policy of the government and reaction in the army see Polievktov, pp. 321–338. The official view is stated in Minister of War Chernyshev's report of 1850 covering the preceding quarter of a century: "Istoricheskoe obozrenie voenno-sukhoputnogo upravleniya s 1825 po 1850 god," SIRIO, XCVIII, 299–447. An excellent recent summary is provided in Curtiss, "The Army of Nicholas I: Its Role and Character," American Historical Review, LXIII (July, 1958), 880–889.

[42] In addition to the comments already cited in this chapter, see, e.g., Schiemann's bitter criticism of the emperor in the Dadian episode (Schiemann, III, 329–330) and of the emperor's misguided reprimand delivered to Moscow merchants (ibid., IV, 16–17).

he himself had imposed. Carried away by the brilliant example of his ancestor, he failed to realize that things have changed since the time of Peter I, that Peter's activity, transferred into our age, becomes an optical illusion; that most affairs, in spite of an apparent direct dependence on the sovereign, become in this manner a prey of the arbitrariness of subordinates, protected by the sacred name of the Tsar and thus unpunishable; or these affairs follow, so to speak, their own course, according to the established pattern, often against His wishes, to the detriment of general welfare, emphasizing the contrast between Russia on paper and Russia in reality.[43]

The principle of autocracy, as taught by the theoreticians of Official Nationality, found manifold expression in the form of Nicholas's rule. The emperor kept supreme power entirely in his own hands, curbing the authority of the existing state institutions and holding them rigidly to the performance of their specific tasks, as defined narrowly by the monarch. By a series of measures, notably the development of His Majesty's Own Chancery, he bypassed repeatedly the regular procedure and obtained immediate control of various aspects of state activity. Above all, as the true father of his people, he tried to participate in everything himself, settling important and unimportant issues and dealing with the high and the low. But autocracy accounted not only for the form of Nicholas's government of Russia, but also for much of the content. For the emperor "considered the preservation of Russian autocracy in its full inviolability as his first and chief duty." [44] In this manner he identified his own person with the existing political system and with the country at large and dedicated himself to the defense of the established order. Liberalism and constitutionalism, the main enemies of the sovereign, were on the rise in Europe during the first half of the nineteenth century, their progress highlighted by the revolutions of 1830 and 1848. Even in Russia autocracy faced the challenge of Alexander I in his liberal mood and of some of his advisers, as well as of the

---

[43] Pogodin, "Tsarskoe vremya," *Istoriko-politicheskie pisma*, pp. 310–313; quoted from p. 312.
[44] Presnyakov, p. 36.

more radically oriented young officers and intellectuals. The latter even staged what came to be known as the Decembrist rebellion at the very moment of Nicholas's accession to the throne. With the new emperor in charge, it became clear that the country would obtain no constitution or liberal reforms from above. And Nicholas was equally determined to prevent their introduction from below. This uncompromising attitude toward liberalism and constitutionalism, and the concomitant fear of revolution abroad and especially at home, determined in large measure the emperor's policies in all their painful rigidity and futility.

Nicholas's treatment of the gentry illustrated the difficult predicament of the government. An autocrat first and foremost, the emperor considered the landlords to be simply servants of the state in the army or in the bureaucracy, and he hated aristocratic independence, distinction, or privilege. Many observers noted the striking difference between the cultivated counsellors surrounding Alexander I and the servile functionaries executing the commands of his brother. Nicholas I demanded absolute and unquestioning obedience from all, and he made it a point to punish the great as well as the small for every transgression he could discover.[45] Besides, it was among the gentry that liberalism grew in Russia in the eighteenth century, and it was members of this class who staged the Decembrist uprising. Still more important, in the social conditions of Russia in the first half of the nineteenth century only the landlords could make a serious bid to curb autocracy and to gain a share in the government of the country. All this more than justified imperial suspicion and hostility. But the arguments on the other side carried an even greater weight. From the rise of the principality of Moscow, the Russian state had been based on the gentry which shouldered the immense burden of state service. In the first half of the nineteenth century the government still could find no alternative. Beyond that, the well-being of the state was intimately connected in every way with the prosperity of the landlords, the one large, powerful, and articulate class in Russia. Furthermore, the gentry controlled the vast serf masses of the

---

[45] See, e.g., the episode with aristocratic youths described in Schiemann, II, 400.

nation, representing law and order in the countryside. Nicholas
I always remembered the Decembrists, but he also appreciated the
implications of the Pugachev rebellion as well as of the lesser
peasant uprisings which totaled several hundred in the course of
his reign.[46] Their success would mean the end of the entire
established system, autocracy and all. Willingly or not, the emperor had to rely primarily on the gentry to support the existing
order.

In these complex circumstances, the sovereign's policies in regard to the landlords tried to attain several goals. For one thing,
Nicholas I wanted to obtain better service from the gentry and at
the same time to bring members of this class, as well as of every
other, under complete regulation and control of his minutely
despotic system. He also wished the gentry to be strong, prosperous,
and conservative in accordance with its key position in his scheme
of things. The landlords, as all other Russians, were to perform
in full their assigned state function. Yet the importance of the
gentry was so great that in moments of danger Nicholas I hastened
to give unqualified recognition to their interests, repressing even
his usual autocratic manner.

The insistence on devoted service to the state within a single,
enormous bureaucratic system affected numerous members of
the landlord class who held positions in the imperial administration. More strikingly, local organizations and leaders of this
estate were largely incorporated into the governmental machine,
with elected gentry representatives becoming assistants to the
governors in such matters as transportation, army draft, and
public health. "So-called gentry self-government is brought fully
into the system of the bureaucratic agencies of the government." [47]
As to the regulations and restrictions so characteristic of Nicholas's
rule, the landlords had their share of them, and sometimes more
than their share. For instance, they were the ones primarily
affected by the various limitations and prohibitions on travel and

---

[46] A recent thorough count notes over seven hundred such risings during
Nicholas's rule. Ignatovich, "Krestyanskie volneniya pervoi chetverti XIX veka,"
Voprosy Istorii, 1950, no. 9, pp. 48–70. The article deals with both the first
and the second quarters of the century. See also Okun, op. cit., p. 44.
[47] Presnyakov, p. 38. See also, e.g., Okun, op. cit., pp. 184–185.

study abroad. The concern of the government with the strength and well-being of the gentry expressed itself in direct financial help to and provisions for the resettlement of some impoverished members of this class, and also in attempts to make the gentry more exclusive by making ennoblement through promotion in state service somewhat more difficult and by providing for entail in the case of large estates. In a broader sense, the government of Nicholas I showed extreme class consciousness, the landlords enjoying every educational and career advantage.

Of all the events which occurred during Nicholas's long reign, the revolutions of 1848 frightened the sovereign most. It was in the spring of that ominous year that he appealed dramatically to the landlords. Speaking to representatives of the St. Petersburg gentry, the emperor described himself and his wife as "local landed gentry," emphasized that the landlords' rights to their estates were sacred and inviolable, and even declared disarmingly: "Gentlemen! I have no police, I do not like them. You are my police. Each one of you is my steward and must, for the sake of peace in the state, bring on his own to my knowledge every evil doing and transgression he has noticed. . . . We shall go step in step, act with one mind, and then we shall be invincible." [48] And, in a more flowery passage: "Extend to each other, as brothers, as children of the fatherland, the hand of friendship so that the last hand reaches to me, and be confident that under my leadership, no earthly power will be able to bother us." [49]

The sovereign's dependence on the gentry determined his attitude toward the gravest economic and social problem of Russia —serfdom. Nicholas I personally disapproved of this institution: in the army and in the country at large he saw only too clearly the misery it produced, and he remained constantly apprehensive of the danger of insurrection; also, as has already been indicated, the autocrat had no sympathy for aristocratic privilege when it clashed with the interests of the state. Yet, as he explained the matter, in

[48] Schiemann, IV, pp. 147–148. As usual, the sovereign went into considerable detail in his instructions to the gentry. Thus he urged them not to discuss political subjects at the table because their words could be misunderstood by and have a noxious influence on the ignorant house serfs. *Ibid.*, p. 147.

[49] *Ibid.*, p. 146.

1842, in the State Council: "There is no doubt that serfdom, as it exists at present in our land, is an evil, palpable and obvious to all. But to touch it *now* would be a still more disastrous evil. . . . The Pugachev rebellion proved how far popular rage can go." [50]

When a member of the Council proposed merely to limit the arbitrary power of the landlords by means of so-called "inventories," that is, formal statements of the serfs' obligations to their masters, the sovereign replied: "I am, of course, autocratic and absolute, but I could never dare to take this step just as I could not dare *to order* landlords to make contracts. This must be, I repeat once more, a product of their own free will, and only experience will tell to what extent it may later become possible to move from the voluntary principle to that of compulsion." [51] In 1842, in 1848, and in fact throughout his reign, the emperor feared, at the same time, two different revolutions. There was the danger of a gentry bid to obtain a constitution which, in the opinion of Uvarov and others, would follow the decision of the government to deprive the landlords of their serfs. There loomed also the threat of an elemental, popular uprising unleashed by such a major shock to the established order as the coveted emancipation.[52]

In the end, although the government paid repeated, almost constant, attention to serfdom, it achieved very little. The emperor himself, as well as most of his ablest associates, including Kiselev, Speranskii, and Kankrin, tried to deal with the cursed issue of human bondage and the attendant economic and social evils. The State Council and many departments and ministries, from police to education, were also concerned with the matter. After the dissolution of the Committee of the Sixth of December, nine

[50] *SIRIO*, XCVIII, 114–115. Italics in the original.
[51] *Ibid.*, p. 119. Italics in the original. The contracts in question were emancipation agreements between individual landlords and their serfs.
[52] Uvarov's views on serfdom and emancipation were discussed in chap. iii. The minister's warning of a gentry revolution contrasted with Pogodin's conviction that the government showed too much concern for this phantom and too little for the real threat of a mass uprising. In contrast to Nicholas I, however, Pogodin came to believe that emancipation was feasible, desirable, and even necessary as the one effective way to eliminate the threat. See especially Pogodin, "O vliyanii vneshnei politiki na vnutrennyuyu," *Istoriko-politicheskie pisma*, pp. 245–271.

special committees were appointed in the course of the reign with
the specific purpose of tackling the problem of serfdom or some
parts of it. But all this activity produced negligible results. New
laws either left the change in the serfs' status to the discretion
of their landlords, thus merely continuing Alexander's well-meaning but ineffectual efforts, or they prohibited only certain extreme
abuses connected with serfdom such as selling members of a single
family to different buyers. Even the minor concessions granted to
the peasants were sometimes taken back. For instance, in 1847,
the government permitted serfs to purchase their freedom, if
their master's estate was sold for debt. In the next few years, however, the permission was made inoperative without being formally
rescinded.[53] Following the revolutions of 1848, the meager and
hesitant government solicitude for the serfs came to an end. Only
the bonded peasants of Western Russian provinces obtained certain substantial advantages in the reign of Nicholas I. They received this preferential treatment because the government wanted
to use them in its struggle against the Polish influence which was
prevalent among the landlords of that area—a policy to be discussed later in this chapter.[54]

Determined to preserve autocracy, afraid to abolish serfdom, and
suspicious of all independent initiative and popular participation,
the emperor and his government could not introduce in their
country the much-needed fundamental reforms. In practice, as well
as in theory, they looked backward, not forward. Important
developments, however, did take place in certain areas where
change would not threaten the fundamental political, social, and
economic structure of the Russian Empire. Especially significant
proved to be the codification of law and the far-reaching reform
in the condition of the state peasants. The new code, produced in

[53] SIRIO, XCVIII, 248–267.
[54] On serfdom in the reign of Nicholas I see especially Dzhivelegov, Melgunov,
and Picheta, eds., *Russkoe obshchestvo i krestyanskii vopros v proshlom i
nastoyashchem*, vol. III and parts of vols. II and IV. See also Semevskii,
Krestyanskii vopros v Rossii v XVIII i pervoi polovine XIX veka, vol. II;
Kizevetter, *op. cit.*; and Kizevetter, *Devyatnadtsatyi vek v istorii Rossii*, pp.
22–35. As one example of the extreme worry and caution displayed by the
government in relation to serfdom see the document published in *SIRIO*,
XCVIII, 270–271.

the late 1820's and the early 1830's by the immense labor of Speranskii and his associates, marked, with all its defects, a tremendous
achievement and a milestone in Russian jurisprudence. Introduced
in January, 1833, it replaced the ancient *Ulozhenie* of Tsar Alexis,
dating from 1649, and was destined to last until 1917. The reorganization of the state peasants followed several years later
and found its protagonist in Count Kiselev who headed, from
1837, the new ministry of state domains. It succeeded in improving the administration and in bettering the economic condition of this vast body of peasants approximately equal in size to
the serfs.

Several aspects of these successful reforms deserve notice. The
codification of law and the reorganization of state peasants did
not interfere with the main problems of the Russian state, such
as autocracy, serfdom, and the position of the gentry. Indeed,
Speranskii abandoned his ambition to recast the legal system of
Russia following the French pattern, which he nourished in the
reign of Alexander I, in favor of an entirely conservative approach.
Both changes stemmed from the energy and the ability of the
individuals in charge—Speranskii and Kiselev—who enjoyed the
confidence of the emperor. Presumably, similar results could
have been obtained by a number of other ministers, had they
been made of the same stuff. Also, these particular reforms fitted
nicely into the general pattern of Nicholas's rule by helping the
government to operate more effectively and directly in two important fields of activity: legislation and the control of state
peasants.[55] Other promising policies in the course of the reign,
for instance, some of Kankrin's financial measures, turned out to
be less important in the long run.

---

[55] On Speranskii see especially Raeff, *Michael Speransky: Statesman of Imperial Russia, 1772–1839.* Chap. xi (pp. 320–346) has as its subject "Codifying Russian Law." The book contains excellent bibliographies. On Kiselev
see Zablotskii-Desyatovskii, *Graf P. D. Kiselev i ego vremya;* Druzhinin,
Gosudarstvennye krestyane i reforma P. D. Kiseleva; or a convenient brief
account, Bogoslovskii, "Gosudarstevennye krestyane pri Nikolae I," *Istoriya
Rossii v XIX veke,* I, 236–260. See also Kiselev's own report of the activities
of his department up to 1850, "Obozrenie upravleniya Gosudarstvennykh
Imushchestv za poslednie 25 let s 20 noyabrya 1825 po 20 noyabrya 1850 g,"
SIRIO, XCVIII, 468–498.

But even partial reform represented the exception rather than the rule in the time of Nicholas. More characteristic by far was the general defensive attitude, an attempt to preserve at all costs the established system. This basic orientation permeated all policies of the government, but it found particularly characteristic expression in the activities of the ministry of education and of the Third Department of His Majesty's Own Chancery, that is, of the special police. The many functions and purposes of the ministry of education were summarized as follows by Shevyrev, on an official occasion at the very end of the reign:

To bring education in our fatherland under the law of state unity; to encompass in this education, as its great center, the fundamental Russian people, and at the same time to include together with it peoples of different languages and religions which are linked to us by means of the state union and which as radii join the central core of the Russian people; to establish the education of the Russian people on those basic principles which have been determined by its history and which constitute the strength of its life; through education and upbringing to draw forth everywhere the consciousness of these principles, to discover and to publish for this purpose all source materials on the fatherland; to create a class of Russian male and female teachers for family education; to shed the light of knowledge over all the estates giving to each one that part which it needs from the general treasury of enlightenment; to raise both the intellectual and the moral level of high schools bringing them closer to the universities; to stimulate in all estates, but especially in the gentry, the spirit of patriotic competition and to multiply the means for the training of youth; having given to our youth a national foundation, to provide for it also all the means necessary to follow the achievements, inventions, and discoveries of the world-wide enlightenment and to transmit these benefits to the fatherland, eliminating harm and evil which are inevitable in all affairs of men; for that purpose to raise the universities and to place them on a level with contemporary European scholarship; to elevate, secure, and reward the difficult calling of scholar, summoning to this calling native

Russians brought up in the midst of their people; to bestow on them all the benefits of learning; to send gifted youths in search of knowledge to all the corners of enlightened Europe, seeing to it stringently that they, like bees, suck only honey from the flowers of world enlightenment, and, with gratitude, bring it into the fatherland hive; to open education to all free estates and, in particular, to convince the gentry of the necessity of enlightenment in the fatherland; to offer this enlightenment at home; to erect school buildings of the beauty, size, and grandeur which correspond to the might, glory, and expanse of the state where they are erected; to stimulate the development of the practical sciences, useful to society, trade, and industry, in order to develop the material forces of the state and thus to keep pace with the better aspects of the progress of scholarship in the West; in another sense, to oppose its materialism, to sanctify the entire temple of popular education by the Lord's altar, the cross, and prayer—these are the problems which have been solved in the course of the last thirty years in the history of education of our fatherland, according to the thought and the will of our indefatigable monarch.[56]

Shevyrev's wordy summation of the activities of the ministry of education contained much empty rhetoric and a good deal of repetition. But it emphasized effectively the importance of the official ideology in the field of education, paying special attention to the principle of "nationality," the implementation of which is to be considered later in this chapter. And it mentioned many significant government policies, some of which advanced while others retarded the growth of enlightenment in Russia.

On the credit side, it should be noted that the ministry of education spent large sums to provide new buildings, laboratories and libraries, and such other aids to scholarship as the excellent Pulkovo observatory, that teachers' salaries were substantially increased—tremendously in the case of professors, according to the University Statute of 1835—that, in general, the government

---

[56] Shevyrev, *Istoriya Imperatorskogo Moskovskogo Universiteta*, pp. 468–470. For a subsequent historian's account of the educational policies of the reign see Rozhdestvenskii, *Istoricheskii Obzor Deyatelnosti Ministerstva Narodnogo Prosveshcheniya*, 1802–1902.

of Nicholas I showed a commendable interest in the physical plant
necessary for education and in the material well-being of those
engaged in instruction. Nor was quality neglected. Uvarov in
particular did much to raise educational and scholarly standards
in Russia in the course of the sixteen years during which he
headed the ministry. Of especially great and lasting value proved
to be the establishment of many new chairs and the corresponding
opening up of numerous new fields of learning in the universities
of the empire, and the practice of sending promising young Russian scholars for extended training abroad. The Russian educational system, with all its fundamental flaws, came to emphasize
academic thoroughness and high standards. Indeed, the government utilized them to make education more exclusive at all levels
of schooling.

Technical and applied education, the emperor's favorite kind
of learning, received exceptional attention. "Practical" schools
founded in the reign of Nicholas I included the following: in
St. Petersburg, in 1828, a technological institute, in 1835 a school
of law, in 1842 a school of architecture, which resulted from a
combination of two other schools established earlier by the
emperor; in Moscow, in 1826, a school of technical drawing, in
1830 a school of arts and crafts, in 1844 an institute for land-
surveyors; also, several veterinary and agricultural schools in
different parts of the realm. The ministry of state domains contributed its share to practical education by operating one agricultural and one forestry institute, eight model farms, three
agricultural high schools, and fourteen schools of gardening.[57]
Technical subjects were similarly introduced or developed in the
universities. The practical emphasis often received priority over
other possible approaches. Law schools, for instance, to cite one
authority, were directed to produce "not learned jurists, but
bureaucrats." [58] Oriental studies stood out as another field of learning which grew and developed in the reign of Nicholas I. Largely
because of Uvarov's special interest and patronage, these studies,

[57] The statistics concerning schools belonging to the ministry of state
domains were taken from "Nikolai I," *Bolshaya Entsiklopediya*, XIV, 74;
and *SIRIO*, XCVIII, 490.
[58] Polievktov, p. 242.

in particular Eastern languages, came to be offered not only in universities, but also in certain high schools.[59]

However, while the government of Nicholas I wanted to provide well for its schools and teachers and while in some ways it promoted learning in the country, several basic state policies tended to restrict and even stifle education and intellectual life in Russia. These included most notably attempts to standardize education and to concentrate the entire educational process in the hands of the central authorities; to limit the individual's schooling according to his social background, so that each person would remain in his assigned place in life; to foster exclusively the official ideology; and, above all, to eliminate every trace or possibility of intellectual opposition or subversion.

The intimate connection between the ministry of education and the doctrine of Official Nationality was discussed in the preceding chapter and needs no further elaboration. The restrictive policies of the ministry expressed, as has been indicated, one aspect of that teaching, as interpreted by the dynastic group. In order to assure that each class of Russians obtained only "that part which it needs from the general treasury of enlightenment," the government resorted to increased tuition rates and to such requirements as special certificates of leave which pupils belonging to the lower layers of society had to obtain from their village or town communities before they could attend high school. Members of the upper class, by contrast, received inducements to continue their education, many boarding schools for the gentry being created for the purpose. Ideally, in the government scheme of things—and reality failed to live up to the ideal—children of peasants and of lower classes in general were to attend parish schools or other schools of the same educational level only,[60] students of middle-

---

[59] Concerning Oriental studies in Russian universities and schools of the period see Uvarov, Desyatiletie ministerstva narodnogo prosveshcheniya, 1833–1843, pp. 23–25.

[60] As an official report put it: "This method of education, being limited exclusively to a religious instruction of the young, must spread and confirm good character in the rising generation, and, together with this, order and obedience—this, so to speak, necessary moral discipline in social and family life." The pupils were not to proceed further where "obtaining academic degrees, they in their new, unusual for them, condition would, not infre-

class origin were to study in the county schools, while high schools and universities catered primarily, although not exclusively, to the gentry. Special efforts were made throughout the reign to restrict the education of the serfs to elementary and "useful" subjects. Schools for girls were under the patronage of the empress and the jurisdiction of the Fourth Department of His Majesty's Own Chancery. Here too, the government stressed the need to correlate the extent and type of instruction and the social background of the students, the desirability of practical subjects, and other characteristic aims.[61]

As to centralization and standardization, Nicholas I and his associates did everything in their power to introduce absolute order and regularity into the educational system of Russia, a policy which reflected closely the general orientation of the government. The state even extended its minute control to private schools and, indeed, education in the home. By a series of laws and rules issued in 1833–1835, private institutions, which were not to increase in number in the future except where public schooling was not available, received regulations and instructions from central authorities, while inspectors were appointed to assure their compliance. "They had to submit to the law of unity which formed the foundation of the reign." [62] Home education came under state influence through rigid government control of teachers: Russian private tutors began to be considered as state employees, subject to appropriate examinations and enjoying the same pensions and awards as other comparable officials; at the same time the government strictly prohibited the hiring of foreign instructors who did not possess the requisite certificates testifying to academic competence and exemplary moral character. As has already been

---

quently, be a burden to themselves and to their families," SIRIO, XCVIII, 480–481. Cf. Charnoluskii, "Narodnoe obrazovanie v pervoi polovine XIX v.," in Istoriya Rossii v XIX veke, IV, 68–128, especially pp. 96–97.

[61] Indeed, in the words of one specialist, the girls were divided not only on the basis of class origin, but also "on the basis of the Table of Ranks" —"They were distributed among the institutes in strict accordance with their social class and the position of their fathers in government service," Kovalenskii, "Srednyaya shkola," in Istoriya Rossii v XIX veke, IV, 140. The chapter contains sections dealing with the education of women.

[62] Shevyrev, op. cit., p. 483.

noted, Nicholas I himself led the way in supervising and inspecting schools in Russia. The emperor's assistants followed his example. To quote from Shevyrev's history of the University of Moscow: "No other reign produced such a bounty of visits to the University by its superior authorities as the reign of Tsar Nicholas. Vigilant and the closest possible supervision on the part of the ministers remained unbroken, so to speak, in the course of the years." [63]

A relentless struggle against all pernicious ideas constituted one of the main activities of the ministry of education. Teachers and students, lectures and books were generally suspect and had to be watched. In 1834 full-time inspectors were introduced into universities to keep vigil over the behavior of students outside the classroom. This treatment of knowledge and education as in large part subversion found expression on several levels of government. Thus, while Uvarov fought revolution, godlessness, and every other form of corruption in the schools and universities of the empire, he in turn had to defend himself and his ministry to the emperor from the charges of being too liberal.[64] The monarch himself held invariably a more limited and suspicious view of education, and so did many of his associates. In fact, this charge of liberalism provided nourishment for intrigues against the minister and contributed heavily to his eventual downfall.

With the revolutionary year of 1848 unrelieved repression set in. Russians were forbidden to travel abroad, an order which hit hard teachers and students. The number of students without government scholarships was limited, except for the school of medicine, to three hundred per university. Uvarov had to resign in favor of a completely reactionary and subservient functionary, Prince P. Shirinskii-Shikhmatov.[65] New restrictions further curtailed university autonomy and academic freedom. Constitutional law and philosophy were eliminated from the curricula, with only logic and

---

[63] *Ibid.*, p. 509.

[64] See Uvarov's annual and other reports to Nicholas I which are remarkably defensive in tone. The reports can be found in the corresponding issues of the *Zhurnal Ministerstva Narodnogo Prosveshcheniya.*

[65] Cf. Shirinskii-Shikhmatov's statement quoted in chap. ii above: "You should know that I have neither a mind nor a will of my own—I am merely a blind tool of the emperor's will."

psychology retained to be taught by professors of theology. In fact, in the opinion of some specialists, the universities themselves came close to being eliminated, only the timely intervention of certain high officials, notably D. Bludov, preventing this disaster.[66] Even Pogodin was impelled in the very last years of the reign to accuse the government of imposing upon Russia "the quiet of a graveyard, rotting and stinking, both physically and morally." [67]

The Third Department of His Majesty's Own Chancery pursued many of the same ends as the ministry of education, only still more openly. Reference has already been made to the key role of the gendarmery in Nicholas I's system of personal government and to the position of the successive heads of the corps, Benckendorff and Orlov, as the emperor's closest associates. The Third Department, which came to symbolize to many Russians the entire reign of Nicholas I, acted as the autocrat's main weapon against subversion and revolution and as his principal agency for controlling the behavior of his subjects and for distributing punishments and rewards among them.[68] The edict of July 3, 1826 declared:

I assign the following field of activity to this Third Department of My Own Chancery:

1. All orders and all reports in every case belonging to the higher police.

2. Information about the number of various sects and schisms which exist in the state.

3. Reports about discoveries of false banknotes, coins, stamping, documents, etc., the search for and the further investigation in

---

[66] E.g., it has been asserted without qualification that Bludov "in 1848 saved our universities from being closed," in "Bludov, Dimitrii Nikolaevich," *Entsiklopedicheskii Slovar* (Brockhaus-Efron), IV, 104.

[67] Pogodin, *Istoriko-politicheskie pisma*, p. 259. For a recent study of "1848" in Russian history see Nifontov, *Rossiya v 1848 godu*. Cf. Berlin, "1848 and Russia," *Slavonic and East European Review*, XXVI, (April, 1948), 85–125.

[68] For the organization of the Third Department and other detailed information about it see especially the works of Lemke and Trotskii. Interesting brief selections from source materials are available in Gershenzon, ed., *op. cit.*, pp. 119–130. A brief official summary of the activities of the Third Department during its first fifty years of existence, 1826–1876, was published in Bogucharskii, "Trete Otdelenie Sobstvennoi E. I. V. Kantselyarii o sebe samom," *Vestnik Evropy*, March, 1917, pp. 85–125.

connection with which remains in the jurisdiction of the ministries
of finance and internal affairs.

4. *Information about all persons placed under police supervision*
as well as all orders in that connection.

5. *Exile and distribution as to place of suspected and noxious*
individuals.

6. *Superintendence, supervision, and management of the econ-*
omy of all the places of incarceration where state prisoners are
confined.

7. *All regulations and orders concerning foreigners who reside*
in Russia, enter, or leave the state.

8. *Reports about all occurrences without exception.*

9. *Statistical information which has police pertinence. . . .*[69]

Instructions to gendarme officers delegated them an even greater
measure of competence and authority. In one case, for instance, a
directive listed all transgressions and abuses of the law, everything
disturbing peace and order, as well as the righting of wrongs by
means of bringing them to the monarch's attention and the discovery of those needy people who are worthy of state help, as lying
within the purview of the officer, and concluded: "However, it
is impossible to name all the occurrences and all the subjects to
which you must turn your attention, or to outline the rules which
should guide you in all circumstances. But I rely in this respect on
your perspicacity and, still more, on the disinterested and noble
quality of your mode of thinking." [70] The final phrase represented
more than mere rhetoric: the government tried hard to make the
gendarmery an elite corps recruited from the best families of the
empire and distinguished by their polish of culture and their excellent manners.

These guardians of the state displayed incessant activity: "In
their effort to embrace the entire life of the people, they intervened actually in every matter in which it was possible to intervene. Family life, commercial transactions, personal quarrels,
projects of inventions, escapes of novices from monasteries—every-

---

[69] Quoted in Trotskii, *op. cit.*, pp. 34–35.
[70] The directive is reproduced in Schilder, I, pp. 468–469; quoted from p. 469.

thing interested the secret police. At the same time the Third Department received a tremendous number of petitions, complaints, denunciations, and each one resulted in an investigation, each one became a separate case." [71]

The Third Department also prepared detailed, interesting, and remarkably candid reports of all sorts for the emperor, supervised literature, ranging from the minute control of Pushkin to the ordering of various "inspired" articles in defense of Russia and the existing system, and fought every trace of revolutionary infection.[72] Yet most of this feverish activity seemed to be to no purpose. Endless investigations of subversion, stimulated by the monarch's own suspiciousness, revealed very little. Even the most important radical group uncovered during the reign, the Petrashevtsy, fell victim not to the gendarmery, but to its great rival, the ordinary police, which continued to be a part of the ministry of the interior. Short on achievements, the Third Department proved to be long on failings. The gendarmes expanded constantly their pointless work to increase their own importance, quarrelled with other government agencies, notably the police, and opened the way to such fantastic adventurers as I. Sherwood, as well as to countless run-of-the-mill informers who flooded them with their reports. The false reports turned out to be so numerous that the Third Department proceeded to punish some of their authors and to stage weekly burnings of the denunciations.

Censorship represented another interest of the gendarmes. This function belonged to the ministry of education, but the Third Department came to play an increasingly important and even dominant role in that field. There existed also various special censorships. Except for a brief liberal interlude of 1828–1830—

---

[71] Trotskii, *op. cit.*, p. 111. As one observer remarked, in Nicholas's Russia: "Fish swam in the water, birds sang in the forest, because they were permitted to do so by the authorities." Quoted in V. Riasanovsky, *op. cit.*, part II, issue I, p. 161.

[72] Some of these reports, for the years 1827–1832, were published in *Krasnyi Arkhiv*, XXXVIII, 138–174; XLVI, 133–159, under the general title: "Gr. A. Kh. Benkendorf o Rossii." The best chronological account of various "cases" handled by the Third Department is in Lemke, *Nikolaevskie zhandarmy i literatura 1826–1855 gg.* The book contains an interesting section on Pushkin (pp. 465–526).

from the appointment of Prince Karl Lieven as minister of education to the outbreak of the July Revolution—the system proved to be extremely oppressive, and it became unbearable after new revolutions broke out in 1848. Then a supreme secret committee on censorship headed by Count D. Buturlin, so-called "censorship over the censors," went into operation, with virtually every printed word becoming suspect. As Nikitenko, himself a censor, complained in 1850:

> And thus, this is how many censorships we now have: general censorship attached to the ministry of education, the main office of censorship, the supreme secret committee, ecclesiastical censorship, military censorship, the censorship attached to the ministry of foreign affairs, theatrical censorship attached to the ministry of the imperial court, newspaper censorship attached to the postal department, the censorship of the Third Department of His Majesty's Own Chancery, and the new pedagogical censorship. In sum: ten censorship agencies. If one adds up all the officials in charge of censorship, their number would exceed the number of books published in a year.
>
> I was mistaken. There are more. There is also the censorship concerned with legal works and attached to the Second Department of His Majesty's Own Chancery, and the censorship of foreign books—altogether twelve.[73]

Ridiculous extremes of Russian censorship in the reign of Nicholas I, especially after 1848, are well-known. It is sufficient to mention some of the instances cited by Nikitenko: the elimination of the "forces of nature" from a textbook in physics, questions probing the hidden meaning of an ellipsis in an arithmetic, changes from "were killed" to "perished" in an account of Roman emperors, and the demand that the author of a fortune-telling book explain why in his opinion stars influence the fate of men.[74] In line with the general tone of Official Nationality, some censors supplemented their decisions with moral lessons. For example, the

---

[73] Nikitenko, I, 396. Nikitenko's list is not complete.
[74] Ibid., pp. 393–417. For government fear that musical notations might conceal secret codes, see Gershenzon, ed., op. cit., p. 105.

notorious A. Krasovskii not only banned certain "Stanzas to Elisa," but explained that the smile of a woman must not be called "heavenly"; that her "one tender look" should not be worth more to the lovestruck poet than "the attention of the entire universe," because the universe includes tsars and other "lawful authorities"; that the desire to retire with the loved one into a desert suggests a shirking of state service; and that in general blessedness can be found only near the Gospel, not near a woman.[75]

If love lyrics sometimes ran into trouble, political discussion was virtually impossible. It became dangerous to give a favorable— let alone an unfavorable—consideration to government actions.[76] As L. Dubbelt, a ranking official of the Third Department, instructed the loyal editor of *The Northern Bee*, Bulgarin: "The theater, exhibitions, guest houses, the market place, inns, confectionaries—this is your territory. And don't you dare take a step beyond it." [77] After 1848 even that territory was beset with perils. No wonder that Nikitenko exclaimed at the end of the reign that there were no new books or manuscripts to be found in Russia,[78] and that Pogodin spoke of a graveyard.

Autocracy represented the very essence of the regime which Nicholas I imposed upon Russia. It guided the monarch's general outlook and determined his particular policies. Still, the other two principles of Official Nationality, "Orthodoxy" and "nationality," also played a certain role in the system of rule instituted by the

[75] Quoted in Trotskii, *op. cit.*, pp. 94–95. A famous example of this moral fervor in censorship was the treatment of Gogol's great novel "Dead Souls." A censor objected to the title on the ground that the human soul was immortal, adding that Chichikov's price of two and a half rubles per soul revolted one's feelings. Eventually the title was expanded into "The Adventures of Chichikov or Dead Souls." See especially Khokhlov, "Rozhdenie Mertvykh Dush," *Russkie Novosti* (Paris), no. 352, Feb. 29, 1952.

[76] " 'Neither blame, nor praise'—observed an imperial note—'is compatible with the dignity of the government or with the order which fortunately exists among us; one must obey and keep one's thoughts to oneself'." And: "It was forbidden to make 'any criticism, even indirect, of the actions and decisions of the government and of established authorities, regardless of their rank in the hierarchy.' " Quoted in Miliukov, Seignobos, and Eisenmann, *op. cit.*, II, 785. For the context of the first statement, see Barsukov, *op. cit.*, X, 525–538, especially p. 538.

[77] Quoted in "Severnaya Pchela," *Entsiklopedicheskii Slovar* (Brockhaus-Efron), LXIII, 250–251, especially p. 251.

[78] Nikitenko, I, 395.

emperor, although their political impact was less direct and ubiquitous. Orthodoxy carried a manifold meaning for the tsar. He considered the Orthodox Church as an essential part of the established order in Russia, and also as a great mainstay of that order. In other words, the church performed, in one sense, the same function as the ministry of education and the Third Department. In that connection, Nicholas I regarded Orthodox church membership as an extremely desirable pledge of good citizenship, stressed religion in the schools and the universities of the empire, insisted on a very close relationship between church and state, and treated the Holy Synod as well as the entire ecclesiastical establishment in his usual authoritarian manner. Count Nicholas Protasov, a despotic cavalry officer who held, from 1836 to 1855, the position of the Ober-Procurator of the Holy Synod, served as the emperor's main agent in church affairs.

Nicholas I proved to be particularly sensitive to every offense, or imagined offense, against religion, as demonstrated, for example, by the case of the unfortunate foreign teacher who was taken to an insane asylum, put into a strait jacket for twenty-four hours and after that ordered to leave the country, because he had sat down during an Orthodox church service.[79] Native Russian dissenters presented a more serious problem. The government divided them into "most pernicious," "pernicious," and "less pernicious," depending on their acceptance or rejection of the state—in particular prayer for the tsar and military service—and of the church with its sacraments, especially marriage, and its hierarchy; and it waged a determined struggle against them. Those assigned to the first category suffered most: their places of worship were closed; large groups were transported to Transcaucasia or to Siberia; the sectarians were barred from high schools and universities; many of them were forced into the army. In 1838 children of the so-called "priestless," a wing of the Old Believers which denied the state and marriage, were declared illegitimate and wards of the state. All dissenters were forbidden missionary activity, specifically the conversion of the Orthodox, and such public display of their faiths as processions and bell ringing.

---

[79] Schiemann, II, 209.

Major denominations, such as the Roman Catholic and the Lutheran, fared much better. But the issue of Catholicism became entangled with the problem of Poland and the Polish influence in Western Russia, while Lutheranism entered as an element into complex rivalries and developments in the Baltic Provinces. These topics will be considered later in this chapter in connection with the concept of "nationality" and its practical implementation during the reign of Nicholas I. The greatest gain for Orthodoxy accrued in 1839, when the Uniates severed their connection with Rome and joined the Eastern Church. However, although official reports boasted of constant victories for the state church, other evidence suggests that the number of sectarians and schismatics increased rather than declined in the course of the period. Intensified persecution led to greater bitterness and hostility on the one hand and to wholesale bribery and corruption of officials on the other. As one historian observed with regard to the religious policies of Nicholas I: "The gulf between the ideology of the Government and that of the people grew and broadened during that reign in perhaps greater dimensions than even the gulf between the Government and the intelligentsia." [80]

Still, the picture of a sovereign who appointed a hussar to run the church and who utilized religion for police purposes tells by no means the entire story of Nicholas I and Orthodoxy. The deep personal piety of the emperor found reflection in various matters of state. Thus it was the religious part of his coronation as King of Poland which worried Nicholas I most and which he arranged so as not to compromise in any manner his exclusive allegiance to

---

[80] Kornilov, op. cit., I, 298. For an official account of the gains of the Orthodox Church in Russia see Protasov's report for the first twenty-five years of Nicholas I's reign: "Otchet Ober-Prokurora Svyateishego Sinoda, 1825–1850," SIRIO, XCVIII, 457–460. Quite a different picture was presented by such intelligent observers as I. Aksakov who made thorough investigations of dissent in various areas of the Russian empire. I. Aksakov, Sochineniya, VII, 834–864. While officially the total number of dissenters was given as under one million, the best scholarly opinion puts the figure at above eight million. This remains, however, no more than an enlightened guess. Works dealing with various aspects of the position of the Russian Orthodox Church in the reign of Nicholas I include: Blagovidov, Ober-prokurory Sv. Sinoda; Kotovich, Dukhovnaya tsenzura v Rossii (1799–1855 gg.); Titlinov, Dukhovnaya shkola v Rossii v XIX stoletii. Vypusk vtoroi. (Protasovskaya epokha i reformy 60-kh godov).

Orthodoxy.[81] In a broader sense, Christian ideals inspired the monarch in his incessant toil to establish justice and well-being in Russia and to defeat revolution and atheism abroad. Christian principles, which as we have seen formed such a substantial part of the doctrine of Official Nationality, were taught in earnest in the schools and even the regiments of the empire. And while they failed to destroy the harshness and the brutality characteristic of the reign, they at least help the historian to classify the Russia of Nicholas I with various European *anciens régimes* and to draw a sharp line between the system of Nicholas and those twentieth-century states which have known no religious or moral inhibitions.

The problem of "nationality" acquired a new meaning in the reign of Nicholas I. To quote a leading authority: "1831 is the date of the birth of the Russification policy in the borderlands; the Western region is its first arena." [82] Other historians stress similarly the rise of Russian national feeling and the suppression of other ethnic groups by the Russians as characteristic of the period. Yet it would be quite incorrect to ascribe imperial actions simply to a new sense of nationalism. Other considerations carried greater weight, although the growth of Russian romantic nationalism should not be ignored entirely. The realities of the Russian politics of the period corresponded, again, to a remarkable extent to the theoretical constructions of the doctrine of Official Nationality.

The adherents to that ideology, it will be remembered, all had a great pride in Russia, the Russian state, and the Russian language. To that extent nationalism did characterize both Nicholas I and his entire reign, revealing itself in general educational and other policies of the government as well as in such details as the order to speak Russian at court receptions and for the ladies to appear in native Russian dress on some such occasions, while the gentlemen retained their glittering Western military uniforms.[83] But beyond this vague general agreement the proponents of the

---

[81] See, e.g., Schiemann, II, 305; Polievktov, p. 125.
[82] Polievktov, p. 141.
[83] Sons of the tsar also sometimes wore Russian dress. But the Slavophiles were forbidden to display their version of popular attire. Schiemann commented that Nicholas I apparently allowed old Russian boyar, but not peasant, dress. Schiemann, IV, 136.

official doctrine split drastically. The dynastic wing set above all the interests of the autocratic state, Russian nationality serving primarily as its bulwark. Romantic nationalists, on the other hand, considered nationality as an ultimate value and goal in itself. The monarch and his associates belonged in general to the first group. In their struggle against Poland and the Polish influence in Western Russia they used nationalism as a weapon against the hated enemy, just as they resorted to such other extraordinary means as a limited championing of the interests of Russian peasants against their Polish or Polonized landlords. Official arguments advanced against the privileged position of the Baltic Germans dwelt not on their alleged anti-Russian and noxious qualities, as Samarin or Pogodin would have it, but on the anachronistic nature of the social, political, and administrative order in their provinces which constituted an unjustified exception to the general structure of the empire.[84] These charges made very good sense in terms of enlightened despotism, and they also had a special appeal to the emperor's rigid and orderly personality. The Jews too were to contribute to the same end of standardization and state unity by renouncing gradually their "Talmudic prejudice" and becoming better integrated into the life of the Russian people.[85] Ethnic groups, for instance, the Finns, who posed no special problems to the monarchy were generally left alone.[86] Moreover, when conservative principles and rising Russian nationalism clashed, notably in the Baltic Provinces, the government decided in favor of conservatism.

The dynastic view thus dominated the policies of Nicholas I

[84] See, e.g., Uvarov, *Desyatiletie ministerstva narodnogo prosveshcheniya,* 1833–1843, pp. 48–56. But cf. the reference to the Baltic Germans in N. Kutuzov's well-known report to the emperor, submitted in April, 1841. Gershenzon, ed., *op. cit.,* p. 170.

[85] Nicholas I and many of his assistants were anti-Semitic in that they had a prejudiced view of the Jews. But their bias lacked the virulence of modern racial anti-Semitism. They considered Jews to be cowards and otherwise bad subjects because of the particular nature of their historical development. Uvarov, for instance, wrote of the need to direct "the rays of enlightenment" to that "people, which until now had been burdened by centuries of oppression." Uvarov, *op. cit.,* p. 74.

[86] On Finland during the period see especially Borodkin, *Istoriya Finlyandii. Vremya imperatora Nikolaya I.* Chapter xiv, dealing with the press and censorship, is of special interest.

and his lieutenants. Still, romantic nationalism grew in importance as a powerful undercurrent, a development reflected in the
writings of the nationalistic wing of Official Nationality. Public
opinion, although it could not express itself freely, apparently
often proved to be more nationalistic than the government.[87] The
tension between the Russians and the Germans in the empire of
the Romanovs increased throughout the period. To some Russians
the emperor himself was a German and as such an enemy of true
Russia.[88] Far-reaching nationalism found a measure of support

---

[87] Both contemporaries and historians noted repeatedly the growth of Russian national sentiment among the educated classes in the reign of Nicholas I
and the resulting tensions and incidents. To select a few examples, Nikitenko
mentions in the first volume of his well-known diary how a student in the
University of St. Petersburg accused a professor with a Ukrainian name, during
his lecture, of "antinational tendencies" and the resulting uproar with students taking sides, adding that there had been other such incidents; he also
dwells on several occasions on the hostility between the Russians and the
Germans, e.g., the struggle of these two parties in the Imperial Russian Geographic Society, or the refusal of those gathered at a banquet marking the
opening of a publishing house to drink a toast to Guttenberg which he had
proposed. Nikitenko even writes gloomily of the coming "tribal struggle" inside Russia. (Nikitenko, I, 221, 289, 308, 394–395. It is not clear what
Nikitenko means by other similar incidents.) Barsukov's enormous study of
Pogodin is a veritable anthology of Russian nationalism at the time of Nicholas I
and immediately after. Materials collected by Schilder in his two volumes on
Nicholas I include a remarkable letter written, in 1826, by a certain, otherwise unknown, Demidov who begged the new emperor "to establish free
access to the august throne of all true sons of the fatherland" and who declared that "courtiers, pupils of foreigners, are not Russians." (The letter is
reproduced in full in Schilder, I, 665–666.) Schiemann emphasizes the rise
of Russian nationalism and the struggle between "the Russian" and "the
German" parties throughout his four-volume standard history of the reign.
This enmity dated from Peter the Great's Westernization of Russia, as well
as his Baltic conquests, and the resulting influx of foreigners, and it was
deepened by the despotic rule of Biren and other Germans in the reign of
empress Anne. It was bound to grow in the nationalistic climate of the nineteenth century. Nicholas I felt on a number of occasions that he was acting
against nationalistic public opinion, and said so.
[88] Those who accused Nicholas I and his government of not being authentically
Russian, ranged from the Slavophiles to Michael Bakunin. Moreover, the
sentiment that the emperor was more a German than a native of his own land
found expression not only among the intellectuals, but also among the common people (Schiemann, IV, 236). Some foreign observers, e.g., Custine,
also shared it (Custine, III, 17). Among the Germans, too, some were willing
to accept the Russian sovereign as virtually one of their own. (The closeness
between Nicholas I and his royal Prussian relatives is discussed in chap. i
above. See also comments by Prussian diplomats and generals, e.g., von Rauch's
statement: "The Emperor is truly and honestly a good Prussian." Von

even within the government where such leading officials as Uvarov, Protasov, and Count L. Perovskii, who in 1844 became minister of the interior, proved on the whole to be much more favorable to it than their predecessors. At times the emperor in person had to apply the brakes on this nationalist trend.

The rebellion of 1830–1831 and its suppression brought tragedy to Poland. The Polish constitution of 1815 was replaced by the Organic Statute of 1832 which made Poland "an indivisible part" of the Russian empire. The Statute itself, with its promises of civil liberties, separate systems of law and of local government, and a widespread use of the Polish language, remained in abeyance, while Poland came to be administered in a brutal and authoritarian manner by its conqueror, the new Prince of Warsaw and Nicholas's viceroy, Marshal Paskevich. The monarch himself carefully directed and supervised his work. The estates of the insurgents were confiscated; Polish institutions of higher learning were closed; the lands of the Catholic Church were secularized, the clergy being given fixed salaries. At the same time, Poland was forced increasingly into the Russian mold in legal, administrative, educational, and economic matters. The most striking steps in that direction included the subordination of the Warsaw school region to the Russian ministry of education in 1839, the abolition of the Polish state council in 1841, and the abrogation of the customs barrier between Russia and Poland in 1850. The Russian language reigned in the high schools as well as in the administration, while a stringent censorship banned most of the leading Polish authors as subversive.[89]

Rauch's report of May 23, 1849 is reproduced as appendix XI in Schiemann, IV, 401–404, quoted from p. 403.) As mentioned in previous chapters, Nicholas I liked on occasion to identify himself with his Prussian relatives or his Prussian troops.

[89] For a summary of the developments in Poland see, e.g., Lenskii, "Polsha v pervoi polovine XIX veka," in *Istoriya Rossii v XIX veke*, I, 260–327. Nicholas I did not conceal his hatred of the rebellious Poles, "a species of animal between man and beast, something indescribable and unfortunately only too real; I mean here what is called the nobility, the clergy, and the gentry." He believed, however, that it was his duty not only to Russify the Poles, but also to make them as materially prosperous and as happy as possible. (See Nicholas I's letters to Frederick William IV published as appendix III in Schiemann, IV, 380–382; quoted from p. 381. Cf. his address delivered

A thoroughgoing Russification developed, however, not in Poland, but in the Western and Southwestern Provinces. That vast area contained an overwhelmingly White Russian and Ukrainian population, but its landlord class had become largely Polonized in the course of history which had linked its fortunes to Lithuania and Poland. Even prior to the insurrection of 1830–1831 the government of Nicholas I moved toward bringing this territory into closer association with Russia proper, a process which corresponded to the emperor's general penchant for centralization and standardization, but antagonized the Poles who maintained their historic claims to the area. After the suppression of the revolution, assimilation grew apace under the direction of a special committee. Rebels from Lithuanian, White Russian, and Ukrainian provinces were denied the amnesty offered to those from Poland. It was in this territory that the Orthodox Church scored its greatest gain when, in 1839, the Uniates severed their connection with Rome and came into its fold. In 1840, the Lithuanian Statute was repealed in favor of Russian law. Because the Polish element was represented by the landlords, Nicholas I and his assistants

---

in 1835 to the deputies of the city of Warsaw and reproduced in Schilder, II, 720–721.) The emperor was determined to eradicate Polish nationality. He wrote to Paskevich in September, 1831: "Order to search in Warsaw for all the flags and standards of our former Polish army and send them to me. Find also those captured from us and dispatch them to the commissary. All revolutionary things, e.g.: the sword, or the sash of Kosciuszko, should be confiscated and sent here to the Cathedral of the Transfiguration; similarly all the Turkish flags should be taken out of the churches. Find and send me all the uniforms of the late emperor as well as all the things in his study which belonged to him personally. Take away thrones and other related items and send them to Brest. After a period of time order General Berg to detail some competent person to seize, pack carefully, and dispatch to Brest the university library and the collection of medals as well as the library of the Societé des belles lettres. In a word, withdraw little by little everything that has historical national value and deliver it here; also the flag from the royal castle. Order to seal up the archives and the bank." (The letter was published in Schilder, II, 589–592; quoted from p. 591.) Paskevich, who in spite of his resounding title commemorating his capture of the Polish capital acted simply as Nicholas's agent, shared fully the views of his sovereign. See, e.g., Paskevich's report on the administration of Poland submitted to the emperor in 1850, "Raport Namestnika Tsarstva Polskogo Ego Imperatorskomu Velichestvu," SIRIO, XCVIII, 592–627. Among other things, the Field Marshal lists thirteen measures or groups of measures designed to bring Poland more fully into the Russian Empire (ibid., pp. 601–604).

changed the usual policy to legislate against their interests. They went so far as to introduce in some provinces so-called "inventories" which defined and regularized the obligations of the serfs to their masters, and to establish, in 1851, compulsory state service for the gentry of the Western region.[90] Thousands of poor or destitute families of the petty gentry were reclassified as peasants or townspeople, some of them being transferred to the Caucasus.[91] But while the Russian government fought against Polish influence, it showed equal hostility to Ukrainian nationalism, as indicated by the destruction of the Brotherhood of Cyril and Methodius, the cruel punishment of its members, and the resulting strictures against local patriotism and general Slavic, as distinct from Russian, sentiments mentioned in the preceding chapter.

The policies of the Russian government in regard to the Jews were also connected with the Western region, where the bulk of the Jews of the empire resided and to which they were largely restricted. The government aimed at an eventual assimilation of the Jews who were to embrace Orthodoxy and become fully integrated into the Russian people. With this goal in view, the authorities both legislated against specifically Jewish institutions and practices and tried to bring this stubborn minority more effectively and directly under the Russian system. For instance, in 1844 Jewish autonomous communities were officially dissolved in many areas,[92] and in 1850 traditional Jewish dress was forbidden. In

---

[90] On the inventories see, e.g., Vasilenko, "Krestyanskii vopros v yugo-zapadnom i severo-zapadnom krae pri Nikolae I i vvedenie inventarei," *Russkoe obshchestvo i krestyanskii vopros v proshlom i nastoyashchem*, IV, 94–109. Cf. peasant legislation of 1846 in Poland proper which was inspired by the fear produced by a massacre of landlords in neighboring Galicia, but which also reflected Nicholas I's bitter dislike of the nationalistic Polish gentry.

[91] Lenskii, "Polskoe vosstanie 1863 g," in *Istoriya Rossii v XIX veke*, III, 268–322, especially pp. 272–273.

[92] Characteristically, this dissolution of autonomous Jewish communities, so-called *kagals*, was explained in an official report as follows: "With the abolition of kagals in the province of Kurland and with cessation, consequently, of a separate existence of Jews within town society, they are given the opportunity to come nearer, in civil life, to other citizens inhabiting the same town. By this edict Jews are becoming gradually accustomed to the general civil order, and, in addition to that, the management of their affairs is now under the control of the general town government which can eliminate

parallel developments Jews were made, in 1827, subject to compulsory military service,[93] while in 1842 all Jewish schools were brought under the jurisdiction of the ministry of education. But in spite of many efforts the harsh policy of Nicholas I toward the Jews proved to be on the whole a failure.

The Baltic Germans presented a different problem as far as Russification was concerned. Far from being underprivileged or downtrodden, they formed an elite in the empire of the Romanovs dominating entirely the Latvian and Estonian natives of their provinces and occupying a tremendous number of important positions in the army,[94] the diplomatic service, and the administration of the Russian state. Both Nicholas I's desire to centralize and modernize the structure of his monarchy and the rising Russian nationalism demanded that the Baltic Germans renounce at least in part their special status. But the descendants of the Teutonic Knights found support in their excellent government and court connections, and, above all, in the fact that they came to be closely identified with the dynastic and conservative principle.

Specific issues included various measures aimed against the exclusive privileges of the Baltic Germans and the unique, still partly feudal, structure of the provinces; proselytizing efforts on the part of the Orthodox clergy in the 1840's among Lutheran Latvian peasants; and the attitudes and activities of the successive governor generals of the area.[95] Although hard pressed at times, the Baltic barons managed, on the whole, to maintain their position, being

---

the irregularities which up to that point had existed in concealment in separate Jewish administrations." *SIRIO*, XCVIII, 659.

[93] Because Nicholas I considered Jews to be cowards, he wanted them to serve in the navy where they would have less opportunity to desert. Schiemann, II, 238.

[94] In 1850, an official report listed 230 Baltic Germans serving in the army with the rank of general of various grades. *SIRIO*, XCVIII, 638.

[95] Schiemann, himself a champion of the Baltic Germans, paid great attention to everything related to them throughout his four-volume study of the reign of Nicholas I. For Schiemann's direct participation in the Baltic problem see his *Die Vergewaltigung der russischen Ostseeprovinzen. Appell an das Ehrgefuehl des Protestantismus.* For a different point of view see, e.g., Lander, "Pribaltiiskii krai v pervoi polovine XIX veka," in *Istoriya Rossii v XIX veke*, II, 327–349.

assisted on occasion by the sovereign himself who declared that he too was a Baltic knight.[96] Their triumph came with the revolutions of 1848. The new governor general, Prince A. A. Suvorov, agreed completely with their point of view; [97] the Orthodox Church had to discontinue its missionary work; and the old German order in the Baltic Provinces was left alone and intact in all its archaic glory.

The victory of "the German party" probably contributed to the dismissal of Uvarov, in 1849, from the ministry of education. The favorite's fall, at the beginning of the last and utterly reactionary period of Nicholas's rule which followed the European revolutions, stemmed from his allegedly insufficient conservatism and vigilance against subversion and, more immediately, from the monarch's displeasure with an article in defense of Russian universities which the minister had sponsored. But there are reasons to believe that the German issue also played a part in the removal of Uvarov from his office.[98]

The doctrine of Official Nationality found manifold application in the policies of Nicholas I and his associates. The state dogma of autocracy both inspired and dominated the activities of the Russian government, in small matters as much as in large. Orthodoxy entered as one element into the general system. It also provided, however, the basic ethical framework and goals which link the Russia of Nicholas I to a particular type of European society and a particular period of European history. Nationality proved to be the most troublesome concept, in practice as in theory. The dynastic interpretation of it, supported by the sovereign, retained its preponderant position. Yet, a more thorough and far-reaching na-

---

[96] Schiemann, III, 404.

[97] See, e.g., Suvorov's report to the emperor in 1850, "Otchet Rizhskogo Voennogo, Liflyandskogo, Estlyandskogo i Kurlyandskogo General-Gubernatora," *SIRIO*, XCVIII, 628–694.

[98] Schiemann thinks so. He quotes Lord Bloomfield, the British ambassador, as follows: "Count Uvarov is represented to have encouraged the publication of writings calculated to encourage the hostility, which has always more or less existed between the Slavonic and the German races in Russia, and he is also accused of permitting the dissemination of principles through the periodical press which are said to be inconsistent with the policy of the Imperial Government and the laws relating to his subjects." Schiemann, IV, 150.

tionalism rose to intrude, with increasing vigor, into Russian politics as well as into Russian thought.

But the principles of Official Nationality received implementation even beyond the borders of Russia; they guided the foreign, in addition to the domestic, policies of the consistent emperor.

V

OFFICIAL NATIONALITY

FOREIGN POLICY

*Throughout Europe the death of the Emperor Nicholas has been
followed by an immediate rise in the value of all public securities,
and by a feeling of increased confidence and hope. The world
stood more in awe of him than we in this country could conceive
possible, and there is hardly a citizen of any continental state who
does not breathe more freely since that incarnate despotism has
ceased to wield the power of Russia. . . . —The Times* [1]

NICHOLAS I would not surrender his rigid principles or bargain
with his exacting conscience. The basic beliefs of Official Nationality found application in Russian foreign policy as well as in
the domestic affairs of the empire of the tsars. Yet, transferred to
the larger and vastly different world stage, these dogmas underwent certain changes to meet the new conditions.

"Autocracy" became legitimism. The two concepts, while by
no means identical, stood naturally together in the minds of the

---

[1] *The Times* (London), March 7, 1855. "Nicholas" is in bold type in the
original.

Russian monarch and of his associates. Nicholas I was determined
to maintain and defend the existing order in Europe just as he
considered it his sacred duty to preserve the archaic system in his
own country. He saw the two closely related as the whole and its
part, and he thought both to be threatened by the same enemy:
the many-headed hydra of revolution which suffered a major blow
with the final defeat of Napoleon, but refused to die. Indeed it
rose again and again, in 1830, in 1848, and on other occasions,
attempting to reverse the decision and undo the settlement of
1815. True to his principles, the resolute tsar set out to engage
the enemy. In the course of the struggle, this policeman of Russia
assumed the added responsibilities of the gendarme of Europe.
It is important to note that Nicholas I's view of the crucial combat between right and wrong in which he played a key role allowed little distinction or discrimination between international
relations proper and the internal affairs of the states: a constitution
in Prussia, or a rebellion in the Austrian Empire represented as
grave a threat to the existing order as outright aggression of one
country against another. Therefore, Russian foreign policy of the
period showed an unusually deep and continuous concern with
the developments within other European states.

It must also be observed that the defense of legitimism and the
status quo acquires a different significance in each specific historical context. In theory Nicholas I's doctrine implied the championing of the established rights of every country on the continent,
from republican Switzerland to autocratic Russia; in practice it
meant largely a determined effort to protect the old conservative
or reactionary order in Europe, eastern Europe in particular,
against the rising tides of liberalism and nationalism. The emper-
or's most persistent international problem was the Poles whose
irrepressible nationalism challenged all three great Eastern monarchies. His best-known foreign intervention was directed against
the Hungarian revolutionaries, in defense of the absolute rule of
the Hapsburgs. Politics, if not political science, linked autocracy
and legitimism firmly to each other.

"Nationality" too had to be adjusted to the world scene. Abroad,
as at home, Nicholas I acted as a convinced patriot, devoted to

his country and dedicated to furthering its interests. Even as a grand duke he had displayed a certain pride in Russia and things Russian which contrasted sharply with the cosmopolitan attitudes and tastes of Alexander I.[2] He proceeded to maintain this patriotic tone throughout the thirty years of his reign. But the issue of nationalism in nineteenth-century Europe involved much more than a sturdy championing of one's own country. It encompassed such questions as the rise of new nations, the unification of Italy, a revamping of Germany, a disruption of Austria, and a possible new role for Russia in Slavic eastern Europe. In all these matters the Russian emperor came out wholeheartedly in support of the old, established order and against the nationalist demands. As has been indicated earlier, he understood "nationality" in the dynastic, not in the radical romantic, sense: his attitude remained the same, inside and outside his native land; it varied in emphasis, and it experienced certain modifications produced by the specific characteristics of every particular situation, but it remained constant in principle. That Nicholas I emerged as a relentless foe of nationalism on the international scene, while his treatment of nationalism at home appeared to be much more complex and ambivalent, can be ascribed to several factors. It has been pointed out, for instance, that the Russian ministry of foreign affairs, headed by Nesselrode, seemed virtually reserved for Baltic Germans and some other individuals of non-Russian origin, and that these high officials had none of the nationalistic urgings of an Uvarov or a Protasov.[3] More importantly, whereas at home nationalism often went hand in hand with such state interests as the suppression of the Poles or the integration of the Western

---

[2] The same was true of the youngest brother in the family, Michael. Observers noticed this contrast between the two grand dukes and Emperor Alexander I especially when all three of them spent several months in Paris after the defeat of Napoleon in 1815. See, e.g., Schilder, I, 54–55; Polievktov, p. 21.

[3] Schiemann notes that in the 1830's and 1840's five out of six immediate assistants of Nesselrode were Baltic Germans. The sixth carried the name of Lavalle. Schiemann, III, 368. This argument became the stock in trade of the Russian nationalist press.

A. Tyutcheva expressed the nationalist dissatisfaction with the emperor's foreign policy in her often-quoted statement that "Nicholas I was the Don Quixote of autocracy"—meaning "legitimism." Tyutcheva, p. 97.

Provinces into the Russian Empire, abroad it posed an immediate and fundamental threat to the established order which the Russian sovereign was determined to uphold. In his own empire only the issue of the Baltic Germans and a few others gave glimpses of the dangers which romantic nationalism might bring to a dynastic state. Elsewhere on the continent nationalism marched openly with liberalism and revolution. No wonder that Nicholas I turned his full force against this revolutionary nationalism, much to the despair of such rabid Russian nationalists as Pogodin and Tyutchev.

The part which "Orthodoxy" played in the foreign relations of the reign paralleled closely its role in domestic affairs. In both areas it provided an ethical framework, a set of ideal standards and goals, if not practical directives. Nicholas I believed in a profound moral unity of Christendom and in a set code of behavior incumbent upon Christian rulers in their dealings with one another. In addition to this basic meaning, however, "Orthodoxy" also had, once again, some special applications. It influenced, in particular, the attitude of Russia toward the Orthodox peoples and interests in the Ottoman Empire, and consequently the Russian position in the entire Eastern Question, an important subject to be considered later in this chapter.

The basic outlines of Russian foreign policy in the reign of Nicholas I are well-known. Inheriting from Alexander I the complex issue of the Greek War of Independence, the new ruler took a firmer stand aginst Turkey and acted with less consideration for the other great powers of Europe. This approach eventually culminated in a war between Russia and the Ottoman state, fought from April, 1828, to September, 1829.[4] Yet, in the opinion of Nicholas I, hostilities against Turkey had nothing to do with any support of the Greeks: they resulted rather from long-range tensions between the two neighboring empires, exacerbated by such recent developments as the naval battle of Navarino and the

---

[4] Except for specialized military histories, Schilder (vol. II) provides the best description of the war and, in particular, of Nicholas I's part in it. The emperor participated personally in the campaign of 1828—for the first and last time in his life.

sultan's militant manifesto to his subjects.[5] The Greeks remained, in the eyes of the Russian autocrat, rebellious and renegade subjects.[6] Although Turkey proved to be more difficult to defeat than expected, the second major campaign of the war brought decisive, if costly, victory to the Russian arms and forced the Ottoman state to agree to the Treaty of Adrianople. This settlement gave Russia the mouth of the Danube as well as considerable territory in the Caucasus; promised autonomous existence, under a Russian protectorate, to the Danubian Principalities of Moldavia and Wallachia; imposed a heavy indemnity on Turkey; guaranteed the passage of Russian merchant ships through the Straits; and, incidentally, assured the success of the Greek revolution. But in spite of these as well as certain other Russian gains embodied in the treaty, it has often and on the whole justly been considered an example of moderation in international affairs. The Russian emperor did not try to destroy the erstwhile opponent of his country, regarding Turkey as an important and desirable element in the European balance of power.

In fact, this decision supporting the preservation of the Ottoman state represented the considered judgment of a special committee appointed by Nicholas I, in 1829, to deal with the numerous problems raised by the defeat of Turkey and the changing situation in the Balkans. Composed of its chairman, Count V. Kochubei, and five other leading assistants of the tsar, the committee discussed several proposals, in particular two by its own members, Nesselrode and D. Dashkov, both favorable to the Porte, and concluded: "the advantages offered by the preservation of the Ottoman Empire in Europe exceed the inconveniences which it presents; therefore, its fall would be contrary to the true interests

---

[5] The manifesto of December 20, 1827, began as follows: "All people of sane mind know that just as each Moslem is a mortal enemy of the infidels, so are the infidels in equal measure mortal enemies of the Moslems, and that, above all, the Russian court is an irreconcilable foe of the Moslem people and of the Ottoman Empire." Quoted in Schilder, II, 427.

[6] "I detest, I abhor the Greeks, I consider them as revolted subjects and I do not desire their independence. My grievance is against the Turks' conduct to Russia." Quoted in Woodhouse, The Greek War of Independence, p. 127. Cf. Schiemann, II, 132.

of Russia; consequently, it would be wise to try to prevent this
fall by utilizing all the possibilities that might yet occur for the
conclusion of an honorable peace." [7]

The emperor himself fully endorsed the judgment. "The decision taken by the Imperial Government on this point in September 1829 became the basis for Russian policy in Turkey until the
outbreak of the Crimean War." [8] In this, as in so many other
cases, Nicholas I opted for the maintenance of the established
order and against unpredictable and fearsome change.

The first years of the new emperor's reign also witnessed a war
against Persia, fought from June, 1826, to February, 1828. Again,
Nicholas to a large extent inherited the conflict from Alexander
who had annexed Georgia in 1801 and had beaten back the
Persian challenge in the course of hostilities which lasted from
1804 to 1813. The resumption of the struggle resulted in a Persian
debacle and in the Treaty of Turkmanchai, General Paskevich—
who was to be so prominent in Nicholas I's reign—emerging as the
hero of the campaigns. While the peace settlement gave Russia
a part of Armenia with the city of Erivan, the exclusive rights to
have a navy on the Caspian sea, commercial concessions, and a
large indemnity, Nicholas I characteristically refused to press his
victory. In particular, he would not support a native movement
to overthrow the shah and destroy his rule. The Kajar dynasty, as
well as its better-known European counterparts, had its legitimate
rights.[9]

---

[7] The complete text of the protocol, from a photostatic copy of the original,
was published in Kerner, "Russia's New Policy in the Near East after the
Peace of Adrianople; Including the Text of the Protocol of 16 September
1829," *Cambridge Historical Journal*, V (1937), pp. 286–290; quoted from
p. 287. Actually Marshal I. Diebitsch terminated the fighting and concluded
the Treaty of Adrianople before he learned of these deliberations and decision;
but his actions were perfectly in accord with the views of his government, and
he received the highest praise from the emperor.

[8] Puryear, *England, Russia, and the Straits Question, 1844–1856*, p. 8. Cf.
Kerner, *op. cit.*, pp. 285–286.

[9] "Unswerving in his strictly legitimist convictions, the sovereign could
not tolerate the thought of a possibility of utilizing the subjects' disobedience
to their lawful monarch. Insisting on satisfaction for Russia, he demanded
at the same time from Paskevich the preservation of both the integrity of
Persia and the inviolability of the shah's lawful authority and throne "
Shcherbatov, *General-Feldmarshal Knyaz Paskevich*, III, 23.

The revolution in Paris in July, 1830, came as a great shock to the Russian emperor, and its impact was increased by the Belgian uprising in September and by unrest in Italy and Germany. Nicholas I sent Diebitsch on a special mission to Berlin to concert action with Prussia and, although this mission failed, assembled an army in Poland prepared to march west. When the regime of Louis-Philippe was promptly accepted by other European governments, the Russian emperor alone withheld official recognition for four months and then treated the new French ruler in a grudging and discourteous manner.[10] The revolution of the Belgians against the Dutch provoked similarly the hatred of the Russian autocrat who regarded it as another assault on the sacred principle of legitimacy and, besides, as a clear violation of the territorial provisions of the Treaty of Vienna. Once again failing to obtain diplomatic support from other powers, Nicholas I had to subscribe to the international settlement of the issue which favored the rebels, although he delayed the ratification of the Treaty of London for several months and did not establish regular diplomatic relations with the new state until 1852. It should be added that the early plans for a Russian military intervention in Western Europe might well have been realized, in spite of objections by some of the tsar's chief advisers, except for the Polish revolution which broke out late in November, 1830. It took the Russian government approximately a year to suppress the uprising. And while this tragic war increased further the gulf and the bitterness between the state of the tsars and revolutionary, or simply liberal, Europe, it also effectively immobilized the Russian army in its own part of the continent.

Unable for one reason or another to influence events in the West, Nicholas I limited himself to bitter comments concerning their course. As he wrote on the subject of the recognition of Louis-Philippe by European powers, and notably by his allies, Austria and Prussia: "However, our allies, without agreeing beforehand with us on a step so important, so decisive, hastened, by their recognition of the established fact, to crown insurrection

---

[10] Nicholas I's attitude towards Louis-Philippe will be discussed later in this chapter.

and usurpation—a fatal, incomprehensible step to which must be attributed the series of misfortunes which have not since ceased plaguing Europe." [11]

Relative stabilization in Europe was followed by new troubles in the Near East. Denied Syria as his reward for help given to the sultan in the Greek war, Mohammed Ali of Egypt rebelled against his nominal suzerain and, during the year of 1832, sent an army which conquered Syria and invaded Anatolia smashing Turkish forces. The sultan's desperate appeals for help produced no tangible results in European capitals, with the exception of St. Petersburg. That Nicholas I rushed to the aid of the Porte in her hour of need found ample justification in the political advantages which Russia could derive from this important intervention. But it should also be noted that such action corresponded perfectly to the legitimist convictions of the Russian autocrat who regarded Mohammed Ali as yet another major rebel, as well as to the Russian decision of 1829 favoring the preservation of Turkey. On February 20, 1833, a Russian naval squadron arrived at Constantinople and, several weeks later, some ten thousand Russian troops were landed on the Asiatic side of the Bosporus. Extremely worried by this unexpected development, the great powers acted in concert to bring Turkey and Egypt together, arranging the Convention of Kutahia between the two combatants and inducing the sultan to yield to its provisions. The Russians withdrew immediately after Orlov signed, on July 8, 1833, on behalf of his emperor, the Treaty of Unkiar Skelessi with Turkey. This agreement, concluded for eight years, contained broad provisions for mutual consultation and aid in case of attack by any third party, a secret article exempting, at the same time, Turkey from helping Russia in exchange for keeping the Dardanelles closed to all foreign warships. Although

---

[11] This selection is taken from an interesting paper which Nicholas I composed late in 1830, which he called his "confession," and which contained an analysis of the catastrophic events of the year, as well as of his attitude toward them. The paper is reproduced in Schilder, II, 311–315; quoted from p. 312. Both Schilder and Schiemann provide valuable detailed accounts of Nicholas I and the Russian policy in 1830 and 1831. For a recent treatment of this subject in English see the chapter on "The Revolution of 1830 and the Alliance of the Three Northern Courts," in Lobanov-Rostovsky, *Russia and Europe,* 1825–1878, pp. 86–115.

the Treaty of Unkiar Skelessi did not provide for the passage of Russian men-of-war through the Straits, contrary to the widespread supposition at the time and since, it did represent a signal victory for Russia: the empire of the tsars became the special ally and, to a degree, protector of its ancient, decaying enemy, acquiring important means to interfere in its affairs and influence its future.[12]

The events of 1830–1831 in Europe, and to a lesser extent recurrent conflicts in the Near East, emphasized to Nicholas I the necessity of close coöperation and joint action of the conservative powers. Austria and in a certain measure Prussia felt the same need, with the result that the three eastern European monarchies drew together by the end of 1833. The meeting at Muenchengraetz attended by the emperors of Russia and Austria and the crown prince of Prussia was followed by agreements concluded there and, soon after, in Berlin. Russia came to a thorough understanding with the Hapsburg empire especially as regards their common struggle against Polish nationalism and their desire to maintain Turkish rule in the Near East. Similarly the Russian agreement with Prussia stressed joint policies in relation to partitioned Poland. More far-reaching in its provisions and its implications was the Convention of Berlin signed by all three powers on October 15, 1833.

Their Majesties: the Emperor of Austria, the King of Prussia and the Emperor of All the Russias, after a full consideration of the dangers which continue to threaten order in Europe, the order established by public law and by treaties, especially the treaties of 1815, and unanimously determined to strengthen the conservative system which constitutes the immutable foundation of their policies. . . .

. . . recognize that each independent Sovereign has the right to call to his aid, in case of internal troubles as well as in case of an external threat to his country, every other independent Sovereign whom he would consider as most appropriate to render this

---

[12] The precise nature of the Straits settlement in the Treaty of Unkiar Skelessi was established in Mosely, *Russian Diplomacy and the Opening of the Eastern Question in 1838 and 1839.*

aid, and that the latter has the right to offer or deny this help according to his interests and circumstances. They also recognize that in the case of such aid being accorded, no power not appealed to or invited by the threatened state has the right to intervene either to interfere with the aid which had been requested and offered or for counteraction.

In the event that the material help of one of the three Courts, the Austrian, the Prussian, and the Russian, is requested, and if any power would want to oppose this by the force of arms, these three Courts would consider as directed against each one of them every hostile action undertaken with this goal in view. They will then resort to the most expeditious and effective measures to repel such aggression.[13]

The agreements of 1833 were meant to protect not only the immediate interests of the signatory powers, but also the entire conservative order in Europe. The three champions of legitimism were to act together in case of need and also to apportion in an efficient manner the task of maintaining law and order on the continent. According to one view, Austria assumed special responsibility for Italy, Switzerland, Spain, Portugal, and, jointly with Prussia, Germany; Prussia, in addition to her leading role in northern Germany, undertook the protection of Holland; Russia served as the reserve of the alliance and at the same time had the paramount role in promoting its policies in relation to Poland and in the Balkans.[14] Nicholas I held steadfastly to his commitment from 1833 to 1848 and, indeed, through the revolutions of 1848 and 1849, invading Hungary in response to the Austrian appeal to suppress the rebellion of that land against Hapsburg

---

[13] The text of the Convention can be found, in French and in Russian, in F. Martens, ed., *Recueil des traités et conventions conclus par la Russie avec les puissances étrangères, IV, part I, Traités avec l'Autriche. 1815–1849,* no. 137, pp. 460–462. The entire fifteen-volume collection is, of course, invaluable for a student of Russian history. The phrase in the second quoted paragraph, "no power not appealed to or invited," agrees both with the official French text of the Convention and with the logic of the situation. The Russian version, which has instead "no power, whether invited or not," must be mistaken.

[14] See, e.g., Polievktov, pp. 159–160.

rule.[15] The system of Muenchengraetz and Berlin collapsed only with the advent of the Crimean War.

The Russian ascendancy over Turkey, reflected in the Treaty of Unkiar Skelessi, proved to be difficult to maintain. The Porte looked eagerly for ways to escape dependence on her mighty northern neighbor. Other European powers, having learned the lesson of 1833, would try to prevent Nicholas I from again playing a lone hand in the issue of the Straits. The climax came in 1839 and 1840 with a resumption of hostilities between Turkey and Egypt and new defeats for the Turks. Under terms of the Treaty of London of July 15, 1840, Great Britain, Austria, Prussia, and Russia agreed to impose a settlement on Mohammed Ali which would save the Ottoman Empire from its ambitious vassal. They enforced their decision by defeating the Egyptians in Syria, and inducing both sides to agree to the prescribed terms. The coöperation of the great powers in the affairs of the Near East found further expression in the Straits Convention of July 13, 1841, in which France also participated. The new agreement reaffirmed the closure of the Bosporus and the Dardanelles to all foreign warships in time of peace, substituting an international guarantee of the five participants for the separate treaty between Russia and Turkey. While it is readily understandable that the other powers considered the settlement to be a significant victory, the satisfaction of the Russian government with the course of events demands explanation. Russian willingness to abandon a special position in the Near East in favor of a multinational settlement was influenced by such particular circumstances as the approaching termination of the Treaty of Unkiar Skelessi which had been concluded for eight years, and the desire to promote antagonism between Great Britain and France, the last-named state supporting Mohammed Ali. But in a more fundamental sense, it stemmed from the essentially conservative attitude of the Russian government in regard to Turkey at the time, as well as from the legitimist

---

[15] Austria and Russia had specifically foreseen the possibility of such an intervention, both in 1833 and in subsequent years, notably in 1837 (*ibid.*, and Pokrovskii, "Krymskaya voina," in *Istoriya Rossii v XIX veke*, III, 8).

and internationally minded orientation of the entire reign. As
Nesselrode informed his sovereign, the new agreement in fact
perpetuated the Treaty of Unkiar Skelessi "in another form." [16]

The policing of Europe which Nicholas I was so eager to undertake in the company of his allies continued to present problems.
In 1846, after an abortive Polish uprising, the free state of Cracow
was annexed to Austria, eliminating the last vestige of Poland
from the political map of the continent. Characteristically, it was
the Russian army that moved quickly to occupy the city and
suppress the uprising, and it was the Russian emperor who insisted
to the somewhat slow and reluctant Austrian government that
this remnant of free Poland must become a part of the Hapsburg
state, as had been previously arranged among the Eastern European monarchies. Nicholas I thought, as usual, in terms of preserving the established conservative order, not of expanding his
own empire or weakening his neighbors.[17]

But particularly disturbing to Nicholas I, in the 1840's, were
the unexpected developments in Prussia. Frederick William IV,
who succeeded to the throne of the Hohenzollerns in 1840, had
a different cast of mind from his conservative and cautious father
as well as from his passionately autocratic and legitimist Russian
brother-in-law. Although varied, vague, and confused, the new
monarch's romantic ideas and aspirations encouraged liberalism
and nationalism which continued to rise in Prussia and Germany.
The Russian ruler watched with particular horror "brother Fritz's"
awkward attempts to move in the direction of a constitutional
government; and, while these efforts produced no significant results, the cleavage between the allies of 1815 and 1833 became
increasingly apparent. Nicholas I's closeness to the Prussian king,
royal family, and court only augmented the bitterness and the
recriminations.[18]

---

[16] *SIRIO*, XCVIII, 292.

[17] As a contrast to Nicholas I's views on Cracow, see Pogodin's opinion, expressed in 1839. Pogodin, *Istoriko-politicheskie pisma*, p. 35.

[18] The attitude of Nicholas I toward Frederick William IV and Prussia is
expertly discussed by Schiemann, notably in his chapter on "Kaiser Nikolaus
und Koenig Friedrich Wilhelm IV" (IV, 1–25), but also throughout his work.
Several appendixes to Schiemann's study contain letters exchanged between

The revolution of February, 1848, in France opened a new chapter in the struggle between the old order and the rising forces of the modern world in nineteenth-century Europe. While the famous story of Nicholas I telling his guests at a ball to saddle their horses because a republic had just been proclaimed in France, is not exact,[19] the Russian autocrat did react immediately and violently to the news from Paris. Although delighted by the fall of Louis-Philippe whom he hated, the tsar turned naturally against the revolution, breaking diplomatic relations with France and assembling three or four hundred thousand troops in western Russia in preparation for a march to the Rhine. But rebellion spread faster than the Russian sovereign's countermeasures: in less than a month Prussia and Austria were engulfed in the conflagration, and the entire established order on the continent began rapidly to crumble into dust.

In the trying months which followed, Nicholas I rose to his full stature as the defender of legitimism in Europe. The remarkable ultimate failures of the initially successful revolutions of 1848 and 1849 still present puzzles to historians; the answers rest largely in the specific political, social, and economic conditions of the different countries involved.[20] Still, the Russian monarch certainly

---

the two monarchs. It may be added that even before the death of Frederick William III Russia and Prussia, with their different interests and positions in Europe, began to draw apart. This deterioration of relations pained Nicholas I greatly. See especially his revealing letter to the empress written on June 16, 1838, after a visit to Berlin. (Schiemann, III, 478–479. Much valuable source material on the attitude of Nicholas I and the Russian government to Frederick William IV and Prussia can be found in Nesselrode, *Lettres*, vols. VIII–XI, in particular in the foreign minister's numerous letters to Baron P. Meyendorff, the Russian ambassador in Berlin. The volumes cover the years 1840–1846, 1847–1850, 1850–1853, and 1854–1856, respectively. See also the correspondence between Nicholas I and Frederick William IV for the years 1848–1850 published by W. Andreas in *Forschungen zur Brandenburgischen und Preussischen Geschichte*, vol. 43, pp. 129–166.

[19] The best account of the reception of the revolutionary news by the tsar and of his response is in Schilder's article, "Imperator Nikolai I v 1848 i 1849 godakh," attached to the second volume of his study of Nicholas I (pp. 619–639, especially pp. 619–622). The article was originally published in *Istoricheskii Vestnik* for 1899. The whole issue of Nicholas I and the Russian government in 1848 and 1849 is discussed in Nifontov, *Rossiya v 1848 godu*.

[20] For a collective analysis of what happened in 1848–1849 and why, see Fejto, ed., *The Opening of an Era, 1848; an Historical Symposium*.

did what he could to tip the balance in favor of reaction. Following the thunderous and strange manifesto against revolution quoted in the first chapter, he proceeded to exercise all the influence he could muster against the numerous uprisings which gripped the continent. Prussia, where the king surrendered to the liberals without a fight, made Nicholas I sick with rage and humiliation; the empress, on her part, wrote to her brother Prince William, the heir to the throne, that she now felt ashamed of Prussia.[21] The subsequent defeat of the revolution in the realm of the Hohenzollerns, while most welcome in St. Petersburg, could never quite eradicate from the heart of the Russian autocrat the bitterness of those early months, especially so because Prussia retained a constitution, even though a very conservative one, and would not return entirely to her old ways.

The policy of the Prussian king and government limited Nicholas I's participation in the revolutionary developments in that country principally to unwelcome advice and admonition, although tsarist troops remained on the border waiting for the invitation. In certain other instances the way was opened for direct Russian action. The first Russian military intervention to suppress revolution occurred in July, 1848, in the Danubian Principalities of Moldavia and Wallachia, where Russia acted both for itself and for Turkey to defeat the Rumanian national movement.[22] The most important action took place in the summer of 1849, when Nicholas I heeded the Austrian appeal to help combat the revolt in Hungary, assigning Paskevich and almost two hundred thousand troops for the campaign. Earlier the tsarist government had rendered the Hapsburgs financial and diplomatic assistance, notably in their struggle to reëstablish their position in Italy,[23] while a Russian detachment had aided the

---

[21] See the empress's letters to Prince William in 1848, especially the letter dated October 28. Schiemann, IV, 393–396.

[22] It may be noted that the sultan accepted at first the new revolutionary settlement in the Principalities, and that it was the tsar who restored order there and led the sultan to reverse his decision.

[23] The Russian government supplied Austria with a loan of six million rubles and pointed out to Great Britain, that, if an outside power were to support an Italian state against the Hapsburgs, Russia would join Austria as a full-fledged combatant. As in the case of Prussia, Nicholas I resented bitterly the

Austrians in Transylvania and, incidentally, had been defeated by the rebels. Russian intervention in Hungary—which earned the undying hatred of the Hungarians—was directed in part against the Polish danger, Polish revolutionaries fighting on the Hungarian side. But its main rationale lay in the Russian autocrat's determination to preserve the existing order in Europe and in the position of the Austrian Empire as one of the principal pillars of that order. The costly Hungarian war proved to be unpopular in Russia [24] and brought no direct gain to that country. Similarly, after accomplishing their purpose, Russian troops were withdrawn, in 1851, from Moldavia and Wallachia, just as they had been withdrawn in 1834. The Convention of Balta Liman, concluded in 1849 between Russia and Turkey, diminished the autonomy of the Principalities, abolishing entirely their elected assemblies.

Two more developments in Russian foreign policy must be mentioned in connection with the revolutionary years: the Russian stand on the side of Denmark in her conflict with Prussia and the Frankfurt Assembly over Schleswig and Holstein; and the Russian support of Austria, once more against Prussia, on the issue of the structure and leadership of Germany. Both diplomatic interventions were significant, and perhaps decisive. The Russian championing of the Danes, backed by the threat of war if Prussia were to continue her military operations and by the dispatching of a naval squadron to the scene of action, played a major role in the stabilization of the situation and in the eventual conclusion of a peace treaty favorable to Denmark. The Russian preference for Austria in her dispute with Prussia helped that

---

concessions which had been made by the Hapsburg government in the early months of the revolutions. He had protested in particular the failure of that government to suppress the revolutionary movement in the Polish-Ukrainian province of Galicia. The Russian autocrat was delighted to witness the remarkable comeback of the Hapsburgs and their absolute rule.

[24] On Russian dissatisfaction with the war see, for instance, Schiemann, IV, 193, and the footnote extending to p. 194 where he quotes the report of a British diplomat: "Indeed this war on behalf of Austria appears to be daily becoming more unpopular amongst the Russians, and I frequently hear it alluded to, amongst them, as a mere act of quixotic chivalry. . . ." Cf. Tyutcheva's statement cited above that Nicholas I was the Don Quixote of legitimism.

country score a major diplomatic victory in the Punctation of Olmuetz, of November 29, 1850, which marked a complete Prussian abandonment of an attempt to change the organization of Germany and a return to the *status quo* and Austrian leadership in that area. Nicholas I's German policy, deeply resented by contemporary and subsequent German patriots, represented a consistent application of the emperor's basic beliefs. It was Prussia that tried to change the established settlement in Europe, while Austria acted as the upholder of the legitimate order. In personal terms too the tsar came to have more confidence in the steadfastly conservative Francis Joseph and Schwarzenberg than in the unpredictable Frederick William IV and his associates.[25]

The extremely impressive and in certain ways dominant position which Russia obtained with the collapse of the revolutions of 1848–1849 on the continent, failed to last. In fact, the international standing of the gendarme of Europe and of the country he represented was much stronger in appearance than in reality: liberalism and nationalism, although defeated, were by no means dead, and they carried European public opinion, from Poland and Hungary to France and England, with them;[26] even the usual friends of the tsar complained of his interference with their interests, as in the case of Prussia, or at least resented his overbearing solicitude, as was true of Austria. Nicholas I himself, on the other hand—in the opinion of some specialists—reacted to his success by becoming more blunt, uncompromising, doctrinaire, and domineering than ever before.[27] The stage was set for a political debacle, if not exactly for the climactic act of a Greek tragedy.

But the circumstances of this debacle turned out to be any-

---

[25] Nicholas I, of course, showed bitter hostility to the revolutionary Frankfurt National Assembly and its far-reaching nationalistic aspirations extending even to the Baltic Provinces of the Russian Empire. In addition to the ideological clash, he naturally considered the creation of a mighty united Germany inimical to Russian interests.

[26] The development of the hatred of the Russia of Nicholas I in one major European nation is presented in Gleason, *The Genesis of Russophobia in Great Britain.* See also T. McNally, "The Origins of Russophobia in France: 1812–1830," *American Slavic and East European Review*, XVII:2 (1958), 173–189.

[27] For an emphatic expression of this not uncommon view see Grunwald, *La Vie de Nicolas I*er, pp. 194–195.

thing but obvious, simple, or straightforward. The crisis which proved fatal to the Russian autocrat's system arose again in the Near East. Following the Straits Settlement of 1841, Nicholas I made a special effort to come to an understanding with England in regard to the future of the Ottoman Empire. Relying on the 1833 treaty with Austria and confident that Prussia, which had no direct interests in the area, would remain a loyal ally, the tsar felt that an agreement with the British would settle the entire matter, isolated France being forced to accept the decision of the other great powers. In the summer of 1844 he traveled personally to England and, in the course of a busy state visit, discussed the Near Eastern situation and prospects with Lord Aberdeen, the foreign secretary. The results of these conversations were summarized in an official Russian memorandum, prepared by Nesselrode, which the British government accepted as accurate. According to its provisions, Russia and Great Britain were to maintain the Turkish state as long as possible, and, in case of its impending dissolution, the two parties were to come in advance to an understanding concerning the repartitioning of the territories involved and other problems of succession.

This victory for Russian foreign policy, however, had an illusory and indeed a dangerous character. The two main points of the understanding were, in a sense, contradictory, and the entire agreement was, therefore, especially dependent on identical, or at least very similar, interpretation by both partners of developments in the Near East, a degree of harmony never to be achieved. Moreover, the form of the agreement also contributed to a certain ambivalence and difference of opinion: while Nicholas I and his associates considered it to be a firm arrangement of fundamental importance, the British apparently thought of it more as a secret exchange of opinions not binding on the subsequent premiers and foreign ministers of Her Majesty's government.[28] The Russian emperor's talks in January and February, 1853, with Sir Hamilton Seymour, the British ambassador, when the tsar dwelt on the

---

[28] This is the majority view. For the argument that the understanding of 1844 represented a lasting treaty which Great Britain failed to honor see especially Puryear, *England, Russia, and the Straits Question, 1844–1856.*

imminent collapse of the Ottoman Empire and offered a plan of partition, served only to emphasize the gulf between the two states. The entire complex and unfortunate entanglement with Great Britain contributed hugely to Nicholas I's mistaken belief that his Near Eastern policy had strong backing in Europe.

In 1850, a dispute began in the Holy Land between the Catholics and the Orthodox in regard to certain rights connected with some of the most sacred shrines of Christendom. Countering Napoleon III's championing of the Catholic cause, Nicholas I acted in his usual direct and forceful manner by sending Menshikov, in February, 1853, with an ultimatum to the Turks: the Holy Land controversy was to be settled in favor of the Orthodox, and the Porte was to recognize explicitly the rights of the vast Orthodox population of its empire. When Turkey accepted the first series of demands, but would not endorse Russian interference on behalf of the Orthodox subjects of the Porte, considering it to be an infringement of Turkish sovereignty, Menshikov terminated the discussion and left Constantinople. Russian occupation of the Danubian Principalities as "material guarantees" added fuel to the fire. While it is probable that Nicholas I wanted to avoid war, there is little doubt that his rash actions precipitated the conflict. However, after the first phases of the controversy described above, the Russian government acted in a rather conciliatory manner, accepting the so-called Vienna Note as a compromise settlement, evacuating the Principalities, and repeatedly seeking peace even after the outbreak of hostilities. The war guilt at this later stage should be divided principally among Turkey, France, Great Britain, and even Austria.[29] In any case,

---

[29] Historical literature on the Eastern Question and the Crimean War is enormous. It is by far the best-studied aspect of Nicholas I's reign. For a convenient recent summary and discussion of the writing in the field, see B. Gooch, "A Century of Historiography on the Origins of the Crimean War," *American Historical Review*, LXII (Oct., 1956), 32–58. As to the responsibility for the war, judgments are many and different. A key issue is the role of Sir Stratford Canning, the British ambassador to Constantinople. He has been accused by numerous historians of promoting the conflict, but ably defended by some others, e.g., Temperley, *England and the Near East. The Crimea.* Gooch concludes: "Essentially, all the principal powers wanted peace. The nature of conditions in the Near East, however, made some sort of action imperative and the cumulative momentum of resulting events pushed matters beyond human control." Gooch, *op. cit.*, p. 58.

after fighting between Russia and Turkey started in 1853, Great
Britain and France joined the Porte in 1854, and Sardinia inter-
vened the next year. Austria stopped just short of hostilities against
Russia, exercising great diplomatic pressure on the side of the
Allies. The Crimean War, in spite of the heroic defense of
Sevastopol, brought a shameful defeat to Nicholas I and an end
to his system both at home and abroad.

The Russian autocrat's championing of legitimism and the
status quo in Europe determined Russian foreign policy not only
in the major developments mentioned above, but also in many
secondary matters. Thus in Italy Russia not only supported in
full the Hapsburg rule in Lombardy and Venetia, but, in general
accord with Austria which had the leading role in the peninsula,
extended its backing to the established order in the various
Italian states, favoring in particular Ferdinand II of the Kingdom
of the Two Sicilies. In Spain, the issues were unusually complex
during a part of Nicholas I's reign because of the struggle for
the throne between the party of Isabella II, Ferdinand VII's
daughter, and Don Carlos, a brother of the late king. The rights
of the two claimants depended on the involved fortunes of the
Salic law in Spanish dynastic history. During the so-called Carlist
War of 1834–1839, the sympathies of the eastern European monarchies remained naturally on the side of the reactionary Don
Carlos in preference to his liberal opponents. The three powers
offered moral encouragement and some financial help to the
absolutist cause, and stood ready to recognize Don Carlos immediately in the event of his victory, although they would not
come out openly against the Spanish government.[30] Nicholas
I's participation in the matter included a violent protest to France
when, in the spring of 1839, Frenchmen were allowed by French
authorities to join, as volunteers, the standard of Isabella. In the
case of Greece, the Russian ruler reacted against the revolution
of 1843, even though the largest group supporting it was pro-
Russian and although he disliked King Otto who favored the
spread of Protestantism in the Orthodox land: the Russian ambassador was withdrawn from Athens, and the post remained in

---

[30] They also hoped for a solution that would be just to all the rights involved:
i.e., the marriage of Isabella to Don Carlos's son.

the care of a chargé d'affaires until the end of Nicholas's reign; Russia recognized the new Greek government much later than did Great Britain or France. Incidentally, on this, as on several other occasions in the reign of Nicholas I, the position of Russia in a foreign country was weakened by the angry recall of its high representative and the handling of its affairs over a long period of time by men of lesser rank.

In northern as in southern Europe the tsar adhered to the same principles of legitimism and defense of the established order, for example, in the already noted instances of his hostility to the Belgian revolution which violated the legitimate rights of the House of Orange and changed the political settlement of Vienna by detaching Belgium from Holland, and of his opposition to Prussia in its attempt to sever the historic ties between Schleswig-Holstein and the Danish crown. As on many other occasions, Nicholas I thought, in connection with these two crises, especially of justice and of maintaining the conservative system in Europe, not of immediate Russian interests.[31] In Germany proper the tsar backed Metternich's policy, supporting especially such reactionary rulers as Ernest Augustus of Hanover.

In the eyes of the Russian autocrat Austria and Prussia stood out as great pillars of the established order and natural allies, a fact that emerges from even the most summary consideration of the emperor's policies. France which, after the overthrow of the restored Bourbons in July, 1830, proceeded to produce a whole series of illegitimate and revolutionary regimes, represented on

---

[31] Nicholas I's relations with Denmark included the interesting episode of the emperor's renunciation, on June 5, 1851, of his rights to the Danish throne. The Romanov claims dated from the reign of Emperor Peter III, originally a prince of the Holstein-Gottorp family, and a treaty between Russia and Denmark drawn in 1773; they acquired some significance after it became apparent that Frederick VII would die without leaving a male heir. The tsar's renunciation in favor of Prince Christian of Schleswig-Holstein-Sonderburg-Gluecksburg helped the prince later to win over his rivals and become King Christian IX of Denmark. By the treaty of 1773 the Russian dynasty had also recognized explicitly the link between Schleswig and the Danish crown. Another reason for the Russian support of Denmark was the desire to maintain a friendly and relatively weak state at the entrance to the Baltic. Much material on the Russian attitude toward Denmark, in particular in relation to Schleswig-Holstein, is contained in Nesselrode, *Lettres*, especially in vol. X.

the whole the enemy. The position of Great Britain remained more ambivalent. Nicholas I resented the British championing of liberalism in Europe and the British opposition to Russian interests in many matters and areas. Similarly, and quite characteristically, he was bitter about the Great Reform Bill of 1832 and about the evolution of British politics and society in general. Yet the tsar retained respect for the strange island state together with a certain confidence in the essential probity of the British and in the possibility of coming to terms with them. This belief inspired, as we have seen, the autocrat's Near Eastern policy, and it found reflection in other less important policies as well. In small things too Nicholas I displayed constantly his hatred of France—or rather of everything France represented after 1830, for he felt differently about the legitimist and aristocratic France of the Bourbons—and his appreciation of Great Britain.[32]

In foreign policy, as in domestic affairs, the Russian autocrat reacted to people and events in a personal and passionate manner. Thus he hated rebels all over the world, whether Polish insurgents, Mazzini, or Mohammed Ali.[33] Beyond them he detected a still more damnable category of men: those individuals who belonged to the side of legitimism and order, but who, for personal profit, betrayed their banner. Louis-Philippe represented well such perfidy.

Nicholas first visited the Duke of Orleans and his family in 1815, in Neuilly, and found himself deeply impressed by his host. He asked permission to come again and returned soon after, for he wanted to learn more about the manner of life of

---

[32] For instance, French universities were the only leading universities not approached by the Russian government in its attempt to find more information about cholera in connection with the dreadful epidemic of 1830 (Schiemann, III, 37); no Frenchmen were to be included among the railroad specialists invited to Russia (SIRIO, XCVIII, 127–128); the British, by contrast, received admission into the empire of the tsars even when, in connection with revolutionary movements in Europe, it was denied other foreigners.

[33] And he considered them all as serving the same enemy. For instance, the tsar declared in 1832, when dispatching N. Muraviev to the Near East, "It is necessary to defend Constantinople from Mohammed Ali's invasion. This entire war is nothing but a result of the spirit of insurrection which has now seized Europe and especially France." Quoted in Istoriya Rossii v XIX veke, II, 600.

this attractive man whom he considered both happy and wise. Later Nicholas maintained his high opinion of Louis-Philippe and even, so the tsar himself asserted, tried to arrange his own family living after the pattern which he had admired in the Duke's household.[34] The July Revolution and "the usurpation of the throne by the Duke of Orleans," who thus revealed himself as "traitor to the King and to the Dynasty,"[35] shook the Russian monarch profoundly. Unable, as explained above, to intervene effectively in the affairs of Western Europe and faced with the acceptance of the new French regime by other powers, Nicholas I recognized the government of Louis-Philippe, rationalizing the matter as best he could:

That country cannot remain without a head, and, in his absence, must fall into the condition of the most horrible anarchy. Therefore, in fact the man nearest to the throne who is present in France, in the absence of those who preceded him, becomes for us actually the king of France. If then my allies judge unanimously that we must agree in this respect on the Duke of Orleans, then, it seems to me, it is better to recognize royal power stemming from such a fact than royal power according to the people's choice: a frightful example, pernicious to every order, and one that would undermine our own existence; I repeat, it would be too revolting for me to recognize him in this manner.[36]

Benckendorff noted on this occasion: "Emperor Nicholas for the first time forced himself to act against his own conviction and, not without deep grief and vexation, recognized Louis-Philippe as the king of the French."[37] The acceptance left much to be desired. "In its essence the sovereign's answer contained a disapproving and conditional recognition of the accomplished fact which was hateful to him, without even observing the forms

[34] On this phase of the relationship between Nicholas and Louis-Philippe see, e.g., Schiemann, III, 16.
[35] This last phrase is taken from the emperor's letter to the empress, written on August 2, 1830. Schiemann, III, 475. See especially the fifteenth volume of Martens, *op. cit.* for a presentation and discussion of Franco-Russian diplomatic relations in the reign of Nicholas I.
[36] Quoted in Schilder, II, 300–301.
[37] *Ibid.*, p. 305.

established for correspondence with royalty," [38] notably avoiding the word "brother" in reference to the new ruler of France.

This letter, "which determined the relations between Russia and France in the course of the following eighteen years," [39] reflected the tsar's unyielding attitude toward the man he considered an usurper. Nicholas I's hostility to the French monarch revealed itself in many matters, ranging from the basic and outspoken anti-French direction of Russian Near Eastern policy to the autocrat's successful efforts to prevent an Austrian marriage for Louis-Philippe's son. Personal bitterness remained extreme: the tsar even tried to avoid the mention of his enemy's name.[40] Finally, after the revolution of 1848, Nicholas I could exclaim in triumph: "Here then the comedy is played out and finished, and the scoundrel is down!" [41] The Russian emperor hated Leopold of Belgium in a similar manner and for somewhat the same reasons as Louis-Philippe.[42]

Considering world politics in his simple and inclusive manner, Nicholas I naturally regarded the proponents of legitimism, law, and order as essentially a single camp, just as he lumped together

---

[38] *Ibid.*, pp. 303–304. The letter is reproduced on p. 304.

[39] *Ibid.*

[40] *Ibid.*, pp. 651–652.

[41] *Ibid.*, p. 305. The emperor also expressed his satisfaction that the King of the French went out "by way of the same door through which he came in." (Lobanov-Rostovsky, *op. cit.*, p. 116.) He had many times predicted this outcome as unavoidable, e.g., in a letter of May 24, 1839, to Orlov where he had asserted that Louis-Philippe could not obtain strength from the element "which had vomited him up," but that, once he repudiated this element, he would find himself suspended in mid-air and would fall from a total lack of support. Schiemann, III, 494. (The emperor's letters to Orlov in 1839 constitute appendix XIII to the volume—pp. 491–494.) Russian court circles had to take into account the tsar's hatred of Louis-Philippe. See, e.g., the worried letter of Countess Nesselrode, the foreign minister's wife, to her son Dmitrii, then in Paris, which was written in February, 1844, and opened with the sentence: "You promised me, at the time of your departure, that you would not present yourself to Louis-Philippe." Nesselrode, *Lettres*, VIII, 238.

[42] The hatred of Louis Napoleon was a different matter, for the Bonaparte prince, president, and emperor never belonged to the camp of legitimism. Nicholas I considered him kindly at one time, apparently as a conservative force in revolutionary France, but the tsar was tremendously provoked by his assumption of the imperial title and the numeral "III" which spelled out his claim to continue the outlawed Napoleonic dynasty. As to the true ruler of France, Nicholas I knew only one after 1830—Henry V. (See, e.g., Schiemann, IV, 419.)

all forms and kinds of revolution and rebellion. The commander in chief of the forces of right and justice was first Frederick William III of Prussia—Alexander I's comrade in arms and Nicholas's "father"—and, after his death in 1840, Nicholas I himself. It was this feeling of the unity of the eastern European conservative world that made the tsar so passionately concerned with developments in the neighboring monarchies. Moreover—a point insufficiently recognized by many modern historians who find it difficult to think in primarily dynastic terms—this attitude had its counterparts on the Prussian and the Austrian sides. Frederick William III's testament, composed with Nicholas's participation, allowed members of the family to protest against any future diminution of royal power in Prussia and gave the tsar an added argument in his attempts to turn Frederick William IV from the constitutional path.[43] Francis I of Austria went much further, enjoining his weak-minded son, Ferdinand I, in his will and otherwise, to follow the advice of Nicholas I, and begging the tsar to support and protect the young ruler.[44]

Joint military policy and action followed logically from this assumption of the unity of legitimist forces. The Russian emperor indicated time and again his eagerness to campaign together with his allies against the exponents of liberalism and subversion. And while these vast plans found only a very limited realization in the Hungarian war, Nicholas I continued to emphasize the military solidarity of the Eastern European courts by constantly exchanging honorary commands, ranks, and decorations with the Hohenzollerns and the Hapsburgs, and by such more extraordinary means as the great maneuvers held jointly, upon the suggestion of the tsar, by the Russian and the Prussian armies in Kalish in 1835. Nicholas I loved to assert that his troops stood at the disposal of his allies,[45] to call himself a subordinate of his father-in-law, or to lecture to Austrian officers on how they should be

---

[43] See, e.g., Presnyakov, p. 67. See also, e.g., Nicholas I's letter to Frederick William IV written early in 1847 (Schiemann, IV, 390–391).

[44] See, e.g., Schilder, II, 711; Schiemann, III, 276.

[45] Earlier, as is well known, Alexander I had proposed to place the Russian army at the service of the congress of European powers to maintain order on the continent.

loyal to their sovereign.[46] Much of this behavior on the part of
the Russian autocrat can be considered a pose or a superficial
display of sentiment, but the nature of the pose and the content
of the sentiment are nevertheless revealing. And there is little
doubt that the tsar's emphasis on military brotherhood strengthened the links between his empire and the neighboring monarchies.[47]

Nicholas I's handling of foreign affairs was quite of a piece
with his management of domestic matters. The Russian ruler
remained always the autocrat who insisted on personal direction
and control of all policies and who treated his associates as junior
officers at best. The task of the tsar's subordinates, in diplomacy
as in other fields, often included efforts to moderate frequently
drastic and extremely blunt decisions and actions of their sov-

---

[46] About this lecture, see, e.g., Polievktov, p. 187.

[47] This point was made in a striking, and in my opinion exaggerated, manner
in a report of Seymour, the British ambassador, to Malmesbury: "Continental
Europe, it is evident, is governed just now by armed masses; the system, it is
not too much to say, is one which the Emperor will always greatly prefer to
constitutional rule, and his conversation and example are well calculated to
give it force and extension. These positions being granted, when the Emperor
is seen to surround himself for weeks together with some of the most influential
Generals of Prussia and Austria, to live on terms of close intimacy with them,
to treat them—according to his own phrase—as *comrades*, it is idle to deny the
strong effect which must be produced from such familiar intercourse. It cannot be otherwise but that any prejudice against the Russian Government (which
means in other words the Russian Court) which may have existed on the part
of the ruling or military classes in Germany must be giving way under the
genial influence to which the distinguished officers summoned hither from
Berlin and Vienna are subjected, and that in both Capitals the services of
powerful friends have been retained. . . . I cannot however but be apprehensive that these military gatherings, presided as they are in Russia, constitute
a danger for the Constitutional liberties of Europe, their direct tendency being
to establish the principle of military force being the basis of social order and to
substitute the word of command for the voice of popular deliberation. It is
accordingly incorrect to say that the Emperor is too much engrossed with Army
matters to devote any time upon political questions. His Majesty may have little
leisure to bestow upon such questions as the occupation of Herat—or the
succession to the throne of Athens but he is engaged in a pursuit which is at
once military and political, and while indulging in a favorite taste may be carrying out an important object." Italics in the original. Seymour's report to
Malmesbury of August 12, 1852, constitutes appendix X in Schiemann, IV,
399–400. For another evaluation of the tsar's peculiar combination of militarism and politics see Presnyakov, pp. 11–12. Honorary field marshals of the
Russian army included such distinguished foreign commanders as the Duke of
Wellington and Radetzky.

ereign. For instance, Russian representatives in France, Count
C. Pozzo di Borgo and N. Kiselev, both evaded, in 1830 and 1848
respectively, the emperor's first impulsive instructions to leave
the French capital gripped anew by revolution.[48] In the opinion
of many students—to which I already had occasion to refer—
a major function performed by Nesselrode, as the man officially
in charge of Russian foreign affairs, consisted in the restraining
influence which he exercised on the tsar.[49] Nicholas I's starkly
straightforward and doctrinaire foreign policy would have been
even more blunt, but for the mitigating effect of these subordinates.

Abroad, as at home, the Russian autocrat relied heavily on
special assignments and extraordinary missions, bypassing regular
procedure. As usual, he delegated different important tasks to
the same small number of trusted assistants. Characteristic and
striking instances included Orlov's mission to Constantinople in
1833, which succeeded and resulted in the Treaty of Unkiar
Skelessi, and Menshikov's mission to the same city in 1853,
which failed and contributed hugely to the outbreak of the
Crimean War. Avoiding regular channels led, in diplomacy as in
domestic affairs, to a certain neglect and relegation in importance
of men formally responsible for imperial policies. To give two
illustrations among many: "When the tsar put his Fourth and
Fifth Army Corps (on the Ottoman border) on a war footing,
neither Orlov, head of the Third Section, Nesselrode, vice-chancellor and foreign minister, nor Dolgorukii, the war minister, knew
about it. Word of the mission of Menshikov to Constantinople
likewise reached the ears of foreign diplomats before Nesselrode
knew of it." [50] But the most common criticism of Nicholas I's

---

[48] Schiemann, III, 13; IV, 178–179.

[49] The relationship between the tsar and the foreign minister is richly, although by no means fully, depicted in Nesselrode *Lettres*. See especially the
appendix to vol. XI (pp. 145–215) which contains informal notes exchanged
between the two. As a major example of the minister's moderating influence
on the sovereign, see his memoir of September 7, 1854, against the proposed
Russian declaration of war on Austria. Nesselrode, *Lettres*, XI, 74–77.

[50] Gooch, *op. cit.*, p. 52. Gooch's account is taken from the Saxon diplomat
C. Eckstaedt's *Saint Petersburg and London in the Years 1852–1864*. Nesselrode was chancellor at the time, not vice-chancellor.

diplomacy by specialists concerns the emperor's inordinate emphasis on the direct approach, above all personal meetings and agreements with different European rulers, and his failure to allow for other elements in the situation, such as public opinion or constitutional procedures in various countries.

The principle—some would say the phantom—of legitimism determined the straight and narrow course of the Russian autocrat's foreign policy. It guided the tsar in his dealings with Belgium as well as with Austria and with Denmark as much as with France; it showed him the way in the early years of his reign no less than in 1848 and 1849. Yet one major aspect of imperial activity did not fit easily into this pattern: the role of Russia in the Near East. In fact, many historians have considered Nicholas I's attitude toward the Ottoman Empire as essentially aggressive, by contrast with the conservative position of Russia in other matters. These critics include a number of prerevolutionary Russian scholars, Soviet historians as a group, and many, though by no means all, Western specialists on the subject. It appears, therefore, imperative to make certain additional comments on the relationship, or possible relationship of the ideology and the Near Eastern policy of the reign, even at the risk of treating some weighty and much studied subjects in a sketchy and tentative manner.

To begin with, it is important to realize that Nicholas I's Eastern policy conformed for a long time and to a large extent to the concept of legitimism. As already indicated, the treaties of Turkmanchai with Persia and of Adrianople with Turkey were both moderate agreements terminating hostilities, which, if continued, might well have resulted in the destruction of these Oriental neighbors of Russia. The decision of the tsarist government in 1829 to work towards the preservation of Turkey apparently represented a sincere effort at stabilizing the situation in the Near East and served as a basis for Russian policy in the years following. Russian intervention to save Turkey from Egypt and the resulting Treaty of Unkiar Skelessi marked in themselves —whatever one may think of the possible future implications or designs connected with them—a most striking and effective instance of Russian action to maintain the Porte and the *status quo* in the East. Russian participation, in 1840 and 1841, in the international guarantee of Turkey and the joint settlement of the Straits question underlined the moderation of Nicholas I's policy in regard to the Ottoman Empire and his conviction that he could work together with other powers in that important area. It should be emphasized that the tsar continuously refused to profit by unrest within Turkey, insisting that all subjects of the sultan, regardless of religion or nationality, must obey their legitimate ruler.[51] Nicholas I respected Turkish sovereignty even in the Danubian Principalities which probably could have been annexed by Russia on more than one occasion. And the tsar's ardent support of the Austrian Empire constituted another contribution to the preservation of order, stability, and the *status quo* in the Balkans and southeastern Europe in general.[52] This legitimist and conservative attitude of Nicholas I toward Turkey

---

[51] As mentioned earlier, the Russian government's support of Turkey and Austria drove such radical nationalists and Pan-Slavs as Pogodin and Tyutchev to despair. The tsarist ministry of foreign affairs took special pains to discourage rebellions in the two neighboring empires. For instance, in 1844 Russian representatives in Turkey and Greece were instructed to inform the elders of Christian communities that they must not hope for any help from Russia, for Russia could not approve an insurrection against Turkey. (Polievktov, p. 180.) It may be added parenthetically that it is quite outside the scope of this chapter to consider the extent to which Russian agents, in the Balkans and elsewhere, understood the intentions or carried out the instructions of their government. Only in 1853, with the coming of the Crimean War, did the tsar think of promoting a rebellion against the Porte, but he abandoned this plan after Nesselrode criticized it as inconsistent with the principles of Russian foreign policy. (For the text of Nicholas I's proposal see Schilder, II, 641–642.) Even this rebellion was to be religious rather than national, or racial. In the words of an American historian of Pan-Slavism: "The most Nicholas was willing to do was to proclaim his country's traditional role as protector of Orthodoxy and to appeal to the Orthodox Christians of Turkey to rise up in common defense of their religion—but not in defense of Slavdom." (Petrovich, *The Emergence of Russian Panslavism, 1856–1870*, p. 31.)

[52] The emperor's associates generally reflected his views. A. Smirnova, for instance, recorded the following conversation with Paskevich at a reception in March, 1845: "I asked him about the Slavic movements in Bohemia. 'You believe these Slavic movements? They are all insurgents, rebels; in my bailiwick I give no freedom of action to these characters; in my Warsaw they dare not speak about it; out with all of them.' 'Well, are the Bohemians also out of your favor?' 'They mutiny against Austria; all this is disobedience'." Barsukov, *op. cit.*, VIII, 452. Cf. Paskevich's comments in Luciani, trans., *Le Livre de la Genèse du peuple ukrainien*, pp. 74–85.

formed an integral part of his total foreign policy and presents no special problems of understanding or interpretation.

Difficult issues arise from the fact that the tsar also developed another approach to the Near East which emphasized a partition of the Ottoman Empire; that this approach became increasingly prominent in his thought, from the decision in 1829 to preserve Turkey, to the Seymour conversations of 1853, when the tsar offered specific plans for its division among European powers; and that the reign culminated in a major war against the Porte, with Russia appearing to many observers as the aggressor. Various hypotheses have been advanced to explain this striking turning of Russian policy in the Near East. Least convincing is the claim that the monarch finally sided with the radical nationalists and the Pan-Slavs: it is based merely on the correspondence, often superficial, between certain aims of the Russian government, notably the partitioning of Turkey, and the ideas of Pan-Slav intellectuals, and it ignores completely the tsar's persistent hostility to revolutionary nationalism and all its proponents. More impressive is the argument that in the case of Turkey Nicholas I, perhaps influenced in particular by the special Russian interest in the Straits, abandoned his customary legitimist position in favor of a grand design of imperial expansion at the expense of the declining Ottoman state, somewhat in the tradition of Catherine the Great. Soviet historians, as well as a few others, have emphasized the importance of economic factors in urging upon the Russian government an aggressive policy in the Near East.[53] It may be that some explanations of this nature are correct and that the tsar's Turkish policy developed according to a rationale of its own in sharp contrast to his general beliefs and orientation. It is possible, of course, to overestimate, as well as underestimate, consistency.

[53] For example, Presnyakov wrote: "Instead of deepening the base of the economic development at home by freeing the working masses from the shackles of the old order, Russian policy took the direction of an external expansion of this base in the Middle and Near East. The protector of 'balance' in the West, Nicholas led, from the very beginning of his reign, an energetic Eastern policy." (Presnyakov, p. 78.) From this point of view, Russian wars against Turkey and Persia, the pacification of the Caucasus, and expansion in Central Asia all formed parts of the same pattern.

It can well be argued, on the other hand, that there existed no such contrast, at least not in the sovereign's own mind. Nicholas I predicated his plans to partition Turkey on the inability of the Ottoman Empire to maintain its life in the changing world. This view has found considerable justification in subsequent history, especially in regard to Turkey in Europe which attracted the particular interest of the tsar. Even the autocrat's faulty time-table may be partly ascribed to the efforts made by European powers to preserve the Ottoman state rather than to its own viability. Nicholas insisted—and in this he adhered firmly to the main line of his political thinking—that the legacy of the Ottomans must be divided clearly and equitably among the guardians of European order to prevent war among them and, above all, to forestall decisions based on popular demand and uprisings. The tsar himself, apparently, felt no inconsistency between his policies in the Near East and elsewhere. And he impressed most observers, from Queen Victoria, Melbourne, and Aberdeen in 1844 in England, to different ambassadors in St. Petersburg, as thoroughly sincere.[54]

One more element should be mentioned in any consideration of the ideology of Nicholas I's reign and its Near Eastern policy: Orthodoxy. It played a part not only in relation to the quarrel among monks in Palestine which led eventually to the Crimean War, but also in the tsar's entire attitude toward the Ottoman Empire. While Nicholas I recognized repeatedly the legitimate nature of the sultan's rule in his own domain, he remained uneasy about the sprawling Moslem state which believed in the Koran and oppressed its numerous Orthodox subjects. In a sense, Turkey simply did not belong to that Christian and traditional international order which the Russian emperor was determined to uphold. To resolve this problem, Nicholas I actually suggested to the Turkish representative, in April, 1830, that the Sultan, in

---

[54] Victoria wrote about Nicholas I: "He is stern and severe—with fixed principles of *duty* which *nothing* on earth will make him change . . . he is sincere, I am certain . . ." (Benson and Usher, eds., *The Letters of Queen Victoria, Vol. II, 1844–1853*, pp. 16–17. Italics in the original.) Puryear, *op. cit.*, pays considerable attention to the impression which the Russian emperor produced on English statesmen.

his own best interest, should become Orthodox![55] While the Russian autocrat had only hatred for national revolts against the Hapsburg rule or liberal movements in different parts of Europe, he could not feel quite the same way about the opposition of the Christian population of the Balkans to their Moslem overlords.

The diplomatic crisis which resulted in the Crimean War contained an abundance of religious ingredients: the initial dispute in the Holy Land, Napoleon III's strong championing of the Catholics and Nicholas I's of the Orthodox, the Turkish rejection of Menshikov's demands on behalf of Orthodox subjects of the sultan. Grunwald notes that Nesselrode was not allowed to exercise his usual influence during the crisis, because, being Protestant, he was considered not entirely competent in the matter.[56] As the sky darkened, Nicholas I could write to Frederick William IV, probably in all sincerity: "Waging war *neither for worldly advantages nor for conquests,* but for a solely Christian purpose, must I be left alone to fight under the banner of the Holy Cross and to see the others, *who call themselves Christians,* all unite *around the Crescent to combat Christendom?* . . . now nothing is left to me, but to fight, to win, or to perish with honor, *as a martyr of our holy faith,* and when I say this I declare it *in the name of all of Russia."* [57]

---

[55] Schilder, II, 271–272. The tsar also mentioned this possibility to General N. Muraviev, when dispatching him, in 1832, on a mission to the Near East. *Ibid.*

[56] Grunwald, *Trois siècles de diplomatie russe,* p. 193.

[57] This letter of June 29, 1854, is reproduced in Schiemann, IV, 429–431; quoted from p. 430; italics in the original. (Appendix XVII to the volume, pp. 425–435, consists of the tsar's letters to Frederick William IV written in January–August, 1854.) While the letter was obviously meant to influence the Prussian king, it also reflected faithfully Nicholas I's character and beliefs. Cf. the tsar's correspondence with Francis Joseph during the same period, e.g., in Levin, ed., *Perepiska Nikolaya I i Frantsa Iosifa.*

VI

CONCLUSION

OFFICIAL NATIONALITY

AND HISTORY

Question: "What reward does our August Monarch deserve for these glorious deeds of his?" Answer: "The astonishment of all the ages."—From a Russian history textbook used in girls' schools at the time of Nicholas I.[1]

The main failing of the reign of Nicholas consisted in the fact that it was all a mistake.—Nikitenko [2]

THE MARVEL—and the mistake—of Nicholas I's long rule is to be found in its extraordinary doctrinaire rigidity and consistency. The steadfast monarch governed his vast empire and participated in the destinies of the world on the basis of a few simple principles which he held with passionate conviction. The ideology of

---

[1] Quoted in Kovalenskii, "Srednyaya shkola," in *Istoriya Rossii v XIX veke*, IV, 144.
[2] Nikitenko, I, 553.

the reign, known as Official Nationality, deserves more attention that it has hitherto received. Far from being mere propaganda or empty talk, it represented the conscious orientation of the Russian government in the course of thirty eventful years. Its roots lay deep in Russian history, most especially in the creation of the modern Russian state by Peter the Great, as well as in the subsequent development of that state. The doctrine of Official Nationality also faithfully reflected a stage in general European evolution, marked by the defeat of Napoleon and the joint effort of victorious powers to restore something like the old order on the continent. As theory, the Russian teaching constituted a typical philosophy of the age of restoration and reaction. In practice it meant a way of managing the enormous and relatively backward Russian state. And while one can easily criticize Nicholas I's desperate effort personally to set everything straight in his far-flung realm, one should at least try to appreciate the difficulties of his position.

The emperor's stubborn loyalty to his convictions taxed the understanding of many of his contemporaries and of numerous subsequent historians. Time and again they have tried to explain Nicholas I's actions more "realistically," notably on the basis of the immediate interests of Russia rather than of the tsar's professed principles. For example, some specialists have maintained that Russian intervention in Hungary in 1849 resulted from the fear of Polish rebels who took an active part in the Hungarian movement, not from the desire to crush revolution, come to the aid of Austria, or honor the treaty of 1833. Even Schiemann, who is in many ways the leading authority on the reign of Nicholas I, argued that the Russian autocrat wanted to manipulate Austria and Prussia so they would serve as a shield against liberalism and revolution and do his fighting for him— this in spite of the fact that the German scholar also repeatedly pointed out in his work the tsar's eagerness for combat and the reluctance of his allies. In fact, this contrast between the recognition of the extremely rigid and doctrinaire nature of the tsar's policy and the attempts, which nevertheless persist, to ascribe its various manifestations to "practical" reasons, constitutes one of the peculiarities of historical writing dealing with this period. A dismissal of "realistic" interpretations does not indicate, however, that Nicholas I ignored Russian interests. Rather he saw these interests in terms of his fundamental beliefs, not apart from them; the effectiveness of the autocrat's service to his native land depended thus largely on the soundness of the beliefs.

Similarly the extreme regimentation and repression of Nicholas I's reign have to be considered in the light of the emperor's convictions and of the aims which he attempted to achieve. While many specific instances of censorship or police interference must be judged ridiculous and stupid, the system as a whole makes good sense provided one accepts the dogma of Official Nationality and the need to impose it upon Russia. Once more Nicholas I stands vindicated or convicted primarily on the basis of his beliefs.

It is necessary to understand the doctrine of Official Nationality in order to comprehend the reign of Nicholas I. But understanding does not imply endorsement. The government ideology of autocracy and of the absolute control of the life of the country by the monarch represented at best one narrow approach to statecraft. It could be called progressive in the age of Peter the Great, in particular in Russia where the mighty sovereign undertook sweeping reforms in the face of an overwhelming popular opposition and indifference. It became increasingly less forward-looking with the passage of time and the social, political, economic, and intellectual evolution of Europe, turning into something of an anachronism in the nineteenth century. The rigid iron rule of Nicholas I tended to obscure the fact that even during his reign, and perhaps especially during his reign, Russia was undergoing fundamental change. The serf economy of the country steadily declined in favor of freer labor, monetary exchange, distant markets, and, in short, the rise of capitalism. Socially too, in spite of all government efforts, new forces were coming to the fore, the Russian intelligentsia of the 1840's being already much more democratic in origin than that of the 1820's. Russian culture, literature in particular, blossomed out in new splendor which offered infinitely more to the reader than the trite and vulgar pages of *The Northern Bee* and *The Reader's Library*. While, as has been indicated above, a number of leading Russian writers contributed in one way or another to the official doctrine, the main currents of this cultural renaissance ran in other directions. The Russia of Pushkin, of Lermontov, of the young Turgenev and Dostoevskii, or, indeed, of Gogol had little in common with the official version.

Ideas also changed. Educated Russians, from Herzen and Belinskii on one wing to Khomyakov and Samarin on the other, espoused views different from and often antagonistic to the teaching of their government. The Slavophiles, the Westernizers, the members of the Brotherhood of Cyril and Methodius, the Petrashevtsy, all saw visions of their native land and made plans for its future which did not fit the prescribed model. The extremist Bakunin and the moderate Granovskii, religious thinkers of the Slavophile camp and atheists such as Butashevich-Petrashevskii, liberals and socialists, constitutionalists and federalists, found themselves in opposition to the Russia of Nicholas I. The revolutionary ideas of the age, notably romantic nationalism, penetrated the official doctrine itself, contending for allegiance with the older dynastic interpretation. Of still greater significance was the fact that the reign of Nicholas I marked not only the flowering but also the beginning of the waning of romanticism in Russia. The romantic emphasis on religion, authority, uniqueness, history, and tradition gradually gave ground to a secular, materialistic, and positivist outlook which the tsar correctly considered as the deadly foe of his system. It is worth noting that the revolutionary movement of the Decembrists, inspired by the ideas of the Age of Reason and by Jacobin practice, had no militant successor in Russia until the 1870's, after the end of the romantic epoch and the advent of realism and the cult of science.

While the split between government and society in Russia continued to increase during the thirty long years of Nicholas I's reign, the gulf between the empire of the tsars and the West widened even more perceptibly. For the leading countries of the West, propelled by the industrial revolution, were undergoing a still more rapid transformation than the state of the Romanovs. Yet the autocrat's only answer to all the change at home and abroad remained a reaffirmation of his old principles, a heroic effort to turn the clock back. Following the revolutions of 1848, government and life in Russia acquired a certain nightmarish quality which forced even many supporters of the existing regime to cry out in despair. The debacle of the Crimean War came both as logical retribution and as liberation.

The historical significance of the reign of Nicholas I and the system of Official Nationality can be judged in several contexts. In the evolution of Russia it meant an attempt, for three decades, to freeze growth and impose stagnation. The liberal hopes of the time of Alexander I, already betrayed by that monarch himself, gave place to outspoken reaction. Abroad, Russia, the recent liberator of Europe, turned definitely into its gendarme. In fairness to Nicholas I it is right and proper to emphasize that his problems were great and his choices limited. Most critics of the emperor knew less about the condition of Russia than he did, and none of them had the awesome responsibility of translating theory into practice. Still, the sovereign's total refusal to consider any other way but his own led to a dead end, all the more so because the existing system was constantly becoming more obsolete and less workable. Although Russia certainly was not Great Britain or France and although it had to find a solution based on its own capabilities, it seems presumptuous to argue that the great reforms of the 1860's could not have been enacted in the fifties and the forties, or that the liberal hopes of the reign of Alexander I were bound to be doomed even if the successor to that emperor believed in constitutionalism, not autocracy. While numerous circumstances delimited the area within which the government system could operate, the fundamental rigidity lay in the system itself.

In a sense Russia never recovered the thirty years lost under Nicholas I. Alexander II instituted reforms; Alexander III appealed to the nationalist sentiment which his grandfather had spurned; in the reign of Nicholas II the country obtained even a shaky constitutional machinery. But all these new departures remained somehow tentative and incomplete. And it was still largely the old order of Nicholas I, the antiquated *ancien régime,* that went down in the conflagration of 1917. In some ways the willful autocrat proved to be more successful than he could have imagined.

In the broader pageant of European history, Nicholas I and Official Nationality deserve attention on a number of counts. The autocratic rule of the Russian sovereign represented a classic example of its kind, comparable to the reign of Louis XIV in France. "Orthodoxy" and "nationality" too, as indicated repeatedly in this study, reflected beliefs, forces, and problems by no means limited to the empire of the tsars. "Orthodoxy," even more than autocracy, linked Russia to the traditional Christian order on the continent which had been undergoing a profound transformation under the impact of the French Revolution and its aftermath. "Nationality," in its romantic interpretation, acted by contrast as a disintegrator of the established system, as a harbinger of a newer, if not a better, world. Official Nationality offers a fascinating picture of the rise of radical nationalism and of its efforts to supersede the older dynastic orientation. In Russia the attempt never quite succeeded: certainly not under Nicholas I and not even under the last of the Romanovs, when the communist victory in 1917 gave a thoroughly new direction to the history of the country. Still, developments in the tsarist state constituted one instance of that basic process and struggle in modern European history which marked the emergence of integral nationalism out of a traditional and dynastic past. It fell to the lot of Germany, the cradle of romanticism, to explore to the end the implications of radical nationalism, and beyond it racism, unhindered by "Orthodoxy" or other moral principles.

The theory and the practice of Official Nationality have something to tell us in a yet larger context. The system of Emperor Nicholas I demonstrated a remarkable coördination between thought and action, a dedication to a set ideal, a determination to mold reality according to an ideological blueprint. It is true that the government doctrine itself originated and could originate only in a certain historical milieu, conditioned by many circumstances of time and place. It is also true that similar circumstances limited its effectiveness and eventually defeated its aims. But, in the last analysis, the student of Nicholas I and Official Nationality in Russia leaves his subject with a sense of the power, not the weakness, of ideas in history, of the importance, not the insignificance, of man's purpose in the shaping of human destiny.

BIBLIOGRAPHY

It has seemed advisable to divide the bibliography into two parts: the ideology of Official Nationality as presented by its intellectual proponents, and other relevant material. The first part, although by no means exhaustive, is meant to provide a substantial list of writings which contributed to the construction and the development of the government doctrine and which were used in this study. No such bibliography exists at present. After a brief mention of the leading periodicals and newspapers, books and pamphlets are grouped alphabetically according to their authors; separate articles, poems, book reviews, notices, and other minor writings are not, however, because of their overwhelming number, entered in the list, except when they are specifically cited in the work. The second, general part is limited to the items directly mentioned in the study. While it is, therefore, in a sense misleading, for it gives only a portion of the material on which this volume is based, it has at least the virtue of being manageable. A scholarly bibliography of such topics related to my main subject as Pushkin, Gogol, intellectual currents in the reign of Nicholas I, or the Crimean War, could exceed this entire study in size. A few references to special bibliographies have been provided in the footnotes, e.g., to B. Gooch's review article of the literature dealing with the Crimean War, or to my own book on the Slavophiles. Comments included in the bibliography are designed to offer some additional information about the works listed and to supplement remarks made in the text or the footnotes.

The Ideology of Official Nationality

PERIODICALS AND NEWSPAPERS

While information about the periodicals of the time can be found in many places, the best single source remains the Brockhaus-Efron *Entsiklopedicheskii Slovar* from which most of the quoted descriptions have been taken. Dementev's study, cited below, provides a substantial recent account which covers much of the subject.

Biblioteka dlya Chteniya (The Reader's Library). St. Petersburg, 1834–1865. "A review of literature, the sciences, the arts, criticism, news and fashions." The first substantial and lasting Russian periodical of the kind which later became very popular. Contained seven sections: Russian literature, foreign literature, the sciences and the arts, industry and agriculture, criticism, the literary chronicle, and miscellaneous. A creation of Senkovskii who served actually, and for the greater part of the time also formally, as its editor from 1834 to 1856, or at least to 1848, at which date his control was reduced to the sections dealing with criticism, that is literary criticism, and the literary chronicle. Senkovskii's own contribution to his periodical was colossal, and, in addition to that, he edited and often changed arbitrarily other writings which appeared in *The Reader's Library*. Indeed the huge file of the review for the first fifteen years and large parts of it for the subsequent eight could be bodily included in Senkovskii's collected works which, unfortunately, are in any case much too voluminous. While *The Reader's Library* deserves attention both as a representative and a promoter of certain trends and attitudes in the Russian reading public during the reign of Nicholas I, its intellectual and ideological content is remarkably slight. Further discussion of Senkovskii and his magazine is contained in chap. ii of this study. I examined the complete file of *The Reader's Library*, from 1834 to 1865.

Literaturnye Listki (Literary Pages). St. Petersburg, 1824. "A review of literature and manners." An independent magazine for a year, it became, in 1825, an appendix to *The Archive of the North* (see below). Interesting as one of Bulgarin's early journalistic ventures. I examined the complete file for 1824, when the periodical appeared twice a month.

Mayak, or, in full, *Mayak Sovremennogo Prosveshcheniya i Obrazovannosti* (The Lighthouse, or The Lighthouse of Contemporary Education and Enlightenment). St. Petersburg, 1840–1845. Edited by S. Burachek and P. Korsakov. Other constant contributors included the historians N. Savelev-Rostislavich and F. Moroshkin. Represented the extreme nationalist and obscurantist Right, much of the periodical reading as a parody of *The Muscovite*. Peculiarities of *The Lighthouse* included patriotic and moral literary contributions by "simple Russian peasants," claims of sweeping scientific and technological inventions on behalf of other such peasants, violent anti-intellectualism, superstition in religion and thought, and Burachek's predilection for naval terminology and subject matter. I examined the complete file, 1840–1845.

Moskvityanin (The Muscovite). Moscow, 1841–1856. Edited by Pogodin, *The Muscovite* enjoyed Uvarov's patronage. An essential source for the ideology of the nationalist wing of Official Nationality, more especially of Pogodin and Shevyrev. Its contributors, however, included the Slavophiles. See N. Riasanovsky, "Pogodin and Ševyrëv in Russian Intellectual History," for the relationship between the two groups. I examined the complete file, 1841–1856.

Severnaya Pchela (The Northern Bee). St. Petersburg, 1825–1864. Bulgarin's and Grech's famous—or infamous—newspaper. Bulgarin was its editor and publisher from its foundation; in 1831 Grech joined him; in 1860, finally, the paper passed into other and strikingly different hands. Although described as "a political and literary newspaper," *The Northern Bee* operated entirely within the confines of Nicholas I's stifling system, with the result that it strikes a modern reader as deficient in interpretation, weak intellectually, and devoted almost entirely to factual, quasi-official summaries of events, superficial literary commentary, and trivial matters. Yet it reflected well Official Nationality in the daily press, and it contains a great abundance of writings, many of them incidental, by Bulgarin, Grech, and their collaborators. I examined the file from 1825 to 1859.

Severnyi Arkhiv (The Archive of the North). St. Petersburg, 1822–1840. Another one of Bulgarin and Grech's journalistic ventures; from 1829 to 1835 it appeared jointly with *A Son of the Fatherland*. "The purpose of this review consists, first, in the dissemination of useful knowledge in the fields of History, ancient and modern, native and foreign, Statistical Data and Political Economy, as related to Russia and other countries; in the second place, in the provision for the reading public of our fatherland of pleasant and edifying reading which is an occupation worthy of enlightened and well-meaning men." Contents ranged from information about the Slavs and the Greeks, and a long discussion of Karamzin's *History* to selections from Bulgarin's own fiction. I examined the file from 1822 to 1828.

Syn Otechestva (A Son of the Fatherland). St. Petersburg, 1812–1852. Founded by Grech who owned and edited it until the late 1830's; Bulgarin joined him in 1825; Senkovskii served as editor briefly in the early 1840's. An exceedingly patriotic publication which illustrates well some links between the reign of Alexander I and that of Nicholas I with its doctrine of Official Nationality. This publication is discussed in chap. iii above. I examined the file from 1812 to 1842.

Zhurnal Ministerstva Narodnogo Prosveshcheniya (The Journal of the Ministry of Education). St. Petersburg, 1834–1917. Founded by Uvarov in 1834, this journal is a basic source for the reign of Nicholas I, as well as for subsequent reigns, containing as it does the minister's annual reports to the emperor, directives to his subordinates, and other valuable documents of the ministry. I also found a scattering of articles dealing with ideological matters. Much of the journal was devoted to scholarly articles in various fields of knowledge. I examined the file from 1834 to 1855.

INDIVIDUAL WORKS

A few writers whose works are included below, Pushkin in particular, cannot be considered to be primarily exponents of Official Nationality; all, however, made some contribution to it. A number of items listed appeared before the government ideology received its formal inauguration. These are either early writings of later proponents of the state creed, or other pieces directly foreshadowing it and cited specifically in my study. Some bibliographical sources for the writings of the different exponents of Official Nationality have been cited in chap. ii above.

Atreshkov, N. "Nekotorye vozrazheniya kritiku naschet izmenenii Petrom Velikim natsionalnosti russkikh," *Severnaya Pchela*, no. 7, Jan. 10; no. 8, Jan. 11, 1833.

"Baron Brambeus" [O. I. Senkovskii]. *Fantasticheskie povesti i rasskazy*. St. Petersburg, 1840. Senkovskii's characteristically unsubstantial and light fiction.

————. *Fantasticheskie puteshestviya Barona Brambeusa*. St. Petersburg, 1835. More of the same.

————. *Listki Barona Brambeusa*. St. Petersburg, 1858. Senkovskii's discussion of various topics of the day in A *Son of the Fatherland* from 1856 to his death in 1858.

The Reader's Library constitutes the best source of Senkovskii's literary and journalistic writings. Senkovskaya, *Osip Ivanovich Senkovskii (Baron Brambeus)*. *Biograficheskie zapiski ego zheny*, a brief personal account of Senkovskii by his second wife, nee Baroness Adelaide Rahl, contains some of his letters to his wife. For a bibliography of Senkovskii's works, notably in the field of scholarship, see Savelev, *O zhizni i trudakh O. I. Senkovskogo*.

Bulgarin, F. *Dimitrii Samozvanets*. 2d ed., rev. St. Petersburg, 1830. 4 vols. A historical novel.

————. *Ivan Vyzhigin*. 3d ed., rev. St. Petersburg, 1830. 4 vols. A work of fiction described by its author in the subtitle as "a moral and satirical novel" (nravstvenno-satiricheskii roman). Quite popular at the time.

————. *Kornet*. St. Petersburg, 1842. Bulgarin published in separate thin booklets a series of such "pictures of Russian manners" (kartinki russkikh nravov).

————. *Letnyaya progulka po Finlyandii i Shvetsii v 1838 godu*. St. Petersburg, 1839. 2 vols. Bulgarin's travels.

————. *Pamyatnye Zapiski Titulyarnogo Sovetnika Chukhina*. St. Petersburg, 1835. 2 vols. Subtitled "a simple history of an ordinary life."

————. *Petr Ivanovich Vyzhigin*. St. Petersburg, 1831. 4 vols. This item bears the description "a novel of manners and a historical novel of the nineteenth century" (nravoopisatelno-istoricheskii roman XIX veka). Bulgarin took pride in the fact that Grand Duke Constantine just had time to read "Petr Vyzhigin" before he died of cholera.

————. *Rossiya v istoricheskom, statisticheskom, geograficheskom i literaturnom otnosheniyakh. Ruchnaya kniga dlya russkikh vsekh soslovii*. St. Petersburg, 1837. Unfinished. I was able to obtain four volumes of history and one, the second, of "statistics" (mostly information about Russian economy and education). The actual author of this *Handbook* was in all probability N. Ivanov, not Bulgarin, but Bulgarin edited the work and appears also to have given it its ideological tone. The *Handbook* and its authorship are discussed in some detail in the article, "Ivanov, Nikolai Alekseevich" cited below.

————. *Salopnitsa*. St. Petersburg, 1842. Another "picture."

————. *Sochineniya*. St. Petersburg, 1830. 12 vols. The *Works* are by no means complete, as the date alone would clearly indicate. The volumes are characteristically thin and small in size.

————. *Suvorov*. St. Petersburg, 1843. A popular and patriotic account of the famous commander, with many illustrations.

————. *Vospominaniya*. St. Petersburg, 1846–1849. 6 vols. Unfinished. Subtitled "Selections from what I have seen, heard, and experienced in life," the *Reminiscences* are autobiographical and interesting, but unreliable, especially so in their accounts of Bulgarin's own exploits.

The *Northern Bee* contains an enormous amount of Bulgarin's writings, particularly the section "Pchelka. Zametki, vypiski i korrespondentsiia F. V." (The Little Bee. Notes, Selections and Correspondence by F. V. —"F. V." were Bulgarin's initials). My only specific reference to Bulgarin's writings in *The Northern Bee*, however, was to No. 78, April 9, 1852, where the journalist defended Kukolnik's play, *The Orderly*, against Pogodin. For a full list of Bulgarin's writings, including translations of his works into foreign languages, see S. Vengerov, *Russkie knigi*, St. Petersburg, 1899, vol. III, part 26, pp. 269–275.

Dal, V. *Polnoe sobranie sochinenii*. 2d ed. St. Petersburg, 1878–1884. Dal, of course, is best known as a lexicographer.

Fedorov, B. "Chuvstva rossiyanina pri vesti o konchine Aleksandra I," *Syn Otechestva*, CI (1826), no. 1, part IV "Rhetoric," pp. 81–93. Boris Fedorov is better remembered in Russian intellectual history for his readiness to accuse his publicistic opponents of subversion than for his contribution to literature or thought. Together with Bulgarin and some others, he may be said to represent the lower depths of Official Nationality.

Glinka. F. *Dukhovnye stikhotvoreniya*. Moscow, 1839.

————. *Opyty svyashchennoi poezii*. St. Petersburg, 1836.

————. *Stikhotvoreniya*. Ed. by V. Bazanov. Leningrad, 1951. Unfortunately this useful Soviet edition of Glinka's poems slights the poet's religious verses which formed such an important part of his output.

Gogol, N. *Materialy i issledovaniya*. Ed. by V. Gippius. Moscow-Leningrad, 1936. A valuable and well-presented volume of Gogol materials, including hitherto unpublished letters of Gogol to Pogodin and Shevyrev and of Pogodin about Gogol.

————. *Sochineniya*. Ed. by V. Kallash. St. Petersburg, n.d. Vol. VIII. *Mistiko-moralisticheskie sochineniya* (Mystical and Moral Works). The volume includes "Selected Passages from Correspondence with Friends" as well as several shorter pieces written in the same spirit.

Grech, N. *Examen de l'ouvrage de M. le Marquis de Custine intitulé la Russie en 1839*. Paris, 1844. There were also a German and two Belgian editions of this quasi-official defense of Russia against Custine. The German version constitutes the original.

————. *Parizhskie pisma s zametkami o Danii, Germanii, Gollandii i Belgii*. St. Petersburg, 1847.

————. *Pisma s dorogi po Germanii, Shveitsarii i Italii*. St. Petersburg, 1843. 3 vols.

————. *Putevye pisma iz Anglii, Germanii i Frantsii*. St. Petersburg, 1839. 3 vols.

Grech, N. *Sochineniya*. St. Petersburg, 1855. 3 vols. The *Works* are incomplete. They include the bulk of Grech's fiction, notably his novels, some of his travel accounts, and a scattering of his journalistic articles.

——. *Zapiski o moei zhizni*. St. Petersburg, 1886.

——. ——. Ed. by R. Ivanov-Razumnik and D. Pines. Moscow-Leningrad, 1930. With an introductory article by Ivanov-Razumnik which is of general as well as bibliographical interest ("N. I. Grech i ego 'Zapiski,'" pp. 9–32). The scholar should use both editions of these important memoirs because the text is not identical: in 1886 large passages, even pages, were excised for reasons of censorship, while in 1930 the editors omitted some sections which they considered to be of little general interest. The references in the text are to the Soviet edition.

I have examined seventeen books by Grech, many of them textbooks, dealing with grammar, language, and literature, especially Russian grammar. But because these specialized works, in contrast, for instance, to similar works of Grech's contemporary, the Slavophile Konstantin Aksakov, contain virtually no broader ideological implications, they are not included in the bibliography.

Kaisarov, A. "Rech o lyubvi k otechestvu," *Syn Otechestva*, XXXVII (1813), part I, pp. 3–20. Professor Kaisarov's speech was delivered at the University of Dorpat in November, 1811.

Kukolnik, N. *Sochineniya*. St. Petersburg, 1852. Vol. III. *Sochineniya dramaticheskie*.

Markov, M. "Russkii Tsar," *Biblioteka dlya Chteniya*, VIII (1835), 5–8. The poem is bad and characteristic of the worshippers of autocracy. Cf., e.g., such versifiers as E. Tregubov listed below, or M. Sukhanov who published in *A Son of the Fatherland*.

Moroshkin, F. *Istoriko-kriticheskie issledovaniya o russakh i slavyanakh*. St. Petersburg, 1842.

Pletnev, P. "O narodnosti v literature," *Zhurnal Ministerstva Narodnogo Prosveshcheniya*, I (1834), part II, pp. 1–30. Again originally a university speech, this time in the University of St. Petersburg, on August 31, 1833.

Pogodin, M. *Borba ne na zhivot, a na smert s novymi istoricheskimi eresyami*. Moscow, 1874. The book contains eighteen separate articles which include a number written in defense of Pogodin's favorite historical thesis, that of the Norman origin of the Russian state, and aimed in particular against Kostomarov and Ilovaiskii; as well as such characteristic pieces as "In Defense of Skopin-Shuiskii," "In Defense of Prince Pozharskii," "In Defense of Minin," and "In Defense of Susanin."

——. *Chernaya nemoch*. Moscow, 1829. One of Pogodin's better-known tales of fiction.

——. *Drevnyaya russkaya istoriya do mongolskogo iga*. Moscow, 1871. 2 vols.

——. *God v chuzhikh krayakh, 1839*. Moscow, 1844. 4 vols. An account of travel, rich in detail.

——. *Historische Aphorismen*. Leipzig, 1836. I was able to find only the German edition of this early work of Pogodin.

―――. *Issledovaniya, zamechaniya i lektsii o russkoi istorii*. Moscow, 1846–1856. 7 vols. The basic arrangement is chronological, from the origin of Russia to the appanage period.

―――. *Istochniki dlya udelnogo perioda russkoi istorii*. Odessa, 1848.

―――. *Istoriko-kriticheskie otryvki*. Moscow, 1846. This collection includes such articles as "A Look at Russian History," "The Parallel between Russian History and the History of Western European States in Regard to the Origin," "About Moscow" (written for the heir to the throne), and "Peter the Great," and offers much valuable material to the student of Pogodin's thought.

―――. *Istoriko-kriticheskie otryvki*. Moscow, 1867. Vol. II.

―――. *Istoriko-politicheskie pisma i zapiski vprodolzhenii Krymskoi Voiny. 1853–1856*. Moscow, 1874. Belying the title, the first three pieces date from 1838, 1839, and 1842, respectively: a patriotic and nationalist letter to the heir to the throne and two reports to Uvarov after trips abroad. This volume includes some of Pogodin's most important political, nationalist, and Pan-Slav writings.

―――. *Istoriya v litsakh o tsare Borise Feodoroviche Godunove*. Moscow, 1868.

―――, ed. *Kirillo-Mefodievskii sbornik*. Moscow, 1865. ("V pamiat o sovershivshemsya tysyashcheletii slavyanskoi pismennosti i khristianstva v Rossii"—To commemorate the passing of a millenium of Slavic writing and Christianity in Russia.)

―――. *Knyaz Andrei Yurevich Bogolyubskii*. Moscow, 1850.

―――. *Kratkoe nachertanie russkoi istorii*. Moscow, 1838. An abbreviated version of a high school text.

―――. *Lektsii po Gerenu o politike, svyazi i torgovle glavnykh narodov drevnego mira*. Moscow, 1835–1836. 2 vols. Pogodin's early lectures in world history at the University of Moscow based on the German historian A. Heeren's (1760–1842) *Ideen ueber Politik, den Verkehr und den Handel der vornehmsten Voelker der alten Welt*.

―――. *Marfa, posadnitsa novgorodskaya*. Moscow, 1830. A historical play in five acts, in verse.

―――, ed. *Nikolai Mikhailovich Karamzin, po ego sochineniyam, pismam i otzyvam sovremennikov*. Moscow, 1866. 2 vols. Materials for Karamzin's biography.

―――. "Neskolko slov po povodu pisma G. Khomyakova ob Anglii," *Moskvityanin*, VI (1848), no. 11, "Scholarship," pp. 1–10.

―――. "Neskolko slov protiv stati, pomeshchennoi v 75 No. Severnoi Pchely 'O yubilee knyazya P. A. Vyazemskogo'," *Severnaya Pchela*, no. 83, April 13, 1861. An attack on Belinskii.

―――. *Nestor, istoriko-kriticheskoe rassuzhdenie o nachale russkikh letopisei*. Moscow, 1839.

―――. *Normanskii period russkoi istorii*. Moscow, 1859.

―――. *O proiskhozhdenii Rusi*. Moscow, 1825. Pogodin's M. A. dissertation, presented in 1823, which determined to a large extent his subsequent scholarly work.

Pogodin, M. *Ostzeiskii vopros.* Moscow, 1869. Subtitled "Pismo k professoru Shirrenu." In its time second only to Yurii Samarin's writings on the "borderlands" as an all-out attack on the Baltic Germans.

————. *Petr I.* Moscow, 1873. A five-act tragedy in verse.

————. *Pisma k M. A. Maksimovichu.* Ed. by S. Ponomarev. St. Petersburg, 1882. The volume consists of one hundred and six letters which contain numerous details of Pogodin's personal life, research, and university work, but little material of a more general intellectual interest.

————. *Povesti.* Moscow, 1832. Vol. II. Consists of five tales. I failed to obtain the first volume.

————, ed. *Pskovskaya letopis.* Moscow, 1837.

————. *Prostaya rech o mudrenykh veshchakh.* Moscow, 1875.

————. *Rechi, proiznesennye v torzhestvennykh i prochikh sobraniyakh, 1830–1872.* Moscow, 1872. A huge and valuable collection of Pogodin's speeches.

————. *Sbornik, sluzhashchii dopolneniem k prostoi rechi o mudrenykh veshchakh.* Moscow, 1875.

————. *Semnadtsat pervykh let v zhizni Imperatora Petra Velikogo. 1672–1689.* Moscow, 1875.

————. *Sobranie dokumentov po delu tsarevicha Alekseya Petrovicha, vnov naidennykh G. V. Esipovym, s prilozheniem rassuzhdeniya.* Moscow, 1861. Documents and a critical essay relating to the episode which, thirty years earlier, formed the subject of Pogodin's play "Peter I"—the trial, condemnation and death of Peter the Great's son Alexis.

————. *Sobranie statei, pisem i rechei po povodu slavyanskogo voprosa.* Moscow, 1878. One of the important volumes in the literature of Russian Pan-Slavism.

————. *Stati politicheskie i polskii vopros (1856–1867).* Moscow, 1876. "Political articles" range from "Disraeli" to the "Revolution in Spain" and from "Good Wishes to Italy" to "Thoughts and Comments on the Subject of the Franco-Prussian War." They represent a running commentary on political events in Europe, including several annual reviews of these events. The part of the book devoted to Poland centers on the Polish revolution of 1863, which marked a milestone both in the "Polish question" and in Pogodin's attitude toward it.

The most important additional collection of Pogodin's writings is in Barsukov, *Zhizn i trudy M. P. Pogodina.* The size and wealth of undigested material make this twenty-two-volume unfinished study unique in Russian biographical literature. Contains hundreds of pages of Pogodin's writings, notably from his diary, many of which remain otherwise unpublished. Pogodin's letters to Prince Vyazemskii were published in Barsukov, ed., *Pisma M. P. Pogodina, S. P. Shevyreva i M. A. Maksimovicha k knyazyu P. A. Vyazemskomu 1825–1874 godov,* pp. 32–107. The seventy-seven letters give much insight into Pogodin's attitude toward Karamzin as well as toward many contemporary writers and publications.

Pushkin, A. *Biblioteka velikikh pisatelei pod redaktsiei S. A. Vengerova. Pushkin.* St. Petersburg, 1907–1915. 6 vols. The third volume contains "The Bronze Horseman."

Senkovskii, O. I. (See "Baron Brambeus.")

Shevyrev, S. "Aus einem Schreiben des Herrn Doctor und Professor Etiénne de Chévireff in Moscau an den Verfasser. d.d. 22 Februar 1840," in F. Baader, *Gesammelte Schriften zur Religionsphilosophie.* Leipzig, 1855. Vol. IV, pp. 204–218. Shevyrev's letter in defense of the Russian Orthodox Church against criticism in the West. This volume is also volume X of F. Baader, *Saemmtliche Werke.*

————. *Istoriya Imperatorskogo Moskovskogo Universiteta, napisannaya k stoletnemu ego yubileyu.* 1755–1855. Moscow, 1855. Developments during Nicholas I's reign take up pages 465–576.

————. *Istoriya poezii.* St. Petersburg. Vol. I, 2d ed., 1887. Vol. II, 1892. University lectures on the histories of Hindu, Hebrew, Greek, and Latin poetry plus two introductory lectures in the first volume, "concerning the character of education and poetry of the leading peoples of modern Western Europe."

————. *Istoriya russkoi slovesnosti.* St. Petersburg, 1887. 4 vols. University lectures on the history of Russian literature from its origins to the early sixteenth century.

————. "Izvlechenie iz pisem ministru narodnogo prosveshcheniya," *Zhurnal Ministerstva Narodnogo Prosveshcheniya,* 1840, part I, sec. IV, pp. 1–14. About Schelling's philosophy.

————. "Khristianskaya filosofiya. Besedy Baadera," *Moskvityanin,* 1841, no. 3, pp. 376–437.

————. *Lektsii o russkoi literature.* St. Petersburg, 1884. Lectures delivered to members of the Russian colony in Paris in 1862.

————. *Ob otnoshenii semeinogo vospitaniya k gosudarstvennomu.* Moscow, 1842.

————. *Poezdka v Kirillobelozerskii monastyr v 1847 godu.* Moscow, 1850.

————. *Stikhotvoreniya.* Ed. by M. Aronson. Leningrad, 1939. The first publication of Shevyrev's poems in book form. The collection is incomplete, concentrating on the years 1825–1831 and slighting especially the later period, for instance, omitting entirely the poems occasioned by the Crimean War. As in the case of the Soviet editor of F. Glinka's poetry, the editor of Shevyrev tries to squeeze as much "progressive" content as he can from his recalcitrant subject. (See his interesting introductory essay.)

————. *Teoriya poezii v istoricheskom razvitii u drevnikh i novykh narodov.* 2d ed. St. Petersburg, 1887. Shevyrev's doctoral dissertation.

————. "Vybrannye mesta iz perepiski s druzyami N. Gogolya," *Moskvityanin,* 1848, no. 1, pp. 1–29.

————. "Vzglyad russkogo na sovremennoe obrazovanie Evropy," *Moskvityanin,* 1841, no. 1, pp. 219–296. An extremely important and well-known article.

————. *Znachenie Zhukovskogo v russkoi zhizni i poezii.* Moscow, 1853. A long speech made at a formal gathering of the University of Moscow.

Shevyrev's letters to Prince Vyazemskii, twenty-seven in number, were published in Barsukov, ed., *Pisma M. P. Pogodina, S. P. Shevyreva i*

M. A. *Maksimovicha k knazyu P. A. Vyazemskomu 1825–1874 godov*, pp. 135–178.

Strakhov, N. "Aleksandr Pervyi, Osvoboditel Otechestva i Evropy," *Syn Otechestva*, XIV (1814), no. XXI, "Contemporary History and Politics," pp. 60–64. A eulogy in prose.

Tregubov, E. "Na vseradostneishii den koronovaniya Ego Imperatorskogo Velichestva Gosudarya Imperatora Nikolaya Pavlovicha," *Syn Otechestva*, CVIII (1826), no. XIV, pp. 180–182. A eulogy in verse.

Tyutchev, F. *Polnoe sobranie sochinenii*. Ed. by P. Bykov. St. Petersburg, 1913. With an excellent introductory article by V. Bryusov (pp. 5–37). See also I. Aksakov, *Biografiya Fedora Ivanovicha Tyutcheva*. This biography of the great poet by his son-in-law, the Slavophile Ivan Aksakov, contains numerous and often lengthy selections from Tyutchev's published works as well as from his letters, drafts, notes, and the like.

Ustryalov, N. *Russkaya istoriya*. 5th ed. St. Petersburg, 1855. 2 vols. The textbook of Russian history in the schools of the empire in the reign of Nicholas I. The fifth edition includes a section on the reign of Nicholas I itself which was checked by the tsar in person. This quasi-official glorification of the reign can be found in works of other contemporary historians, e.g., in those of Zotov which are listed below. It outlived the monarch as attested by such authors and books as K. Yarosh, *Imperator Nikolai Pavlovich*, Kharkov, 1890; V. Nazarevskii, *Tsarstvovanie Imperatora Nikolaya I*. 1825–1855, Moscow, 1910; or—in a more limited area, that of education—M. Lalaev, *Imperator Nikolai I, zizhditel russkoi shkoly*, St. Petersburg, 1896. For a more scholarly and sophisticated work in praise of the emperor see L. Strakhovsky, *L'Empereur Nicolas I* et *l'ésprit national russe*, Louvain, 1928.

Uvarov, S. *La Certitude historique est-elle en progrés?* St. Petersburg, 1850.

———. *Desyatiletie ministerstva narodnogo prosveshcheniya*. 1833–1843. St. Petersburg, 1864. Uvarov's decennial report to the emperor.

———. *Discours du Président de l'Académie Impériale des Sciences prononcé dans la séance solennelle du 29 décembre 1826, à l'occasion de la Fête séculaire de l'Académie*. St. Petersburg, 1827. A translation of the Russian original.

———. *Eloge funèbre de Moreau*. St. Petersburg, 1813.

———. *L'Empereur Alexandre et Buonaparte*. St. Petersburg, 1814.

———. *Esquisses politiques et littéraires*. Paris, 1848. The book is divided into three parts: "Politics" consisting of essays on Napoleon's attitude toward Italy, Stein and Pozzo di Borgo, and the Prince de Ligne; "Literature" devoted primarily to ancient Greece, but including also a discussion of the philosophy of literature; and "Travels" dealing with Venice and Rome.

———. *Essai sur les mystères d'Eleusis*. Paris, 1816. Also published in the *Études*.

———. *Études de philogie et de critique*. 2d ed. Paris, 1844. The largest collection of Uvarov's writings within the covers of a single volume. Some pieces were also published separately or in the *Esquisses*, or both.

————. *Examen critique de la fable d'Hercule*. St. Petersburg, 1820. Published later both in the *Études* and in the *Esquisses*.

————. *Mémoire sur les tragiques grecs*. St. Petersburg, 1825. This study can be found also in both the *Études* and the *Esquisses*.

————. *Nonnos von Panopolis der Dichter*. St. Petersburg, 1817. Also published in the *Études*. Dedicated to Goethe.

————. *Projet d'une Académie Asiatique*. St. Petersburg, 1810. One of Uvarov's earliest and best known pieces. Included in the *Études*.

————. *Stein et Pozzo di Borgo*. St. Petersburg, 1846. Included in the *Esquisses*.

————. "Tsirkulyarnoe predlozhenie G. Upravlyayushchego Ministerstvom Narodnogo Prosveshcheniya Nachalstvam Uchebnykh Okrugov, 'o vstuplenii v upravlenie Ministerstvom,' " *Zhurnal Ministerstva Narodnogo Prosveshcheniya*, I (1834), "Ministerial orders," pp. xlix–l. Uvarov's circular of March 21, 1833 (old style) to those in charge of educational districts in Russia marking his assumption of the ministry and the inauguration of Official Nationality. It can also be found in *Sbornik rasporyazhenii po Ministerstvu Narodnogo Prosveshcheniya*, Vol. I, 1802–1834, St. Petersburg, 1866, pp. 837–839. Of the four volumes of the *Sbornik*, the first three contain materials from the reign of Nicholas I. *Zhurnal Ministerstva Narodnogo Prosveshcheniya*, from its foundation by Uvarov in 1834 to his resignation as minister in 1849, represents, of course, an invaluable source for the writings and the activities of Uvarov as the man in charge of education in Russia.

Further material on Uvarov can be found in *Goethe und Uwarow und ihr Briefwechsel*, ed. by G. Schmid, St. Petersburg, 1888; and in Stepanov and Vermale, "Zhozef de Mestr v Rossii," *Literaturnoe Nasledstvo*, vol. 29/30 (1937), 577–726. Pages 677–712 of the latter contain an introductory article concerning the correspondence between De Maistre and Uvarov and the correspondence itself which consists of four letters by De Maistre and one by Uvarov.

"Vzglyad na Severo-Amerikanskie Soedinennye Shtaty," *Syn Otechestva*, CLXXX (1836), 172–192. The author of this article on the U. S. A. is not given.

Zagoskin, M. *Polnoe sobranie sochinenii*. St. Petersburg, 1889. 7 vols. *Yurii Miloslavskii* is his best-known novel.

Zhukovskii, V. *Polnoe sobranie sochinenii v odnom tome*. Ed. by P. Smirnovskii. Moscow, 1915.

————. "Vera i um. Istina. Nauka. Stati iz nenapechatannykh sochinenii," *Zhurnal Ministerstva Narodnogo Prosveshcheniya*, LXXXI (1854), part II, pp. 1–9. Selections from the papers left at the time of Zhukovskii's death.

Zotov, R. *Istoricheskie ocherki tsarstvovaniya Imperatora Nikolaya I*. St. Petersburg, 1859. Adulation of Nicholas I.

————. *Tridtsatiletie Evropy v tsarstvovanie Imperatora Nikolaya I*. St. Petersburg, 1857. 2 vols. Other European countries as well as the Russia of Nicholas I are surveyed.

LITERATURE ON OFFICIAL NATIONALITY

Aksakov, I. *Biografiya Fedora Ivanovicha Tyutcheva.* Moscow, 1886. Perceptive, intimate, and interesting.

———. *Sochineniya.* Moscow, 1887. Vol. VII.

Ammon, N. "Nikolai I." *Entsiklopedicheskii Slovar.* St. Petersburg: Granat, n. d. Vol. XXX, cols. 211–221.

Andreas, W. "Der Briefwechsel Koenig Friedrich Wilhelms IV. von Preussen und des Zaren Nikolaus I. von Russland in den Jahren 1848 bis 1850," *Forschungen zur Brandenburgischen und Preussischen Geschichte.* Vol. 43 (1930), 129–166.

Arendt, H. *The Origins of Totalitarianism.* New York, 1951.

Baader, F. *Gesammelte Schriften zur Religionsphilosophie.* Leipzig, 1855. Vol. IV. Pages 204–218 contain Shevyrev's letter in defense of the Russian Orthodox Church. Also vol. X of F. Baader, *Saemmtliche Werke.*

Barsukov, N. *Zhizn i trudy M. P. Pogodina.* St. Petersburg, 1888–1910. 22 vols.

Belinskii, V. *Sobranie sochinenii v trekh tomakh.* Moscow, 1948. 3 vols.

Benois, A., and N. Lanceray. "Dvortsovoe stroitelstvo imperatora Nikolaya I," *Starye Gody* (July–Sept., 1913), 173–197.

Benson, C., and Viscount Usher, eds. *The Letters of Queen Victoria. A Selection from Her Majesty's Correspondence Between the Years 1837 and 1861.* London, 1907. 3 vols. Vol. II covering the years 1844–1853 is of special interest.

Benz, E. *Die abendlaendische Sendung der oestlich-orthodoxen Kirche. Die russische Kirche und das abendlaendische Christentum in Zeitalter der Heiligen Allianz.* Wiesbaden, 1950. Especially important for the relationship of Baader to Official Nationality.

Berlin, I. "Russia and 1848," *Slavonic and East European Review,* XXVI (April, 1948), 341–360. A stimulating article.

Blagovidov, F. *Ober-prokurory Sv. Sinoda,* 2d ed. Kazan, 1900.

"Bludov (Dmitrii Nikolaevich, graf)." *Entsiklopedicheskii Slovar.* St. Petersburg: Brockhaus-Efron, 1891. Vol. IV, pp. 103–104. Author not given.

Bogoslovskii, M. "Gosudarstvennye krestyane pri Nikolae I," in *Istoriya Rossii v XIX veke.* Vol. I, pp. 236–260.

Bogucharskii, V. "Trete Otdelenie Sobstvennoi E. I. V. Kantselyarii o sebe samom," *Vestnik Evropy,* (March, 1917), 85–125. A publication, with Bogucharskii's discussion, of "Obzor deyatelnosti III otdeleniya sobstvennoi vashego imperatorskogo velichestva kantselyarii za 50 let 1826–1876 gg." (pp. 90–122).

Borodkin, M. *Istoriya Finlyandii. Vremya imperatora Nikolaya I.* Petrograd, 1915.

Botsyanovskii, V. "Bulgarin, Faddei Venediktovich," *Russkii biograficheskii slovar.* St. Petersburg, 1908. Vol. "Betankur" to "Byakster," pp. 476–479.

———. "Senkovskii (Osip-Yulian Ivanovich)." *Entsiklopedicheskii Slovar.* St. Petersburg: Brockhaus-Efron, 1900. Vol. XXIX^A, pp. 531–532.

Bowra, C. "Pushkin," *Oxford Slavonic Papers,* I (1950), 1–15.

Bryusov, V. "Mednyi Vsadnik," in Pushkin, *op. cit.,* vol. III, pp. 456–476.

Charnoluskii, V. "Narodnoe obrazovanie v pervoi polovine XIX v.," in *Istoriya Rossii v XIX veke.* Vol. IV, pp. 68–128.

Cherniavsky, M. " 'Holy Russia': a Study in the History of an Idea," *American Historical Review*, LXIII (April, 1958), 617–637.

Chizhevskii, D. "Baader i Rossiya," *Novyi Zhurnal* (New York), XXXV (1953), 301–310. An extensive review of E. Benz, *Die abendlaendische Sendung der oestlich-orthodoxen Kirche.*

————. *Gegel v Rossii.* Paris, 1939.

Curtiss, J. "The Army of Nicholas I: Its Role and Character," *American Historical Review*, LXIII (July, 1958), 880–889.

Custine, A. *La Russie en 1839.* Brussels, 1843. 4 vols. My references are to the edition published by "Société Belge de Librairie. Hauman et Companie." In 1843, and again in Brussels, the same book was also published by "Wouters et Companie." *La Russie en 1839* is probably the best known account of the Russia of Nicholas I by a visiting foreigner and the only one to which I had occasion to refer directly in my study. But I found items of interest in many other similar descriptions and reminiscences. See, e.g., Georgiana Baroness Bloomfield, *Reminiscences of Court and Diplomatic Life*, New York, 1883, 2 vols.; A. Gurowski, *Russia as It Is*, 2d ed., New York, 1854; and Baron von Haxthausen's famous *Studien ueber die inneren Zustaende des Volksleben, und inbesondere die laendlichen Einrichtingen Russlands*, Hanover, 1847. Cf. such contemporary or near-contemporary foreign historical accounts of the reign as W. Kelly, *The History of Russia from the Earliest Period to the Present Time*, London, 1855, vol. II; and P. Lacroix, *Histoire de la vie et du règne de Nicolas I*, Paris, 1864–1875, 8 vols.

Dementev, A. *Ocherki po istorii russkoi zhurnalistiki 1840–1850 gg.* Moscow-Leningrad, 1951.

Driesen, N. "Iz starykh arkhivov," in *Krestovyi Pokhod vo Imya Pravdy. Russkaya Zhizn* (San Francisco), no. 167, Jan. 30, 1958.

Druzhinin, N. *Gosudarstvennye krestyane i reforma P. D. Kiseleva.* Moscow-Leningrad, 1946. Vol. I.

Dvoichenko-Markov, E. "Americans in the Crimean War," *Russian Review*, XIII: 2 (April, 1954), 136–145.

Dzhivelegov, A., S. Melgunov, and V. Picheta, eds. *Velikaya reforma. Russkoe obshchestvo i krestyanskii vopros v proshlom i nastoyashchem.* Moscow, 1911. 6 vols.

Fallmerayer, J. *Geschichte der Halbinsel Morea im Mittelalter.* Stuttgart, 1830. Vol. I.

Fejto, F., ed. *The Opening of an Era, 1848; an Historical Symposium.* London, 1948.

Florinsky, M. *Russia. A History and an Interpretation.* New York, 1953. Vol. II.

Fomin, A. "Pushkin i zhurnalnyi triumvirat 30 kh godov," in Pushkin, *op. cit.*, vol. V, pp. 451–492.

Gershenzon, M., ed. *Epokha Nikolaya I.* Moscow, 1911. A selection of varied and interesting materials which provide a good, brief introduction to the reign of Nicholas I; also has a short, but perceptive preface by the editor.

Gleason, J. *The Genesis of Russophobia in Great Britain. A Study of the*

Interaction of Policy and Opinion. Cambridge, Mass.-London, 1950. There are no similar comprehensive studies of other countries, but some interesting investigations of a more limited scope are available. See especially D. Petrov, *Ocherki po istorii politicheskoi poezii XIX v. Rossiya i Nikolai I v stikhotvoreniyakh Espronsedy i Rossetti.* St. Petersburg, 1909, as well as McNally's article listed below.

Gogel, S. "Krug vedomstva i ocherk deyatelnosti Pravitelstvuyushchego Senata," in *Istoriya Pravitelstvuyushchego Senata za dvesti let, 1711–1911 gg.* St. Petersburg, 1911. Vol. III. *Pravitelstvuyushchii Senat v XIX stoletii do reform 60-kh godov.* Pp. 404–505.

Gooch, B. "A Century of Historiography on the Origins of the Crimean War," *American Historical Review,* LXII (Oct., 1956), 33–58.

"Gr. A. Kh. Benkendorf o Rossii," *Krasnyi Arkhiv,* XXXVII (1929), pp. 138–174; XLVI (1931), pp. 133–159. Reports of the Third Department to the emperor; the first reference covers the years 1827–1830, the second 1831–1832.

Grunwald, C. de. *La Vie de Nicolas Ier.* Paris, 1946. An English translation: *Tsar Nicholas I,* London, 1954.

———. "Nesselrode et le 'gendarme de l'Europe,'" in *Trois siècles de diplomatie russe.* Paris, 1945. Pp. 173–198.

Herzen, A. *Byloe i dumy.* Leningrad, 1946. A great, if one-sided, description of the Russia of Nicholas I. Cf. I. Golovin, *Russia under the Autocrat, Nicholas the First,* London, 1846, 2 vols.; and N. Turgenev, *La Russie et les russes,* Paris, 1847, 3 vols.

———. *Sochineniya i perepiska s N. A. Zakharinoi.* St. Petersburg, 1905. 7 vols.

Ignatovich, I. "Krestyanskie volneniya pervoi chetverti XIX veka," *Voprosy Istorii,* 1950, no. 9, pp. 48–70.

Istoriya Rossii v XIX veke. St. Petersburg: Granat, n. d. 9 vols. A very useful collective work.

"Ivanov, Nikolai Alekseevich." *Entsiklopedicheskii Slovar.* St. Petersburg: Brockhaus-Efron, 1894. Vol. XIIᴬ, p. 763. Author not given.

Karamzin, N. *Istoriya gosudarstva rossiiskogo.* 6th ed. St. Petersburg, 1851–1853. 12 vols.

———. "O drevnei i novoi Rossii v ee politicheskom i grazhdanskom otnosheniyakh," appended to Pypin, *Obshchestvennoe dvizhenie v Rossii pri Aleksandre I,* pp. 479–534.

Karnovich, E. *Tsesarevich Konstantin Pavlovich.* St. Petersburg, 1899.

Kerner, R. "Russia's New Policy in the Near East after the Peace of Adrianople; Including the Text of the Protocol of 16 September 1829," *Cambridge Historical Journal,* V (1937), 280–290.

Khokhlov, E. "Rozhdenie 'Mertvykh dush'," *Russkie Novosti* (Paris), no. 352, Feb. 29, 1952.

Khomyakov, A. *Polnoe sobranie sochinenii.* Moscow, 1900–1914. 8 vols.

Kizevetter, A. *Devyatnadtsatyi vek v istorii Rossii.* Rostov on the Don, 1903. A very small book composed of separate studies, the second of which deals with Nicholas I's secret committees, and the third with serfdom in Russia in the first half of the nineteenth century.

————. "Vnutrennyaya politika v tsarstvovanie Nikolaya Pavlovicha," in *Istoriya Rossii v XIX veke*. Vol. I, pp. 169–231. An acute survey and analysis.

Kornilov, A. *Modern Russian History from the Age of Catherine the Great to the End of the Nineteenth Century*. New York, 1943. 2 vols.

Korsakov, D. "Senkovskii, Osip Ivanovich." *Russkii biograficheskii slovar*. St. Petersburg, 1904. Vol. "Sabaneev" to "Smyslov," pp. 316–325.

Koshelev, A. *Zapiski* (1812–1883 gody). Berlin, 1884.

Kostomarov, N. (See Luciani, G.)

Kotovich, A. *Dukhovnaya tsenzura v Rossii* (1799–1855 gg.). St. Petersburg, 1909.

Kovalenskii, M. "Srednyaya shkola," in *Istoriya Rossii v XIX veke*. Vol. IV, pp. 128–185.

Koyré, A. *La Philosophie et le problème national en Russie au début de XIX* siècle. Paris, 1929.

Krylov, I. *Basni. Polnoe sobranie*. Warsaw, 1913.

Lander, K. "Pribaltiiskii krai v pervoi polovine XIX veka," in *Istoriya Rossii v XIX veke*. Vol. II, pp. 327–349.

Lednicki, W. *Pushkin's Bronze Horseman. The Story of a Masterpiece*. Berkeley and Los Angeles, 1955.

Lemke, M. *Nikolaevskie zhandarmy i literatura 1826–1855 gg*. St. Petersburg, 1908. Based on the case records of the Third Department of His Majesty's Own Chancery.

————. *Ocherki po istorii russkoi tsenzury i zhurnalistiiki XIX stoletiya*. St. Petersburg, 1904. The second part of the book deals with the "epoch of censorship terror (1844–1855)" and the fourth with Bulgarin.

Lenskii, Z. "Polsha v pervoi polovine XIX veka," in *Istoriya Rossii v XIX veke*. Vol. I, pp. 260–327.

Levin, I., ed. *Perepiska Nikolaya I i Frantsa Iosifa*. N. p., n. d.

Lobanov-Rostovsky, A. *Russia and Europe. 1825–1878*. Ann Arbor, Mich., 1954.

Luciani, G., trans., *Le Livre de la Genèse du peuple ukrainien*. Paris, 1956. Translated from the Ukrainian original of N. Kostomarov, *Knihi bitiya ukrainskoho narodu*, with additional material.

Lukacs, J. "Russian Armies in Western Europe: 1799, 1814, 1917," *American Slavic and East European Review*, XIII: 3 (Oct., 1954), 318–337.

McNally, T. "The Origins of Russophobia in France: 1812–1830," *American Slavic and East European Review*, XVII: 2 (April, 1958), 173–189.

Malia, M. "Schiller and the Early Russian Left," *Harvard Slavic Studies*, IV (1957), 169–200. An excellent article.

Mandt, M. *Ein deutscher Arzt am Hofe Kaiser Nikolaus I von Russland*. Munich-Leipzig, 1917. With an introduction by Schiemann. An informative and interesting account by the man who served for many years as the chief physician of the emperor and the imperial family.

Martens, F., ed. *Recueil des traités et conventions conclus par la Russie avec les puissances étrangères*. St. Petersburg, 1874–1909. 15 vols.

Masaryk, T. *The Spirit of Russia. Studies in History, Literature, and Philosophy*. New York, 1955. 2 vols.

Mazour, A. *The First Russian Revolution, 1825; the Decembrist Movement, Its Origins, Development, and Significance.* Berkeley, 1937.

Melgunov, S. "Epokha 'ofitsialnoi narodnosti' i krepostnoe pravo," in A. Dzhivelegov, S. Melgunov, and V. Picheta, eds. *Velikaya reforma.* *Russkoe obshchestvo i krestyanskii vopros v proshlom i nastoyashchem.* Vol. III, pp. 1–21.

Mickiewicz, A. *Digression.* Tr. by Marjorie Beatrice Peacock. In *Poems by Adam Mickiewicz.* Ed. by G. R. Noyes. New York, 1944. Also in Lednicki, *Pushkin's Bronze Horseman,* pp. 109–139.

Miliukov, P. *Gosudarstvennoe khozyaistvo Rossii v pervoi chetverti XVIII stoletiya i reforma Petra Velikogo.* St. Petersburg, 1905.

Miliukov, P., C. Seignobos, and L. Eisenmann. *Histoire de Russie.* Paris, 1932–1933. 3 vols. The reign of Nicholas I is discussed in vol. II.

Monas, S. "Šiškov, Bulgarin and the Russian Censorship," *Harvard Slavic Studies,* IV (1957), 127–147.

Mosely, P. *Russian Diplomacy and the Opening of the Eastern Question in 1838 and 1839.* Cambridge, Mass., 1934.

Motley, J. *Correspondence.* London, 1889. Vol. I.

Nesselrode, C. *Lettres et papiers du chancelier Comte de Nesselrode. 1760–1856.* Paris, 1908–1912. 11 vols. A very valuable collection of documents from the Nesselrode archives, ranging from important and abundant diplomatic correspondence to social gossip contained especially in the letters of the chancellor's wife.

Nifontov, A. *Rossiya v 1848 godu.* Moscow, 1949.

Nikiforov, D. *Vospominaniya iz vremen imperatora Nikolaya I.* Moscow, 1903.

Nikitenko, A. *Moya povest o samom sebe i o tom "chemu svidetel v zhizni byl." Zapiski i dnevnik.* (1804–1877 gg.). 2d ed. St. Petersburg, 1905. 2 vols. The first volume is devoted almost entirely to the years of Nicholas I's reign. A well-known autobiographical work which is of exceptional interest and significance to students of Russian education, censorship, and, in general, the relationship between the tsarist government and the intellectuals.

"Nikolai I." *Bolshaya Entsiklopediya.* St. Petersburg, 1904. Vol. XIV, pp. 70–74. Author not given.

"Nikolai I." *Entsiklopedicheskii Slovar.* St. Petersburg: Brockhaus-Efron, 1897. Vol. XXI, pp. 119–124. The article is signed "N."

Nolde, B. *Yurii Samarin i ego vremya.* Paris, 1926.

Okun, S. *Ocherki istorii S.S.S.R. Vtoraya chetvert XIX veka.* Leningrad, 1957.

Petrovich, M. *The Emergence of Russian Panslavism, 1856–1870.* New York, 1956.

———. "Russian Pan-Slavists and the Polish Uprising of 1863," *Harvard Slavic Studies,* I (1953), 219–247.

Picheta, V. *Vvedenie v russkuyu istoriyu (istochniki i istoriografiya).* Moscow-Petrograd, 1923.

Pipes, R. "Karamzin's Conception of Monarchy," *Harvard Slavic Studies,* IV (1957), 35–58.

Polievktov, M. *Nikolai I. Biografiya i obzor tsarstvovaniya.* Moscow, 1918. One of the very best studies of Nicholas I and his reign; better on domestic than on foreign affairs.

Pokrovskii, M. "Krymskaya voina," in *Istoriya Rossii v XIX veke*. Vol. III, pp. 1–68.

Presnyakov, A. *Apogei samoderzhaviya. Nikolai I*. Leningrad, 1925. Brief, but interesting.

Puryear, V. *England, Russia and the Straits Question, 1844–1856*. Berkeley, 1931. Excellent, especially in its treatment of Nicholas I and the Russian government.

Pypin, A. *Kharakteristiki literatyrnykh mnenii ot dvadtsatykh do pyatidesyatykh godov*. 3d ed. St. Petersburg, 1906.

———. *Obshchestvennoe dvizhenie v Rossii pri Aleksandre I*. 3d ed. St. Petersburg, 1900. An appendix (pp. 479–534) contains Karamzin's treatise "concerning Old and New Russia."

Raeff, M. "An American View of the Decembrist Revolt," *Journal of Modern History*, XXV: 3 (Sept., 1953), 286–293.

———. *Michael Speransky: Statesman of Imperial Russia, 1772–1839*. The Hague, 1957.

Rath, R. "Training for Citzenship in the Austrian Elementary Schools during the Reign of Francis I," *Journal of Central European Affairs*, IV: 2 (July, 1944), 147–164. Austrian "Official Nationality."

Rauch, G. "J. Ph. Fallmerayer und der russiche Reichsgedanke bei F. I. Tjutčev," in *Jahrbuecher fuer geschichte Osteuropas*. Munich, 1953. Vol. I, no. i, pp. 54–96.

Riasanovsky, N. *Russia and the West in the Teaching of the Slavophiles. A Study of Romantic Ideology*. Cambridge, Mass., 1952.

———. "Pogodin and Ševyrëv in Russian Intellectual History," *Harvard Slavic Studies*, IV (1957), 149–167.

Riasanovsky, V. *Obzor russkoi kultury*. New York, 1947. Part II, issue I.

Rozhdestvenskii, S. *Istoricheskii obzor deyatelnosti ministerstva narodnogo prosveshcheniya, 1802–1902*. St. Petersburg, 1902.

Rubinstein, N. "Istoricheskaya teoriya slavyanofilov i ee klassovye korni," in *Trudy Instituta Krasnoi Professury. Russkaya istoricheskaya literatura v klassovom osveshchenii. Sbornik statei*. Ed. by M. Pokrovskii. Moscow, 1927. Vol. I, pp. 53–118.

Sakulin, P. *Iz istorii russkogo idealizma. Knyaz V. Odoevskii*. Moscow, 1913.

———. "Russkaya literatura vo vtoroi chetverti veka," in *Istoriya Rossii v XIX veke*. Vol. II, pp. 443–508.

Savelev, P. *O zhizni i trudakh O. I. Senkovskogo*. St. Petersburg, 1858. A separate printing of Savelev's eulogistic introduction to the first volume of Senkovskii's *Works*. The full bibliography of Senkovskii's writings occupies pages cxiii–cxxxviii. Contains 440 items. Savelev, a noted orientalist, was one of Senkovskii's students.

Sbornik Imperatorskogo Russkogo Istoricheskogo Obshchestva. St. Petersburg, 1867–1917. 148 vols. For a student of the reign of Nicholas I, the most important volume of this basic Russian collection of historical materials is vol. 98, often mentioned in the course of my study. It consists of M. Korff's compilation of biographical information on the tsar's childhood and adolescence, of a detailed record, again by Korff, of Nicholas I's participation in committee and State Council work, and of the reports of the following branches of administration, with an account of their activities during the first twenty-five years of the reign: the ministry of foreign affairs; the ministry of war; the navy; the Holy Synod; postal service; state domains; state control; communication and public buildings; Poland; Finland; and the Baltic Provinces. Other important volumes include: Vol. 31—the education of the heir to the throne, later Emperor Alexander II; vols. 74 and 90—records of the committee of December 6, 1826; vol. 113—materials on the Orthodox church in Russia in the reign of Nicholas I; vol. 122—materials on Chernyshev, the minister of war, including his reports and correspondence; vols. 131 and 132—correspondence between Nicholas I and Constantine.

Schiemann, T. *Geschichte Russlands unter Kaiser Nikolaus I.* Berlin, 1904–1919. 4 vols. A study of fundamental significance; the volumes contain very numerous and very valuable documentary appendixes.

————. *Die Vergewaltigung der russischen Ostseeprovinzen. Appell an das Ehrgefuehl des Protestantismus.* Berlin, 1886.

Schilder, N. *Imperator Nikolai Pervyi, ego zhizn i tsarstvovanie.* St. Petersburg, 1903. 2 vols. A documentary emperor- and court-centered history which is extremely valuable because of the rich source material it contains. Remained unfinished, going only to, and largely including, 1831. Possesses numerous documentary appendixes and, in addition to them, a special addendum to the second volume which consists of two articles by Schilder, "Emperor Nicholas I in 1848 and 1849" and "Emperor Nicholas I and the Liberation of the Christian East," and of Benckendorff's *Memoirs* for the years 1832–1837. The articles were published originally in *Istoricheskii Vestnik* in 1899 and in *Russkaya Starina* in 1892, respectively. Schilder occupies a uniquely important position as a historian of several Russian emperors and their courts. In English a summary of the subject can be obtained in E. A. Brayley Hodgetts, *The Court of Russia in the Nineteenth Century,* New York, 1908, the reign of Nicholas I taking up pp. 141–303 of vol. I, part II.

Sechkarev, V. *Schellings Einfluss in der russischen Literatur der 20er und 30er Jahre des XIX Jahrhunderts.* Berlin, 1939.

Semevskii, V. *Krestyanskii vopros v Rossii v XVIII i pervoi polovine XIX veka.* St. Petersburg, 1888. 2 vols.

[Senkovskaya, A.] *Osip Ivanovich Senkovskii (Baron Brambeus). Biograficheskie zapiski ego zheny.* St. Petersburg, 1858. Invaluable for an understanding of Senkovskii.

"Severnaya Pchela." *Entsiklopedicheskii Slovar.* St. Petersburg: Brockhaus-Efron, 1901. Vol. LXI!I, pp. 250–251. Author not given.

Shcherbatov, A. *General-Feldmarshal Knyaz Paskevich. Ego zhizn i deyatelnost.* St. Petersburg, 1888–1904. 7 vols. in 9. Possesses numerous and valuable documentary appendixes, including many letters of Nicholas I to Paskevich.

"Shevyrev, Stepan Petrovich," *Russkii biograficheskii slovar.* St. Petersburg, 1911. Vol. "Shebanov" to "Shyutts," pp. 19–29. The article is signed "N. Ch."

"Shevyrev (Stepan Petrovich, 1806–1864)." *Entsiklopedicheskii Slovar.* St. Petersburg: Brockhaus-Efron, 1903. Vol. XXXIX, pp. 361–364. The article is signed "Shch."

Shtakelberg, N. "Zagadka smerti Nikolaya I," *Russkoe Proshloe*, I (1923), 58–73.

Soloviev, S. *Moi zapiski dlya detei moikh, a, esli mozhno, i dlya drugikh*. St. Petersburg, n. d. The famous historian's reminiscences were also published in *Vestnik Evropy* in 1907.

Stepanov, M. and F. Vermale. "Zhozef de Mestr v Rossii," *Literaturnoe Nasledstvo*, vol. 29/30 (1937), 577–726. A long article by Stepanov plus documentary material, mostly De Maistre's letters, presented with introductions and annotations.

Strakhovsky, L. "Pushkin and the Emperors Alexander I and Nicholas I," *Canadian Slavonic Papers*, I (1956), 16–30.

Stremoukhov, D. *La Poésie et l'idéologie de Tiouttchev*. Paris, 1937. One of the better studies of Tyutchev.

Struve, P. "S. P. Shevyrev i zapadnye vnusheniya i istochniki teorii-aforizma o 'gnilom' ili 'gniyushchem' Zapade," in *Zapiski Russkogo Nauchnogo Instituta v Belgrade*. Belgrade, 1940. A valuable study.

Susini, E. *Lettres inédites de Franz von Baader*. Paris, 1942. Pages 451–461 contain Baader's letters to Uvarov.

Svod Zakonov Rossiiskoi Imperii. St. Petersburg, 1832. 15 vols.

Tarasov, E. *Nikolaevshchina (Vremya Nikolaya I)*. Petrograd, 1917. A very brief and superficial denunciation of Nicholas I written in the popular language.

Temperley, H. *England and the Near East. The Crimea*. London-New York-Toronto, 1936. An acknowledged masterpiece, but surprisingly weak in places in its treatment of Russia.

Thaden, E. "The Beginnings of Romantic Nationalism in Russia," *American Slavic and East European Review*, XIII: 4 (1954), 500–521.

The Times (London), March 7, 1855.

Titlinov, B. *Dukhovnaya shkola v Rossii v XIX stoletii. Vypusk vtoroi. (Protasovskaya epokha i reformy 60kh godov.)* Vilno, 1909.

Trotskii, I. *Trete otdelenie pri Nikolae I*. Moscow, 1930. Rather brief, but interesting and valuable.

Tyutcheva, A. *Pri dvore dvukh imperatorov*. Moscow, 1928. Rather brief, but extremely interesting and perceptive. With a valuable introductory article and notes by S. Bakhrushin (pp. 6–57).

Vasilenko, N. "Krestyanskii vopros v yugo-zapadnom i severo-zapadnom krae pri Nikolae I i vvedenie inventarei," in A. Dzhivelegov, S. Melgunov, and V. Picheta, eds. *Velikaya reforma. Russkoe obshchestvo i krestyanskii vopros v proshlom i nastoyashchem*. Vol. IV, pp. 94–109.

Vernadsky, G. "'Mednyi Vsadnik' v tvorchestve Pushkina," *Slavia*, II: 4 (1924), 645–654.

[Viskovatyi, A.] *Nikolai Ivanovich Grech. Biograficheskii ocherk*. St. Petersburg, 1854. A brief and formal summary of Grech's life. The booklet itself gives no author, but Viskovatyi is listed as the author in K. Polevoi, ed., *Yubilei pyatidesyatiletnei literaturnoi deyatelnosti Nikolaya Ivanovicha Grecha. 27 dekabrya 1854 g.*, St. Petersburg, 1855, p. 20.

Weidle, V. *Zadacha Rossii*. New York, 1956. The perceptive essay "Tyutchev i Rossiya" occupies pp. 169–200.

White, A. *Autobiography*. New York, 1905. Vol. I.
Woodhouse, C. *The Greek War of Independence*. London, 1952.
Zablotskii-Desyatovskii, A. *Graf Kiselev i ego vremya*. St. Petersburg, 1882.
    4 vols. By Kiselev's collaborator.
Zetlin, M. *The Decembrists*. New York, 1958.

INDEX